THE HERMITAGE

THE HERMITAGE

The Biography of a Great Museum

Geraldine Norman

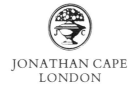

JONATHAN CAPE
LONDON

First published 1997

3 5 7 9 10 8 6 4 2

© Geraldine Norman 1997

Geraldine Norman has asserted her right
under the Copyright, Designs and Patents Act 1988
to be identified as the author of this work

First published in the United Kingdom in 1997 by Jonathan Cape,
Random House, 20 Vauxhall Bridge Road, London SW1V 2SA

Random House Australia (Pty) Limited
20 Alfred Street, Milsons Point, Sydney,
New South Wales 2061, Australia

Random House New Zealand Limited
18 Poland Road, Glenfield,
Auckland 10, New Zealand

Random House South Africa (Pty) Limited
Endulini, SA Jubilee Road, Parktown 2193, South Africa

The Random House Group Limited Reg. No. 954009

www.randomhouse.co.uk

A CIP catalogue record for this book is available from the British Library

ISBN 0-224-04312-9

Typeset by Deltatype Ltd
Printed and bound in Great Britain
by Mackays of Chatham Plc

Contents

List of Illustrations

WORKS OF ART

PORTRAITS

INTERIORS AND EXTERIORS

NEWS PHOTOS

A Note on Transliteration of Russian Names and Reference Sources

*I*n a text that is so crowded with Russian and other foreign names, several of which have variant spellings, it is difficult to impose a rigid consistency. There is no single universal style of Russian transliteration, but in general, Russian names and places have been transliterated following the system of *Oxford Slavonic Papers*, with variant spellings given in the bibliography and index where appropriate. In the case of names of Russian tsars – such as Alexander, Nicholas, Paul – and prominent figures – such as Boris Yeltsin – the convention of using the popular, anglicised spelling is followed.

The city of St Petersburg has changed its name several times this century. It held its current name from its foundation in 1703 by Peter the Great to 1914. Between 1914 and 1924 it was named Petrograd, and from 1924 to 1991 Leningrad. In 1991 it reverted to its original name. The text refers to the city in the relevant name for the historical context being described.

Footnotes have not been included in the text on the assumption that they would interfere with the narrative. Where the source of a quotation is not obvious, it will be found in the bibliography, which is divided up by chapters.

Acknowledgements

$\mathcal{T}$his book could not have been written without the support of three people, Mikhail Borisovich Piotrovsky, director of the Hermitage, Tom Maschler, Publisher of Jonathan Cape, and Catherine Phillips, my research assistant. I consider it little short of miraculous that they should have come into my life simultaneously and cannot begin to thank them enough.

I could not have started if Tom Maschler had not warmed to the project and commissioned it and I would not have started without Mikhail Borisovich's permission. In the event, Mikhail Borisovich's help went much further than allowing me to work in the museum. He encouraged his staff to help me and spent a most generous amount of his own time answering my questions and reading my drafts.

Catherine was much more than a research assistant. A fluent Russian speaker with a first class degree in art history and several years' experience in publishing, she educated me about Russia, interpreted, provided intelligent synopses of books I should have read in Russian, combed libraries for useful sources, criticised what I wrote and corrected my spelling. She also made very good jokes and seldom complained. Her mind is responsible for this book along with mine.

The typescript of *Hermitage Collections and Collectors*, by Oleg Neverov and Mikhail Piotrovsky, to be published by Slavia, provided an invaluable guide for me and I thank both authors for letting me see it before publication. Oleg Neverov, the curator of antique gems, has made a special study of eighteenth- and nineteenth-century St Petersburg art collections and shared his knowledge with me most generously. Lyudmila Voroni-khina, the author of the most recent guide to the museum and a member of the Education Department, also gave me invaluable help on the history of the collections and the buildings.

Many people have helped me piece together the more recent history of the museum and I am particularly grateful to the former director, Vitaly Suslov, and the two deputy directors, Georgy Vilinbakhov and Vladimir Matveev. (The latter proved also to be an inspiring authority on Peter the Great.) Vadim Zuev, an archaeologist recently recruited by the Hermitage to research the museum's history, helped me to clarify the complicated interactions of politics and personnel in the Soviet period and I extend to him and his wife Lena, who is also a curator, very special thanks.

I have received generous and friendly help from a very large number of Hermitage staff and I thank them all. I should like particularly to mention the kindness of Sergey Androsov, Boris Asvarisch, Sergey Avramenko, Asya Cantor-Gukovskaya, Albert Kostenevich, Alexandra Kostsova, Marta Kryjanovskaia, Alexey Larionov, Marina Lopato, Boris Marshak, Vsevolod Potin and Galina Smirnova.

My visit to the Hermitage excavations at Kerch was made possible and enjoyable through the kindness of Sergey Solovev and his archaeologist wife Natasha. The staff of the Hermitage Library have been particularly helpful to me as have the staff of the Hermitage Archive, notably Lena Solomakha.

Outside the museum, I have made two particular friends in St Petersburg, Marina and Alexander Kozyrev, who have had me to stay, talked tirelessly about my problems and helped me to find solutions. I should also like to thank Ripsime Djanpolodyan Piotrovsky, the mother of the present director of the Hermitage and widow of his predecessor, for several very enjoyable conversations. Both Professor Oleg Artamonov, whose father was director of the museum in the post-war years, and his wife have been very helpful to me, as has his father's old pupil, Professor Abram Stolyar.

I should also like to thank Professor Igor Diakonoff, Venyamin Joffe of Memorial, Professor Boris Starkov, Dr Petr Gryaznevich, Sergey Kuznetsov, Vladimir Uflyand, Mikhail Chemiakin, Natasha Smirnova, Pavel Tichtchenko, Dr Yaroslav Vasilkov, Stanislav Chernichov, the staff of the Galitzine Library, Vadim Znamenov, director of the Peterhof State Museum Reserve, and Irina Zolotinkina, archivist at the Benois Museum in Peterhof.

I have received most valuable assistance from many people outside Russia and I am particularly grateful to Larissa Haskell, Bill Clarke, Jasper Gaunt, Gocha Tsetskhladze, Peter Batkin, John Stewart, Konstantin Akinsha, Grigori Kozlov, Valery and Galina Panov, Professor Dr Irena Zerbst-Borovka, Nikita Lobanov and Tatiana Orloff.

Introduction

*T*he State Hermitage in St Petersburg is Russia's premier museum. It has one of the greatest collections in the world, on a par with the Louvre, the British Museum or the Metropolitan Museum in New York. Prior to the opening of the extended Grand Louvre in the 1990s the Hermitage was the world's largest museum. If its development plans, currently stalled for lack of funds, are ever completed, it will regain its pre-eminence.

The museum began life as the private collection of the Russian tsars, housed in two pavilions built onto their Winter Palace in central St Petersburg by Catherine the Great, which are known today as the Small Hermitage and the Old Hermitage. Catherine's grandson, Nicholas I, had the idea of building a museum extension on to the palace and sharing his own art treasures with the public. This building is known as the New Hermitage and first opened its doors in 1852.

After the Revolution in 1917 the whole of the palace complex was gradually turned over to the nationalised museum, thereafter known as the State Hermitage. It was swollen by accretions from confiscated private collections but depleted by the requirement to share its treasures with Moscow and other regional museums. In the 1930s some great paintings were sold abroad to bolster the national treasury.

The imperial collection, as it existed before the Revolution, comprised Old Master paintings, Classical antiquities, coins and medals, an Arsenal and some medieval and Renaissance works of art. In the 1920s an Oriental Department was added, in the 1930s an Archaeological Department and in the 1940s a department devoted to Russian works of art.

The collection today is encyclopaedic. In addition to superb works of art, it contains many imperial eccentricities, such as Peter the Great's underwear and Catherine's coronation coach. The architectural complex in which it is housed, lining a bank of the River Neva, is one of the wonders of the world.

This book attempts to sketch the museum's turbulent history, laying special emphasis on the twentieth century and the interaction of the museum with Russia's seventy-year experiment with Communism.

1

Catherine's Hermitage and Peter's City

*H*ermitage is pronounced with a French accent in Russia. It loses its 'H' and the stress falls on the last syllable. It should be spelt 'Ermitazh', if one follows the standard rules for converting Russian Cyrillic script into our own. It is one of the many French words that entered the Russian language during the reign of Peter the Great (1682–1725), the crude, seven-foot genius who built St Petersburg and forced his people to shift their mental orientation from East to West.

Both Peter and Catherine the Great (reigned 1762–96) prided themselves on introducing French culture and habits into their country. As a result, Russia's premier museum takes its name from an aspect of country living which became popular in France in the seventeenth century and turned into a pan-European landscape gardening fashion in the eighteenth. A Hermitage, with or without a hermit, sometimes in ruins and sometimes intact, was a required feature of a fashionably landscaped park of the Romantic era. When Peter began to build his great country palace of Peterhof, a seaside imitation of Versailles complete with fountains and garden pavilions, he naturally included a Hermitage – the first Russian Hermitage. It was a two-storey building with an upstairs dining-room lined, edge to edge, with Dutch seventeenth-century paintings and Peter used it for private parties.

So when Catherine built a pavilion on to her Winter Palace in St Petersburg, as a private place where she could entertain her friends without ceremony and hang her pictures, she called it her Hermitage. And the name stuck. Her original pavilion is now known as the Small Hermitage and a second extension she built to accommodate her overflowing art collection is known as the Old Hermitage. The theatre she later tacked on to them is known as the Hermitage Theatre. When a museum was built on to the palace complex in the nineteenth century it was dubbed the New Hermitage. Since 1917 the collections have gradually spread to fill all the former palace buildings and the whole, magnificent complex is now known as the State Hermitage Museum.

As with their other borrowings from European culture, the Russian idea of a Hermitage differed considerably from the models that inspired it. The first Hermitages had been constructed in Italy during the Renaissance by princes with a genuine desire to mix piety with pleasure on their country estates. Buen Retiro in Madrid, built between 1636 and 1639, was the first royal palace to have custom-built hermitages, with chapels and fountains, in its park – the Spaniards saw no contradiction in serving God and Mammon simultaneously. From Spain the fashion spread to France but with a shift in emphasis. In the late seventeenth century Louis XIV built the Château de Marly as a place of retreat, where he could escape the rigid etiquette he had instituted at Versailles, and called it his Hermitage.

According to the Duc de Saint Simon, whose memoirs paint a vivid picture of life at the French court, the king 'sickened with beauty and tired at last with the swarm of courtiers, persuaded himself that from time to time he needed a small place and solitude . . . so the Hermitage was built. The plan was to spend there three nights only, from a weekday to a Saturday, two or three times a year, with a dozen or so courtiers for necessary attendance. But what actually happened was that the Hermitage was enlarged, building after building sprang up, hills were removed, waterworks and gardens were put in.'

This was where the Russian idea of a Hermitage came from. Peter the Great visited Versailles and Marly in 1717, shortly after Louis XIV's death, and was delighted with them. He saw a Hermitage as a place where you could entertain your friends without fuss or ceremony. The Hermitage that he built at Peterhof was a small, moated, two-storey building with a system of pulleys which allowed the dining table on the first floor to be supplied from below, thus making the presence of servants unnecessary during his carousals.

When Peter's daughter, the Empress Elizabeth, was laying out the park of her own great country palace, Tsarskoe Selo, in the 1740s, she naturally included a Hermitage, this time a Baroque dining pavilion with another mechanical table. Elizabeth Dimsdale, the wife of a British doctor, has left an account of how it worked. There were 'four dumb waiter plates with silver rims and something of the slate kind in the middle of them and a pencil fixed to each plate. You wrote on the plate what was ordered, then pulled another string and the plate sunk down and returned again with the order, dishes the same.'

This was the kind of Hermitage that Catherine had in mind when she commissioned the French architect Jean-Baptiste Vallin de la Mothe to add a small pavilion to the majestic Winter Palace she had inherited from the Empress Elizabeth. The buildings were connected by a covered bridge and both look out over the broad waters of the River Neva just before it splits in two to flow either side of Vasilevsky Island.

The Empress Elizabeth had referred to the rooms in the Winter Palace that she used for private entertainment as her 'Hermitage'. Catherine was thus following her lead when she added a Hermitage pavilion to the palace – but it was still connected in her mind with a garden. Her original idea was to have a first-floor 'hanging garden' built over her stables. At one end, which connected directly with her private apartments, there were to be rooms for her lover, Count Grigory Orlov. At the other, there would be the Hermitage proper, a suite of rooms looking out over the river which she would use for entertaining her friends. There was also a conservatory which opened on to the hanging garden, which she kept bustling with songbirds. Before the building was completed, Catherine had begun collecting paintings on a massive scale, so she had picture galleries added down the sides of the garden.

The galleries quickly proved inadequate for her collection – she bought 2,000 pictures in the first ten years of her reign. So she had the German-trained architect, Yury Velten, build her a second, larger extension to the palace. As well as galleries, it contained a library, a medal cabinet and a billiard room – Catherine was very fond of billiards. It was tacked on beyond Vallin de la Mothe's small pavilion and the two buildings came to be known as the 'Small Hermitage' and the 'Old Hermitage'.

Like its namesakes in the parks of Peterhof and Tsarskoe Selo, Catherine's Small Hermitage had *tables volants* – dinner tables which could be mechanically raised or lowered from the ground floor by a system of pulleys. 'In the dining-rooms, there are two tables side by side laid for ten,' the German writer Friedrich Melchior Grimm explained in a letter to society hostess Madame Geoffrin in 1774. 'Waiting is done by machine. There is no need for footmen behind chairs, and the Provost of Police is distinctly at a disadvantage as he is unable to report to Her Majesty anything that is said at these dinners.'

Catherine regarded her Hermitage as a sort of private club, whose members she personally selected, and as a place where she could forget her rank and relax. She particularly enjoyed small dinners for a dozen or so people and would often carry off her guests to watch a play in her private theatre afterwards. She held soirées known as *Petits Hermitages* for sixty or eighty people several times a month and, more rarely, *Grands Hermitages* to which she invited up to 200 guests, providing them with dinner and a ball.

To ensure that everyone behaved properly in the intimacy of her Hermitage, she drew up a set of rules which she had mounted on the wall:

1 All ranks shall be left behind at the doors, as well as swords and hats.
2 Parochialism and ambitions shall also be left behind at the doors.
3 One shall be joyful but shall not try to damage, break or gnaw at anything.
4 One shall sit or stand as one pleases.
5 One shall speak with moderation and quietly so that others do not get a headache.
6 One shall not argue angrily or passionately.
7 One shall not sigh or yawn.
8 One shall not interfere with any entertainment suggested by others.
9 One shall eat with pleasure, but drink with moderation so that each can leave the room unassisted.
10 One shall not wash dirty linen in public and shall mind one's own business until one leaves.

That Catherine needed to ban drunken brawls at her soirées underlines how superficial the French polish adopted by the Russian court remained at this period. It was only a matter of fifty years since Peter the Great had visited London, Paris and Vienna and brought home with him the vision of how a European court should look and behave – a vision that he proceeded to impose on Russia. He forced his nobles, the boyars, to abandon the long fur robes they had worn for centuries and adopt European dress. He cut their flowing beards with his own hands, ignoring pleas for mercy; the Russians believed that their beards, so similar to those worn by the Apostles in icon paintings, were passports to heaven and several carried the severed relics in their pockets after Peter's scissors had put their salvation at risk.

Above all, it was Peter who moved the Russian capital from Moscow to St Petersburg, in the far north, where he built a new, European-style city on the marshy delta of the River Neva. He wanted it to look like Amsterdam but since he and his successors used mainly Italian architects, it ended up looking more like Venice.

Peter was also an art collector and founded Russia's first public museum, the so-called Kunstkammer, whose elegant Baroque building can still be admired from the windows of the Hermitage, a little downriver, on the banks of Vasilevsky Island. While the treasures of the Hermitage include imperial acquisitions dating back as far as the reign of Ivan the Terrible (1547–84), its first great works of art were acquired by Peter. It is with him, rather than Catherine, that the history of the Hermitage museum really begins.

Peter's posthumous fame rests almost equally on cruelty and culture. He tortured his eldest son Alexey to death in an effort to obtain evidence of a non-existent plot against himself, and executed his subjects on a lavish scale, but he also succeeded in introducing the most up-to-date developments of European science, engineering and art to Russia. He was a passionate 'improver' of his people.

Peter became co-tsar at the age of ten in 1682, in partnership with his half-brother Ivan V who was to die in 1696. Ivan's sister Sophia became Regent and Peter was banished from the court, growing up with little education. He loved to play games of war, constantly ordering arms for the use of his young playmates, and, more significantly from the point of view of St Petersburg, which was to be Russia's first significant sea port, he developed a passion for boats and boatbuilding.

At first Peter learned what he could about boats from knowledgeable locals and the inhabitants of the foreign quarter of Moscow – in old Muscovy foreigners lived apart from the rest of the population. Then he sent agents abroad to study the techniques of seafaring nations. Finally, he went abroad to learn for himself. In 1697–8, he embarked on his first foreign journey, known as the 'Great Embassy', travelling 'incognito' with a retinue of 250. No one was taken in by his disguise but it enabled him to avoid pomp and formality which he disliked. He spent several weeks living with a Dutch blacksmith-turned-fisherman in Zaandam working as a carpenter in the dockyard there.

Firm in the knowledge of his limitless power, Peter liked to play the humble citizen. In Zaandam he lived in two rooms with a stove and a mattress that could be packed away in a cupboard. The rooms have been preserved as a sort of Petrine shrine – which has been visited over the centuries by a succession of tsars. From Holland, Peter moved on to Britain to investigate the naval shipyards of Greenwich where another of his characteristics became apparent. Here, he was lent the diarist John Evelyn's house but devoted so much time to hard drinking with his companions that the house and garden were virtually destroyed – floors and furniture used as firewood, trees cut down and bushes uprooted. After his departure, Sir Christopher Wren had to be sent down to Greenwich to rebuild the house.

On his return to Russia, Peter built two navies, one to attack the Turks in the south and the other to attack the Swedes in the north, but he built them on rivers since, at the time, Russia's only access to the sea was its Arctic coast, where the water was frozen for most of the year. It was thus of enormous significance to Peter when, in 1703, he defeated the Swedish army and captured a stretch of coast on the Gulf of Finland. He immediately ordained the construction of a fortress on the mouth of the Neva to protect the territory from Swedish reprisals – and this became the very first building of St Petersburg, the so-called Peter and Paul fortress.

Peter's absolute power as autocrat enabled him to draft 20,000 men to work on its construction. According to an account given by the Hanoverian ambassador, Friedrich Christian Weber, some of them came 'Journies of 200 to 300 German Miles. There were neither sufficient provisions to furnish them with the necessary Tools, as Pickaxes, Spades, Shovels, Wheelbarrows, Planks and the like, they even had not so much as Houses or Huts; notwithstanding which the Work went on with such Expedition, that it was surprising to see the Fortress raised within less than five Months time.'

Peter's contemporaries considered it crazy to build a city in the far north of the country in harsh climatic conditions. Its inhabitants had to contend with snow and ice for five months a year, then floods, and finally hot summers when the steaming marshes spread disease. Nevertheless, by 1704 Peter was referring to the new settlement as his 'capital'. And his spectacular defeat of the Swedes at the battle of Poltava in 1709 confirmed his determination to make it the first city of the empire.

He built himself a log and mud cabin on the north bank of the Neva where he lived while directing the construction of the city. His principal architect, Domenico Trezzini, came from Switzerland but had studied architecture in Rome; he arrived in Russia in 1705 and drew up overall plans for the city as well as designing its principal buildings. The government was moved from Moscow in 1712 and Peter populated his city by decree. In 1710 he demanded that 40,000 workmen a year should be sent from the provinces with their tools. All nobles owning more than thirty families of serfs were required to settle in St Petersburg and build houses there. Those who owned more than 500 serfs had to build stone houses of at least two storeys. In order to secure enough stonemasons, he issued an embargo on the construction of stone buildings elsewhere in the country.

The ambassador of Hanover, Friedrich Christian Weber, has left a classic account in his *The Present State of Russia*, published in 1723, of how the diplomatic corps was drafted into clearing woodland in 1715. It provides a glimpse of the Petrine life-style:

His Majesty, who was restrained in his own drinking, gave us a well matured Hungarian wine at dinner. We could hardly stand, having drunk such a quantity already, but it was impossible to refuse another pint glass offered by the Tsarina herself. This reduced us to such pitiful circumstances that our servants chose to throw one of us into the garden, and another in the wood where we stayed till four p.m. in the afternoon, and where we were sick. We were woken up at four p.m. and we went back into the Palace where the Tsar gave us each an axe and ordered us to follow him. He took us into a wood, planted with young trees.

Wanting to reach the sea, he had marked out a cutting and immediately started cutting wood down alongside us. Hardly able to cope with this type of work, especially after a debauch which had made us very tired, the seven of us, not counting His Majesty, finished off the alley in three hours. This violent exercise sweated us out of our alcoholic haze. No accident happened except that Mr—, one of His Majesty's Ministers, lurching hither and thither, was knocked over by a tree which fell on him.

Having thanked us for our work, His Majesty paid for our supper that night. A second debauch followed; this time we fainted away and were put to bed. After one hour's sleep, one of the Tsar's favourites woke us up to visit the Prince of Circassia, in bed with his wife. We had to drink brandy and wine by his bed till four o'clock when we found ourselves at home, ignorant of how we got there. At eight a.m., we went to Court to drink coffee but the cups were full of brandy.'

Peter was dedicated to hard drinking and considered it necessary to offer visitors a choice of vodka, Hungarian wine, or coffee when he opened Russia's first museum, the so-called Kunstkammer. His henchman Alexander Menshikov, the first governor of St Petersburg, objected but Peter insisted that making alcohol available was vital in order to attract attendance. Neither his theatres nor his museum were immediately popular with the boyars who had reluctantly settled in St Petersburg.

Many exhibits from Peter's Kunstkammer have ended up in the Hermitage, but art was not its main focus. As the German term Kunstkammer implies, it was a 'cabinet of curiosities' of the kind accumulated by both scholars and monarchs in the sixteenth and seventeenth centuries, a combination of found objects, such as shells and minerals, scientific specimens, curiously wrought craft works, jewels and paintings. Peter was inspired by the cabinets he saw in Holland and Germany on his Great Embassy in the 1690s; he spent three days in detailed study of the Elector of Saxony's Kunstkammer in June 1698. His first purchases are recorded in the Embassy accounts: 'Bought at Amsterdam from the merchant Bartholomew Vorhagen, a marine animal, a "Korkodil", also a sea fish called Swertfish, for his Highness the Tsar's personal household, and the animal and the fish have been handed to bombardier Ivan Hummer for taking to Moscow.'

Peter was less interested in painting but he admired the meticulously rendered sea pictures of Ludolf Bakhuizen, sat for his portrait to Godfrey Kneller in The Hague – at the request of William III of Holland – and learned engraving from Adriaan Schoonebeeck in Amsterdam. It was on the Great Embassy that he first met Gottfried Wilhelm Leibniz, the German philosopher and mathematician, whom he later described as his 'intimate adviser'. In 1708 Leibniz wrote Peter a memorandum on his museum plans: 'Concerning the Museum, and the cabinets and Kunstkammern pertaining to it, it is absolutely essential that they should be such as to serve not only as objects of general curiosity, but also as means to the perfection of the arts and sciences.' His advice perfectly accorded with Peter's desire to 'improve' his subjects.

The Kunstkammer was first housed in a garden pavilion beside the small Summer Palace that Domenico Trezzini built for Peter about a mile up the Neva from the Winter Palace. The palace survives to this day, a modest Dutch-style home with gardens stretching along the banks of the Neva and Fontanka rivers. Besides the Kunstkammer pavilion, which has now vanished, the gardens were 'peopled' with more than one hundred sculptures imported from Rome and Venice, including recently excavated antique pieces. Among them was one of the Hermitage's most treasured possessions, the *Tauride Venus*, a Roman copy of a third century BC Greek original.

The life-size marble lady has no arms but is otherwise remarkably complete, with a sensitively carved face and sensuous body. She was unearthed in Rome in 1718 and bought secretly on Peter's behalf by Yury Kologrivov who was in Rome in charge of a group of young painters. But the civil governor of Rome forbade its export. Kologrivov appealed to the vice-chancellor of the Vatican, Cardinal Ottoboni, for help and a deal was finally struck whereby the Pope donated the *Venus* to Peter while he, in return, undertook to try to obtain the relics of the fourteenth-century nun St Bridget from Sweden. They were kept in the town of Vadsten a good way from the frontier and it is unclear whether Peter intended to obtain them through diplomacy or conquest. In any case, they were never delivered. But a series of letters from Cardinal Ottoboni to Peter and others in authority in St Petersburg bear witness to the fact that the Vatican expected to receive them. The *Venus* travelled to St Petersburg overland in a specially sprung coach ordered by the tsar himself. She was number one on the list of treasures that were removed for safekeeping to the Urals at the outbreak of World War II.

Peter's museum collection, as opposed to his private Kunstkammer, was first opened to the public in 1718 in the Kikin Mansion which had conveniently become available after the arrest and execution of its owner. Alexander Kikin was an early friend of Peter's, accompanied him on the Great Embassy in the 1690s, learned shipbuilding in Holland and was given charge of the Admiralty in St Petersburg. But he befriended Peter's estranged son Alexey and they were both tortured to death in 1718 for allegedly plotting to overthrow the tsar. The ceremonial opening of the museum in Kikin's elegant Baroque manor house – which also survives, now in central St Petersburg – took place in 1719.

By this time Peter had commissioned the museum building on the bank of Vasilevsky Island which is today known as the Kunstkammer, a blue and white confection centred by a four-tier, polygonal tower that doubles as a skylight. Peter was particularly proud of his skill in pulling teeth and intended to give demonstrations in the well of the tower; the public would be able to watch from a balcony. His dental equipment is today on display at the Hermitage, among a collection of his other tools, while some of the teeth he drew are on show at the Kunstkammer with labels that identify whose they were – 'a person who made tablecloths', for example, or 'a fast-walking messenger'.

The museum building was not completed by the time Peter died in 1725. Both his private collection and the museum collection from the Kikin Mansion were combined there in 1734 and an inventory compiled in 1741 reveals the original character of its exhibits. The scientific section included anatomical specimens, embryos, freaks, animals, plants and minerals; in the 'man-made' section there were craftsmen's tools, an ethnographic collection and a large display of 'wares from China'; there was a section containing gold, silver, gems and coins and another with 'pictures in colours thinned with oil' which was subdivided into representations of faces, representations of single figures, groups, symbolic paintings, landscapes and still lives.

An entirely original feature of Peter's Kunstkammer was the presence of live exhibits, such as a young hermaphrodite, who later escaped, and Foma, the son of a peasant from Irkutsk who was born with only two digits on each hand and foot. After Foma's death, Peter had him stuffed and exhibited in the Kunstkammer next to the skeleton of another of his old associates, a French giant called Nicholas Bourgeois. Like earlier monarchs, Peter kept dwarfs and giants at his court to entertain him.

After Peter's death, a new gallery was added to the museum which contained a wax figure of Peter himself, made by Carlo Rastrelli, the leading court sculptor, together with the stuffed skins of Peter's dog and his horse Lisetta, 'a stallion of Persian stock'. Carlo Rastrelli, father of the architect Bartolomeo Rastrelli who built the Winter Palace, had been recruited in Paris. On Louis XIV's death, Peter realised that many artists would be out of work in the French capital and instructed his envoy to try to recruit the best of them into his service. He thus obtained the services of Jean-Baptiste Le Blond, the French architect and garden designer, and Carlo Rastrelli, the sculptor – both were required to sign contracts stating that they would teach their craft to Russian pupils 'without any secrets or deceptions'.

In addition to bronzes – including a magnificent bust of Peter now in the Hermitage – Carlo Rastrelli had made Peter waxworks of several members of the court in the style now mainly associated with Madame Tussaud of London. The waxwork he made of the tsar after his death has become one of the most famous images of Peter in Russia – along with Etienne-Maurice Falconet's equestrian statue, the *Bronze Horseman*, later commissioned by Catherine.

In the eighteenth century, portraits were always expected to flatter, and often imbued the sitter with some allegorical significance – Peace, Victory, Freedom or something of the kind. But a waxwork was expected merely to be lifelike. Rastrelli's wax figure of Peter has a direct realism, quite untypical of the period, which still speaks powerfully of the subject's character. It is now the centrepiece of a special exhibition illustrating the age of Peter the Great in the basement of the Hermitage Theatre building – where the remains of Peter's original, much smaller, Winter Palace were recently excavated.

Peter's own museum, the Kunstkammer building on Vasilevsky Island, today contains only a few minor leftovers of the original exhibits, which have been gradually dispersed over the centuries. Most popular with tourists are the remains of his collection of anatomical freaks. Having studied the collection of the professor of anatomy Fredrik Ruysch in Amsterdam, which he subsequently purchased, Peter issued a decree that 'human monsters', unknown animals and birds found anywhere in the country should be saved for him. Dead specimens had to be preserved in vinegar or vodka, which was reimbursed by the imperial pharmacy on delivery of the exhibits. The collection still includes Siamese twins, a two-faced baby and a two-headed calf.

Another of Peter's decrees brought in a collection which is now one of the glories of the Hermitage, comprising gold buckles and ornaments in the Scytho-Siberian animal style made around the seventh to the third century BC. Peter's attention was first drawn to these artefacts when Akinfy Demidov, who had mined for precious metal in Siberia, presented twenty marvellous golden objects to his wife Catherine to celebrate the birth of an heir in 1715. Peter was fascinated by the imaginative animal figures which include eagles with ears, lion-griffins, eagle-griffins, wild cats with manes, tails and griffin's heads and other exotica. He gave Prince Matvey Gagarin, the governor of Siberia, strict instructions that all the antiquities found in local burial mounds should be collected and sent to St Petersburg. The following year, Gagarin was able to send Peter another one hundred pieces and the collection continued to increase steadily.

The gold objects had mainly been found by tomb robbers who made a professional, or part-time, living from the tall burial mounds left behind by the Scythians, Sauromatae, Sakae and other ancient inhabitants of the Eurasian steppes. Prior to Peter's decree the gold objects, once looted, would have been melted and resold as bullion, their artistry lost for ever. Peter is thus largely responsible for our knowledge of the extraordinary aesthetic achievements of craftsmen in this remote period. Luckily, he had picked up an interest in archaeology on his European travels.

A miscellany of other leftovers of Peter's Kunstkammer have found their way to the Hermitage. These include architectural drawings for the early buildings of St Petersburg, scientific instruments, commemorative medals, pottery, textiles and furniture. The contents of his turning shop are particularly interesting since they cast an unusual sidelight both on the monarch and his age. Ingenious machines, known as lathes, capable of imparting barley sugar twists and other geometric mouldings to wood or ivory, as well as accurately copying relief carvings, became popular with European monarchs in the seventeenth century and many, including Maximilian of Bavaria, the Medici Grand Duke Ferdinand III of Florence and Louis XV of France, turned their hands to lathework. It was one of Peter's favourite hobbies, satisfying simultaneously his artistic sensibility and his fascination with technology.

The turning shop was run by one Andrey Nartov, a Russian craftsman and inventor who worked 'to devise new and as yet unknown applications for turning skills', according to a contemporary. Peter gave one of his lathes to Louis XV but the Hermitage still has twelve of the machines Nartov invented, together with articles that Peter made with them from bone, ivory and wood: drinking cups, snuffboxes, candlesticks, sundials, a compass, portrait medallions and an amazingly elaborate ivory chandelier.

Peter's Kunstkammer does not appear to have housed much in the way of paintings, though some 150 were recorded in the 1741 inventory. Most of Peter's picture collection, which ran to over 400 works by the time of his death, was housed at Peterhof, his country palace on the Gulf of Finland. Early inventories leave some doubts over which imperial purchases he was responsible for but it is clear that he preferred Dutch pictures and that he bought most of them during, or after, his second foreign trip in 1716–17.

After spending a month and a half in Paris in 1717, he is known to have returned to Russia with works by Jean-Baptiste Oudry, Jean-Marc Nattier, Nicolas de Largillière and Hyacinthe Rigaud. His agent in Holland bought Rembrandt's *David and Jonathan*, a touching scene of the two friends parting, painted in 1642, at the Amsterdam sale of Jan van Beuningen's collection in 1716, and other notable works by Jan Steen, Simon de Vlieger and Adriaen Van Ostade which are now in the Hermitage collection are thought to have belonged to Peter.

Peter's death brings to a close the first era which had a significant impact on the Hermitage collections. Between his reign and that of Catherine the Great, such notable objects as found their way into the collection did so more or less by mistake – they were either very grand examples of the applied arts purchased for daily use, or gifts from foreign potentates.

At this time in Russian history, either a tsar named his heir or the nobles elected a successor from among the previous tsar's close relations. Peter had left no instructions and was succeeded by his second wife, Catherine, who was popular with his friends. Born Martha Skavron-skaya, the daughter of a Lithuanian peasant, she was left an orphan at an early age and became a camp follower of the Russian army in 1702, progressing from bed to bed – she was exceptionally beautiful – until she became the mistress of Peter's favourite, Prince Alexander Menshikov. Peter first saw her in 1703, pouring wine for the guests at Menshikov's table.

They were soon lovers and Peter married her privately in 1710, then publicly in 1712 with their two daughters, Anna and Elizabeth, as bridesmaids. Catherine also bore him several sons but all of them were sickly and died young. Her reign lasted only two years. Worn out by hard drinking, the birth of ten children and venereal disease which she had caught from Peter, she died in 1727. Menshikov's ascendancy died with her. In 1728 he was found guilty of treason, stripped of his possessions and exiled.

The nobles' selection then fell on Peter's eleven-year-old grandson by his first marriage, who ascended the throne as Peter II. He was the only child of Alexey, the son Peter I had tortured to death in 1718. The little boy was keen on hunting and moved the court back from St Petersburg to Moscow where he thought the sport was better. But he, too, only lasted for three years, unexpectedly dying of smallpox in 1730.

The next choice was more enduring, Anna Ivanovna, the daughter of Peter the Great's half brother Ivan. Anna had been married at seventeen to the Duke of Courland in order to add this little Baltic province to Russia's sphere of influence. Her nineteen-year-old husband drank so much at the celebrations that he died on the journey home and Anna remained an impecunious dependant of the imperial household until finding herself empress at the age of thirty-seven. Her ten-year reign (1730–40) is considered one of the darker pages of Russia's history.

She reigned by fear, relying on the secret police and their torture chamber to impose her will. She was also noted for her cruel practical jokes, the most famous being the enforced marriage of Prince A. M. Golitsyn, a middle-aged widower, with a very ugly Kalmyk peasant. Anna organised the wedding procession which included goats, pigs, cows, camels, dogs, reindeer and an elephant with a cage on its back enclosing the bridal couple. After the wedding they were forced to consummate the marriage in a palace built entirely of ice which Anna had erected on the Neva, all the furniture, including a four-poster bed, also being carved from ice.

Anna's unpopularity was compounded by the power she placed in the hands of her lover, Ernst Johann Biron, the handsome son of a groom in her late husband's stables. She made him a count on her accession in 1730 and Duke of Courland, when her in-laws died out, in 1737. Both Anna and Biron's principal interest was hunting. According to the Austrian ambassador Count Ludwig Cobenzl, 'when the Count Biron talks of horses, or to horses, he speaks like a man, when he speaks of men, or to men, he speaks as a horse might do.'

Anna and Biron shared a taste for the ostentatious and commissioned the top goldsmiths and silversmiths of London, Paris and Augsburg to make them glittering adjuncts to daily living, mostly very large. Anna's commissions stayed, naturally, in the imperial collection while Biron's were confiscated and added to it after his exile in 1740.

Anna's most sumptuous commission was the throne she ordered from the London goldsmith Nicholas Clausen in 1731, its wooden frame encased in silver-gilt of scrolling, Baroque design. The arms end in eagles' heads and the feet in eagles' claws clutching silver balls. It can be admired today in the small throne room of the Hermitage. The throne was so popular with Anna's successors that they had several carved and gilded wooden copies made for other rooms that were used for ceremonial occasions.

Anna also commissioned a solid gold toilet set from the greatest Augsburg craftsman of his day, Johann Ludwig Biller. There are still forty-three pieces in the Hermitage collection, including a mirror, combs, brushes, boxes, perfume bottles and part of a breakfast service – though the set must originally have been much larger. It is one of the most impressive exhibits in the high-security exhibition of the museum's 'Special Collection' of gems and items wrought from precious metal.

Among the Biron treasures is a magnificent wine cooler made by the English silversmith Paul de Lamerie in 1726, still in the Baroque style which Britain's most famous silversmith favoured before he got caught up with the Rococo. It is exceptionally large.

Anna's most important contribution to the Hermitage, however, was the discovery of the young architect Bartolomeo Rastrelli who later designed the Winter Palace. After her coronation in Moscow Anna determined to move the court back to St Petersburg and she commissioned Rastrelli, then virtually unknown, to build her a wooden Summer Palace in Peter the Great's Summer Gardens. She and Biron were delighted with it and showered Rastrelli with commissions. He built an opera house, a riding school so large that it could accommodate seventy-five horsemen simultaneously, and two palaces for Biron in Courland. Anna also commissioned him to rework the old Winter Palace but nothing remains of this building. Under Anna's successor, the Empress Elizabeth, Rastrelli built the Catherine Palace at Tsarskoe Selo and entirely rebuilt the Winter Palace, giving it the appearance that it has today.

Anna's death in 1740 sparked the most confused succession of the century. Six days before she died she named as her successor the newly born son of her German niece, Anna Leopoldovna. Ivan VI was only two months old when he became emperor on 8 October 1740. Biron had himself named as Regent in order to assure his continuing power. But he was immensely unpopular and one month later, in a palace coup, he was replaced as Regent by Ivan's mother, Anna Leopoldovna, Princess of Brunswick-Wolfenbuttel-Bevern. Biron was arrested in the middle of the night, ripped from his bed by guards who stuffed a handkerchief into his mouth, bound his hands and took him to prison naked, but for a cloak lent him for decency's sake. He was subsequently exiled to Siberia and his possessions were confiscated.

The Regency went to Anna Leopoldovna's head. She was pregnant when she became Regent but began a passionate affair with one of her ladies-in-waiting, Julie Mengden. The British ambassador Edward Finch wrote to William Stanhope, Lord Harrington: 'I should give your lordship but a faint idea of it by adding that the passion of a lover for a new mistress is but a jest to it.' After her baby was born, Anna switched her affections to the Saxon ambassador Count Maurice Lynar, and then became obsessed with the idea of marrying Mengden to Lynar.

Meanwhile, Peter the Great's illegitimate daughter Elizabeth was waiting in the wings and the pressure on her from various nobles to oust the baby Ivan and his mother grew in line with Anna's follies. The news that Anna had decided to have herself declared empress in place of her son finally stung Elizabeth and her supporters into action. In the early hours of 25 November 1741 she arrived by sleigh at the palace accompanied by 360 élite Preobrazhensky guards. The Palace Guard joined them and Elizabeth took over in a bloodless coup.

Elizabeth was much loved, partly on account of her great beauty. 'Her physical charms are marvellous to behold, her beauty indescribable,' the Duke of Liria had written in 1728. She loved festivities and kept the court busy with fancy dress balls. As she looked very good dressed as a man, she insisted that men should come to her balls dressed as women and women as men – a directive which was not popular with either sex. She had a passion for clothes and is reputed never to have worn the same dress twice.

The museum contains the mementoes of an extraordinary event which coincided with Elizabeth seizing power in 1741. Nadir Shah, the ruler of Iran (1736–47), had sent an embassy to St Petersburg from India after his conquest of the Mogul Empire in 1739; the journey took two years, as the Shah's representatives travelled by elephant. They arrived in St Petersburg on 8 October 1741 carrying with them twenty-two elaborate jewelled objects, including plates and bottles, together with fifteen signet rings, all from the colossal booty that Nadir Shah seized from the Mogul treasuries.

These jewelled gifts had been intended for the Empress Anna but the ambassadors quickly took advantage of the confused situation and divided them between the baby Ivan VI, his mother, the Regent, and Elizabeth, who was to seize power the month after their arrival. In the first inventory of the Hermitage collections the jewels were mistakenly described as 'Persian' and they were not the focus of any special study until the 1980s – when it was realised that the pieces were Indian and that the Persian embassy must have come direct from Delhi. Most of the Mogul jewels and jewel-encrusted ornaments which Nadir Shah took home with him to Iran had the precious stones gouged out of them for reuse. Today the group of Mogul jewelled objects in the Hermitage is the largest in the world to have survived in their original form. Only three mounted pieces have survived in the Iranian treasury and there are none in Indian museums.

The Mogul emperors, then the richest rulers in the world, were the main customers of the Colombian emerald mines after the Spanish conquest of South America in the sixteenth century; Colombian emeralds then, as now, were considered finer than those from any other source. All the emeralds used in the Hermitage pieces came from Colombia via India. There are two bottles whose outer surfaces are encrusted with emeralds – emeralds, rubies and diamonds are the principal stones used in all the pieces. There are several other jewel-encrusted bottles, some plates, a casket, a small table, turban pins and ankle bracelets. They are all wrought from gold but almost all the surfaces are covered over, either with colourful floral enamels or patterns of encrusted precious stones. From the original gift, seventeen jewelled items and one signet ring have survived. The signet ring is inscribed with a commemoration of the birth stars of Shah Jehan who ruled India from 1631 to 1657 and built the Taj Mahal.

The fourteen elephants that accompanied the embassy were also a gift to the imperial family. In advance of their arrival several of St Petersburg's bridges had to be rebuilt or reinforced in order to carry the elephants' weight. A new elephant yard was constructed near the Fontanka river and a square was cleared beside it for them to walk in. On 16 October, however, three of the elephants got away from their keepers in the yard. Two were soon restrained but the third broke the wooden fence, escaped into the Summer Palace gardens and got all the way across to Vasilevsky Island where he wrought havoc in a village before being caught.

The crowning glory of Elizabeth's reign, as far as the Hermitage is concerned, was the construction of the Winter Palace itself, one of the most beautiful Baroque buildings in the world. It grows out of the ground like a giant's wedding cake on a platter. The white columns, in two ranges, connect the earth with the sky in soaring lines. It has changed colour several times over the centuries, starting life yellow and white, shifting to green and white in the mid-nineteenth century, and temporarily turning brick-red all over in the early twentieth century. Today the building is faced in plaster painted a soft, sea green, against which the white columns and window surrounds stand out. Above the windows are masks and shell mouldings picked out in bronze paint. The coppered roof has turned green to match the walls, as have the double life-size bronze statues that embellish the balustrade that runs round it – gods, goddesses, nymphs and urns.

The Russian imperial family had built several previous Winter Palaces at different locations along the banks of the Neva. The present building is the sixth, if one counts the wooden Winter Palace that Rastrelli made for use while his masterpiece was under construction. His plans were approved in 1754 and it took a year to clear the jumble of buildings that already existed on the site.

To quote the architectural historian Audrey Kennett:

> By 1757 the scene of building activity almost resembled that of the earliest days of the city. Thousands of soldiers were used as labourers. Artisans and craftsmen were gathered from far and wide. Two thousand masons from Yaroslavl and Kostroma were at work. All were camped in the meadows. Rastrelli was acting under imperial orders, but they were not sufficient to release the money that was needed for such a vast enterprise. He himself had to appeal to the Senate – arguing that the palace was being built for the glory of all Russia.

The Winter Palace was completed in 1762, six months after Elizabeth's death, and was first used by Peter III and Catherine the Great.

2

Catherine's Collections

*C*atherine the Great is still the presiding genius of the Hermitage. Most histories date the foundation of the museum to her purchase of 225 Old Master paintings from the Berlin dealer Johann Gotzkowski in 1764. And, while her 'gluttonous' – to use her own word – purchase of 4,000 Old Master paintings has drawn visitors from all corners of the world to the Hermitage for over 200 years, there is almost no field of the fine or applied arts which is not represented in the museum collection by some extraordinary masterpiece that she acquired.

She was not much interested in sculpture but she bought the only Michelangelo marble in the collection – the unfinished *Crouching Boy* – and commissioned Jean-Antoine Houdon's *Voltaire*, which depicts the famous French philosopher in old age, life-size, seated in an armchair. The greatest sculptor of the eighteenth century has brilliantly conveyed the personality of the crusty old genius. It is also Catherine's doing that the Hermitage has the best collection of French eighteenth-century bronzes outside France.

Engraved gems were probably her greatest love, a collecting field to which little attention is now paid. In antiquity, precious and semi-precious stones were often carved in relief or engraved, most often with portraits but also with emblems and little pictures commemorating special events. Some were made as personal ornaments, some as amulets or charms and some as seals. They were rediscovered in the Renaissance and new gems began to be carved. Catherine, who was fascinated by history, loved the historical references she found in these little carvings. She collected Greek and Roman examples, as well as Renaissance pieces and brand new commemorative items – many of which were carved at her court. She was probably the greatest gem collector the world has ever known.

She also bought Classical sculpture and set the scene for Russia's great archaeological discoveries of the nineteenth century by annexing the Crimea in 1783 and territory north of the Black Sea which had previously belonged to the Turks. The ancient tombs of the Crimea did not begin to yield their treasures until the early years of the nineteenth century, but General A. Melgunov, a local military governor, had a barrow of the late seventh or early sixth century BC – the Litoi or Melgunov Barrow – near modern-day Kirovograd (formerly Elizavet-grad), opened in 1763, and donated its contents to Catherine. They included part of an iron sword with a finely wrought gold sheath and the gold lion-headed arms of a throne and are among the earliest in date of the museum's Scythian treasures.

In the field of the applied arts Catherine commissioned silver, jewels, porcelain, furniture, tapestries and other artefacts from the leading craftsmen of the day – dinner services from Sèvres and Wedgwood, tapestries from the Gobelins factory in France, furniture from David Roentgen in Germany – Marie Antoinette's favourite cabinetmaker – and silver from Roettiers in Paris. She also patronised her own Imperial Porcelain Factory, and the local goldsmiths and cabinetmakers of St Petersburg. The scale of her commissions was always grandiose. Faced with furnishing the Winter Palace at the outset of her husband's reign, for example, she ordered from Paris 'eighty-five giltwood mirrors and sixty-seven carved and gilded sidetables with marble tops'. When planning a surprise gift for her lover Grigory Orlov in 1765, she ordered a 300-piece breakfast service from the Imperial Porcelain Factory decorated with scenes from his military career.

While the Russian imperial family produced many big spenders, Catherine was probably the biggest – but her spending was driven by political calculation. She realised early on that the splendour of her court would enhance her reputation in Europe and have a direct impact on diplomatic relations. It was no coincidence that the paintings she purchased from Gotzkowski in 1764 had been accumulated by the dealer on the instructions of Frederick the Great of Prussia – who could not afford to buy them after his financially crippling Seven Years War with Austria, Russia and France. Her husband Peter III made a highly disadvantageous, unilateral peace with Frederick, his hero, which Catherine did not renege on – but she got her own back by buying

Frederick's pictures. The spectacular bulk purchase was a way of demonstrating her superiority in a manner that all Europe would understand.

She continued this strategy of lavish artistic patronage throughout her thirty-four-year reign, making St Petersburg a financial honeypot that attracted artists, designers and art dealers from all over Europe. Nowhere else was so much money being lavished on the arts. St Petersburg in the second half of the eighteenth century played a role similar to that of New York in the second half of the twentieth.

In a letter she wrote to her agent and friend Friedrich Melchior Grimm in 1790, six years before her death, Catherine was able to congratulate herself on having a collection that outclassed those of all the other monarchs of her day. 'Besides the paintings and the Raphael Loggia,' she wrote, referring to her 4,000 Old Masters and the copies she had commissioned of frescoes Raphael painted for the Vatican Palace in Rome, 'my museum in the Hermitage contains 38,000 books; there are four rooms filled with books and prints, 10,000 engraved gems, roughly 10,000 drawings and a natural history collection that fills two large galleries.' She forgot to mention her collection of roughly 16,000 coins and medals.

But it was not as an art collector and patron that Catherine earned the historical privilege of having 'Great' tacked on to her name. Through well calculated alliance and war she significantly extended Russia's frontiers to the west and south. In a series of three annexations she gobbled up most of Poland and, fighting the Turks in the south, she acquired rich new farmlands, the strategic northern coast of the Black Sea, and a bite of the Caucasus. At home she tackled a thoroughgoing reform of Russia's antiquated legal system and looked long and hard at the possibility of turning Russia into a constitutional monarchy – like Britain – but finally opted for autocracy. She was a stateswoman of no mean order.

Not unnaturally, Catherine fascinated her generation and many different accounts of her appearance and character survive. According to Austria's ambassador, the Prince de Ligne, she was:

pretty rather than beautiful. Her eyes and her agreeable smile made her large forehead seem smaller. But this forehead still told all . . . it betokened genius, justice, precision, boldness, depth, equanimity, tenderness, serenity, tenacity, and its width testified to her well developed memory and imagination. It was clear that there was room for everything in this forehead.

Her chin, slightly pointed but neither projecting nor receding, was noble in shape. As a result, the oval of her face did not stand out unduly and was most agreeable on account of the direct and cheerful expression on her lips . . . entering a room she always followed the Russian tradition and bowed three times like a man: first to the right, then to the left and finally straight ahead. Everything about her was measured and orderly.

Other observers took a more jaundiced view. In 1772 the British ambassador Robert Gunning wrote that 'the Empress, whatever may have been reported, is by no means popular here, it is not indeed in this country that she aims at becoming so. She neither bears any affection to the People of it, nor has she acquired theirs. The Principle which in her supplies the want of these motives to great undertakings is an unbounded desire of Fame.' The creation of the Hermitage Museum is, perhaps, one of the happiest results of Catherine's 'unbounded desire of Fame'.

The first indications of this governing 'Principle' can be read in her childhood. On a visit to her relations in Brunswick, a canon who practised palmistry asserted that he saw three crowns in her palm. She interpreted this reading as a sign that she was to marry Karl Peter Ulrich of Holstein-Gottorp, heir to the Russian throne. 'Child that I was,' she wrote in her memoirs, 'the title of queen delighted me. From then on my companions teased me about him and little by little I became used to thinking of myself as destined for him.' Catherine first met Peter when she was ten, became affianced to him at fourteen and was married at fifteen.

Born on 29 April 1729, she was the daughter of Prince Christian August of Anhalt-Zerbst, a major-general in the Prussian army, and was baptised Sophia Frederika Augusta according to the Lutheran rite – she took the name Catherine when she converted to the Russian Orthodox religion before her marriage. It was her mother's connections that rendered 'Sophia' a suitable bride for her cousin Karl Peter Ulrich, the nephew of the childless Empress Elizabeth of Russia. Catherine's mother, Johanna, had been born a Holstein-Gottorp and one of her brothers was King of Sweden. Another had been engaged to marry Elizabeth but died before the wedding could take place and the Empress remembered him with nostalgia.

Catherine was brought up at Stettin, a Baltic port where her father was Governor. The most important influence on her childhood was a French governess, Elisabeth Cardel, who made her read Corneille, Racine and Molière and taught her to love the speed and wit of the French language. This Francophile orientation later became the keynote of her court, and the Hermitage Museum has the best collection of French painting outside France. Catherine recognised her debt to her governess even in old age, proudly describing herself in a letter to Voltaire as the 'pupil of Mlle Cardel'.

After her marriage to Peter in 1744, she spent seventeen years at the court of the Empress Elizabeth. The Grand Duke Peter was sickly and mentally retarded, with a passion for all things German, especially military parades. He idolised Frederick the Great of Prussia on account of his prowess as a military commander and the discipline of his troops. Peter loved dressing up in Prussian uniform and drilling his footmen and servants. Contemporary accounts suggest that he may also have been sterile. In which case the future Tsar Paul I was the son of a handsome courtier called Sergey Saltykov with whom Catherine says she fell in love in 1752 – according to the *Memoirs* which she wrote in old age, describing her life up to the beginning of her reign as empress.

Catherine's son Paul was born on 20 September 1754. The Empress Elizabeth was present at the birth and immediately took the child back to her own rooms. 'I did not see a living soul for the rest of the day,' wrote Catherine, 'nor did anyone send to enquire about me. The Grand Duke was drinking with anyone he could find and the Empress was busy with the child.' To comfort herself, she turned to her books, and devoured Tacitus' *Annals*, Voltaire's *Essay on the Customs and Spirit of Nations* and Montesquieu's *Spirit of the Laws*, she tells us. After she recovered, she hardly saw her son, who was effectively adopted by Elizabeth. Saltykov also abandoned her and her daughter Anna, born three years later in 1757, was fathered by Count Stanislaw Poniatowski, the future King of Poland. Elizabeth removed and adopted this second child as she had done the first.

While they started out as friends, Peter and Catherine grew rapidly apart. Unlike her husband, Catherine groomed herself to rule. She learned Russian, studied Russian history, and went out of her way to demonstrate her devotion to the Orthodox Church. While she had a succession of lovers, the mainstay of her life was study. According to the Chevalier d'Eon, a French diplomat, writing at the time of her accession:

The Empress has a great love of reading. And the greater part of her time since her marriage has been spent devouring those modern French and English authors who have written the most influential works on ethics, the natural sciences and religion. It is enough for a book to be condemned in France for her to give it her full approbation. She is never without the works of Voltaire, the *De l'esprit* of Helveticus, the writings of the *Encyclopédistes* and of Jean-Jacques Rousseau. She is, in fact, a natural bluestocking.

The famous French *philosophes* – Voltaire, Montesquieu, Diderot, Rousseau – were keen advocates of political reform which would give ordinary citizens rights in the running of their countries, for which they were from time to time imprisoned or exiled. It was no doubt their political ideas that first caught Catherine's imagination but, after her accession, their friendship helped stimulate and instruct her taste for art. Her *Memoirs* do not reveal that she had any interest in collecting art before 1762, but within a year of her accession she was corresponding with Voltaire, and Diderot became her chief buying agent in Paris.

By the time of the Empress Elizabeth's death in December 1761, Peter's feelings for Catherine had shifted from unromantic friendship to acute dislike. He had fallen in love with one of her ladies-in-waiting, Elizaveta Vorontsova, the daughter of Elizabeth's vice-chancellor, who tried to persuade him that he should announce little Paul's illegitimacy, divorce Catherine and marry her instead. Well aware of this danger, Catherine retired to the seaside pavilion of Mon Plaisir at Peterhof where she began to plot a *coup d'état* with her new lover, Count Grigory Orlov, a handsome officer in the palace guards, his four brothers and a few close friends in the army.

All was well prepared and, on 29 June 1762, she was fetched before dawn by Grigory's brother Alexey Orlov and driven to St Petersburg where the Ismailovsky Guards proclaimed her their *matushka* – which is usually translated 'little mother' but in Russian implies the respect and reverence that a devoted son feels for his mother, who has the right to command him as she sees fit. They marched triumphantly through the city, with other regiments joining them, and at the Kazan Cathedral the Archbishop of Novgorod received Catherine as sovereign and gave her his blessing. She went on to the Winter Palace where, pausing to collect her eight-year-old son to provide added legitimacy, she made her first public appearance on a balcony overlooking the pillared entrance on Palace Square. Six regiments were gathered below, with their artillery, while priests passed among them distributing blessings. The army and the church had endorsed Catherine's accession.

Meanwhile, a manifesto, hastily printed the night before, was distributed in the streets of the capital. In it Catherine explained that Peter's disdain for the church and his alliance with Prussia, 'our mortal enemy', had made her move necessary. 'For these reasons we have felt ourselves obliged, with God's help, and on the clear and sincere wishes of our subjects, to take the throne as sole and absolute sovereign.'

Only a week later a crumpled note was brought her from Alexey Orlov stating that over supper with the Emperor an argument had arisen and he 'was no more'. 'We cannot even remember what we did, but every one of us down to the last man is entirely guilty,' wrote Alexey. Catherine is said to have fallen into a faint, horrified by the idea that her husband had been assassinated by her friends. But she recovered quickly enough to issue a manifesto the next day covering up what had happened: 'On the seventh day of our accession to the throne of Russia, we have been advised that the ex-tsar Peter III suffered another of his habitual haemorrhoidal attacks, together with a violent colic. Aware of our duty as a Christian, we immediately gave the order to supply him with all necessary care. But to our great sadness we received, last night, the news that God's will had put an end to his life.'

Only nine days after her *coup d'état* she wrote to Denis Diderot offering to continue printing his famous *Encyclopédie* in Russia – its publication had just been banned in France. The *Encyclopédie* was one of the great intellectual achievements of the eighteenth century, the first of the multi-volume encyclopaedias which have continued to be compiled and published in almost every country up to the present day. It was edited by Diderot with the help of the mathematician Jean d'Alembert, with Jean-Jacques Rousseau among its many distinguished contributors. Diderot turned Catherine down on this occasion, preferring to publish in Switzerland.

Next she tried inviting d'Alembert to come to Russia as tutor to her son Paul – she offered him a salary of 20,000 roubles, a palace and the rank of ambassador. But d'Alembert also refused. Foreigners were initially nervous of associating with a regicide. Referring to Catherine's manifesto on Peter III's death, d'Alembert explained to Voltaire why he turned down her offer: 'I am also prone to Haemorrhoids; they take too serious a form in that country and I want to have a painful bottom in safety.'

She had better luck with Voltaire himself. Having just completed a two-volume *History of Russia*, a paean of praise to Peter the Great, he was intrigued by a sovereign who positively wanted to help publish the *Encyclopédie*. He wrote a poem dedicated to Catherine who was overwhelmed with delight when she received it. Her reply, dated 15 October 1763, tells him:

> I was so eager to read your ode that I have abandoned a heap of petitions, and many people's fortunes have been set aside. I am not even sorry ... I must assure you that since 1746 I have felt the greatest obligation towards you. Before that time I read only novels; then by chance your works came into my hands; since then I have never stopped reading them, and would not have wished for books better written, or where there was as much to learn.

It was the beginning of a correspondence that lasted until Voltaire's death in 1778. After which, Catherine paid his heirs 135,398 livres for his library – 7,000 volumes bound in red morocco and annotated by the sage himself, together with most of his papers and her own letters to him. They remained at the Hermitage until the mid-nineteenth century when they were transferred to the Public Library on Nevsky Prospect. She even considered building a replica of Voltaire's château at Ferney, on the French–Swiss frontier, in the park at Tsarskoe Selo as a memorial. She had careful scale drawings and a model made for her but the idea came to nothing. The Hermitage still has the model.

While Voltaire offered his friendship – in fulsome verse – Diderot had to be bought. In 1766 Catherine heard from her ambassador in Paris, Prince Dmitry Golitsyn, that Diderot's financial affairs were in such disorder that he was forced to offer his library for sale for 15,000 livres. She offered 16,000 on condition that the books remained in Diderot's home in Paris and he acted as her librarian during his lifetime – with a salary of 1,000 livres a year to be paid for fifty years in advance, in other words a further lump sum of 50,000 livres. Diderot was overcome with gratitude. 'Great Princess,' he wrote, 'I bow down at your feet; I stretch my arms towards you but my mind has contracted, my brain is confused, my ideas jumbled, I am as emotional as a child, and the true expression of the feeling with which I am filled dies on my lips . . . Oh Catherine! Remain sure that you rule as powerfully in Paris as you do in St Petersburg.'

In Diderot Catherine had acquired not only a counsellor and friend but also a well connected artistic adviser with impeccable taste. For the next eight years, the most active of Catherine's collecting career, Diderot busied himself finding great paintings and securing them on Catherine's behalf.

Her first major acquisition had, however, been made two years earlier when she bought the collection of 225 Old Master paintings from the Berlin dealer, Johann Gotzkowski, which had been intended for Frederick the Great of Prussia. The most cultivated monarch of his age, and another of Voltaire's correspondents, Frederick had filled his palace, Sans Souci, near Berlin with paintings by modern masters – Watteau, Boucher, Lancret, Chardin and others. He then decided that he wanted a group of Old Masters and in 1755 commissioned Gotzkowski to buy them for him. The dealer combed Europe for the finest Italian, Dutch and Flemish paintings money could buy and Frederick purchased a few works in 1756. But the outbreak of the Seven Years War with Austria, France and Russia turned his mind to more urgent problems – in 1760 the Austrian and Russian armies briefly occupied Berlin – and he refused to buy the rest.

As a result, Gotzkowski found himself in financial difficulties. He managed to exacerbate them by the speculative purchase of bread shops left behind in Prussia by the Russian army in 1762. On the verge of bankruptcy, he turned to the Russian ambassador, Vladimir Dolgoruky, and asked if Catherine would take the paintings in discharge of his debts. She decided to accept the offer and the Hermitage collection was born with a flourish. She acquired three Rembrandts, *The Incredulity of St Thomas*, *Potiphar's Wife* and a *Portrait of a Turk*. There was a handsome Frans Hals *Portrait of a Man with a Glove*, and notable examples of Dutch genre painting, such as Jan Steen's *Revellers* and Bartholomeus van der Helst's *Market in Amsterdam*.

She was quick to follow up on her first collecting initiative. Paris was the centre of the art market at the time and she was lucky in having Prince Dmitry Golitsyn as her ambassador in France. He had been brought up there, knew Diderot, attended the famous salon of Madame Geoffrin and was very much at home in the intellectual circle that had long fascinated Catherine. He bought her the works of contemporary painters such as Greuze and Chardin and a miscellany of Old Masters, but his greatest coup was the 1766 purchase of Rembrandt's *Return of the Prodigal Son* from a certain M. d'Amezun for 5,400 livres. The painting, with its extraordinary psychological sensitivity, is regarded by some as the greatest work of art in the Hermitage.

It was also in 1766 that Golitsyn helped introduce Catherine to her two most influential artistic advisers, Denis Diderot and Etienne-Maurice Falconet. He had alerted Catherine when Diderot put his library up for sale and handled the negotiations over its purchase. Later in the year she asked Golitsyn to find her a sculptor capable of creating a fitting monument to her predecessor Peter the Great. Catherine regarded herself as Peter's political heir – he had begun to open Russia to Europe and the modern world, a task which she saw herself completing. She pointed this out with a pretty play on words in a Latin inscription she placed on the sculpture's pedestal once it was completed: *Petro Primo Catharina Secunda* ('To Peter the First from Catherine the Second').

Golitsyn tried out a succession of fashionable sculptors but they quoted exorbitant prices – Guillaume Coustou 450,000 livres, Louis-Claude Vasse 400,000 livres and Augustin Pajou 600,000 livres. Then Diderot took a hand and asked Falconet, who had written an article on sculpture for his *Encyclopédie*, for a quotation. Falconet had been working at the Sèvres factory for the previous nine years, modelling small classical figures that could be reproduced in porcelain and was enthusiastic at the idea of working on a monumental scale. He said he would execute the statue for a salary of 25,000 livres a year and was prepared to devote eight years to it, thus undercutting his colleagues and securing the commission. In fact, the *Bronze Horseman* which dominates the banks of the Neva in front of St Isaac's Cathedral – and has become a popular venue for newly weds to get themselves photographed – took Falconet twelve years to complete, a period during which he acted as a crucial link between Catherine and her artistic advisers in Paris, counselled her on the quality of the pictures she was buying and helped to hang them in her new galleries.

By 1782, when his bronze was finally completed after three attempts at casting the vast sculpture, Falconet had fallen out with Catherine and he returned to France without her even bidding him goodbye. She was the first to honour his monument, however, stifling local criticism of Peter being depicted – three times life size – wearing only a Roman toga. She went to fantastic lengths to obtain a pedestal that would suitably support his rearing horse, a vast lump of granite shaped like a wave about to break, 22 feet high, 42 feet long and 34 feet wide, which she had seen on a visit to Finland in 1768. She offered a reward of 7,000 roubles to the person who devised the best way of moving it to St Petersburg and it ended up being rolled on brass balls with one hundred horses pulling it. The journey lasted a year on a road built specially for the purpose.

In terms of enhancing Catherine's fame, the whole enterprise was an outstanding success. The sculpture, Falconet's masterpiece, has been hailed as one of the most imposing of all equestrian statues. Furthermore, it inspired Pushkin in 1833–4 to write his poem *The Bronze Horseman*, thus earning the statue a significant place in literature as well as art history.

One of the first picture purchases engineered by the Falconet-Diderot team was from the Gaignat collection. When Louis XV's secretary Louis Jean Gaignat died in 1768, Diderot immediately wrote to Falconet urging him to alert Catherine, since Gaignat, he said, 'had collected some wonderful works of literature almost without knowing how to read, and some wonderful works of art without being able to see any more in them than a blind man'. In the event there was fierce competition and Diderot only managed to buy Catherine three canvases by Gerard Dou, and one each by Bartolomé Murillo and Jean-Baptiste Van Loo.

Falconet and Catherine exchanged views on the paintings, once they arrived in St Petersburg, by letter. 'What a charming picture,' Falconet wrote of the Van Loo *Galatea*, 'What magnificent brushwork! What beautiful tones! What a sweet little head of Aphrodite! What an admirable consistency! As for the Murillo we should fall on our knees before it. Anyone who dares to think otherwise has neither faith nor morals. The three pictures by Gerard Dou are all jewels, notwithstanding the wretched dry drawing and the colour of the flesh' – they depicted bathers – 'After all, I do know something about it. It is practically my profession.' He was referring to his expertise in depicting the human form. Catherine replied: 'I think you are right. It is only the Van Loo I cannot approve and I am well aware of the reason; it is because I don't understand enough to see in it all that you do.' What humility on the part of an empress!

Golitsyn, meanwhile, had been transferred from Paris to The Hague and in 1768 secured two small but significant collections of Dutch and Flemish paintings, those of Charles-Joseph, Prince de Ligne and Johann-Philipp, Count Cobenzl, the Austrian emperor's minister at the Belgian court. The purchase of the Cobenzl collection was particularly important in that it also contained Old Master drawings – some 4,000 of them were thrown in on the deal, thus founding the Hermitage collection. Cobenzl's taste appears to have been erratic. There were twenty-five Rubens drawings and some splendid Van Dycks, as well as a quantity of drawings with very ambitious attributions which turned out to be wrong. Catherine does not appear to have been much interested in drawings herself but bought them along with collections of paintings, when necessary, on an imperial scale.

Three years later Golitsyn prepared a 'peaceful triumph' for Catherine – then engaged in war with Turkey – by purchasing the best paintings from the collection of Gerrit Braamcamp at an auction in Amsterdam, including works by Rembrandt, Gerard Terborch, Ostade, Steen, Esaias van de Velde and Gabriel Metsu. He sent them by sea to St Petersburg but unfortunately the captain was a man of exceptional piety. While navigating tricky waters in the Baltic he joined the ship's company at prayers leaving a junior in charge of the sounding line. The ship ran aground and all the pictures were lost. Catherine took it stoically. 'I only lost 60,000 *chervontsy*,' she wrote to Voltaire. 'I shall have to get by without them. This year I have had several successes in such cases; what can I do?'

She had one of her biggest successes in 1769 when she acquired the collection of Count Heinrich von Brühl who had been chancellor to Augustus III of Saxony. Anxious that his collection should keep up with that of his royal master, Brühl had used both treasury money and the king's agents to make his purchases. When he died in 1763, his property was sequestered on account of his huge debts and it was not until 1768 that his heirs were given the right to sell. Catherine was alerted by her ambassador in Saxony, A. N. Beloselsky, and pronounced herself ready to buy the paintings as long as they were really by the artists to whom they had been attributed.

They were. She got four paintings by Rembrandt and five by Rubens – including a dazzling *Landscape with a Rainbow* – four great Jacob van Ruisdael landscapes, five Adriaen van Ostades, a charming Terborch interior called *The Letter*, and twenty-one paintings by Philips Wouwermans. Besides Old Masters, there were contemporary works, including Watteau's *The Embarrassing Proposal* and a fine group of Dresden views by Bernardo Bellotto – which Catherine admired so much that she invited the artist to St Petersburg. Maybe the Venetian Bellotto felt it was too far north; after hesitating for a while, he turned Catherine down in favour of her former lover Stanislaw II of Poland and went to work in Warsaw.

The Brühl collection cost Catherine 180,000 Dutch guilders and arrived by boat from Hamburg slightly the worse for sea water – over

600 paintings and 1,076 drawings carefully mounted in fourteen leather-bound albums. Unlike Cobenzl, Brühl had impeccable taste in drawings. He focused primarily on the seventeenth century, buying Dutch, Italian and French masters. He had a large group of Poussins, many Rembrandts and other important Dutch masters, and works by Paolo Veronese and Titian. He also had a large number of engravings which became the core collection of the Hermitage – there were albums devoted to Raphael, Titian, the Carracci and all the major artists admired in his day, a mix of original prints and reproductive engravings.

Catherine's next sensational acquisition was the collection of the French banker Pierre Crozat, the most important private collection formed in France in the early eighteenth century. Pierre and his brother Antoine grew up in Toulouse and moved to Paris around 1700. Antoine was known as '*le riche*' – his house on the Place Vendôme is now the Ritz – while Pierre was '*le pauvre*', despite his château at Montmorency and Paris home on the Rue Richelieu. The latter became the centre of artistic and intellectual life in the capital. Pierre was a bachelor and allowed several artists to live in his home for extended periods, including Watteau and Rosalba Carriera.

Crozat himself died in 1740 but his paintings only came on the market in 1770, following the death of his nephew Baron Thiers, who had extended the collection with a few choice acquisitions of his own. These included Rembrandt's *Danaë*, probably the most admired painting in the Hermitage until an unbalanced Lithuanian stabbed the painting twice and threw acid at it in 1985. It has been carefully restored but the acid removed the fine glazes; much of the detail has disappeared, leaving unfinished areas of underpaint open to view.

When Diderot heard of the forthcoming sale he 'exploded like a volcano', as he later commented, and gathering up his collector friend François Tronchin, a Geneva banker, dramatist and art lover, set him to work on preparing a catalogue for Catherine. Tronchin rejected 158 paintings as unworthy of her and she ended up buying 500 paintings for 460,000 livres. As a thank-you present she sent Tronchin a sack of sable skins to make a fur coat with. The paintings arrived at St Petersburg in June 1772 aboard a ship called *The Swallow* and Catherine found herself the mistress of eight more paintings by Rembrandt, six by Van Dyck, including a *Self-portrait*, some outstanding Rubens oil sketches and three finished paintings, a Raphael *Holy Family*, Giorgione's *Judith* – a powerful, female study by one of the rarest masters of the Renaissance – and Veronese's *Lamentation over the Dead Christ*.

There was an outcry over the sale in France, which Diderot described in a letter to Falconet: 'I arouse the most genuine public hatred, and do you know why? Because I am sending you paintings. Art lovers cry out, artists cry out, the rich cry out . . . The Empress plans to acquire the Thiers collection in the midst of a ruinous war: that is what humiliates and embarrasses them.' The contract of sale was signed on 4 January 1772, at a time when Catherine was precariously negotiating the partition of Poland with Austria and Prussia as the price of peace on her western flank, while still fighting the Turks in the south.

Catherine also, of course, acquired paintings in ones and twos, sometimes taking advantage of a lucky chance – as in the case of two canvases that Diderot bought for her. The steward of the Marquis de Conflans lived in the apartment above Diderot's in Paris. When the Marquis lost vast sums at cards and ordered his steward to sell two paintings he had no use for, Diderot secured them. They cost 1,000 écus the pair and turned out to be by Poussin.

An even more exotic stroke of fate put a *Perseus and Andromeda* by Anton Raffael Mengs in her possession. It had been commissioned in Rome by a rich English baronet, Sir William Watkin, and was much admired when it was displayed to the public in Mengs' studio. It was shipped to England from Livorno but captured off the French coast by pirates and subsequently confiscated by the French government.

Catherine's agent, Melchior Grimm, managed to acquire it for Catherine through the French minister for foreign affairs, though the Empress had some qualms over the deal. 'I see that you and M. de Vergennes, in order to give me pleasure, are doing down an honest English gentleman,' she wrote to Grimm. 'I have a slight conscience over it. If the good Englishman asks me, I will give him back his painting.' Apparently, he never asked for it, though it is recorded that his son saw the picture in St Petersburg in 1792. In his *A Tour of Russia, Siberia, and the Crimea*, John Parkinson described visiting Catherine's galleries in the 1790s with his friends: 'Sir Watkin recognised here the *Perseus and Andromeda* by Mengs,' he wrote, 'which having been ordered by his father at Rome, was taken on its way to England by a Spanish vessel and sold to the Empress.'

By 1773 Catherine's first enthusiasm for collecting paintings was on the wane. The period 1772–4 saw a watershed in her life on many fronts and may have reoriented her priorities. Grigory Orlov, her lover *en titre* for the last thirteen years, became so brazen in his infidelities that he was dismissed in 1772 and replaced, in December 1773, by Grigory

Potemkin – Catherine had toyed with a twenty-eight-year-old ensign in the Horse Guards for a few months in between. It was also over these years that her first military campaigns were successfully concluded by the 1772 partition of Poland and the 1774 peace treaty with Turkey. The only major rebellion of her reign erupted in 1773; led by a Cossack called Emelyan Pugachev, who claimed to be her murdered husband Peter III, but was successfully repressed the following year.

It was in 1773 that Catherine ordered the Green Frog Service from Josiah Wedgwood's factory at Burslem in Staffordshire – the largest and most important service this famous factory ever produced. Each piece is decorated with a different view, faithfully recording castles, abbeys, stately homes, gardens, towns and landscapes throughout Britain. It was intended to serve fifty people and 1,222 different views were painted on the creamware pieces in grisaille. A green frog was added to each since the service was intended for the Kekerekeksinen or 'Frog Marsh', Palace (later known as the Chesma Palace). This was typical of the scale on which Catherine issued her commissions.

In 1777 she ordered the so-called Cameo Service from Sèvres, a porcelain dinner and dessert service for sixty people including silver-gilt cutlery. Incorporating an antique cameo design, on a turquoise blue ground, it was the factory's first fully Neoclassical design and one of the most expensive services ever made there. Catherine confided to Grimm that it was intended for Potemkin 'and so that they will make it more beautiful, I have told them it is for me'.

It was also in 1773 that Diderot gave way to Friedrich Melchior Grimm as Catherine's chief agent in Paris, both having visited St Petersburg in person that year. It was a struggle for the ageing Diderot to manage the long journey from Paris to St Petersburg. Although he was well received and spent many hours talking to Catherine, he was disappointed at her lack of interest in his advice. 'Monsieur Diderot,' she told him, 'I have listened with great pleasure to the outpourings of your brilliant mind; your great principles, which I understand perfectly well, make fine theory but hopeless practice.' She sped him on his way with the gift of a ring, a fur, his own carriage and three bags of a thousand roubles. 'But,' he wrote to his wife, 'if I deduct from that the price of an enamel plaque and two paintings which I am giving to the Empress, the expenses of the journey and the presents I must give . . . we will only be left with five or six thousand francs, perhaps even less.'

Grimm was in St Petersburg at the same time, having come for the wedding of Catherine's son Paul to a German princess. Friedrich

Melchior Grimm was a well born German courtier who arrived in Paris in 1748 escorting a young member of the Schoenberg family, then worked for the Prince of Saxe-Gotha and the Duc d'Orléans. He became a close friend of Diderot and joined the circle of the *philosophes*. This enabled him to launch a fortnightly newsletter, his *Correspondances littéraires*, aimed at keeping the crowned heads of Europe up to date with the latest thinking in Paris. Catherine had long been among his subscribers. He was more of a gossip than a philosopher and their racy correspondence indicates how well the two got on. Grimm performed a wide range of services for Catherine, from buying cosmetics to dealing unofficially with the French government – and collecting art.

It was a sign of her waning enthusiasm for pictures that he could not interest her in the sale of the Jean-Pierre Mariette collection in 1775. Mariette came from a long line of engravers, was a patron of Watteau and had a collection whose fame was second only to that of Crozat. It was not until 1779 that Catherine made another major paintings purchase when she bought the pictures amassed by Sir Robert Walpole, Britain's first prime minister, for his gallery at Houghton Hall in Norfolk. Her motive, in this case, seems to have been strictly political.

Britain was then at the zenith of its power with an empire stretching from India to North America. The French *philosophes*, moreover, had hailed its political structure as the ideal for a modern country. In the words of Voltaire, Britain was a place 'where the Prince is all powerful to do good and, at the same time is restrained from committing evil . . . and where the people share in the Government without confusion'. Catherine had admired Britain since the days of the Empress Elizabeth, when she had been a close friend of the British ambassador. By buying the ex-prime minister's pictures she was demonstrating that the Russian Empire could upstage the British . . .

The Walpole scholar, Robert Ketton-Cremer, has described Sir Robert's Houghton Hall as a house which 'matched the man', with 'room after room filled with pictures from floor to ceiling, the Gallery, the Salon, the Carlo Maratti Room and all the other rooms with their profusion of pleasant family portraits, indifferent hunting scenes, and unrivalled masterpieces by every painter whose work was admired by the cognoscenti in the reign of George II.' There were twenty Van Dycks, nineteen Rubens, eight Titians, five Murillos, three works each by Veronese and Guido Reni, two by Velasquez, a Frans Hals, a Raphael and a Poussin. John Wilkes, the politician and reformer, advised the British parliament to turn it into a National Gallery – 'a noble gallery ought to be built in the garden of the British Museum for the reception of this invaluable collection'. Instead, the finest pictures – not including the family portraits – were bought by Catherine for a sum variously reported as £35,000, £40,000 and £45,000.

If Catherine's picture purchases were primarily motivated by political considerations rather than a love of art, her interest in building was a genuine passion. 'Building is a devilish affair,' she wrote to Grimm in 1779. 'It eats money and the more one builds, the more one wants to build; it is an illness like drunkenness.' Within weeks of her 1762 coup she had ordered a Chinese pavilion at Oranienbaum, the country estate where she and Peter had been living, from the Italian architect Antonio Rinaldi. She was so delighted with it that she asked Rinaldi to build a palace for her lover Grigory Orlov in the heart of St Petersburg, using the coloured marbles that had recently been found in the Urals. The Marble Palace, built between 1768 and 1785, a couple of hundred yards up the bank of the Neva from the Winter Palace, is a masterpiece of Neoclassicism and one of the loveliest buildings in the city. The façade and interiors sound subtle colour harmonies by juxtaposing different marbles.

In 1759 the French architect Jean-Baptiste Vallin de la Mothe had been invited to St Petersburg to design an Academy of Arts. Catherine approved his plans and construction began in 1764 – the huge and handsome building was one of the first Classical revival buildings in Russia. Indeed, she was so impressed that she commissioned him to design her first extension to the Winter Palace – the Small Hermitage. Its pillared façade repeats the design of the Academy on a miniature scale.

These early commissions already underline the Classical orientation of Catherine's taste which became more pronounced as her reign continued. The Small Hermitage, incorporating a hanging garden built over the stables with apartments at either end, was ready for use in 1769, but Catherine's imagination moved faster than her architects. She immediately asked for picture galleries to be added down each side of the garden and in 1770 she decided that she needed a major museum building for her rapidly expanding collection. She commissioned a much larger Classical building from Yury Velten, a St Petersburg-born architect of German extraction. The three-storey, ten-window extension was completed in 1776 and then she enlarged it again; the seventeen-window version, now known as the Old Hermitage, was finished in 1787. The design is severe – it has no pillars or ornaments –

and relies for its impact on perfectly balanced Classical proportions. Velten also masterminded the cladding of the Neva banks with granite to produce the present embankments.

Catherine's last extension of the Hermitage was entrusted to the Italian architect Giacomo Quarenghi, a great master who has left his mark all over St Petersburg. In the early 1780s he added a loggia to Velten's Old Hermitage to contain the painted copies of Raphael's Vatican frescoes which Catherine had ordered from Rome. The copies were painted on canvas under the direction of the Austrian artist Christoph Unterberger between 1778 and 1785, then rolled up and sent to St Petersburg where they nearly, but not quite, fitted Quarenghi's building. After the Loggia, Quarenghi was commissioned to build a theatre on the other side of the Winter Canal, connected to the Old Hermitage by a bridge; it took four years to complete, from 1783–7.

Catherine had gone theatre-mad in the 1780s and even wrote plays herself. An Englishman who visited St Petersburg described one of her plays called *Olga* as 'a tragedy with choruses, like the ancients: there are no less than 30 personages in the play, two emperors and the rest of proportionate rank; the suite consists of 600 people who are all to be on stage at once'. This must have been an exaggeration – 600 people would not fit on the stage, flanked by pink marble columns and classical statues, of Quarenghi's theatre, an imitation of the famous theatre Palladio built in Vicenza, Italy, a hundred years before – which, in its turn, had been copied from the Roman theatre at Orange in France. Like a Roman theatre it has semicircular banks of seats looking down on the stage. The building has a pillared façade, finely proportioned and more ornamental than Velten's.

Catherine's interest in architecture rubbed off on her collections. In 1773, using the good offices of Falconet, she commissioned a series of drawings for a garden pavilion from the French architect and decorator Charles Louis Clérisseau, who had spent twenty years in Rome and was one of the pioneers of Neoclassical design. He loved Roman ruins, which he incorporated into many of his designs and gained an international reputation – he advised Thomas Jefferson on the construction of the Capitol building in Virginia.

Catherine wanted her pavilion to look just like a Roman villa on the outside and to have interiors furnished as nearly as possible after the Antique. She stipulated that it should be 'neither very large, nor very small'. The commission went to Clérisseau's head and he sent eighteen large cases of drawings for a huge Roman palace, accompanied by a correspondingly large bill. Prince Golitsyn, Diderot and several other notables were dragged into the conflict over the fee which outraged Catherine. But five years later she had forgiven Clérisseau and was buying more drawings. She made him an honorary member of the St Petersburg Academy and First Architect to the Court, ending up with over 1,000 of his drawings – but no buildings. She hung seventeen of his gouaches of ancient Roman monuments round her boudoir in the Winter Palace.

Rome, rather than Paris, was the crucible in which Neoclassicism was fired. From there the writings of the German art historian Johann Joachim Winckelmann and the paintings of his disciple Anton Raffael Mengs attracted the attention of Europe's connoisseurs, naturally including Catherine. Her enthusiasm for Classical and Neoclassical art is reflected in both her buildings and her collections. However, she was not as well connected in Rome as she was in Paris. Her most useful contact proved to be Ivan Shuvalov, the last lover *en titre* of the Empress Elizabeth and the founder and first president of the St Petersburg Academy of Arts.

Some unforgivable action – hinted at in Catherine's letters but not spelt out – led Shuvalov to accept voluntary exile in the early days of her reign, moving to Rome in late 1762. He did not expect to return and gave his remarkable collection of paintings to the Academy, whence they were transferred to the Hermitage after the 1917 Revolution. From Rome he sent back plaster casts of antiquities for 'his' Academy, which Catherine much admired and had copied in bronze for the park at Tsarskoe Selo. Their relations began to improve and he sent her twelve volumes of engravings by Piranesi; she was delighted and wrote to Grimm regretting that Piranesi had not done more work. In 1785 she purchased the collection of Antique sculpture Shuvalov had bought for himself in Rome.

To these she added, in the same year, some 250 Antique sculptures from the collection of John Lyde-Brown, a director of the Bank of England, at a cost of £23,000. He had acquired his collection over a period of thirty years, mainly in Rome, and established a museum-quality display in his villa at Wimbledon, just outside London. There was a great fashion for collecting newly excavated sculptures in Italy in the mid-eighteenth century but collectors and dealers liked to improve the fragmentary remains that were found – adding heads to torsos that didn't really match and supplying missing body parts with newly carved marble. Oskar Waldhauer, the scholar who was in charge of the

Classical collection at the Hermitage just before and after the Revolution, ripped the Lyde-Brown statues apart and reassembled them, without their eighteenth-century additions, making many remarkable discoveries in the process.

Lyde-Brown had also purchased a few Renaissance sculptures in Italy. That is how Michelangelo's *Crouching Boy* arrived in Russia, also a puzzle sculpture of a *Cupid on a Dolphin* in Renaissance style. It was published as the work of Raphael's associate, Lorenzetto, when in the hands of the fashionable eighteenth-century sculptor and restorer, Bartolomeo Cavaceppi, but in the 1960s the American scholar Seymour Howard proclaimed it a fake, cooked up by Cavaceppi himself, possibly with the assistance of the English sculptor Joseph Nollekens. The latter, who lived in Rome and restored ancient sculptures for English tourists, made no fewer than four copies of the statue – for David Garrick, Lord Palmerston, the Earl of Exeter and the Earl of Bristol. The Hermitage has yet another theory – that Lyde-Brown got his hands on a sculpture described as '*Un Puttino morta sopra un Delfino ferito*' in the 1633 inventory of the Ludovisi family's art collection in Rome. If so, it is by a little-known sculptor called Giulio Cesare Conventi whose only claim to fame is having taught the great Baroque sculptor Alessandro Algardi. It seems likely that someone will eventually work out whether the sculpture was made in the fifteenth, seventeenth or eighteenth century.

Catherine kept these pieces, along with Lyde-Brown's Antique sculptures, in her lakeside Grotto at Tsarskoe Selo, an elegant domed pavilion whose interior was originally encrusted with 250,000 shells. In subsequent years the sculptures were dispersed to other palaces but the best were gathered up again in 1852 to decorate the Classical galleries of the New Hermitage.

Antique gems, carved with portrait and other images, were, however, Catherine's greatest enthusiasm in the Classical field. In the spring of 1782 she wrote to Grimm:

> My little collection of engraved gems is such that yesterday four people could only just carry two baskets filled with drawers containing roughly half the collection; and, so that you don't get the wrong impression, you should know that they were using the baskets that carry wood for the fires in winter and that the drawers were sticking out a long way; from that you can judge the gluttonous greed that we suffer from under this heading.

Her most important acquisition in this field came in 1787 when she bought the collection of the Duc d'Orléans, revolutionary politician and father of King Louis-Philippe of France. It contained 1,500 gems and was one of the most famous in Europe. After this Catherine was able to confide to Grimm that: 'All the cabinets of Europe are only childish accumulations compared to ours.'

She loved her gems so much that she took them with her to the country in summer in a special carriage, along with the necessary reference books. And she commissioned a series of rich cabinets to contain them from the most renowned furniture maker of the day, David Roentgen – who lived in Germany but worked for all the courts of Europe, notably for Marie-Antoinette. His furniture combined architectural design, fine marquetry and inlays, and ingenious mechanical devices. While most of the furniture Catherine commissioned was not regarded as art by the curators sorting the imperial possessions after 1917, they kept twenty-two Roentgen pieces which are now rated among the highlights of the applied arts collection.

All the court came to share in Catherine's enthusiasm for engraved gems and many of them even tried their own hands at engraving them. The Empress employed an artist chemist, Georg König, and a gem cutter, Karl Leberecht, to carve new gems recording her family, her friends and her victories – they also made glass reproductions of her Antique pieces. She ordered glass reproductions of all the most famous collections of Europe from James Tassie in London, a total of some 10,000 items, delivered in elegant cabinets designed by James Wyatt. In a letter to the most influential of all her lovers, Grigory Potemkin, then fighting the Turks in the south, she wrote: 'I am sending you a portrait, engraved after a gem, of the conqueror of Ochakov; both the gem and the portrait have been cut in my Hermitage.'

The 'conqueror' she referred to was, of course, Potemkin himself – Ochakov was a strategically crucial Black Sea fort he won from the Turks in 1788. In another letter she reports that her new lover Alexander Dmitriev Mamonov 'cut with his own hands the carnelian seal sent with the present testimonial'. Her daughter-in-law, Maria Fedorovna, cut portraits of her husband, the future Paul I, their sons Alexander and Constantine and of Catherine herself as Minerva – which the Empress graciously described as 'a very good likeness and excellently cut'. They were later copied by Wedgwood in jasper ware.

Catherine's many lovers and favourites had an influence on the Hermitage collections that went far beyond carved gems. She was immensely generous, showering them with serfs, palaces, jewels and every luxury, and developed the habit of buying back the collections of those who died. The French diplomat J. H. Castera, who published a life of Catherine in 1797, drew up an approximate account of what she had spent on them:

The five Orlov brothers	17,000,000 roubles
Vysotsky	300,000 roubles
Vasilchikov	1,110,000 roubles
Potemkin	50,000,000 roubles
Zavadovsky	1,380,000 roubles
Zorich	1,420,000 roubles
Rimsky-Korsakov	920,000 roubles
Lanskoy	7,260,000 roubles
Ermolov	550,000 roubles
Mamonov	880,000 roubles
The Zubov brothers	3,500,000 roubles

Not only was Grigory Orlov her longest-running lover, but she also owed a special debt to his family, who were the architects of her coup – and the executioners of her husband. The silver dinner service made by Jacques-Nicolas Roettiers in Paris, now known as the Orlov Service, was one of her most spectacular presents to him. She had originally intended it for her own use.

In February 1770 she wrote to Falconet: 'I've heard that you have some designs for a silver service; I would love to see them if you would show me them since it is quite possible that I might dream of ordering one large enough to serve 60 or so persons.' The drawings found favour and Falconet selected the Paris silversmith Jacques-Nicolas Roettiers, who had made a service for Louis XV which he admired just before leaving France for St Petersburg.

The service Catherine ended up ordering was so large that Roettiers had to farm out the commission to selected colleagues – there were 3,000 pieces and most of them were made in the space of eighteen months. There were, for example, forty-eight dozen plates, eighty-four chandeliers and thirty-six candelabras. She gave the service to Orlov in 1772 when they were reconciled after a lovers' tiff and shipments from Paris continued to be made to his Marble Palace up to 1775. Catherine got it back in July 1784, one year after his death. Much of the service got lost, melted down or muddled up with other services during the first century of its existence – only 1,041 pieces were recorded in the 1859 inventory of the Winter Palace. There are now 230 pieces from the service recorded in collections outside Russia – items sold off to earn the Soviets foreign currency in the 1920s and 1930s – and 169 recorded pieces in Russia itself, of which 123 are in the Armoury Museum in the Kremlin and forty-six in the Hermitage.

Beside Potemkin, however, Catherine's generosity to the Orlovs takes a modest second place. Grigory Potemkin was the only lover whose brains qualified him to share with Catherine the responsibilities of state, a forceful, moody character to whom Catherine may have been secretly married. He was her lover for only two years, from 1774 to 1776, but remained her close adviser and the most powerful man in the Empire until his death in 1791, even helping her to choose her subsequent lovers. He commanded her armies in the south in their campaigns against the Turks and she made him governor of the new territories he had helped her to acquire there. In 1787 she gave him a new title – Prince of Tauris. In Greek mythology the Crimea was known as Tauris, its fame assured by Euripides' play *Iphigenia in Tauris*.

The palace that Potemkin built in St Petersburg is known to this day as the Tauride Palace. It was designed by Ivan Starov, a Russian pupil of Vallin de la Mothe, with a central dome and single-storey pillared portico, connected, left and right, to two-storeyed pavilions. This Neoclassical design was so admired that it was adapted for the construction of more modest villas all over Russia. The palace was to play a key role in the Revolution – both the Provisional Government and the Petrograd Soviet first met there, although both moved out in the course of the year.

Potemkin's most important impact on the Hermitage collection lies in his partiality for British art – both pictures and objects. Catherine bought no fewer than three paintings by Joseph Wright of Derby in the 1770s – an artist whose importance has only been fully appreciated in Britain in the twentieth century – including one of the first industrial scenes ever depicted, *An Iron Forge Viewed from Without*. She acquired it through her London agent Alexander Baxter in early 1774, when Potemkin was the dominating force in her life, both in bed and outside it. In 1785 both of them commissioned paintings from Sir Joshua Reynolds, the president of the Royal Academy – historical scenes rather than the portraits that are found in British country houses. Catherine got *The Infant Hercules Killing Snakes* and Potemkin *The Continence of Scipio* and *Cupid Untying the Zone of Venus*. All three are now in the Hermitage.

A *Landscape with Dido and Aeneas* by Thomas Jones, a *Seashore* by William Marlow and a Godfrey Kneller portrait also arrived in the museum from Potemkin's collection after his death. In the field of the applied arts, the most spectacular impact of his taste is reflected in objects he purchased from the infamous Duchess of Kingston, a beautiful bigamist who arrived in St Petersburg with a boatload of family treasures. His Kingston purchases included a vast wine cooler made in London in 1705–6 by Philip Rollos and a musical clock in the form of a life-size gilt metal peacock standing under a small gilt-metal oak tree. They provide a vivid illustration of his taste for the flamboyant and theatrical.

Potemkin's most famous achievement in this vein was a journey to the Crimea that he orchestrated for Catherine, her court and the entire diplomatic corps – a total suite of 3,000 people – in 1787. They travelled down the Dnieper by boat in seven enormous red and gold barges – for the Empress and her most important guests – and seventy smaller ones. Potemkin packed the banks with loyal subjects performing – Cossacks on horseback and maidens dancing. 'Groups of peasants enlivened the beaches; innumerable boats, with young girls and boys on board, singing rustic local tunes, surrounded us all the time; nothing had been forgotten,' wrote the Comte de Ségur. It was reported that Potemkin even had fake villages erected to suggest settlements where there were none – as a result the term 'Potemkin villages', meaning show without substance, has entered the Russian language.

The silver wine cooler Potemkin bought from the Duchess of Kingston was used as a container for fish soup at a famously lavish party he threw for Catherine in April 1791. 'On both days there were quadrilles and small balls,' wrote a contemporary, 'when 180 and never less than 100 places were laid and at which the fish soup alone cost more than 1,000 roubles. It filled a vast seven or eight pood silver chalice. Two people standing served the whole table and when the serving was finished there was still enough soup left for the same number of guests.' In 1996 when the wine cooler was being restored for exhibition in America, the Hermitage conservators found they were unable to clean its interior – until they were told about the soup. It had retained a thin veil of grease for 200 years which the conservators, once alerted, found they could remove with ordinary kitchen soda.

The arrival of the Duchess of Kingston in St Petersburg in her so-called *bateau-musée* is one of the most curious incidents of Catherine's reign. Born Elizabeth Chudleigh in 1720, she achieved a *succès de scandale* in London. Among her many escapades was that of attending the Venetian ambassador's ball naked. In 1744 she secretly married a young naval lieutenant, Augustus Hervey, who later became third Earl of Bristol, and in 1769 the fabulously wealthy Duke of Kingston who died four years later. In 1776 she was arraigned for bigamy before Britain's High Court of Parliament and found guilty – but let off with a fine.

The deceased Duke's nephew launched a lawsuit with the aim of wresting the Kingston fortune from her hands. The Duchess escaped to the Continent where she set about dazzling Rome, Paris and Vienna while she fought the case through lawyers, and eventually won. In 1777 she determined to visit Russia and 'had built a ship with very splendid accommodation', according to a contemporary biographer. 'There was a drawingroom, diningroom, kitchen and bedroom and every convenience to be found in a suite of family chambers.'

Catherine was much taken with the Duchess, giving her a fine house in St Petersburg and a nearby estate. The Empress was busy laying out new gardens at the time – in the English style – so the Duchess summoned the Kingston gardener from Thoresby, in Yorkshire, to work for the court. 'Mr Mowat', who now styled himself 'Gardener to Her Imperial Majesty Empress of all The Russians', wrote home describing the splendour of the Duchess's life-style. 'Her Grace has fitted up a very large House here in the most Ellegant manner possible, Crimson Damask hangings, Do. Window Curtains, Most splendid five Musical Lustres! Grand Organ, plate, paintings! and other ornaments displayed to the greatest advantage.'

Many of these are now in the Hermitage. When the Duchess died in Paris in August 1788 she left an elaborate will with a series of blanks where she had failed to fill in the beneficiaries' names. There were two contestants for her Russian property but Colonel M. Garnovsky, who had been Potemkin's personal aide, was backed by Catherine and won the day. Through him Potemkin got hold of many Kingston possessions. The organ referred to by Mr Mowat can almost certainly be identified with the one now displayed in the Grand Salon of the Hermitage out-station in the Menshikov Palace and regularly used for concerts. In fact it is two organs, a clock with a mechanical organ above a boxed organ which can be played in the ordinary way; both are English and cased in mahogany with gilt embellishments. Both organs played at the last great party Potemkin threw for Catherine in 1791, shortly before his death. The Russian poet Gavriil Derzhavin was there and noted the 'two gilded great organs that share our attention and deepen our joy'.

According to him, 'the Empress left after one o'clock. As she was leaving the room, you could hear soft singing accompanied by the organ. They were singing an Italian cantata.'

Other Kingston pieces which embellish the museum galleries include Pierre Mignard's painting of the *Magnanimity of Alexander the Great*, a series of cartoons for tapestries by Rubens' pupils and, of course, the Peacock Clock. For anyone who passes through the Small Hermitage around midday, the clock is one of the most memorable experiences of today's museum. It was made by the Duchess's favourite London jeweller James Cox, best known for the elaborate, jewel-encrusted clocks he made for the Oriental market. First a chime of bells starts to play and an owl moves his head from side to side. Then the peacock, which stands on a metal hill, begins to spread his tail while nodding his head in a most realistic manner; he executes a 180-degree turn to display his tail feathers from behind. And finally a metal cock lifts his head and begins to crow. The clock face is on the head of a mushroom under the gilt-bronze oak tree; a dragonfly sitting on the mushroom marks the seconds.

The Duchess brought the clock to St Petersburg carefully disassembled, with hundreds of delicate pieces of mechanism packed separately. Potemkin acquired it in 1788 in this state and so it passed to Catherine. It took a gifted Russian mechanic and inventor, Ivan Kulibin, two years, from 1792 to 1794, to make it work.

3
Paul and Alexander

*B*y the end of Catherine's reign the Hermitage was beginning to take on the character of a museum. The lower orders were, of course, denied entrance but no well-bred traveller's account of a visit to St Petersburg in the last decade of the eighteenth century omits a tour of the galleries. And a special room, on the eastern side of the hanging garden, was set aside for artists to copy in.

An English visitor called John Parkinson was shown around in 1792 by the Italian architect, Giacomo Quarenghi, who had designed Catherine's Hermitage Theatre and the Raphael Loggia. His account catches the feel of the times:

> The Empress having graciously permitted all the foreigners in Petersburg to see the Hermitage – this morning we repaired thither between the hours of ten and eleven . . . We were not permitted to enter with swords or sticks; but they were required to be delivered up before we went in. Quarenghi joined us there and was of great service to us in pointing out what particularly deserved our attention. In so short a time, however, and in such a crowd, it was impossible to see such a profusion to any good purpose or with any satisfaction.
>
> We first saw the Royal apartments, which occupy that side of the building which fronts towards the river, we then passed through the picture Galleries which form the three other sides of a square. Afterwards we went by Raphael's Gallery to the Cabinet of Medals, Mineralogy and what I must call for want of a better word

'bijouterie' . . . The Apartments as well as the Galleries are crowded with paintings, good and bad placed promiscuously together.

At this period visitors were required to use a side entrance under the arch over the Winter Canal. They took the stairs to the first floor where three doors led out of a vestibule embellished with a statue of *Cupid and Psyche*. One door led to the theatre foyer which was hung with paintings, the second to the Raphael Loggia and three adjoining rooms which contained the minerals collection, precious objects – such as Catherine's engraved gems – and more paintings, and the third opened onto the suite of fourteen picture galleries in the Old Hermitage which Velten had built for Catherine along the banks of the Neva.

Catherine's death in 1796, four years after John Parkinson's visit, severed the highly personal relationship between ruler and art. The collection as it existed in 1796 was almost entirely her own making and it was housed in buildings which she had planned and commissioned. In the hands of her son Paul I, who reigned from 1796 to 1801, and her grandson Alexander I (1801–25) it became institutionalised. The collections were cared for by an administrator and professional staff – the tsars treated them as a responsibility rather than a source of personal delight.

For Paul, who felt a bitter antipathy to his mother, it was a trial to use or touch anything that had been hers. He would not live in the Winter Palace, preferring to build himself a new home, the Mikhail Castle, on the other side of town. Nevertheless, he was a man of culture with a strong interest in art, architecture and the applied arts – he liked to visit craftsmen and know how things were made – and many purchases he made for other homes have now been incorporated into the Hermitage collections. The silver console tables and candelabras he commissioned from the St Petersburg silversmith Ivor Buch for the throne room in the Mikhail Castle have, for example, joined Anna Ivanovna's English silver throne in the Winter Palace small throne room.

His son Alexander, in contrast, was devoted to the memory of his grandmother but had little time for art. He began his reign with a burning interest in social reform which he later regretfully abandoned as impractical; combating Napoleon then became his chief concern and, after Napoleon's defeat in 1812, the remodelling of Europe; Christian mysticism was the dominating interest of his later years – there is even a legend that he faked his death in 1825 and started a new life as a holy man in Siberia. The care he took to restructure the Hermitage administration, in his reforming mode, and the acquisition of art from the collection of Napoleon's estranged wife, the Empress Josephine, were his two major contributions to the museum.

Both Paul and Alexander were subject to the kind of psychological pressures which would land a modern man jittering on the analyst's couch. Indeed, it is arguable that Paul had lost his reason by the time he succeeded to the throne. He had been taken from his mother within minutes of his birth and brought up by the Empress Elizabeth. He was eight when she died and, within six months, his mother's friends had assassinated his father, Peter III. Alexander was also removed from his mother as a baby and brought up by the Empress – this time by Catherine the Great. At the age of twenty-three he collaborated in a plot to oust his father, though he was probably unaware that his friends intended assassination.

Paul was Peter III's legitimate heir and Catherine was wary of any signs of popular support for him, aware that he was the natural focus for any plot to oust her. She gave him no responsibilities or opportunities to shine in public life. And she removed his first two children so as to bring them up herself – just as the Empress Elizabeth had removed Paul. There is little wonder that Paul hated her and refused to live in the shadow of her art collections.

Catherine, for her part, doted on Paul's two sons, Alexander born in 1777 and Constantine in 1779 – she even designed the perfect baby garment. Sending a sketch to Grimm, she wrote: 'It is all stitched together, you put on all at once, and it closes at the back with four or five little hooks. There are no bindings and the child hardly notices that he is being dressed; one pushes his arms and legs into the costume all at once, and that's it. This garment is a stroke of genius on my part. The King of Sweden and the Prince of Prussia have asked for and obtained copies of Master Alexander's costume.'

To celebrate Alexander's birth Catherine gave Paul and his wife Maria Fedorovna a vast tract of country to the south of the imperial palace of Tsarskoe Selo, 1,500 acres of virgin forest. In adapting the wild terrain into an exquisite pavilioned park with a small but exceptionally beautiful Neoclassical palace, to be known as Pavlovsk, the couple discovered their interest in architecture, sculpture and interior decoration. They collected Neoclassical art and artefacts, a taste which remains well represented in the Hermitage Museum as a result.

Paul and Maria were exposed to the very finest in European art, old and new, during a fourteen-month tour which Catherine bullied them into making in 1781–2. Paul feared that it was an excuse to get him out of the way so that Alexander might be declared her heir and almost refused to go, but it turned out a great success. The imperial couple travelled incognito as the Comte and Comtesse du Nord, but every court in Europe had been alerted to their visit and they took a large retinue. It may have been the happiest period of Paul's life. He was treated everywhere as a future emperor, entertained with splendour and showered with gifts.

In Venice he entered into negotiations to buy the important sculpture collection formed by Filippo Farsetti (1704–74), which contained a mix of casts of Antique sculptures and terracotta models by leading seventeenth-century sculptors, such as Algardi and Bernini. It was the casts that had made the collection famous in Venice – Tiepolo, Giovanni Battista Pittoni and Canova had all visited Farsetti to sketch them – but today's connoisseurs come to the Hermitage to see the terracottas. It was the imperial family's first major acquisition of modern sculpture since Peter the Great's purchases at the beginning of the century.

So important did the Venetians consider the collection that they initially refused to allow its export. Paul left without it but did not forget his enthusiasm. After the annexation of Venice by France in 1797, when the Republic's old export laws were jettisoned, he completed his purchase. The first shipment of 308 cases of sculpture arrived in St Petersburg in March 1800; a second shipment of sixty-three cases arrived in October of the same year. Paul donated the collection to the Academy of Arts, whence the best pieces were removed to the Hermitage after the 1917 Revolution.

In Paris the imperial couple indulged in an epic spending spree. They visited the Sèvres factory where they received over one hundred pieces as gifts from its patron Louis XVI and bought as much again on their own account. They acquired several dinner, tea and toilet services, as well as sets of vases, figures and medallions. Most of the surviving pieces are exhibited at Pavlovsk but among those that found their way to the Hermitage is the most expensive of all Louis XVI's gifts to the imperial couple – a *Vase Bachelier beau bleu Emaillé*, valued by the factory at 1,800 livres.

The couple's connoisseurship and appetite for detailed information was remarked upon at every stop on their journey. The Austrian Emperor Joseph II, who had entertained them in Vienna, wrote his brother Leopold, Grand Duke of Tuscany, a letter of advice on how to

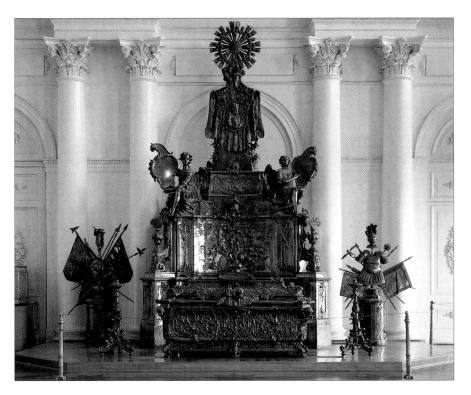

The Alexander Nevsky sarcophagus commissioned by the Empress Elizabeth and designed by the court painter Georg Christoph Grot. It is made from sheet silver over a wooden carcass and stands sixteen foot high.

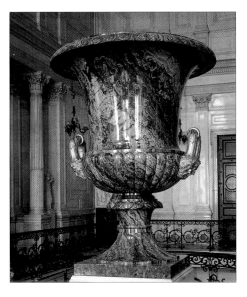

The largest malachite vase in the world, six foot high, the veneer pieced together from a mosaic of matched slivers of malachite at the Ekaterinburg lapidary factory between 1839-42.

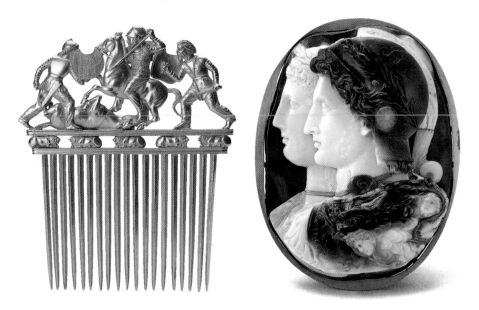

Above left: Scythian gold comb of the early 4th century BC, excavated in the Dnieper valley in 1913.

Right: The so-called 'Gonzaga Cameo' carved from sardonyx in the 3rd century BC and believed to depict King Ptolemy II of Egypt and his wife Arsinoë.

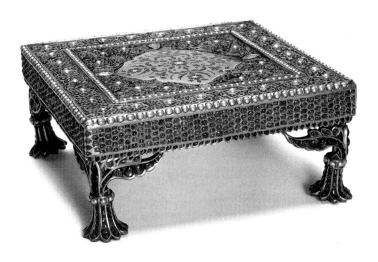

Small table (24 cm square and 10 cm high) from the Mughal treasury, encrusted with rubies, emeralds, pearls and enamels. A gift from Nadir-Shah, who sent it from Delhi to St Petersburg by elephant in 1740-41.

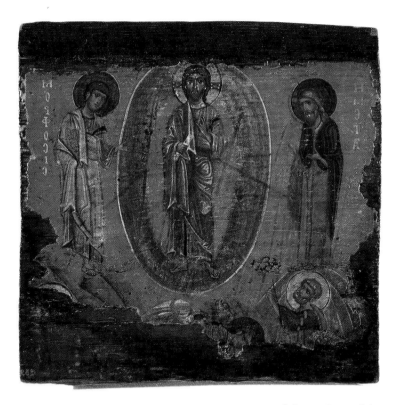

The Transfiguration, a 12th-century icon painting acquired from Mount Athos
through P.I. Sevastyanov in 1860.

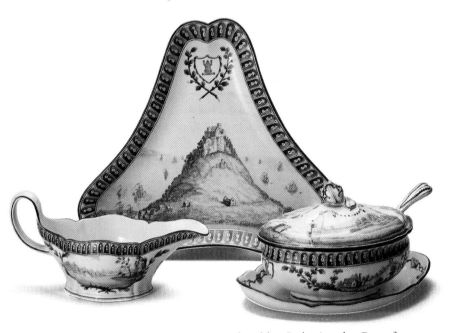

Pieces from the Green Frog Service ordered by Catherine the Great from
Josiah Wedgwood's factory at Etruria in 1773-4.

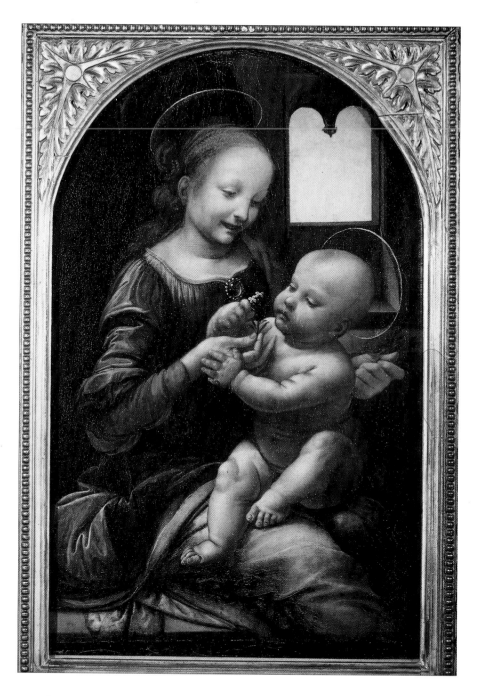

The *Benois Madonna*, an early work by Leonardo da Vinci, 'rediscovered' in
St Petersburg in 1908 and acquired by the Hermitage in 1914.

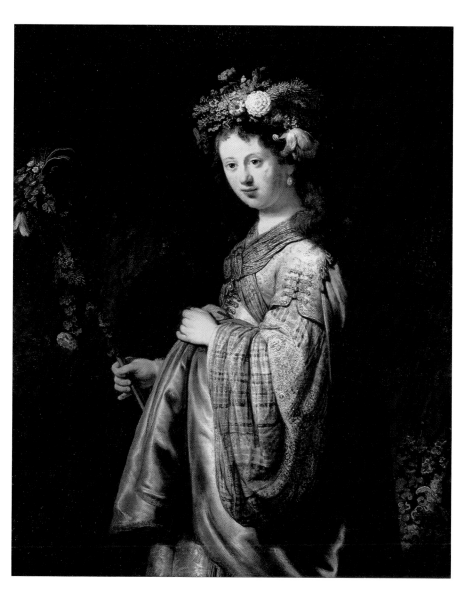

Rembrandt's portrait of his wife Saskia as *Flora*, painted in 1634 and acquired by Catherine the Great in around 1776.

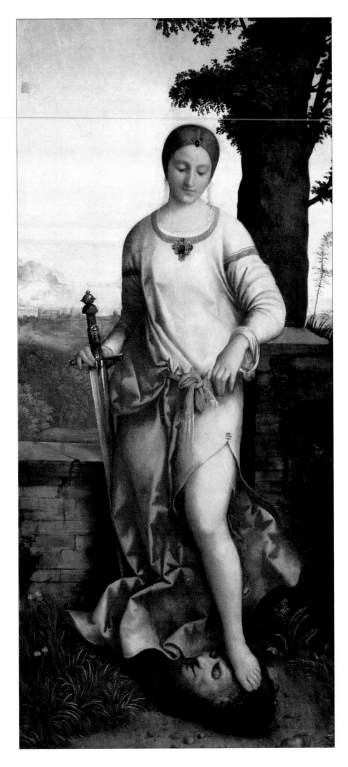

Giorgione's *Judith*, formerly attributed to Raphael, one of the stars of the Crozat collection which was acquired by Catherine the Great in 1772.

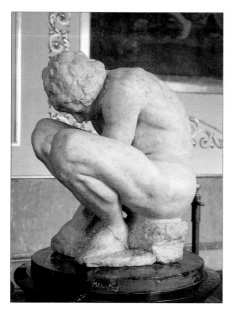

Michelangelo's unfinished *Crouching Boy*, dated circa 1530-34, acquired with the Lyde-Browne collection in 1787.

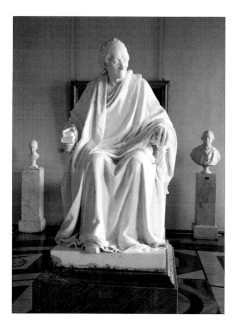

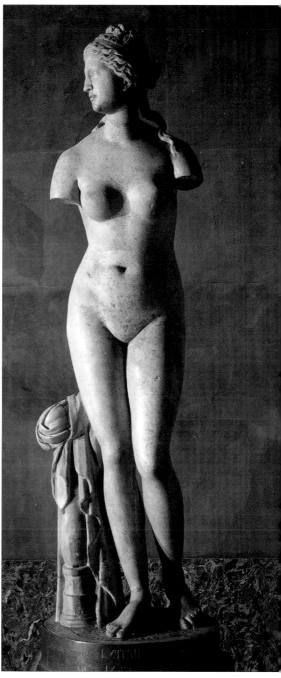

Above left: A life size, marble statue of *Voltaire*, commissioned by Catherine the Great from Jean-Antoine Houdon in 1780, banished from the palace by Nicholas I with the memorable words 'destroy this old monkey'.
Right: The *Tauride Venus*, a Roman copy of a Greek original of the 3rd century BC, acquired by Peter the Great from Rome in 1719 as a gift from the Pope – after considerable diplomatic hassle.

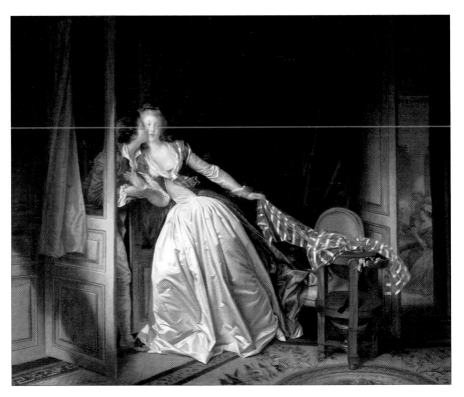

The Kiss by Jean-Honoré Fragonard, from the collection of Catherine the Great's lover Stanislaw Poniatowsky.

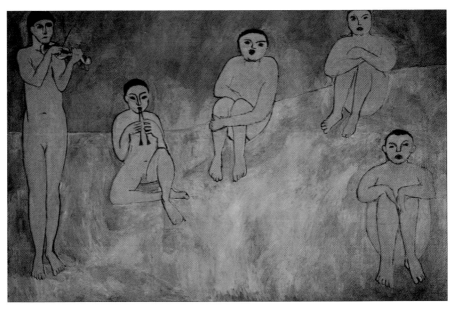

Music, one of a pair of monumental paintings by Henri Matisse commissioned by Sergey Shchukin for the stairwell of his Moscow home. Shchukin got cold feet about the nudity of the figures and painted out the flute-player's private parts.

handle their visit to Florence. 'They are particularly interested in anything that is old or curious and in buildings which are at all remarkable either for size or beauty. And that is why they must not be over-wearied by seeing too many things the same day, but have, if possible, the opportunity of examining all that is remarkable and interesting in detail.'

Following their visit to Paris, the Chevalier du Coudray wrote a similar account of their enthusiasm. 'M. the Comte and Mme the Comtesse du Nord have surprised everyone with their extensive knowledge of all the arts and trades. In our factories they enter into the tiniest details with the workers, using technical words and employing artistic terms as well as the craftsmen.'

The couple patronised the furniture merchant Dominique Daguerre, the leading supplier of rich furnishings to the court and the aristocracy. On 25 May 1784 they spent 35,093 livres at his shop, coming away with four pieces of furniture made by the great *ébéniste* Martin Carlin who specialised in encrusting his furniture with Sèvres porcelain plaques painted with brightly coloured flowers on a white background. Maria Fedorovna placed a little library table with a frieze of porcelain plaques, edged with gilt bronze mouldings, in her bedroom at Pavlovsk. It was sold off by the Soviet government in the 1930s and has passed through the auction rooms twice since World War II, setting a new record auction price for any piece of furniture at 165,000 guineas in 1971 and selling for £918,000 to the Getty Museum in 1983. Among the finest pieces that remain in St Petersburg are a secretaire and four commodes attributed to Adam Weisweiler, another great Neoclassical furniture maker, all with Wedgwood and Sèvres plaques cunningly incorporated in their design.

The furnishings that the Grand Duke and Duchess brought back from Paris started a craze for French furniture in St Petersburg. Catherine had tended to favour English and German furniture over French – she bought many mahogany and ormolu *chefs-d'oeuvres* by David Roentgen which were the inspiration of the following generation of Russian cabinetmakers. So imported French furniture had rarity value – but not for long. Captured by the elegance of the pieces that Paul and Maria brought back with them, the Russian aristocracy besieged Paris merchants with their orders and French imports poured into St Petersburg. The nationalisation of private collections after the Revolution landed some of the most outstanding pieces in the Hermitage.

Not all the imperial couple's purchases were equally well received.

Maria returned with '200 cases filled with chiffon, pompoms and other toiletries from Paris', according to the British ambassador, Sir James Harris. Catherine considered this excessive and made her return them to the famous Paris modiste, Mlle Bertin, who, according to Grimm, was enraged and 'defended her flounces'.

Maria was not, however, a feather-brained princess who was only interested in clothes. She was a notable connoisseur and artist in her own right and through the good taste she passed on to her two sons, the emperors Alexander I and Nicholas I, she contributed significantly to the flowering of the applied arts in Russia in the early nineteenth century; Russian furniture, tapestry, glass, porcelain and silver all recorded splendid aesthetic and technical achievements at this time. Even Catherine admired Maria's skill at cutting engraved gems. The portrait cameo she cut of Catherine herself was sent to Wedgwood to be copied in jasper. Maria also painted, designed furniture and tried her hand at lathework. In 1795 she wrote a detailed description of how she had furnished Pavlovsk.

The way in which she dwells on the details of furniture, textiles, porcelains and other rich materials clearly demonstrates her fascination with the decorative arts. The description she gives of her husband's desk reveals both her own skills and her taste for the sumptuous:

Almost under the archway of the study is a very large writing table like that by Roentgen. It is supported by twelve ivory columns which I turned on a lathe. A sort of raised desk of an elegant shape covers one third of the table and provides a base for an ivory temple, square in shape, of fine architecture; on the pediment of the temple is a cameo of the Grand Duke, mounted in clear glass on which I have painted a trophy in grisaille. On the other side of the pediment is the Grand Duke's monogram. On the base of the temple are more paintings in grisaille; in the middle of the temple is an eight-sided altar made of amber and ivory; on the central one is my monogram in a medallion, painted on glass and mounted in amber; on the other sides are medallions of my seven children, starting with Alexander, whose monogram is linked with that of Elizabeth, and finishing with the late dear Olinka. (I gave this present to the dear Grand Duke last year when dear Olinka was still alive and Annette was not yet born.) I have painted all the children's monograms in roses and myrtles.

When Maria gave birth to the first of her six daughters, Alexandra

Pavlovna, in 1783 Catherine commented, 'I love boys far more than girls' and left them to bring up their own daughters. She even gave Paul another palace to celebrate Alexandra's birth, Gatchina, the Neoclassical jewel built by Antonio Rinaldi for Grigory Orlov, some twenty miles south of Tsarskoe Selo. Catherine's former lover had died in 1781 and Catherine bought the presents she had lavished on him, such as Gatchina, back from his heirs.

Denied the opportunity to take any part in government, Paul retired to Gatchina, a flourishing estate with more than 6,000 serfs, and began to run it as a sort of mini-kingdom, a testing ground for his political theories. He secured a battalion of troops to defend it and appointed a goose-stepping Prussian, Baron Steinwehr, to command them. That seems to have been his undoing. Like his father – indeed, imitating his father – Paul hero-worshipped Frederick the Great and now sought to apply the same rigid disciplines that Frederick had developed for the parade ground on his own troops, brutally castigating any soldier with so much as a button out of place.

Paul drilled and paraded as if his life depended on it and began to apply the same discipline to other spheres of life, including his family. He alienated his wife and – which may have been worse for Russia – infected his sons Alexander and Nicholas with his military mania. Plasterwork arms and trophies abound in the interior decoration of the Winter Palace, mostly created on the instructions of Paul's son, Nicholas I. Nicholas also bought battle paintings by the score, most of them now sold off or consigned to the Hermitage storerooms.

When Catherine died in 1796, Paul's long period of waiting in the wings was over. He emerged from Gatchina embittered, suspicious, determined to contradict all Catherine's policies and to impose Prussian-style discipline on his empire. Alexander, his son and heir, watched with dismay. In a letter to his former tutor he expressed his concern:

My father, on succeeding to the throne, wished to reform everything. The beginning, it is true, was sparkling enough but what followed did not fulfil expectations. Everything has been turned upside down at once; something which has served only to increase the already too great confusion which reigned in our affairs. The military take up almost all his time, and that in parades. For the rest he has no plan to follow; he orders today what a month later he countermands; he never permits any representation except when the harm has already been done.

One of Paul's first initiatives was to order his father's bones to be exhumed from their resting place at the Alexander Nevsky Monastery. It was an insult to Peter's memory that he should lie there since the Peter and Paul Cathedral, within the walls of the ancient fortress of the same name, was the official burial ground for monarchs. Paul ordered that his father's coffin should lie in state beside his mother in the Winter Palace. He placed a banner above them that read, 'Divided in life, united in death'. Then he ordered a joint funeral. Peter's assassin, Alexey Orlov, now an old man, was made to carry his victim's crown on a cushion at the head of the procession.

Paul now also began to play musical chairs with his art works. The Hermitage was initially neglected since he had moved his residence elsewhere, but in 1797 he appointed Prince Nikolay Yusupov administrator of the 'museum'. Yusupov was a connoisseur and collector much valued by Catherine, who had appointed him director of her Tapestry Works in 1789 and director of the Imperial Glass and Porcelain Factories in 1792. But he had also accompanied Paul and Maria on their European trip in 1782 and Paul apparently trusted him. Yusupov persuaded Paul to allocate funds for the upkeep of the Hermitage galleries, even including the birds, trees and flowers in the hanging garden.

Then he changed his mind. He sent 200 paintings each to Gatchina and Pavlovsk; he moved eighty paintings to the Mikhail Castle – which came back after his death; he sent twenty-eight paintings to Tsarskoe Selo, seventy-two to Peterhof and twenty-three to a new palace that he was building on Kamenny Ostrov, an island on the Neva delta which the imperial family reserved for their own use. He removed the sculptures that Catherine had kept in the beautiful lakeside grotto pavilion at Tsarskoe Selo – including the great Antique pieces from the Lyde-Brown collection – and installed them in the Mikhail Castle; he moved the statuary from the Chinese Pavilion that Catherine had built at Oranienbaum, Menshikov's seaside palace, to Gatchina and some statuary from Tsarskoe Selo to Pavlovsk.

And, for some reason, he ordered his collector's mark, a single 'P', to be appended to all the drawings in Catherine's collection – a move which has proved very useful to latter-day scholars researching the provenance of drawings. Paul's mark indicates that a drawing reached the Hermitage before 1801 – the year when his subjects could stand his erratic behaviour no longer and he was assassinated.

Paul had offended both the officer corps and the nobility. During his five-year reign he ordered the arrest of seven field marshals, 333 generals and 2,261 officers. The conspirators who plotted his overthrow were highly placed in the government and army – Count Nikita Panin, the vice-chancellor, Count Petr von Pahlen, governor-general of St Petersburg and foreign minister, Prince Platon Zubov, Catherine's last lover *en titre*, his brother Nikolay Zubov, and General Levin Bennigsen. The latter led the group of soldiers who invaded Paul's bedroom in the Mikhail Castle on the night of 23 March 1801. Paul was struck down by Nikolay Zubov and strangled by one of the officers.

Alexander, Paul's eldest son, had supported the conspirators' plan to wrest power away from his father but had believed it would be achieved without violence. He was apparently not privy to the planned assassination and Paul's death filled him with horror. 'I am the unhappiest man on the earth', he told the Swedish ambassador, Count Karl Stedingk, on the first day of his reign.

He was young, handsome, idealistic, not hugely intelligent, but initially much loved. In his accession manifesto he promised to rule 'according to the spirit and laws' of his grandmother, Catherine the Great, and immediately set about undoing his father's follies. He granted an amnesty to 12,000 prisoners. Together with a group of young friends, whom he laughingly referred to as his 'Committee of Public Safety', he began to draft wide-ranging constitutional reforms. But they never became law. Like Catherine before him, he began to back-pedal on reform as he realised the damage it would inflict on his own position.

A new administrative system for the Hermitage was one result of his reformist zeal. In 1802 he appointed a well-known art collector and bibliophile, Count Dmitry Buturlin, administrator of the museum. Buturlin set about preparing a 'most humble petition' to the Emperor about the Hermitage which became the blueprint for its reform. Pointing out that an art collection is rightly judged by the quality of paintings it contains rather than their number – a consideration which Catherine in her pursuit of prestige had tended to overlook – Buturlin noted that the Hermitage was richly supplied with Dutch and French pictures but lacked Italian and Spanish works. 'If we make good use of our opportunities to enlarge the collection of the Italian school – which has ever been the most difficult to assemble – ours will be the most outstanding collection in existence,' he told the Emperor. He also advised that the Hermitage should be open to the public 'at a fixed season of the year, on condition that certain inviolable rules be observed and under the supervision of specially appointed staff'. At last the collection was beginning to adopt the character of a museum rather than a private collection.

Alexander accepted Buturlin's recommendations and in 1805 promulgated a 'Rule on the Hermitage'. Under this decree the Hermitage was formally divided into five separate departments, each with its own curator. The 'First Department' comprised the library, engraved gems and medals, the 'Second Department' the picture gallery, bronzes, marbles and *objets de vertu*, the 'Third Department' engravings, the 'Fourth Department' drawings and the 'Fifth Department' natural history specimens and the collection of minerals.

The precedence given to the library no doubt reflected Buturlin's own preoccupation with books. The 'Second Department' comprised the core of the museum, as we know it today, and was run by an artist called Franz Labensky who had been recruited in 1796 to take charge of the inventory of paintings in the Hermitage, Tauride and Marble Palaces ordered by Paul I – the Marble Palace built by Catherine for Grigory Orlov and the Tauride Palace for Grigory Potemkin were bought back by the crown after their deaths along with the best of the art they contained. Labensky acted as director of the picture gallery up to his death in 1849 and proved a notable connoisseur and enlightened administrator. Buturlin soon lost interest, moving first to Moscow, then to Florence.

One of Labensky's first successes lay in persuading Alexander that the Hermitage should collect Russian painting. Catherine had only bought Old Masters and a few contemporary paintings by French and British artists, while Paul favoured artists that he had got to know in France, such as Joseph Vernet and Hubert Robert. It was only in 1802, on Labensky's urging, that Russian paintings began to be bought by the Hermitage in any numbers.

This was not as surprising as it may seem at first sight. Up to 1700 or so there was no Russian school of painting, unless one counts icons, which were mainly painted by monks in monastic workshops. In painting, as in many other fields, Russia joined the stream of European endeavour as a result of a sharp kick up the backside from Peter the Great. Peter imported artists, mainly from France, and required them to teach their skills to young Russians as part of their contract of employment. And it was only during the reign of his daughter Elizabeth that an Academy of Art was established in St Petersburg.

The first significant achievements of Russian painting lay in the field of portraiture – for which there was a good demand at court. It was not until the nineteenth century that Russian artists began to tackle history, landscape and genre painting with outstanding success. The first Russian artists represented in the Hermitage included Andrey Martynov, Fedor Alekseev, Fedor Matveev, Vasily Shebuev and Aleksey Egorov.

In 1824 the collection was rehung in order to devote a gallery exclusively to Russian painting. The Emperor scoured his other palaces in order to bring together the best Russian works that he owned and made the attractive decision that this gallery, in particular, should always be run by an artist – recruited, of course, from the Imperial Academy of Arts. The gallery survived until 1898 when Nicholas II established what is now known as the Russian Museum, calling it the Alexander III Museum in memory of his father. While the Hermitage still has a good collection of Russian painting, the Russian Museum, magnificently housed in the Mikhail Palace, is now the national showcase.

It was Alexander's dealings with Napoleon and his estranged wife Josephine that resulted in his reign's most spectacular enrichment of the Hermitage. Napoleon himself was no mean connoisseur. As he crossed and recrossed Europe as a conqueror, he annexed the greatest art treasures of his enemies and sent them back to Paris to form the Napoleonic Museum in the Louvre. This short-lived institution was probably the greatest accumulation of art treasures ever gathered in one place – it was effectively a Supra-National Gallery of Europe. After Napoleon's defeat the Allies, against Alexander's advice, ordered the restitution of the treasures to their original owners. Most were duly returned, though a few of Napoleon's trophies are still in Paris and thirty-eight paintings that Alexander purchased from Josephine's heirs, while the other allied rulers were not looking, are now in the Hermitage.

Alexander changed sides in the Napoleonic wars more often than any ruler is supposed to do who comes out of an imbroglio smelling of roses – which was exactly what he, somewhat surprisingly, achieved. In 1814 he personally led the Russian army into Paris and was hailed as the Liberator of Europe. He also inadvertently coined the French word *bistro*; the Russian word *bystro* means 'fast' and the Russian soldiers' constant call for fast food left behind a new name for the cheerful little restaurants of France.

In 1801, however, Alexander sided with the French. He told their ambassador, General G. Duroc: 'I have always desired to see France and Russia as friends; these are the great and powerful nations . . . which must agree to put a stop to the little disagreements of the continent.' In

1805 he changed his allegiance, joining Britain and Austria in an alliance against France. Austria and Russia were routed at the battle of Austerlitz where Alexander was leading the Russian army in person and was nearly captured.

Two years later, in February 1807, Napoleon won a bitter victory over Russia at Eylau – both sides lost about 20,000 men killed, wounded or captured – and suggested peace. So Alexander changed sides. The two emperors met on the only neutral territory they could find – a raft in the middle of the River Nieman at Tilsit. Alexander is said to have opened the conversation with the words: 'Sire, I hate the English no less than you do and I am ready to assist you in any enterprise against them,' and Napoleon is said to have replied: 'In that case everything can be speedily settled between us and peace is made.' Peace was to last for five years – until Napoleon with an army of 400,000 men invaded Russia in June 1812.

In 1808, in the wake of the Tilsit agreement, Alexander sent the Hermitage curator of paintings, Franz Labensky, to Paris in search of new acquisitions. Through the good offices of Napoleon, he was introduced to the director of the Napoleonic Museum at the Louvre, Dominique Vivant Denon, one of the most universally gifted connoisseurs of the period. Before the revolution Vivant Denon had been an attaché at the French embassy in St Petersburg and served as a diplomat in Sweden and Naples. He studied engraving and was subsequently taken up by Napoleon and Josephine. Having accompanied Napoleon on his Egyptian campaign, he published one of the first serious works on Egyptian archaeology, with his own text and engravings; he also was given charge of organising Napoleon's military parades and the Musée du Louvre.

Labensky secured some important acquisitions, but better still he managed to recruit Vivant Denon himself as a buying agent for the imperial collection. The paintings of the Roman Giustiniani family had recently been sent to Paris for sale and before they were catalogued and offered elsewhere, Vivant Denon managed to secure a great Caravaggio, *The Lute Player* – a young boy playing the lute at a table spread with flowers, fruit and music. He bought a second work attributed to Caravaggio from the same collection, *The Crucifixion of St Peter*, which turned out to be a masterpiece by Caravaggio's contemporary Lionello Spada.

Labensky went home with twenty-three paintings, including the first Dutch interior by Pieter de Hooch to reach the Hermitage collection,

A Mistress and Her Maid. After his departure Vivant Denon took over, dispatching crate after crate of pictures to St Petersburg – two Murillos, a Francesco Bassano, a Guercino, a Luca Giordano and, from the Northern schools, a rare triptych by Maerten van Heemskerck, among many, many other works. The stream of new acquisitions only dried up when Napoleon invaded Russia and the two nations were once again at war.

Alexander was at a ball in Vilnius when the news of Napoleon's invasion reached him on 24 June 1812 and he 'suffered intensely in being obliged to show a gaiety which he was far from feeling', according to his confidant Madame Choiseul-Gouffier. Napoleon defeated the Russians at the battle of Borodino, seventy-two miles west of Moscow, on 7 September and, advancing on Moscow, found the city evacuated and burning. Alexander, holed up in St Petersburg, fought as little as possible, aiming to starve Napoleon out of the country. For safety's sake, however, he evacuated the Hermitage art collection to three small northern towns, Vytegra, Lodeinoe Pole and Kargopol. The division presumably reflected a hope that if one cache of art were found by Napoleon, the others might escape detection.

With a depleted army and no food – the Russian peasants destroyed their stores rather than hand them to the French – Napoleon was forced to retrace his steps. His army was worn down by the cold, snow and ice and harassed by guerrillas. He had entered Russia with an army of 400,000 in June but there were fewer than 40,000 left when he again reached the frontier on 13 December.

Now came Alexander's hour of triumph. He took personal command of the Russian forces and pursued Napoleon into Prussia in January 1813. By June he had persuaded Austria and Prussia into an alliance and the three powers defeated Napoleon at Leipzig in October. And it was on Alexander's urging that the Allies pursued the war into France itself. On 31 March 1814 the Russian army entered Paris with Alexander at its head.

The handsome young Tsar was soon more popular with the Parisians than the former Emperor. 'Napoleon is my sole enemy,' Alexander told them. 'I promise my special protection to the town of Paris. I will guard and preserve all the public establishments. It is for yourselves to secure your own future happiness. I must give you a government that will ensure your own repose and that of Europe.' Alexander played a key role in helping to establish a new order in France. He was initially in favour of a republic, as opposed to the restoration of the Bourbon monarchy, and after Louis XVIII and the émigré nobles returned, was careful to see that the rights of those who had come to prominence during the Consulate and Empire were protected. The tender protection he extended to Napoleon's first wife, the Empress Josephine, was a striking example of this policy.

When Napoleon had divorced Josephine in 1809 she received a magnificent settlement. She was allowed to keep the title and prerogatives of an Empress and was granted an annual allowance of three million francs and the Duchy of Navarre, over and above the palace of Malmaison, to the west of Paris, where she had lived with Napoleon. She also had estates in Switzerland and her native Martinique. Whether she would be allowed to retain her income and estates, following the defeat of her former husband, was naturally her overriding anxiety in April 1814. Alexander came out to Malmaison to reassure her and the two were soon firm friends. Josephine had the King of Prussia to dinner and Alexander was invited to come and help entertain him. He met Josephine's daughter Hortense, the ex-Queen of Holland, and bounced her little son Louis Napoleon – the future Emperor Napoleon III of France – on his knee. Alexander wrote to his brother Constantine that Josephine reminded him of their grandmother Catherine the Great, both in her voice and appearance – she had become very stout in her old age.

Josephine was anxious to make a gesture which would adequately express her immense gratitude to her Russian protector. When Alexander visited Malmaison on 4 May 1814 she pressed one of the wonders of Antiquity into his hand – the Gonzaga cameo. The massive cameo is a double portrait exquisitely carved from an oval of sardonyx that measures roughly $6\frac{1}{4}$ by $4\frac{3}{4}$ inches. The style is Hellenistic and the two heads have traditionally been identified as the King of Egypt, Ptolemy II, who reigned from 285 to 246 BC, and his wife Arsinoe II. Some scholars have recently suggested that it may be a Roman imitation, dating from around AD 50 and depicting the military commander Germanicus and his wife Agrippina – but the Hermitage expert, Oleg Neverov, does not agree. It was already famous in the Renaissance when it belonged to Isabella d'Este and it subsequently passed to Queen Christina of Sweden, another avid collector, and from her to Pope Pius XII. It was stolen from the Vatican by a French soldier when Napoleon sacked Rome but was subsequently purchased by Napoleon himself as a present for Josephine.

At first Alexander refused to accept so valuable a present, telling

Josephine that he would much prefer a porcelain cup decorated with her portrait which stood on a nearby table. But he was persuaded to accept, and the Gonzaga cameo is now one of the great treasures of the Hermitage.

Alexander also exerted himself on behalf of Hortense, Josephine's daughter by her first husband, the Vicomte Alexandre de Beauharnais. Hortense had been unhappily married to Napoleon's younger brother Louis who became king of Holland and had already escaped to Switzerland. She now found herself without a husband or title. Alexander persuaded Louis XVIII, much against his will, to make her a duchess in her own right. Adopting the name of an estate she owned near Paris, Hortense became the Duchesse de St Leu. It was St Leu, however, that was her mother, Josephine's undoing. Hortense threw a ball there one chilly evening in late May. Josephine, scantily clad as was the fashion, opened the ball by dancing with Alexander, then walked with him for a long time in the garden discussing family affairs. She caught a chill and died five days later on 29 May. Alexander sent an aide-de-camp to attend her funeral and a guard of honour from the Russian army, a degree of attention which reputedly much annoyed Napoleon.

Josephine died three million francs in debt, which provided Alexander with the opportunity to secure another artistic coup on behalf of the Hermitage. Malmaison had been turned into a *château-musée* by Josephine, who was a knowledgeable and enthusiastic art collector – she had recently built on an art gallery to contain her large picture collection. Its crowning glory was a group of forty-eight pictures from the collection of the landgraves of Hesse-Kassel. The eighteenth-century ruler, Wilhelm VII, had put together one of the finest collections in Europe; Vivant Denon had difficulty selecting the 299 best pictures to take back to the Louvre as war booty after the battle of Jena in 1806. However, the cunning landgrave of the time had hidden forty-eight of the finest in a forester's hut where they were found by General Lagrange who gave them directly to Josephine. Of these paintings, Rembrandt's *Descent from the Cross*, a marvellous piece of realist narrative painting, is today considered one of the most important Old Master pictures in the Hermitage; Kassel also provided four of Claude Lorrain's finest landscapes, a suite titled *Morning, Noon, Evening* and *Night*. Alexander bought thirty-eight paintings for which he paid 940,000 francs – while insisting that four white marble statues by Canova, the greatest sculptor of the Neoclassical age, should be thrown in as well.

The following year, as part of the peace settlement, the Allies directed that the Napoleonic Museum in the Louvre should be dismantled and the art works returned to their original owners. The representatives of the landgrave of Hesse-Kassel retrieved the 299 paintings taken to the Louvre, but when they got to Malmaison to collect the rest they found to their astonishment that the paintings had already been shipped to Russia. The landgrave demanded them back from Alexander who told him that he would only return them if his own expenses were refunded. Announcing that it was not his intention to pay double for his own pictures, the landgrave left the paintings in St Petersburg.

Despite his weighty responsibilities, Alexander made two other significant purchases for the Hermitage at this time. He bought a collection of Spanish paintings formed by the English banker William Coesvelt which came up for sale in Amsterdam – no doubt remembering Buturlin's advice that the Hermitage was short of good Spanish works. For 100,000 guilders he got fifteen paintings, including a *Portrait of Olivares* and two others by Velasquez, three Murillos, two Francisco Ribaltas and a much praised *Childhood of the Virgin* by Francisco de Zurbarán.

Around the same time Alexander bought a vast collection of English caricatures, mainly devoted to Napoleon and incidents during the Napoleonic wars. There is no record of where Alexander bought them or why. One presumes that his own close involvement in the Napoleonic saga gave the engravings their appeal. But the collection must have been bought *en bloc* and no trace has yet been found of their original owner. Alexander visited England in June 1814 – the first Russian sovereign to do so since Peter the Great – and may have bought them there. He was acclaimed by the crowds as a hero, much to the chagrin of the Prince Regent who described himself as 'worn out with fuss, fatigue and rage' after the first week of the visit. The prime minister, Lord Grey, described Alexander as 'a vain, a silly fellow'.

In September 1814 Alexander, together with most of the crowned heads of Europe, and all its leading politicians, arrived in Vienna for the Congress which was to resolve the shape of Europe in the wake of Napoleon's defeat. Cities, islands, even countries changed hands in long sessions of hard bargaining while the younger generation danced the nights away. Alexander played a leading role in both the negotiations and the festivities, but the most significant event from the point of view of the Hermitage was the arrival of the British portrait painter Sir Thomas Lawrence, who had been commissioned to paint full-length portraits of all the leaders of the campaign against Napoleon for Windsor Castle. The twenty-four portraits, which are considered Lawrence's masterpieces, hang in what is known as the Waterloo Gallery. Lawrence's fluid, impressionistic style was admired throughout Europe as a result. His influence can be traced in the work of Delacroix in France and the leading artists of the Austrian school, such as Peter Krafft and Peter Fendi.

Lawrence began his portrait of Alexander in London in 1814 and finished it at Aix-la-Chapelle, where the allied leaders met after the battle of Waterloo to complete the negotiations begun in Vienna. His admiration for Lawrence inspired Alexander to construct a gallery of his own in the Winter Palace, known as the Gallery of 1812. It runs between the Armorial Hall and the vast St George's Hall, leading the visitor down towards the Cathedral. The barrel-vaulted gallery, designed by Carlo Rossi, contains 332 head and shoulders portraits of the Russian generals who fought in the wars against Napoleon. An English artist called George Dawe was awarded this vast commission. Now largely forgotten in England, Dawe was a celebrity in his day. He won the Royal Academy gold medal in 1803, attended surgical operations to study anatomy, wrote a treatise on the theory of colour, became 'First Portrait Painter of the Imperial Court' and the subject of an ode by Pushkin. According to Lawrence, his chief competitor, Dawe 'prowled' and 'crept' around the Congress of Aix-la-Chapelle in search of clients, thus winning the tsar's attention and an invitation to St Petersburg. He had two assistants, Alexander Polyakov and Vasily Golike but painted nearly half the portraits himself, as well as a full-length portrait of Alexander to decorate the wall at the north end of the gallery.

The paintings were still not completed in 1825, the year that Alexander died, and it fell to his brother Nicholas I to complete the undertaking. He decided to add large-scale portraits of Russia's two principal allies, Friedrich Wilhelm II of Prussia and Francis I of Austria, commissioning the leading portraitists of Berlin and Vienna, Franz Krüger and Peter Krafft, to make the paintings. Krüger's meticulously painted Friedrich Wilhelm caused such a sensation in St Petersburg when it arrived in 1832 that he was asked to take away Dawe's rendering of Alexander and paint a new one. A Russian traveller who saw him at work in Berlin in 1837 confessed himself 'rather surprised, for Krüger was to paint the first faithful portrait of the deceased, whom he had never seen before, guided only by the somewhat inferior portrait by Dawe and a rather splendid death mask'. The circumstances of the picture's creation have now been forgotten and it looks very splendid at the end of the gallery, where it is frequently photographed as a faithful likeness of the Emperor.

An attentive observer to the Gallery of 1812 will notice that there are thirteen blank spaces on the postage stamp walls, now filled with green silk. They were intended for generals who inconveniently died before they could be painted and not, as is often claimed, for generals who disgraced themselves by taking part in the Decembrist uprising of 1825. Alexander died on 1 December 1825 and the so-called 'Decembrist' revolt took place on 26 December. Only one portrait of a Decembrist was ever included in the gallery, that of Prince Sergey Volkonsky. It was banished by Alexander's brother Nicholas in 1826 but was found in one of the palace storerooms in 1903 and restored to its place.

The Decembrist uprising was essentially a demonstration in favour of the succession passing to Alexander's brother Konstantin rather than Nicholas. The conspirators believed that Konstantin would make a reformist tsar and give Russia a 'constitution' like those which Alexander himself had helped to establish in France and Poland after the defeat of Napoleon. A constitution, they believed, would exert a crucial restraint on autocratic power; the Decembrist Mikhail Fonvizin has left an eloquent assessment of the causes of the uprising:

> During the campaigns in Germany and France our young people became acquainted with European civilisation, which made a strong impression on them so that they could compare everything that they had seen abroad with that which presented itself at every turn at home – the slavery of the vast majority of Russians who had no rights, the cruel treatment of subordinates by their superiors, all manner of the abuse of power, everywhere arbitrary rule – all this excited the discontent and outraged the patriotic feelings of educated Russians.

The Decembrists did not know, however, that Konstantin had renounced his claim to the throne in 1819 following his marriage to a Polish woman who was not of royal birth. In 1823 Alexander had prepared a secret manifesto recognising his younger brother Nicholas as heir. In St Petersburg some 3,000 demonstrators gathered in the Senate Square around Falconet's statue of Peter the Great on 26 December 1825 and one of the first decisions of Nicholas's reign was to have his guards fire on them, mowing down around eighty and dispersing the rest in pandemonium. 'Dear, dear Konstantin,' he wrote to his brother a few hours later, 'Your will has been done. I am Emperor, but, my God, at what price! At the price of my subjects' blood!'

4

Nicholas I and the New Hermitage

*N*icholas I, who reigned from 1825 to 1855, was the last tsar profoundly to affect the evolution of the Hermitage. In December 1837 the Winter Palace was gutted by fire and the Hermitage pavilions, containing the imperial art collection, were only saved by the guards and palace servants who destroyed the two connecting passages, built a dividing wall between the buildings while the fire blazed and continuously doused it with water pumped from the frozen Neva and Moika rivers.

Nicholas had to rebuild and refurbish the palace. Luckily he seems to have inherited both his mother Maria Fedorovna's interest in the applied arts, including architecture, and her clever artistic eye. His elder brother Alexander I had hired Alexander Sauerweid, Russia's first important battle painter, to teach him drawing and painting and the examples of his work that have survived demonstrate that Nicholas had a definite talent in this field. On a loftier scale, central St Petersburg – Palace Square, the Admiralty, St Isaac's Cathedral and the Senate – bear witness to his fascination with architecture. The sequence of magnificent Neoclassical buildings which linked the older palaces and completed the elegant symmetry of the city centre were all commissioned by Nicholas or his brother Alexander I, and completed under Nicholas's eagle eye – he was a martinet of no mean order. His contemporaries called him 'the rod', referring simultaneously to his deportment and his dedication to corporal punishment.

He took a close interest in the reconstruction of the Winter Palace and, apart from the furnishings, most of its rooms have survived almost unchanged from his time. While the rebuilding was still in progress he had the idea of adding a purpose-built museum to the palace complex – the New Hermitage – which was cunningly tucked into a space between the Small and Old Hermitage pavilions. And after he had moved the best of the imperial art collection into the museum in 1852, he commissioned the architect Andrey Stakenschneider to redecorate the interiors of the Old and Small Hermitages in flamboyant, historicist style. Stakenschneider's white marble Pavilion Room at the Neva end of the Winter Garden is one of the finest expressions of this style anywhere, combining slim columns and arches borrowed from an Arabian mosque, medieval fountains and a Classical Roman mosaic.

Nicholas's involvement with the interiors of the museum building went far beyond the normal relationship of sovereign and architect – in this case, Leo von Klenze from Germany. The Emperor oversaw every detail, from the choice of marbles, to the design and arrangement of show cases. He chose the paintings that should hang there and he pooled the collections of antiquities spread around his other palaces to form the galleries of Greek, Roman and Scythian art. Major archaeological finds were made in the Crimea early in his reign and he saw that these discoveries were handsomely displayed in his new museum.

Nevertheless, Nicholas's conviction that he knew what was best in every sphere – he regarded himself as God's chosen representative in Russia – led to his making several eccentric, and some disastrous, decisions about the Hermitage collection. He sold off 1,220 paintings, some of them of the first importance; he had others destroyed. He melted down several of Catherine's gold and silver dinner services, some 3,300 lb of metal in all, and had new ones made in a style he preferred. His London Service, which was intended to serve around fifty people and included 1,680 pieces, was ordered from Garrards, Hunt and Roskell and other British silversmiths after his state visit to England in 1844. It included seven sculptural groups to decorate the centre of the table, one of them being a copy of the 'Queen's Cup' which had been made for presentation at the Ascot races of 1844.

Nicholas dismissed Houdon's great full-length statue of the seated Voltaire with the famous words: 'Destroy this old monkey' – luckily, his staff disobeyed him. The statue was first removed to the Hermitage library, where Nicholas, presumably, rarely ventured, and later in the nineteenth century, when the books themselves were sent to the Public Library on Nevsky Prospect, Voltaire went along for the ride.

Nicholas's character as a ruler was profoundly influenced by the Decembrist uprising and the shock of its bloody suppression in the first hours of his reign. 'No one can fully comprehend that burning pain which I feel and will continue to feel throughout the rest of my life whenever I remember this day,' he told the French ambassador at the time. The Decembrist conspirators included the flower of Russian youth – there were thirteen sons of senators and seven of provincial governors – five were eventually executed and another 200 or so were imprisoned or sent to Siberia.

Nicholas was convinced that he was dealing with a highly organised plot aimed against the Romanov regime itself – with the conspirators maybe seeking to replay the French Revolution in Russia. He commissioned an in-depth investigation of the conspirators in order to understand, on the one hand, what might be wrong with the running of his empire that had provoked them and, on the other, how to prevent future insurrections. His investigating commission interrogated some 580 suspects over a period of five months in the Winter Palace and the Hermitage. Ivan Yakushkin, who was active in the uprising in the Moscow garrison, describes in his memoirs being 'led into one of the rooms on the lower floor of the Winter Palace. There was a soldier with a naked sabre by each door and window. Here I spent the night and the next day. In the evening I was taken upstairs and to my extreme surprise I found myself in the Hermitage.' He had been taken to a large room overlooking the Neva, where the Leonardos are now exhibited but which then displayed lesser Italian paintings. Nicholas and General Levashev were seated at a folding table, under a portrait of Pope Clement IX, questioning a succession of Decembrists. 'It was quite easy being questioned by Levashev and during the whole interrogation I admired Domenichino's *Holy Family*,' Yakushkin wrote.

Nicholas was to keep a summary report of the Decembrists' criticisms on his desk for the rest of his life, regarding it as a fundamentally important description of the problems of his empire. And, in order to prevent a repetition of trouble, he instituted a secret service, known as 'the Third Section of His Majesty's Own Chancellery', to spy on his subjects. Secret denunciations were encouraged and the department expanded and flourished on the basis of fictitious, or semi-fictitious, plots uncovered by ambitious employees. Russia became, in effect, a police state and the seeds of the Bolshevik Revolution were sown. The same fear of insurrection dictated Nicholas's foreign policy. He allied himself with the conservative rulers of Austria and Prussia, and regarded France, with its history of revolution, and Britain, with its taste for democracy, as dangerously subversive. He became known as 'the gendarme of Europe'.

Queen Victoria of England gave a perceptive reading of Nicholas's character in a letter she wrote to her uncle Leopold, King of Belgium, after the tsar visited England in 1844:

> He is stern and severe – with fixed principles of duty which nothing on earth will make him change; very clever I do not think him, and his mind is an uncivilised one; his education has been neglected; politics and military concerns are the only things he takes great interest in; the arts and all softer occupations he is insensible to, but he is sincere, I am certain, sincere even in his most despotic acts, from a sense that that is the only way to govern.

The Queen clearly failed to discover artistic leanings under Nicholas's stern exterior. She described him as 'a very striking man; still very handsome; his profile is beautiful and his manners most dignified and graceful; extremely civil – quite alarmingly so, as he is full of attentions and politenesses . . . He seldom smiles and when he does the expression is not a happy one.'

Nicholas's upbringing had reflected his father's military tastes. On the day after his own accession Paul appointed the four-month-old Nicholas to his first command – as Colonel of the Imperial Horse Guards. Nicholas wore his colonel's uniform at his brother Mikhail's christening eighteen months later – he was only two. When he was four his father appointed Count Matvey Lamsdorf as governor of his two youngest sons, a man who had no intellectual accomplishments but had pleased Paul while Governor of Courland and director of the First Cadet Corps.

With so much of his education taken up with military matters, it is not surprising that Nicholas followed his brother Alexander's campaigns against Napoleon with vivid interest, burning to be allowed to play a part himself. At the beginning of 1814, Alexander permitted his two youngest brothers, Nicholas and Mikhail, to join the army in the field – Nicholas was just short of eighteen. 'I cannot even begin to describe our happiness or, more accurately, our mad joy,' he later wrote. 'We began to live and, in a single moment, crossed the threshold from childhood into the world, into life.'

On their way home from the wars in 1815 the brothers visited Berlin where Nicholas fell in love with Princess Charlotte, the daughter of Friedrich Wilhelm III, King of Prussia. For the first, and only, time in his life he took to writing poetry. The young couple wandered happily around the Potsdam countryside and Nicholas proposed on the famous Pfaueninsel, or Peacock Island, a marvellous garden with a fake Gothic castle in the middle of Lake Havel. It was a rare, royal love match and their affection never dimmed. 'Happiness, joy and repose – that is what I seek and find in my old Mouffy,' he wrote in later life. He was not above having affairs with other women, however, most notably Pushkin's wife. According to some accounts, the young Frenchman Georges d'Anthès, who killed the poet in a duel over her honour in 1837, had, in fact, been covering up for the Emperor.

Nicholas and Princess Charlotte became formally engaged in October 1815 but did not marry until July 1817 – after Nicholas had made an eight-month tour of Europe at Alexander's behest, spending four months in England to learn at first hand the unspeakable dangers of democracy. Like the other German princesses who married into the imperial family, Charlotte converted to the Russian Orthodox religion and changed her name in the process, becoming known as Alexandra Fedorovna. Her taste, formed in the artistic milieu of early nineteenth-century Berlin, profoundly influenced Nicholas. German painters flocked to his court, a German architect built the New Hermitage, and he made an extensive collection of contemporary German sculpture – white marble gods and goddesses by followers of the Danish sculptor Bertel Thorwaldsen and the Italian, Antonio Canova.

The couple started their married life in the Anichkov Palace on Nevsky Prospect which had been built by the Empress Elizabeth in the 1740s for one of her lovers but which had been extensively and frequently altered over the years. They moved into the Winter Palace when Nicholas became Emperor and their alterations of the interior began with the completion of the 1812 Gallery initiated by Alexander. Its formal opening took place in 1826 and they subsequently added portraits by Krüger, the Berlin court painter. Nicholas himself lived and worked in a ground-floor room facing the Admiralty whose spartan furnishings became so famous – he slept on an iron campaign bed – that the room was preserved intact, as a memorial, up to the time of the Revolution. He wanted his wife to be housed in splendour, however, and commissioned Alexander Bryullov to redesign her suite of rooms on the first floor. His *chef-d'oeuvre* was the Malachite Room, where the mix of bright green malachite pillars with gilded plaster work and mirrors still makes a gloriously rich effect.

Meanwhile the French architect Auguste Montferrand rebuilt the

Field Marshal's Hall, one of the largest state rooms, and constructed a throne room beside it as a memorial to Peter the Great. It is still furnished according to Montferrand's designs, with a portrait of Peter hanging behind the massive silver throne that the Empress Anna Ivanovna ordered from London, the walls hung with red brocade embroidered with silver thread and, below, silver side tables and candelabras that Nicholas's mother had ordered – and perhaps designed? – for the throne room in the Mikhail Castle. Montferrand, who was trained as a miniature painter, not an architect, had arrived in St Petersburg from Paris, seeking his fortune. He wheedled his way into Nicholas's good graces by presenting him with a small volume of exquisite architectural views. The great fire of 1837 is generally blamed on his lack of architectural training.

Nicholas and Alexandra Fedorovna were at the Bolshoy Theatre attending a performance of the ballet *Dieu et la Bayadère* when news of the fire was brought. It had started in a chimney hidden in the wall between the Field Marshal's Hall and the Throne Room – Montferrand is thought to have left inflammable pieces of wood irresponsibly close to this large chimney connecting the apothecary's stove on the ground floor, and several subsidiary fireplaces, with the roof. Without telling his wife what was happening, Nicholas hurried home to inspect the fire which took hold relatively slowly – all the portraits in the nearby 1812 Gallery were successfully saved. Nicholas had his young sons taken to the Anichkov Palace, then took command of a massive evacuation of paintings and furniture.

Everything was first dumped in the snow in Palace Square – one of the Empress's favourite gold ornaments was only found when the snow melted in the spring. Sailors carried out the contents of the vast silver stores. The palace guards threw themselves into the burning building with such enthusiasm that Nicholas was eventually forced to restrain them. He is reputed to have found a crowd of guards wrestling with a firmly fixed wall mirror and, when they ignored his command to leave, to have thrown his opera glasses and shattered it. 'You see, lads,' he then told them, 'your lives are dearer to me than the mirror and I now ask you to leave the building.' The poet Vasily Zhukovsky described the scene as 'a vast bonfire with flames reaching the sky'. The fire burned for several days and the Winter Palace was completely gutted.

The reconstruction was completed within eighteen months where it had taken Rastrelli eight years (1754–62) to build the original edifice. This Herculean task was achieved through the massive recruitment of manpower and disregard for human life which is so characteristic of Russia's great endeavours. Some 8,000 building workers camped in the snow. According to the highly coloured account of Edward Jerrmann, writing in the 1840s:

> the work went on literally day and night; there was no pause for meals; the gangs of workmen relieved each other. Festivals were unheeded; the seasons themselves were overcome. To accelerate the work, the building was kept, the winter through, artificially heated to the excessive temperature of 24 to 26 degrees Réaumur. Many workmen sank under the heat, and were carried out dead or dying; a painter, who was decorating a ceiling fell from his ladder struck with apoplexy. Neither money, health, nor life, was spared.

The work was directed by the distinguished Neoclassical architect, Vasily Stasov, but, on Nicholas's instructions, the main state rooms and staircases were restored as they had been before the fire. Thus Rastrelli's Jordan Staircase – so called on account of the annual ceremony of blessing the waters of the Neva as a celebration of Christ's baptism in the River Jordan – was reconstructed from his original plans, complete with its exuberant Baroque plasterwork. Stasov replaced the gilt bronze handrails with white marble, and the pink columns with polished grey granite, but otherwise there was little change. He followed Rossi's designs for the 1812 Gallery, Rastrelli's for the cathedral and Montferrand's for the Small Throne Room. He got Alexander Bryullov to redesign the rooms facing Palace Square, however, incorporating, on Nicholas's instructions, military themes in the grisaille ceiling paintings and plasterwork arms and armour in the new Alexander Hall, named after Nicholas's brother.

During 1838, the year of intensive reconstruction work on the Winter Palace, Nicholas paid a visit to Munich where Ludwig I of Bavaria was in the midst of a major building programme. The connoisseur king, who had come to the throne, like Nicholas, in 1825, was determined to turn Munich into the greatest art centre in northern Europe. He was tearing down the city and raising majestic new public buildings, mostly designed by Leo von Klenze. At the time of Nicholas's visit Klenze had completed the Glyptothek, a temple-style building constructed to house Ludwig's collection of Classical sculpture, and the Alte Pinakothek, or picture gallery, designed in the new 'Renaissance' style inspired by the old palazzi of Florence.

Nicholas, with his mind already bent on building problems, was excited and impressed. He was shown round by Klenze and immediately invited him to St Petersburg to design new buildings for the Russian capital. In the event, Klenze only designed one building, but a very grand one – the New Hermitage, a custom-built museum tucked on to the back of Catherine's Old Hermitage. The idea of constructing a museum where the imperial collection could be displayed to the public was, no doubt, encouraged by Nicholas's seeing the splendid new galleries that Ludwig had built for his own and his family's collection.

Klenze had been trained in Berlin and Paris, where he developed his special interest in the ornamental detail of interiors. He started out as a Neoclassicist, basing his early designs on Greek temples, but later adopted a neo-Renaissance style. By the time he designed the New Hermitage he was a thoroughgoing eclectic, and incorporated elements of Greek, Roman, Renaissance, Baroque and Gothic styles, skilfully combining them to achieve a very grand and ornamental effect. The New Hermitage was not merely to be a museum, but the museum extension of an imperial palace, and that is what Klenze made it look like.

Klenze's first design involved pulling down the Small Hermitage and creating a square between the Winter Palace and the proposed New Hermitage. This was turned down and he had to have his building's main façade looking on to Millionnaya Street – which runs parallel to the Neva at the back of the Winter Palace and leads into Palace Square. The public entrance he designed was spectacular. The Greek-style portico is supported by ten, five-yard, granite giants, known by the French term 'Atlantes', carved by the Russian sculptor Alexander Terebenev. According to classical myth Atlante, or Atlas as he is known in English, supported the heavens and the Hermitage statues put the same effort into supporting the roof of the entrance.

Klenze was much too busy in Munich to stay in St Petersburg to superintend work on his building, so Vasily Stasov, who had so ably overseen the reconstruction of the Winter Palace, was put in charge of a building commission which directed the work. This commission modified Klenze's designs and introduced ideas of their own, especially in the interiors. Klenze had designed new furniture for all the galleries but not much of it was made – there are still some of his extraordinary obelisk-shaped show cases in the Antique galleries. Nicholas ordained that furniture from the imperial store in the Tauride Palace should mainly be used. There were some handsome suites of furniture which had been designed for the Winter Palace by Rossi and Montferrand before the fire, and not reused afterwards, and they were brought into the museum. The marvellous mahogany chairs, richly embellished with giltwood carving, that Rossi designed in 1818–20 to furnish the guest rooms used by Wilhelm Friedrich of Prussia are still in the museum galleries; visitors are even allowed to sit on them!

Nicholas and Alexandra were so delighted with the museum that one of the first-floor galleries, now the Michelangelo room, was converted into a rest room where the Empress could happily while away the afternoon. The finest *objets de vertu* and the Scythian gold were displayed there in Klenze's obelisk-shaped show cases and Nicholas ordered a new suite of sofas and easy chairs for the Empress from St Petersburg's leading cabinetmaker Peter Gambs. The gallery seems to have been returned to the museum after Nicholas's death but when Florian Gilles, the librarian, wrote an account of the Hermitage in the 1860s it was still known as 'the Empress's cabinet' and contained jewels and gold.

One of Nicholas's happiest ideas for the museum's decoration was the extensive use of monumental vases carved from the richly coloured hardstones of Siberia. While decorative items were carved from hardstones all over Europe, the scale and sophistication of Russian vases are unique. Most of the finest ones are in the Hermitage since the three main factories worked almost exclusively for the imperial household. Leading architects designed the vases as well as their intricate ormolu mounts – they generally echo the French Empire style but the Russians added an extra richness.

The first hardstone factory had been established at Peterhof by Peter the Great in 1721 as part of his efforts to introduce European decorative arts to Russia but it was during Catherine's reign that the great deposits of coloured stone were discovered – the first jaspers in 1765, green breccia in 1780, rhodonite, marble and further jaspers in 1781–3, amazone-stone in 1784, lazurite in 1785, and a deposit of violet, red and black porphyries in the Altai mountains in 1786. Initially the stones were rough cut on site, and shipped to Peterhof for finishing. However, it was obviously more economic to work where the stone was found and new factories were established at Ekaterinburg, in the Urals, and in the small village of Kolyvan in the Altai. Most of the very large vases came from the latter and had to be transported to St Petersburg over a distance of some 3,000 miles.

The carving of a single vase often took between ten and twenty years. First the stone would be found and its measurements sent to the Imperial

Cabinet. The Cabinet would commission a design from an architect, sometimes one of the famous architects who were at work on the imperial palaces, such as Quarenghi, Rossi or Andrey Voronikhin, but more often, in Nicholas's day, the design was supplied by Ivan Galberg, the official architect attached to the Cabinet. The design was sent back to Ekaterinburg or Kolyvan where the vase was carved and shipped to St Petersburg. It went into the 'Cabinet Store of Stone Objects' in the Anichkov Palace and the ormolu mounts would be added.

Every Christmas and Easter an exhibition of the new vases was arranged on the Jordan staircase and the Emperor himself picked out the pieces he wanted for the Winter Palace or the Hermitage. The rejected vases would be used as diplomatic gifts – there is a particularly fine one at Windsor Castle – or just sent back to languish in store. The most famous of all the items Nicholas installed in the New Hermitage is the vast 'Kolyvan vase' – its elliptical bowl is five yards long and three yards wide – and its history perfectly illustrates the labour involved in creating these ornamental pieces. The jasper came from Revnevskaya, high in the mountains above Kolyvan – jasper was first found there in 1789. Workers would live in huts at the quarry during summer and rough-cut the stones they found, then slide them down to Kolyvan after the first snows had fallen.

The vast stone from which this vase was cut was unearthed in 1819. The dimensions were sent to St Petersburg and a design, incorporating elaborate carved mouldings on the underside, was supplied by the architect Abram Melnikov. The Cabinet approved his design in 1824 but it turned out not to be realisable; Kolyvan pointed out the difficulties and asked for a plaster model to carve from. At this point the stone was still at the quarry and the rough cut, on which up to forty men were working at any one time, was not completed until 1831. Then came the problem of moving the stone over twenty miles of mountain back to Kolyvan – its transport is said to have involved between 500 and 1,000 men.

Work started on the vase at the Kolyvan factory in December 1831 and took eleven-and-a-half years at a cost of 30,284.43 silver roubles. In 1843 it took 154 horses to drag the completed vase to the port at Barnaul where it was put on a ship for St Petersburg. The transport to Barnaul had to be done during winter to avoid using bridges which might have collapsed under the weight of the vase; instead it was taken across the ice. When it arrived in the capital the vase was found to be too large to be moved into the marble store in the Anichkov Palace so a special hut was built for it under the palace colonnade. It stayed there until 1850 or so when it was moved to the New Hermitage whose walls were literally built around it. It has a gallery to itself among the rooms of Greek and Roman antiquities on the ground floor.

The display of antiquities was the most important innovation in the New Hermitage, inspired by Nicholas's visit to Munich and the great impression that Ludwig's Glyptothek had made on him. Catherine the Great had established the Hermitage picture gallery and allowed visitors to admire it but the imperial collection of Classical antiquities had never been gathered together or put on show. Antique sculptures, vases and jewellery had been acquired from the time of Peter the Great onwards and some gold items were exhibited in Peter's Kunstkammer. But sculptures had habitually been used as decoration and were spread around the imperial palaces and their parks, or stored in various palace basements. Nicholas gathered the best together in order to establish his new galleries. As today, the ground floor of the New Hermitage was devoted to antiquities and the upper floor to pictures.

The most exciting and original feature of the display of antiquities, then as now, was the range of gold and silver artefacts, some exquisitely wrought, that had been found in Scythian tombs in southern Russia. The Scythians, a nomadic people who originated in Central Asia, arrived in the Black Sea area in the eighth century BC and remained politically dominant there for the next 400 years. They became immensely wealthy through trading corn, grown on the fertile plain to the north of the Black Sea, with the Mediterranean world. Their princes went to their graves decked out with rich gold ornaments. Mostly these were made by Greek craftsmen, who were the most sophisticated jewellers of the ancient world. The Scythians either imported their gold jewellery from Greece or commissioned Greek craftsmen who had settled locally to make it for them – Greek colonies were established in the Crimea and along the north coast of the Black Sea from the seventh century BC onwards.

At the time the New Hermitage was being built, Russian archaeology was still in its infancy. The Academy of Science, founded in 1725, had sent expeditions to Siberia in the eighteenth century but they were essentially treasure hunters. The tall burial mounds that remain one of the curiosities of the south Russian landscape only began to attract attention at the end of the eighteenth century. The first purposeful excavations were made on the orders of the Russian military governors – the territory had only been acquired by Russia during Catherine's reign and the governors were busily building roads and towns. A burial mound at Litoi was opened by General Melgunov, another at Taman by General Vandervelde, mounds near Kerch by General Gangeblov while General Suchtelen began to excavate the ancient city of Olbia.

There was also a most influential influx of French émigrés who had been ousted from France by the Revolution. The most notable was Paul Dubrux who spent three years in the Russian army from 1797 to 1800, and then became a Commissioner of Health in the Crimea. He began to excavate on his own account in 1816 and spent all his free time exploring and mapping ancient remains – he received a small subsidy from Count Nikolay Rumyantsev, chancellor of the empire, and gave some of his early finds to the Dowager Empress Maria Fedorovna, Nicholas's mother. Thus home-grown archaeology began to attract the attention of the court. New museums were established in Kerch and Odessa in 1823 to house local finds and it was ordered that the finest pieces should always be sent to the Hermitage. The Hermitage collection is thus extraordinarily well documented – most other museum collections of antiquities were bought from dealers who rarely knew, or wished to reveal, the exact location and date at which pieces had been found.

In 1830 came the sensational opening of the burial mound at Kul Oba, close to Kerch, which stirred the imaginations of the intelligentsia and nobility throughout Russia. The Governor of Kerch, Colonel Ivan Stempkovsky, was a keen amateur archaeologist and on 19 September 1830 he invited his friend Paul Dubrux to come and watch 200 soldiers who were removing stones from two burial mounds to build a barracks. Dubrux realised from the shape of the stone structure that was revealed that the site contained an unexplored tomb.

It turned out to contain a Scythian king of the fourth century BC who had been buried with his wife and servant. Round his neck he wore a magnificent gold torque ending in figures of Scythian horsemen; beside him lay a gold libation bowl, its lobes embossed with twelve gorgons' heads, twelve panthers, twenty-four bearded heads of deities, forty-eight boars' heads and ninety-six bees. His wife wore an elaborate gold pendant embossed with the head of Athene, copied from the famous statue of the goddess by Phidias in the Parthenon. At her feet was a five-inch gold flask worked by a Greek master with scenes from life – two seated warriors chatting, a man stringing a bow, a man treating another's mouth ailment and another bandaging his friend's wounded leg. They all wear patterned trousers and belted tunics – in contrast to the naked, or lightly draped, heroes of native, Greek imagery. The vase is one of the highlights of the Hermitage collection of Scythian gold.

It has been suggested that the scenes around its sides illustrate the Greek myth concerning the founding of the Scythian kingdom, as reported by Herodotus, the fifth-century BC historian. Herodotus writes that 'the Greeks who dwell about the Pontus' say that 'Heracles, when he was carrying off the cows of Geryon . . . being overtaken by storm and frost, drew his lion's skin about him, and fell fast asleep. While he slept, his mares, which he had loosed from his chariot to graze, by some wonderful chance disappeared.' They had been taken by 'a strange being, between a maiden and a serpent, whose form from the buttocks upwards was like that of a woman while all below was like a snake' and she would not give them back before he had intercourse with her.

The result was triplets and before Heracles left her, the snake lady enquired: 'When your sons grow up, what must I do with them?' Heracles replied: 'When the lads have grown to manhood, do thus, and assuredly you will not err. Watch them, and when you see one of them bend this bow as I now bend it, and gird himself with this girdle thus, choose him to remain in the land. Those who fail in the trial send away.'

In a book on the Scythians published in 1977, D. S. Raevsky suggests that the scenes on the queen's little vase depict the three brothers attempting to string Heracles' bow. Two have failed and hurt themselves in a manner common when stringing a bow, one on the jaw and the other on the calf of his leg, which is being bandaged. Meanwhile the youngest son, Scythes, who was to inherit the kingdom, is quietly, and successfully, attaching the bow string.

The so-called 'Kerch Room' was one of the most popular highlights of the New Hermitage when it opened to the public in 1852. It had been artistically arranged with gold objects, bronzes, vases, terracottas and stone sculptures from the burial mounds of southern Russia. The excavated jewellery was upstairs in Alexandra's rest room – there were eighteen crowns, four diadems and the gold death mask of a queen. In all, almost 1,500 objects from Kerch were put on show.

From the very start the antiquities galleries were thus of a high standard, suitably matching the extraordinary riches of the paintings collection which Nicholas had inherited. He took the same close personal interest in the preparation of the picture galleries but, in this case, to less happy effect. He began by setting up a commission of three artists to review all the paintings in the imperial collection and divide them into four classes: those worthy of display in the new galleries (815), those suitable to be used as decoration elsewhere in the imperial palaces (804), those that should be kept in store (1,369) and those of no importance (1,564). The keeper of the picture gallery, Fedor Bruni, tells us in his memoirs that the Emperor would visit the museum from 1 to 2 p.m. every day to supervise the work of the commission. 'If he had once defined a painting as a work of this or that school, it was no easy matter to make him change his opinion,' Bruni writes and quotes a typical exchange between the two of them: 'This is Flemish,' Nicholas pronounced. 'But it seems to me, Your Majesty . . .', 'No, Bruni. Don't argue. Flemish it is.'

Nicholas had the pictures in the last category – those condemned as of 'no importance' – sent to the Tauride Palace where he picked out a few as suitable gifts and ordered that the rest should be auctioned off. Naturally enough, the commission of painters, under the eccentric direction of Nicholas himself, had missed many pearls. An astute art dealer, A. A. Kaufmann, acquired the wings of a Lucas van Leyden triptych for thirty roubles and sold them back to the Hermitage in 1885 for 8,000 roubles. Other paintings which returned to the Hermitage as a result of confiscations and sales after the Revolution are Chardin's *Still Life with Attributes of the Arts* in 1926, Charles-Joseph Natoire's *Cupid Sharpening an Arrow* in 1932, and Pieter Lastman's *Abraham on the Road to Canaan* in 1938. Others got away for good, including a José de Ribera now in the National Gallery, Warsaw, a Kneller now in the National Gallery, London, and a Terborch in the Philadelphia Museum of Art.

Nicholas's own acquisitions were heavily influenced by Alexandra Fedorovna and the taste of the Berlin court. Her father was an enlightened patron of Berlin's Biedermeier artists whose particular strengths lay in portraiture, architectural views and pictures of military parades. One of Franz Krüger's greatest masterpieces, *Parade on the Obernplatz, Berlin, in the Year 1824*, now in the Berlin National Gallery, was commissioned by Nicholas I – it was given to Kaiser Bill by Nicholas II in 1912. It depicts the Brandenburg cuirassiers whose command Nicholas I had been given by his father-in-law. The Hermitage still owns twenty portraits by Krüger. Another Berlin master, Eduard Gärtner, a specialist in architectural views and genre, was commissioned to supply a replica of the masterpiece he painted for Alexandra Fedorovna's father, *Panorama from the Roof of the Friedrichswer-derkirche* – a 360-degree view of Berlin, made up of six separate panels; the replica is now in the Palace at Peterhof. Gärtner came to St

Petersburg in 1837 and was commissioned to paint interior and exterior views of imperial palaces.

Watercolours depicting the interiors of houses and castles became very popular in Berlin in the Biedermeier period and Gärtner was one of the pioneers of the genre. Alexandra's sister Louise had commissioned paintings of her favourite rooms in the Berliner Schloss from him as early as 1821 and the fashion now spread to Russia. Nicholas commissioned watercolours of palace interiors from many different artists and, after the New Hermitage museum was completed in 1852, he commissioned a special series to record its elegant arrangements from Eduard Hau, Konstantin Ukhtomsky and Luigi Premazzi. His son, Alexander II, followed up by ordering a major series of watercolours recording the appearance of the rooms in the Winter Palace. They are still in the Hermitage and, together, make up a fascinating portrait of gracious, imperial living in the mid-nineteenth century.

The biggest catch from Germany, however, was Caspar David Friedrich – now regarded as the most important German painter of the Romantic movement. His landscapes, with their lonely figures, twisted trees, ruins and dramatic effects of light, were a transcription of his religious beliefs; he saw God in nature, which gives his paintings a powerful spiritual impact. The Hermitage has nine paintings and six drawings, all specially commissioned or carefully selected from his studio. Nicholas bought the first of them, *On Board a Sailing Ship*, on a visit to Friedrich's studio in 1820 – presumably at the behest of Alexandra Fedorovna whose father and brother were already Friedrich's patrons. The connection was fostered by the poet Vasily Zhukovsky, who was first employed to teach Alexandra Fedorovna Russian and subsequently became Alexander II's tutor and mentor. He visited Friedrich in 1821 at Alexandra Fedorovna's suggestion and became a lifelong friend of the artist.

By marrying into the Prussian royal family, Nicholas allied himself with the very source of his father's and grandfather's militarism – it was the parades, uniforms and manoeuvres of Frederick the Great's armies which both had endeavoured to emulate in Russia. Alexandra Fedorovna had also inherited this taste. Writing of the day she first arrived in St Petersburg, the homesick princess recorded: 'I was delighted to see again the Semenovsky, Ismailovsky and Preobrazhensky Regiments which I remembered from a military review in Silesia . . . during the armistice of 1813. And when I saw the Chevalier Guards drawn up near the Admiralty, I could not restrain a small cry of pleasure because they reminded me of my beloved Guards of the Berlin Regiment.' The couple's fascination with military matters is reflected in two collections – that of arms and armour which ended up the most extensive and important in Europe and is still in the Hermitage, and that of paintings of military subjects, most of which were either consigned to storage or actually got rid of after the Revolution. Nicholas's passion for such paintings verged on mania.

The catalogue of his private collection, made after his death, included 666 paintings, of which 650 were military scenes. In his idle days at the Anichkov Palace, before he became Emperor, he not only tried his hand at making military paintings himself, but also painted figures of soldiers into the Old Master landscapes hanging on his walls. One entry in his catalogue reads: 'Van Goyen: Landscape with the manoeuvre of Russian troops. Figures painted in by His Imperial Majesty when Crown Prince.' Jan van Goyen was a seventeenth-century Dutch landscapist, a masterly interpreter of the flat fields, waterways and windmills of Holland set off by low horizons and big skies – a landscape where Russian troops never penetrated except in the imagination of Nicholas himself.

After the 1837 fire in the Winter Palace imposed on him a duty to rebuild and redecorate, Nicholas conceived the idea of a 'War Gallery', to be composed of paintings depicting the most famous battles of Russian history. In the wake of the Napoleonic wars, battle painting had become a popular genre throughout Europe and Nicholas was inspired by the example of the *Galerie des Batailles* at Versailles – which opened in 1836 – and the *Schlachtensaal* in the royal palace at Munich, the Residenz. Peter Hess of Munich supplied the principal masterpieces of the War Gallery. He painted with almost photographic realism, lovingly delineating smoking cannon, bloodstained bandages, dying horses and staggering soldiers, all in the correct uniforms – he had accompanied the Bavarian army in campaigns against Napoleon in his youth. He was invited to St Petersburg by Nicholas in 1839 and spent the next thirteen years of his life on a series of eight large paintings and four smaller ones depicting famous Russian engagements with Napoleon's army. He visited the battlefields and took the most painstaking care to achieve absolute 'realism' – copies of twenty generals' portraits from the 1812 Gallery were sent to Munich for him to work from.

He had, however, met his match in his imperial patron. Nicholas's criticism of the first canvas Hess sent from Munich, *The Battle of Vyazma*, did not dwell on aesthetics: '1. The officers' coats in the picture are buttoned down the left front; our officers all button theirs down the right front. 2. The cloak of a non-commissioned officer should not be trimmed with galloon. 3. No white edging to the cravat . . .' Once these important matters had been seen to, the paintings were received with overwhelming enthusiasm in Russia. Many copies were made for the administrative offices of towns near the battlefields and other interested institutions. Several of the paintings were reproduced as complete books – the detail in Hess's panoramas made this kind of treatment possible. But today only two of them are on view, *Crossing the Berezina River* and *The Battle of Borodino*. They were added to the display in the 1812 Gallery after World War II. The rest are tucked away in store awaiting their return to fashion.

Nicholas also decorated a suite of five rooms overlooking Palace Square with battle paintings – the rooms are now filled with masterpieces of the French eighteenth century. The ceilings painted in grisaille with guns, banners and other military motifs, provide a gentle echo of past times. Most of the paintings were sold off by the Soviet government in the 1920s and 1930s.

Nicholas's collection of arms and armour, or Arsenal, was undertaken in a similar, romantic spirit but to much more interesting effect. In his introduction to the magnificent catalogue of the collection produced between 1835 and 1853, its keeper Florian Gilles highlights Nicholas's debt to historical novels. 'Thanks to Walter Scott and some other famous writers, the study and classification of fifteenth, sixteenth and seventeenth century arms came into favour,' he says. Historical novels were, indeed, central to the early nineteenth-century Romantic movement – Scott and his ilk brought chivalry and its trappings into fashion. Nicholas was interested in all the trappings. In addition to weapons of war, he bought wonderful carved ivory hunting horns, wriggling with deer, wild boar and rabbits amidst rich foliage, as well as medieval stained glass and metalwork.

As a child, Nicholas knew and admired the collection of arms his father had at Gatchina, his country palace near St Petersburg, and it was probably a desire to emulate his father that started him collecting. The Gatchina arsenal had, in fact, been begun by the first owner of the palace, Count Grigory Orlov, Catherine the Great's lover. She had ordered hunting equipment for Orlov from the leading European armourers in the late eighteenth century – on an exceptionally lavish scale, since Orlov liked large hunting parties. Nicholas made his first acquisition at the age of thirteen when General Lageron gave him a

Turkish sabre taken by him in the 1811 campaign against the Turks; arms captured in war were always a useful source for imperial collectors.

Nicholas, however, collected in the spirit of the new century. He did not buy arms either for decoration or for use but in the scientific spirit of an antiquary. He wanted the best makers of East and West to be represented in his collection and the history of arms manufacture to be illustrated by his pieces, with all its by-ways and cul de sacs. The collection includes, for instance, an interesting group of medieval torture instruments as well as superb Mannerist helmets from Milan, Russian hatchets, their blades patterned with inlaid gold, and jewelled Indian daggers. His collection contains 6,000 European arms, 2,000 items of Russian manufacture and another 7,000 or so pieces from the Orient, principally Turkey, Persia and India, a reminder that Russia is as much an Oriental as a European country.

Once he had become emperor, Nicholas moved his collection of arms and armour into a fake medieval castle that his brother Alexander had built in the park of his country palace at Tsarskoe Selo – a little jewel, faced in pink plaster, with four towers and a crenellated parapet. In Nicholas's time it could be lived in. There was a bedroom, dining-room, study and library. The latter, according to Florian Gilles, contained a 'small but precious' collection of works on chivalry, heraldry and the Middle Ages.

Gilles explains that the collection was guarded by a group of twenty retired officers from the Imperial Guard – 'old soldiers covered in wounds from many different fields of battle . . . who happily remember, as they clean the arms, their own glorious careers. They often have the pleasure of seeing their Sovereign who loves to visit his arsenal and on such occasions is not above chatting familiarly with these brave old men.'

By the time the Arsenal was moved from Tsarskoe Selo to the Hermitage in 1885 it also contained a group of Colt pistols from America which latterday collectors make pilgrimages to St Petersburg to see. Samuel Colt had taken out patents in the 1830s on the multi-chambered rotating breech which he invented, but it was the Mexican War of 1846–8, and the resulting vast US government orders for his pistols, that led to the mass production of Colts and made his fortune. When the Crimean War broke out in 1854, Colt scented new opportunities. The richly ornamented, presentation pistols he made for Nicholas I, his son Alexander II, and Alexander's two brothers, the Grand Dukes Konstantin and Mikhail, form a unique series. They are pretty toys, the steel parts blued, embellished with engravings and damascened in gold, the grip mounts sculptural arabesques of gilt bronze. The first two of the series, a five-shot and a six-shot revolver, were presented to Nicholas in 1854.

The Crimean War, which pitted Russia against Turkey, Britain, France and Piedmont, revealed to Nicholas that his precious army was trained and equipped for the parade ground, not for real war. Its equipment was technologically out of date and hurried efforts to bring it up to standard resulted in Colt receiving the bulk orders his presentation pistols were designed to attract. Curiously, despite his fascination with military matters, Nicholas had comparatively little experience of real war.

When he came to the throne in 1825 the defeat of Napoleon was still fresh in every memory and the Russian army was bathed in an aura of glory. In July 1826, just as Nicholas arrived in Moscow for his coronation, the Persian army invaded Russian territory in the Caucasus. After a rather incompetent campaign, the Russian army drove them back and peace was signed in January 1828. Three months later, when the Sultan refused to allow Russian ships to pass through the straits from the Black Sea to the Mediterranean, Nicholas declared war on the Ottoman Empire. This limited war was concluded in August 1829 with the defeat of the Sultan's forces. Thereafter, the principal role of the Russian army was the suppression of revolt, in Poland in 1830 and Hungary in 1849.

The bitter aftermath of the Polish revolution, which Nicholas regarded as a betrayal, revealed his aptitude for destroying art – presumably an act of ritual revenge. The Hermitage archives contain a report from the chief restorer, Alexander Mitrokhin, to Franz Labensky, keeper of the picture gallery: 'In fulfilment of Your Excellency's instructions of this 26 July concerning the destruction, by His Imperial Majesty's command, of certain portraits, pictures and other things brought from Warsaw in seventeen boxes, we have the honour to report that on this 31 July . . . the said portraits, pictures and other things have been annihilated and burnt, with the exception of a portrait of the Emperor Alexander I which we intend to rub out with pumice stone.'

Nicholas's high-handed attitude to art, including, when he deemed it necessary, its destruction or sale, has often led to his being depicted as a philistine. There is no doubt, however, that Nicholas loved the Hermitage museum in a very intimate way. He is said to have paid it a farewell visit a day or two before his death. Broken by the failure of his

Crimean campaign, and the ignominious revelation that his cherished army was incompetent in the field, he may have committed suicide. Alexander Herzen, the dissident intellectual, repeatedly claims this in his writings, though official reports stated that Nicholas died of pneumonia after reviewing his troops in the snow. As he wandered through the Hermitage galleries for the last time, he was heard to murmur: 'Yes. Here is perfection!'

5
Twilight of the Romanovs

*T*he second half of the nineteenth century or, more precisely, the period from Nicholas's death in 1855 to the outbreak of revolution in 1917, was marked in Russia by massive social change. This period witnessed the belated industrialisation of the nation, underground agitation for political reform which cut the tsars off from the people and put their lives at risk (Alexander II was actually assassinated in 1881), and extraordinary achievements in the spheres of literature, music and the arts. From now on, the tsars took only a limited interest in the Hermitage, which they came to regard rather as an 'institution' than their own, private collection.

The museum itself, after the fanfare that accompanied its opening in 1852, entered a period of stagnation – relieved by occasional bursts of activity when new directors were appointed. From the 1850s onwards, the moulding of the museum's character slipped out of the hands of the imperial family and into those of professional administrators. In 1863 the post of 'director' of the museum was instituted and filled by Stepan Gedeonov, who was also given charge of the Imperial Theatres four years later. He cultivated the acquaintance of collectors and found some great works of art which he persuaded the emperor to buy – but it was now the administrator's taste and ingenuity that led the way, not the emperor's.

Even the emperors became muddled over the status of their collection. In 1905, the Ministry of the Imperial Court asked the Hermitage to clarify 'whether we can consider the artistic works located in the Imperial Hermitage as the property of the museum, or if, in the collection, there are works which form the property of His Imperial Majesty'. To this enquiry the museum replied:

> The administration of the Imperial Hermitage has the honour to tell you that the pictures and other treasures of the Hermitage have always, from the time of Catherine II, formed the property of the reigning emperors, in the same way as objects decorating imperial palaces, only allocated from among their artistic possessions to be shown in the said museum. Everything kept in it must be considered the property of His Imperial Highness.

This, no doubt, was true in juridical terms. But, as the Ministry's enquiry highlights, the museum had already come to be regarded more in the light of a National Gallery than an imperial collection. To understand how it evolved from one to the other in the course of the nineteenth century, it is necessary to look at the changing character of Russia in general and of St Petersburg in particular.

The hands-on government of Nicholas I had required a vast army of clerks to shuffle paper and they poured into St Petersburg from all over the empire, hoping to make their fortunes but ending up impoverished, overworked and disillusioned. The mysterious appeal that St Petersburg exerted over provincial Russia is described in Mikhail Saltykov-Shchedrin's *Diary of a Provincial in Petersburg*, published in 1872:

> We provincials somehow turn our steps towards Petersburg instinctively . . . A particular individual will be sitting around and suddenly, as if a light had dawned, he begins to pack his things. 'You're going to Petersburg?' – 'To Petersburg!' is the answer. And that is all that needs to be said. It is as if Petersburg, all by itself, with its name, its streets, its fog, rain and snow could resolve something or shed light on something.

In the wake of the clerks came factory workers as the industrial revolution finally reached Russia. Until the 1860s they were principally serfs, single men who were still required to send a percentage of their earnings to their owner back home.

St Petersburg soon began to run out of space to accommodate its vast new population. The habit of living in an apartment, rather than a house, was adopted by the nobility around the 1820s and became the norm with St Petersburg's new middle classes; large quantities of apartment blocks began to mingle with the city's imperial monuments. Then, in the second half of the century, the imperial city was gradually ringed by an industrial quarter, combining factories and slums – some industrial workers rented no more than a bed-sized space on the floor of a large room.

The spread of education brought a new class known as the 'intelligentsia' into existence. Nowadays the term only means people with higher education, but when the Russians first invented it, 'intelligentsia' carried a connotation of radical opposition to the existing regime – the police state had turned the educated elite against the government. Nervous of the revolutions which shook a succession of European countries in the mid-nineteenth century, the Russian tsars imposed censorship and diligently sought to suppress free thought. It is a curious reflection on Russia that the intelligentsia were censored, arrested, sentenced to exile and hard labour under the tsars just as they were under the Soviets – though conditions in Siberia were better in the nineteenth century than the twentieth.

The museum became a department of the Ministry of the Court in the 1860s and thus, formally, one of the responsibilities of Russia's vast and highly structured civil service. In nineteenth-century street direc-tories it was not listed among museums but with the other institutions of the Imperial Court – the Imperial Hunt, the Stables, the Palace Police, the Library and so on. Thus, even if the tsars were taking little interest in its collections, the Hermitage remained within their close sphere of influence and, as in all other periods, politics dictated both the museum's opportunities and its limitations. In the succession of Nicholases and Alexanders who ruled Russia in the decades leading up to the Revolution each, naturally, had his own impact on the museum's development.

Nicholas I had instituted his infamous 'Third Section' in the late 1820s in reaction to the Decembrist 'uprising', a secret police force with a licence to spy on the ordinary citizen. And it was left to his heir, Alexander II, to unscramble the social ills of his father's policies – as well as deal with the Crimean War, which had broken out in 1853. Alexander was thus driven, despite his conservative upbringing, to a radical legislative programme, later known as the Great Reforms. He emancipated the serfs in 1861 and within a decade of his accession had instituted a new elective system of local government, replaced trial by secret tribunal with trial by jury and made the judiciary independent of government.

He was not thanked for it. Political opposition, suppressed for so long, broke out in a flood of revolutionary activity. In 1866 a disaffected student shot at Alexander in the Summer Gardens, but missed, and the Emperor spent the rest of his life under threat. In 1881 a group of terrorists, calling themselves the Party of the People's Will, who had opened a cheese shop on a St Petersburg street frequently used by the emperor's carriage, succeeded in killing him with homemade hand grenades.

Alexander's significance, from the point of view of the Hermitage and its collections, lies in his having bought a miscellany of contemporary European paintings under the guidance of his tutor Vasily Zhukovsky, in having commissioned a major series of watercolour paintings of the Winter Palace interiors, in being the recipient of some of Colt's most spectacular presentation pistols, in founding the Imperial Archaeological Commission, and in appointing the first professional director of the museum. The two last were easily Alexander's most important legacy.

The foundation of the Imperial Archaeological Commission in 1859 was to have far reaching significance for the museum. Many of the important treasures held in today's Oriental, Archaeological and Antiquities Departments reached the museum through the agency of the Commission. Before it came into existence there had been little distinction between archaeology and tomb robbing. Anyone with an amateur interest could try their hand at excavating.

After 1859 the Commission controlled which archaeological sites were excavated and by whom; all chance finds, which were made quite frequently during farming or the building of roads and railways, were supposed to be reported to the Commission; the Commission decided where newly discovered artefacts should be housed and channelled all discoveries of special artistic merit to the Hermitage. The commissioners were a mix of scholars and cultured noblemen with a keen amateur interest in archaeology. They had a small support staff with an office, first in the Stroganov Palace, and later in the Hermitage itself.

The Commission started small and grew in importance. Towards the end of the century, in addition to licensing digs and allocating discoveries, they became increasingly involved in archaeological publications. This was of great advantage to the Hermitage. Unlike the archaeological collections of other museums, most of the pieces in the Hermitage have a known find spot and the circumstances of their discovery are documented. In other words, they have a history.

The vast territories of the Russian empire were rich in ancient sites, the Black Sea area having close connections with Classical Greece, and the regions east of the Urals with a succession of Oriental civilisations. The ancient Silk Road, which carried textiles between China and Europe, passed through Russia's Asian provinces while the fur trade route ran from the Kama basin in the north, down to the Volga in the south.

The early fur traders came mainly from Central Asia, and they traded silver vessels with the fur trappers of the north – with the result that much of the finest surviving Sassanian silver was found in Russia and passed by the Archaeological Commission to the Hermitage. The embossed silver dishes and ewers made in Persia during the Sassanid period (third to seventh century AD) with their lively decoration of kings and princes, wild and domestic animals, and mythical beasts, are considered among the finest historic achievements of metalworking. Along with similar silver vessels made by neighbouring peoples, some imitations and some quite original, they were traded up the fur road into north-east Russia where they were incorporated into pagan shrines and used in religious ceremonies.

The primitive local peoples sometimes used the silver dishes as body parts of their idols. Other dishes were used at feasts, since there was a rule that sacrificial meat should only be eaten from metallic vessels. In the lonely forests of the north such practices have survived right up to the present day – a tenth-century silver vessel was found in an active shrine in the 1980s. In these primitive communities, silver had no monetary value since no currency circulated. As a result, it did not get melted down as it did elsewhere.

Most of the Sassanian silver in the Hermitage was found by chance, sometimes at the sites of ancient shrines, sometimes in hoards buried by individuals for their personal use in the afterlife. In the second half of the nineteenth century Russian farmers moved into the forest areas, cutting down trees and turning the land over to cultivation. Most of the finds date from this period, though they began in the eighteenth century and continue today.

As well as founding the Archaeological Commission, Alexander II instituted the post of 'director' of the Hermitage Museum and appointed its first two incumbents, Stepan Gedeonov, in 1863 and Prince Alexander Vasilchikov in 1879. Both had a vivid interest in art and sought out unusual opportunities for the museum.

Gedeonov had spent almost twenty years in Italy working for Russia's

Commission on Archaeological Finds in Rome, where he also had responsibility for looking after visiting students from the St Petersburg Academy of Arts. And it was in Rome, before he joined the Hermitage staff, that he pulled off his first coup on behalf of the museum – the acquisition of 760 pieces of Antique art from the Campana collection. The Papal Government had allowed him first pick from this extraordinary assemblage, despite howls of rage from the British Museum and the Louvre.

The Marchese di Cavelli, Giampietro Campana, was the intimate friend and patron of Italy's nineteenth-century tomb robbers and formed the century's largest collection of Classical antiquities, mostly unearthed from Etruscan tombs around the ancient city of Caere (now Cerveteri), north-west of Rome. There were 3,791 ancient Greek vases in Campana's printed catalogue of 1857 – which omitted many more thousands of vase fragments. He went on to add paintings, sculpture, majolica and other decorative arts to his collection on a lavish scale. But it turned out that his spending power reflected the embezzlement of deposits at the Monte de Pietà Bank of which he was director. When he was arrested and sent to a papal prison in November 1857 he owed the colossal sum of five million francs.

Campana had first offered his collection to the Russian government as far back as 1851, but the price was considered too high. After his arrest, the Papal authorities sold off the collection piecemeal to pay his debts. London's South Kensington Museum got his collection of Renaissance works of art for a modest £5,856 (roughly 146,000 francs) in 1860. Next, Gedeonov picked out a group of choice items for which the Russian government paid some 650,000 francs. Finally, the French acquired the remainder of the collection for a total expenditure of 4.8 million francs. The French purchase reflected the direct intervention of Napoleon III who thus lavishly paid off a debt of honour. Campana's mother-in-law had helped him escape from the Château of Ham, in Picardy, when he was imprisoned there in 1846 after a failed military coup. In addition to buying up the remainder of the collection, Napoleon III managed to negotiate Campana's early release from prison.

In February 1861 an angry article in the *Nazione*, the leading Italian newspaper, revealed that the Russians had managed 'to skim the cream off the collection'. The French purchase was finalised in May, accelerated by the fear that Gedeonov might get his hands on more. There was indeed a lot of cream – he had selected 500 vases, 193 bronzes and seventy-eight sculptures. Gedeonov also secured a group of frescoes attributed to Raphael which had been painted for the Villa Spada on the Palatine but carefully removed from the walls and transferred to canvas by the artist Antonio Zucchi in the 1850s. They are now regarded as the work of Raphael's studio assistants but nevertheless have an honourable place in the museum's Italian gallery. Gedeonov was so mesmerised by the frescoes that he paid no attention to the rest of Campana's paintings, which are now in the Louvre.

The Campana vases which came to the Hermitage include examples by most of the great painters of Hellenic Greece and, combined with the vases discovered at Kerch and elsewhere in southern Russia, make up one of the finest museum collections in the world. The hydria, or water vessel, from Cumae with its three-dimensional frieze of Grecian ladies at play, was described in the 1850s as 'the crowning jewel of Campana's famous museum' and is known in the Hermitage as the *Regina Vasorum* or 'Queen of Vases'. The Roman sculpture also helped give the Hermitage a collection of particular distinction. Gloating over a relief sculpture of *The Slaughter of the Niobids*, Gedeonov wrote: 'It is a poem in marble! Alexander II got it for 125 scudi, whereas Napoleon III would have had to pay 812,000!' It was only one of his many bargains.

The display of the Campana collection caused a problem, however. The architect Leo von Klenze's designs for the New Hermitage had left no room for such an influx. After serious discussions, it was decided to move the library out of the Hermitage altogether and to give the space to Campana's antiquities. The public library on Nevsky Prospect thus received Catherine the Great's library, including both Voltaire and Diderot's books. And, since Houdon's portrait sculpture of the seated Voltaire had been hidden in the Hermitage library to avoid the angry gaze of Nicholas I, it too followed the books down the road.

It was the Campana collection that earned Gedeonov his appointment as director of the Hermitage in 1863. And he continued to work his Italian contacts to spectacular effect. In 1864 the Milanese collector Count Litta offered his collection to the Hermitage and Gedeonov bought four paintings, including the magical Leonardo *Madonna and Child*, now known as the *Litta Madonna* – behind the two figures, arched windows open on a blue Tuscan landscape echoing the tone of the Madonna's robe. Then, in 1869, the Roman collector Count Connestabile offered his paintings to the Hermitage and Gedeonov managed to negotiate the acquisition of his Raphael *Madonna* on behalf of the Empress, Maria Alexandrovna. It initially hung in the Winter Palace and only came to the Hermitage at her death in 1880. After he was made director of the St Petersburg and Moscow theatres in 1867, however, Gedeonov had less time to spend on the Hermitage – the attractions of live actors and actresses were apparently more compelling than dead art. He made no more major acquisitions.

In 1879 Alexander II appointed a new director of the museum, a young diplomat called Prince Alexander Vasilchikov who was a close friend of the imperial family and had a special interest in archaeology. He was additionally appointed to the post of President of the Imperial Archaeological Commission in 1882, but there was no problem in combining these two jobs since the Commission worked closely with the museum.

Alexander II was assassinated in 1881 and succeeded by his second son Alexander III. Born in 1845, the new tsar had only become heir to the throne in 1865 on the death of his elder brother Nicholas. He inherited his brother's fiancée, Princess Dagmar of Denmark and, despite its unromantic start, the marriage was exceptionally successful; he was the only Romanov emperor who didn't take a mistress. A giant of a man – he is famous for holding up the ceiling of the imperial carriage after a train crash so that his wife and children could escape – he was frugal, hard working and conservative. He undermined all his father's Great Reforms and reinstituted a police state which successfully suppressed all revolutionary activity – for a time.

Alexander III was a keen patron of Russian painting, which reached its first period of outstanding achievement during his reign but the pictures he bought never became part of the Hermitage collection. He planned a museum of Russian painting which was opened after his death by his son Nicholas II. Housed in the early nineteenth-century Mikhailovsky Palace, it is now known as the 'Russian Museum' – though up to 1917 it was called the Alexander III Museum in memory of the tsar who planned its creation.

Alexander Vasilchikov had been director of the Hermitage for two years when Alexander III came to the throne. He presented the new government with a report on the condition of the museum. 'Twenty-five years ago,' he wrote, 'the Hermitage was very nearly the world's first museum but as soon as no steps are made forward, a step is thereby made backward.' The museum had stagnated, he said – though he acknowledged a certain revival in the 1860s when Gedeonov was pulling off his Italian coups – and blamed its condition on the lack of funds made available by the court. He asked for an acquisition fund of

50,000 roubles a year but was granted a paltry 5,000 – a figure which remained unchanged up to the Revolution.

Alexander III did not accord the museum a high priority but he financed a couple of major purchases out of his personal fortune. In 1885 the cabinet secretary, Alexander Polovtsov, who was an art connoisseur, and the Russian artist, Alexander Bogolyubov, then resident in Paris, enlisted Alexander's support for the purchase of the Basilewski collection of medieval and Renaissance art. Alexander Basilewski was a Russian then living in Paris; his collection was paid for by the Emperor personally, rather than the government, and cost 2.2 million gold roubles. A Paris auction of the 750-piece collection had already been announced and an unnamed American collector had offered almost double this figure. But Basilewski's patriotism led him to prefer the Hermitage and the Emperor.

'The Basilewski collection was sold yesterday evening on the basis of a simple telegram,' exploded the Paris daily newspaper, *Le Figaro*, on 29 November 1884. 'The Russian government has paid six million francs ... What a devastating disappointment for the collectors who were already getting their ammunition together to do battle in March! . . . All the intelligentsia of Europe who love the arts would have been present.'

Basilewski had started collecting in the 1850s when the fashion for medieval art, launched by Walter Scott's novels, was beginning to spread across Europe. He decided to concentrate on forming a documentary collection of Christian art, tracing its evolution from the earliest times up to the sixteenth century. The collection included carved ivories, medieval and Renaissance metalwork – some of the sumptuous silver from the Basel cathedral treasury was bought back by the city of Basel from the Soviet government in the 1930s – Limoges enamels, Italian majolica, Venetian and German glass, medieval furniture and woodwork, arms and armour and Byzantine icons.

In every field Basilewski had bought the very best examples available. The fame of the collection in France was such that he was asked to contribute pieces for display to the *Expositions Universelles* of 1865 and 1867, and in 1874 he published a catalogue with the help of a curator friend at the Louvre, Alfred Darcel. The magnificent gallery in his home in the Rue Blanche was opened to the public once a week – and was besieged by visitors after the sale to Russia was announced. Among them were the president of the Republic, Jules Grévy, escorting the wife of Woodrow Wilson, the American President.

The arrival of the collection in St Petersburg posed another accommodation problem, but Vasilchikov resolved it in the grand manner. The State Council had recently moved out of the ground floor of the Old Hermitage to take up residence in the Mariinsky Palace. He persuaded the Emperor that the Tsarskoe Selo Arsenal which, under Nicholas I, had acquired a few medieval works of art, and the Basilewski collection, should be combined to create a new display of medieval and Renaissance art filling the former council rooms. This occupied twenty rooms on the ground floor of the Old Hermitage and was dressed up in theatrical manner – there were fully armed knights on horseback and on foot, wall displays of armour, cases densely packed with ivories and bronzes. 'The decorative element was developed to such a degree that it could produce a certain giddiness in the viewer', according to Alfred Kube, a later keeper of the collection. Some Russian works of art were also transferred from the Antiquities department. The exhibition was changed after the Revolution.

The following year Vasilchikov again enlisted Alexander III's support, this time for the purchase of Moscow's Golitsyn Museum *en bloc* for 800,000 roubles – roughly one third of the price paid for Basilewski's collection. It comprised the collection of paintings formed in the eighteenth century by Princes A. M. and D. M. Golitsyn through purchases in Vienna and Paris – including the wonderful early Venetian *Annunciation* by Cima da Conegliano – and a superb library. Most of the books went to the St Petersburg Public Library and, as a *quid pro quo*, Vasilchikov negotiated the return of Houdon's statue of the seated Voltaire. Nicholas I having joined his fathers, it went back on display at the Hermitage.

The death of Alexander III, on 20 October 1894, from a rare kidney disease, had not been expected. His son Nicholas II, the last Emperor of Russia, was twenty-six when he ascended the throne. Only a year before, the Finance Minister, Count Sergey Witte, had suggested to Alexander that Nicholas might chair the Committee for Constructing the Trans-Siberian Railway. 'Have you ever tried to discuss anything of consequence with him?', Alexander had asked and, when Witte admitted he hadn't, explained that Nicholas was still an 'absolute' child. 'His judgements are still truly childish. How could he be chairman of a committee?', his father enquired.

Within a year he was not only a chairman but an emperor. At his side stood a strong-minded but intellectually blinkered woman, his young wife Alexandra, whose influence over her doting husband was to prove disastrous. Born Princess Alix of Hesse-Darmstadt, Queen Victoria's granddaughter became engaged to Nicholas in April 1894. 'I cried like a child and she did too,' Nicholas wrote to his mother. 'But her expression changed,' he added. 'Her face was lit up by a quiet content.' They were married quietly in the large church of the Winter Palace, surrounded by the Baroque splendour designed by Rastrelli, a week after Nicholas's father's death and were the last Romanov rulers of Russia.

The young couple's tragedy stemmed fundamentally from their piety. Nicholas believed, very literally, that a tsar was anointed by God and was thus a divinely inspired source of wisdom and order. In 1900, after celebrating Easter in the Kremlin cathedrals, he wrote to his mother: 'I never knew I could be in such a state of *religious ecstasy* as I have experienced this Lent . . . Everything here makes for prayer and spiritual peace.' His antagonism to democratic principles and his repeated rejection of his advisers' suggestions stemmed from a belief that he was the chosen instrument of God's will; an inner voice told him what to do.

Alexandra, who had converted to Russian Orthodoxy from the Lutheran church at the time of her marriage, shared his piety. After bearing four daughters she gave birth to a precious son, Aleksey, in 1904 who turned out to have haemophilia. At the slightest scratch, he bled and the bleeding would not stop. Aleksey's health became Alexandra's overriding preoccupation. When a wild, holy man from Siberian peasant stock, Grigory Rasputin, proved able to heal Aleksey's bleeding, Alexandra welcomed him into her family circle and listened obediently to his every pronouncement. Meanwhile Rasputin's debauchery – he had an insatiable sexual appetite – outraged the capital.

When Nicholas took over command of the army at the outbreak of war in 1914, on God's instructions and to the despair of his advisers and allies, he left Alexandra to rule the country in his place – which she did, leaning heavily on Rasputin's advice. In 1916 Rasputin was assassinated by a group of extreme conservatives who believed that in this way they were saving the monarchy from itself.

In all the events of his reign Nicholas saw only the workings of God's will – even in the Revolution of 1905 which was, as it were, a trial run for 1917, and the disastrous Russo-Japanese war of 1904–5 whose incompetent handling gave a foretaste of the disasters of World War I. Nicholas astonished his foreign minister by his calm reception of the report of a naval mutiny at the Kronstadt Fortress in 1905, telling him: 'If you find me so little troubled, it is because I have the firm and absolute faith that the destiny of Russia, my own fate and that of my family are in the hands of Almighty God, who has placed me where I am. Whatever may happen, I shall bow to his will.'

A Duma, or elected parliament, was forced on Nicholas after the 1905 Revolution but he quickly moved to limit its powers. In 1917 he attempted to close it down altogether but the Duma instead forced him to abdicate and formed a Provisional Government. Six months later, in the second revolution of the year, the Bolsheviks came to power. The Provisional Government had kept Nicholas and his family under arrest at Tsarskoe Selo. The Bolsheviks now moved them first to Tobolsk, then to Ekaterinburg in the Urals, where they were shot in the cellar of the Ipat'ev House on 17 July 1918. Attempts were made to destroy the bodies, which, together with an assortment of jewels sewn into the ladies' corsets, were thrown in a mineshaft. A whole industry rapidly grew up to sift the evidence of how the Romanovs perished.

During his reign, Nicholas and his government were keenly criticised by connoisseurs for not taking more interest in the Hermitage Museum. Its displays were hardly changed; it was given no money for new acquisitions; it was staffed by a small group of scholarly courtiers which meant that young art historians could not gain employment. However, the museum has subsequently benefited from some of the schemes which did attract Nicholas's patronage. A striking example is provided by the treasures recovered in 1908–9 from excavations of the lost city of Khara Khoto on the Edsin-Gol river delta, near the border between China and the Mongolian People's Republic, by the explorer Petr Kozlov – 3,500 works of art, all dating from before 1387. They were transferred to the Hermitage from the Ethographical Department of the Russian Museum in 1933 when the curator Iosif Orbeli was building up the new Oriental Department.

The turn of the nineteenth and twentieth centuries was a great era for explorers and Kozlov gained worldwide recognition for his work, receiving the Gold Medal of the Royal Geographical Society of London, the Gold Medal of the Italian Geographical Society and the Chikhachev prize of the French Academy of Sciences, among other honours. His major achievement lay in his comprehensive study of Central Asia, its peoples, its history and its natural phenomena – botanical and zoological museums gained from his expeditions as well as the Hermitage. In 1905 Nicholas II dispatched him to Urga to meet the Dalai Lama. They got on particularly well and the expedition's artist made sketches of the Dalai Lama which are now in the Hermitage.

Kozlov met the Dalai Lama again in Xining in 1908, after the discovery of Khara Khoto, which fascinated the Dalai Lama so much that he invited Kozlov to come to Lhasa and explore Tibet – an invitation he was never able to take up.

The existence of the ruins of Khara Khoto had first been mentioned to the Russian explorer Grigory Potanin in 1886 by a local Torgut tribesman and fired the imagination of Kozlov when he heard of it, but the Torguts subsequently tried to conceal its location from the Russians. The city had been recorded by Chinese geographers in the fifth century BC and later became a flourishing oasis on the Silk Road connecting Europe with China. It was abandoned after its river dried up, turning the whole area into desert, some time after 1400. Kozlov would probably never have found it if a Mongolian prince had not provided him with a guide in order to spite the Torguts. The ruins lay a short distance from a dry river bed. There were mosques and stupas outside the town walls, then a huge rectangular open space covered with the remnants of buildings, piles of rubbish and the foundations of temples. Kozlov found fragments of manuscripts, paintings, beads and clay figures which he despatched to St Petersburg for study in March 1908.

It took almost ninth months to get a reply – though the arrival of Kozlov's parcels in St Petersburg had caused a sensation. Friends and colleagues from the Imperial Geographical Society explained to him the enormous academic significance of his finds, how significantly they were going to contribute to an understanding of Tangut culture, about which little or nothing was hitherto known, and the unique nature of the documents he had found written in Tangut script – he had also found manuscripts in Chinese and Persian with which to compare them. It was imperative that he return to Khara Khoto immediately.

He arrived back in May 1909 and his team opened a stupa some 300 yards outside the city wall which 'yielded a truly prodigious treasure', to use the words of Hermitage curator Kira Samosyuk. There were manuscripts, books, scrolls, miniature stupas, bronze and wooden statues – all jumbled together. 'I shall never forget those blissful moments,' Kozlov wrote, 'as I shall equally never forget, in particular, the powerful impression made on myself and my companions by two Chinese icons on a muslin-like material. As we unrolled them, we were enthralled to see magnificent seated figures, bathed in a soft pale blue and pink radiance. From these sacred Buddhist relics there emanated something living, something expressive, something unalloyed; we simply could not take our eyes off them.'

The stupa was the burial chamber of a member of the Tangut imperial family. A female skull was found and the most likely guess is that this was the burial of Empress Lo, the Chinese-born widow of the Tangut Emperor Ren-zong who died in 1193. As a result of this extraordinary find, the Hermitage has 200 paintings on silk, canvas, paper and wood, more than half of them complete, as well as drawings, seventy sculptures in clay, wood and bronze, textiles, paper banknotes and coins and literally thousands of pottery and porcelain fragments.

On his return Kozlov was promoted to the rank of Colonel and invited by Nicholas II to give a lecture on Khara Khoto to the imperial family and an audience of specially invited guests at Tsarskoe Selo. The lecture was accompanied by lantern slides.

While the art works from Khara Khoto went to the Russian Museum – and on to the Hermitage – the books and manuscripts were given to the Asiatic Museum of the Russian Academy of Sciences which had been run since 1900 by Sergey Oldenburg, the greatest Orientalist of his time. It was Oldenburg, a specialist on Buddhism, who had recognised the importance of the first documents and artefacts that Kozlov had sent back from Khara Khoto in 1908. He ran several expeditions himself – his 1914–15 expedition to the ancient monastery outside the Chinese city of Dunhuang, the so-called 'Cave of a Thousand Buddhas', has provided the Hermitage with a group of wall paintings, sculpture and votive banners which, although smaller than the Dunhuang collections at the British Museum and Musée Guimet in Paris, are of comparable importance to the study of Buddhist art.

Oldenburg is a pivotal link between the old regime and the new. He was a friend of Lenin and became the most important figure in the Russian world of scholarship after the Revolution. He was elected to the governing Council of the Hermitage Museum in 1918, helped launch the new Oriental Department in the early 1920s and fought tirelessly to prevent the sale of the museum's treasures in 1928–30. He will make many appearances in later chapters and deserves to be properly introduced.

Sergey Oldenburg was born in 1863 and was a university student in St Petersburg in the early 1880s, the period of most extreme police censorship which followed Alexander II's assassination. Large gatherings of students were forbidden by law; if they did get together for any purpose, such as a literary society or for a drink, their names were taken – even if they had only assembled to read essays to each other. Oldenburg was often in trouble over meetings with students and colleagues and continued to battle for a relaxation of the regulations after he became a professor in the Oriental Faculty at St Petersburg university in 1897. He finally resigned from the university in 1899, considering it impossible to work there given the repressive atmosphere. His Orientalist friends got him the job of running the Asiatic Museum of the Academy of Sciences.

In the following years he climbed to the very top of his profession, always seeking to reform and improve the world around him. He became the permanent secretary of the Academy of Sciences in 1904, an Academician in 1908 and a member of the State Council in 1912. At the time of the Revolution he was a left-wing member of the Kadet party and served, for six months, as the Provisional Government's Minister of Education. He spent seventeen days in prison in 1919 when the Bolsheviks were busy stamping the Kadet party out of existence.

He had been a friend of Lenin's brother, Alexander Ulyanov, before his execution in 1885 for plotting an attempted assassination of the tsar Alexander III, and first met Lenin himself in 1891. When the Bolsheviks considered closing the Academy of Sciences in 1919, it was Oldenburg's appeal to Lenin that saved it. For a decade he was the most powerful figure in the Soviet academic world; but, under Stalin, his star was eclipsed. In 1929 he was summarily sacked from the Academy of Sciences. It was a time when the secret police arrested a swathe of Academicians and Oldenburg's name was on their list – but, for some reason, struck through with a red pencil. He died a natural death in 1934. As will be seen, Oldenburg's career closely echoes the fate of scholarship, in general, in the turbulent years before and after the Revolution.

6

St Petersburg Collectors
and Connoisseurs

*T*o understand what happened to the Hermitage in the twentieth century, it is necessary to look at the history of art collecting in St Petersburg, not just the collecting activity of the tsars but also that of noblemen, scholars, artists and the newly rich merchant class. As a result of the Revolution, the museum was to inherit the fruits of their endeavours. All private collections became State property at a stroke of Lenin's pen, including university and private museum collections. The best pickings came to the Hermitage.

The imperial capital was home to the greatest aristocratic families of Russia, many of whom formed magnificent collections. Most were begun in the eighteenth century and some in earlier times. None of these families seem to have seen the threat of confiscation coming – unlike the French aristocrats who managed to ship their collections to London for sale by James Christie at the end of the eighteenth century. And, in the nineteenth century the ranks of collectors were swelled by newly rich merchants and industrialists who developed a passion for art and had the resources to indulge it.

In nineteenth-century Russia, as elsewhere in Europe and America, appalling living conditions for the poor went hand in hand with an explosion of high-minded, charitable activity. Rich benefactors not only founded orphanages, schools and hospitals, but also turned their hands to setting up museums. There were many of them in St Petersburg, founded for a variety of idiosyncratic purposes – from the study of the Byzantine church, to the display of cuneiform tablets and the popularisation of modern French art. They were all nationalised by the Bolsheviks and parts of their collections came to the Hermitage.

And in the last two decades before the Revolution there was an explosion of artistic activity in both St Petersburg and Moscow which had a major impact on the rest of Europe. Alexandre Benois, Sergey Diaghilev and their friends mounted ballets and operas, started magazines and organised exhibitions which helped put Russia at the forefront of the world art scene. Diaghilev's Ballets Russes had a sensational success in Paris while Kandinsky, Kasimir Malevich, Chagall, Natalya Goncharova and Mikhail Larionov are counted among the pioneers of twentieth-century painting. Several of the people who participated in this renaissance of artistic activity also became involved with the Hermitage just before or just after the Revolution.

Among the great aristocratic collections of St Petersburg pride of place must be given to the Stroganov Palace and its art gallery which was briefly turned into an outstation of the Hermitage after the Revolution. The collection, sadly, did not survive intact. In 1928 the palace was closed to the public and a selection of treasures were incorporated into the Hermitage collection. The rest were auctioned off in 1931 in a spectacular sale at the Lepke Gallery in Berlin in order to earn foreign exchange for the Soviet government.

The Stroganovs were the richest noble family in Russia. They began mining salt at Solvychegodsk in the far north in the early sixteenth century, built a cathedral there and helped found many other towns and villages. In the late sixteenth and early seventeenth century, two pious Stroganovs commissioned many small icons for their homes – the first icons painted for private individuals rather than churches – giving rise to the so-called Stroganov School of icon painting, noted for its rich colour and exquisite draughtsmanship. The family's salt and iron mines in the Urals enabled them to maintain a private army with which they helped obtain the annexation of Siberia by Russia in the 1580s. They also helped the government out when its coffers were empty and backed the accession of Michael, the first Romanov, in 1613. They were faithful servants of the tsars and in the eighteenth century they took to art collecting.

Rastrelli, the architect of the Winter Palace, built them the greatest private house in St Petersburg on the corner of the Moika Canal and Nevsky Prospect. Count Alexander Stroganov filled it with art during the eighteenth century. He travelled all over Europe, buying Old Masters and commissioning paintings and sculpture. He commissioned a

Houdon bust of Catherine the Great, bought a great Poussin – *The Flight into Egypt* – which now adorns the Hermitage, and decorated a whole room with Hubert Robert landscape panels – which have also ended up there. Pavel I appointed him President of the Academy of Arts.

But Alexander Stroganov's greatest gift to St Petersburg was bringing up and educating the son of a peasant girl from his estates, Andrey Voronikhin, who became a leading architect – legend has it that Alexander was his father. He launched Voronikhin's career by getting him to redesign the interior of the Stroganov Palace, adding a picture gallery and an adjoining Egyptian room for the display of Russia's first collection of Egyptian antiquities. Voronikhin went on to design St Petersburg's Kazan Cathedral, a northern adaptation of St Peter's in Rome, which took eleven years to build, from 1800 to 1811, employing thousands of serfs. He also became a noted furniture designer, working for Maria Fedorovna, Pavel I's widow, and designing some of the finest hardstone vases in the Hermitage.

Alexander Stroganov's legitimate son and successor, Pavel, was also a picture collector, while Pavel's cousin and heir, Sergey, collected icons, Renaissance furniture and coins and medals. Sergey's three sons were also collectors; Grigory and Pavel collected Old Masters while Alexander collected coins. The break-up of the collection housed in the Stroganov Palace thus enriched virtually every department of the Hermitage. Stroganov treasures are to be found in many surprising places around the museum. In the rotunda at the end of the Dutch Picture Gallery, for instance, there are two side tables from the Egyptian Gallery that Voronikhin designed for Alexander Stroganov. Topped with slabs of rich blue lapis lazuli, the tables are wrought from ebony, bronze and ormolu, with mirror backs and blue and white painted friezes reminiscent of Wedgwood. The front legs are columns, topped and tailed by Egyptian priestesses – their bronze torsos, with gilded hairdos and bare bronze bosoms, connect the columns to the table top while, at the bottom of the column, their brown bronze feet peep out of ormolu drapery.

Among the other important family collections that found their way to the Hermitage after 1917 were those of the Shuvalovs and Yusupovs. In the mid-eighteenth century Ivan Shuvalov had been the Empress Elizabeth's lover *en titre* and became a great patron of art and education; he founded both the St Petersburg Academy of Arts and Moscow University. Catherine the Great considered the Baroque pomp of his palace and art gallery exaggerated. 'This house,' she wrote, 'which is large in itself, is so ornamented that it reminds one of cuffs made from Alençon lace.' He gave his picture collection to the Academy of Art, whence it was removed to the Hermitage in the 1920s. Meanwhile, from the family palace came the rich collection of medieval and Renaissance applied arts – silver, majolica, bronzes, Limoges enamels – formed by Elizaveta Shuvalova in the last years of the nineteenth century and the beginning of the twentieth.

Nikolay Yusupov was a friend of Catherine the Great, who sent him on many diplomatic missions. He commissioned paintings and bought Old Masters in Rome and Paris. He brought two of the Hermitage's great Canovas back to St Petersburg, the *Cupid and Psyche* and the *Winged Cupid*. In 1798 he became director of the Imperial Tapestry Works, in 1792 director of the Imperial Glass and Porcelain Manufactory and in 1797 administrator of the Hermitage – an honorary post awarded him by Paul I who wanted to have nothing to do with his mother's collection. The great art collection Nikolay Yusupov formed was, of course, extended by subsequent generations of the family and by 1917 it was housed in their Palace on the Moika river – in whose cellars Rasputin was assassinated in 1916 by a group of Felix Yusupov's friends.

In 1919 a Komsomol patrol was given the job of searching the Yusupov palace where the family had literally walled up their treasures. The leader of the group, one Pavel Usanov, wrote an account of how they bullied the forty servants who remained into revealing the hiding places. Last, and most difficult to find, were the paintings, a better collection than graces most European 'National Galleries', both in number and quality, despite the fact that Felix Yusupov had left Russia with two Rembrandts in his baggage.

> Trembling with fear, the manager agreed to show the place where the pictures were hidden. Turning a plate that was virtually invisible he pushed a part of the wall which was faced with tiles. It turned out to be a door leading to a storage room in which there were numerous cases full of paintings. There it was, the goal of our quest, a collection of paintings famous all over Europe! It took the young members of the Komsomol team a whole day to clear the storage room of paintings. Specialists and artists came to the palace to see them.

The Shuvalov and Yusupov Palaces were opened to the public as museums after the Revolution, as were palaces all over Russia. Art became the property of the people after 1917 and the first curators were filled with idealism. The government did not, however, have the resources to support hundreds of small museums and decided to keep only the bigger ones open, amalgamating collections. In the mid-1920s most of St Petersburg's palace museums were closed down and, since the government was now desperate for foreign exchange, many of their treasures were sold abroad.

Most private museums were also closed down at that time, with the best pieces passing to the Hermitage. The sheer number of such museums is a remarkable measure of Russian cultural achievement. There was the Museum of Old St Petersburg set up by Petr Weiner, publisher of the art magazine *Starye Gody*, the Museum of Old Russian Art attached to the Academy of Art, the Museum of the Russian Archaeological Society, the Archaeological Museum attached to the St Petersburg Religious Seminary, the Likhachov Museum of Palaeography, the Ethnographic Museum attached to the Academy of Science, a second Ethnographic Museum attached to the Russian Museum, the Kushelevskaya Gallery of contemporary paintings attached to the Academy of Art, the Museum of Artistic Craftsmanship sponsored by the Society for the Encouragement of the Arts and the Stieglitz Museum – the St Petersburg equivalent of the Victoria and Albert Museum in London – to name but a few. Their stories are various and colourful.

Petr Sevastyanov, the son of a merchant from Penza, who collected icons and early church art for the Academy's Museum of Old Russian Art, was a particularly notable figure. His interest lay in tracing the sources of Christian art and he attempted to construct an encyclopaedia of Christian iconography based on his own collection. That such an endeavour should have brought him fame and worldly success underlines the fundamental importance of the Orthodox Church in nineteenth-century Russia. From the autocrats, who believed themselves appointed by God to dictate the fate of Russia, down to the poorest peasant, the church filled every individual life with hope and fear. In 1861 the Academy acquired 135 icons and frescoes and 125 items of applied art from Sevastyanov's collection, including a 1363 icon of *Christ Pantocrator* from Mount Athos, in Greece – now one of the stars of the Hermitage collection.

Where Sevastyanov was far ahead of his time, however, was in the use of the camera as an aid to research. In 1857–8 he spent half a year in the ancient monastic community on Mount Athos photographing Byzantine objects and manuscripts – photography had only been invented in the 1830s and had never previously been used in this way. He compiled some 5,000 photographs which caused a sensation when they were exhibited, along with drawings and copies of works of art, in Paris in 1858. In 1861, at the Emperor's request, he set up an exhibition in the White Hall of the Winter Palace and an enlarged version of the exhibition moved to the Academy of Arts later in the year.

In 1862 the Academy of Arts received a spectacular bequest in quite a different field – a whole museum collection of paintings and contemporary art together with a private palace, built in the eighteenth century by Quarenghi, in which to display them. Count Nikolay Kushelev-Bezborodko died in Nice, leaving the Academy 466 paintings and twenty-nine sculptures, together with his house on Pochtamtskaya, in his will – a will which was immediately, but unsuccessfully, contested by his relatives. The Museum was opened to the public in 1863 and became known as the Kushelevskaya Gallery. Its particular significance for St Petersburg was the collection of contemporary French painting, over 200 works of the Romantic school including pieces by Delacroix, Courbet, Théodore Rousseau, Millet, and Corot.

Some of them had been shown in a big exhibition of art from private collections organised in 1851 by the Duke of Leuchtenberg – Nicholas I's son-in-law and President of the Academy of Arts – where they met the kind of critical hostility traditionally reserved for works of the extreme avant garde. By 1922, however, when they arrived in the Hermitage, the collection had been recognised as the most important repository of nineteenth-century European painting in Russia. The pictures had been evacuated to Moscow during the 1914–18 war and it took a lot of political arm twisting to secure them for the museum.

The Kushelevskaya Gallery also included, through inheritance, part of the Old Master collection formed by Catherine the Great's chancellor, Prince Alexander Bezborodko – a famous collection compiled with a determination to impress by a great *arriviste*. Bezborodko himself wrote the best description of it: 'By dint of hot zeal, my friends' aid, and approximately 100,000 roubles spent in the course of less than three years, I have formed a good collection, surpassing that of Stroganov's both in numbers and in quality.' The collection passed to his brother, Nikolay's great-grandfather, and was split up among descendants through whom, by various different routes, some 300 of the chancellor's paintings eventually reached the Hermitage.

Bezborodko particularly liked buying works of art that had formerly graced French royal collections. Among his treasures was a marble statue of Cupid which Falconet had made for Louis XV's mistress, Madame de Pompadour – both Catherine the Great and Stroganov had copies of it, but Bezborodko claimed to have the original. The poet Gavriil Derzhavin wrote a poem about seeing it in his house:

> I saw a Cupid in the home of Croesus.
> He sat Crying in a marble grotto
> Amidst a forest of arrows . . .
>
> Is his flame powerless?
> Vain the stream of his tears?
> Alas, he now owns himself defeated
> For Croesus has no love to give.

The most ambitious of the institutional collections which later came to be incorporated in the Hermitage was that of the Stieglitz Museum. In 1876 Baron Alexander Stieglitz, a privy councillor, merchant and banker to the court, asked the Ministry of Finance to accept a donation of one million roubles to finance the foundation of a new School of Industrial Arts. The then Emperor, Alexander II, wrote him a personal letter of thanks and agreed that the school should be named in memory of the Baron's father – a German émigré who had made a vast trading fortune in Russia. The idea for this amazingly generous gesture seems to have come from Stieglitz's son-in-law, Alexander Polovtsov, who later became Alexander III's cabinet secretary and was the chairman of the school board. There is a revealing entry in his diary which he made during a visit to London in 1875: 'Russia will be happy when businessmen donate their money for schooling and educational purposes without any hope of reward.'

His father-in-law's School of Industrial Arts opened in 1881 with a small Museum and Library on the first floor. The museum exhibits were fairly miscellaneous since all had come as gifts from local collectors, mainly noble friends of Polovtsov's, such as Prince Sergey Trubetskoy, the 'acting director' of the Hermitage, and Count A. V. Bobrinsky. Polovtsov even got a gift of artefacts from Schliemann's excavations at Troy after meeting the archaeologist on board ship in the Dardanelles.

But, on the death of Baron Stieglitz in 1884 the resources of the School were dramatically multiplied. He left the institution 9,690,642 roubles and 32 kopeks in silver. Polovtsov immediately commissioned the director of the School, a noted architect called Maximilian

Mesmacher, to design a new museum building. Mesmacher travelled all over Europe in search of inspiration and finally erected one of the most elaborate and magnificent realisations of the Historicist style. He borrowed designs from Pompei, from Renaissance Venice, from medieval Germany, from Baroque France and put them all together, with pillared halls, stairways, and galleries, into a brightly painted stucco and marble shell to contain the collection; it was opened by Nicholas II in April 1896.

Polovtsov, meanwhile, embarked on a tremendous spending spree, purchasing treasures for the museum in Paris, Vienna and Italy. Among the highlights of his acquisitions, now in the Hermitage, is a series of marble reliefs by the Venetian sculptor Antonio Lombardo which were made to decorate the marble rooms of Alfonso d'Este's palace in Ferrara and a series of five huge wall panels, depicting scenes from the history of the Roman Empire, by Giovanni Battista Tiepolo which were commissioned in the 1720s for the Palazzo Dolfin in Venice. By 1902 the museum owned 15,000 items, reflecting the decorative arts of every historic period. Polovtsov's son, who was also a collector, was responsible for adding a huge Oriental collection. He had worked for the government in the Caucasus, bringing back many Middle Eastern treasures, and later became interested in the art of China and Japan. Most of the contents of the Stieglitz museum came to the Hermitage, in stages, between 1925 and 1941, along with its curators.

While the arrival of such collections at the Hermitage was to radically alter its profile, there had been a brief renaissance of museum activity just before the Revolution, following the appointment of Count Dmitry Tolstoy as director in 1909 – after decades of neglect. When Vasilchikov resigned as director for health reasons in 1888 the museum had entered a period of stagnation. Prince Sergey Trubetskoy was appointed 'acting director', a title he retained for eleven years since he never chose to live in St Petersburg. He had served in the army in the Caucasus and made a home in Tbilisi, Georgia, where he remained. His salary as 'acting director' of the Hermitage was transferred to Tbilisi – 979 roubles and 99 kopeks a month, of which 326 roubles and 66 kopeks was specifically identified as payment for food. His deputy ran the museum.

In 1899 Trubetskoy was replaced by Ivan Vsevolozhsky, a former diplomat who was also director of the Imperial Theatres. But it made little difference since the government made no money available for purchases and Nicholas and Alexandra more or less ignored the museum. Visitors were further discouraged by new entry regulations instituted after the 1905 revolution to ensure that no revolutionary 'meetings' took place there. It became necessary to show a passport or identity document at the entrance and write your name and title in a special book in the vestibule.

Then in 1909 Count Tolstoy took over. He was a lawyer who had worked for the Ministry of Foreign Affairs and who was already assistant director of the Russian Museum – he combined the two jobs. A popular figure in St Petersburg's artistic community, he managed to persuade several private collectors to donate paintings to the museum. In 1911–12 the two Stroganov brothers, Grigory who lived in Rome, and Pavel who lived in St Petersburg, each gave an important group of paintings to the Hermitage, the first by donation, the second by bequest. Among Grigory's were a Simone Martini *Madonna of the Annunciation* and a shrine decorated by Fra Angelico; Pavel's bequest included a Cima da Conegliano, a Filippino Lippi and a Domenichino. In 1914 the museum acquired its second Leonardo da Vinci, the so-called *Benois Madonna*, by purchase – at a bargain price – from the Benois family. The painting belonged at the time to the widowed mother of Alexandre Benois, the artist, art historian and pundit who was to play a key role in the Hermitage's affairs at the time of the Revolution. We will come back to the painting later.

Benois, more than any other, was responsible for the explosion of artistic activity in St Petersburg in the last years of the nineteenth century and the beginning of the twentieth. Born in 1870 in St Petersburg, he was a typical product of the city's foreign community; his grandfather had been Paul I's French chef and his father, the godson of Paul I's widow, Maria Fedorovna, was educated at her expense to become one of Russia's leading architects. Alexandre's maternal grandfather was also an architect, Alberto Cavos, who specialised in building theatres and opera houses. He built the Mariinsky in St Petersburg and the Bolshoy in Moscow and had been chosen to build the Paris Opéra when he died unexpectedly. Cavos was a Venetian by birth and a passionate art collector; the young Alexandre Benois grew up glorying in the remains of his collection. In addition, Alberto Cavos's father, a successful composer, had moved from Venice to St Petersburg where he became Director of Music to the Imperial Theatres. Thus music and theatre and design were woven into Benois's background.

It was while he was still at the May School that Alexandre Benois and a group of friends founded a society called the 'Nevsky Pickwickians' who met at each other's houses and passionately debated art, literature and music. Benois was their leading spirit and proselytiser. In 1890, the year when they all left school and moved on to the university, Benois met a young artist called Léon Bakst, and introduced him to the group; later in the same year Benois's school friend Dmitry Filosofov introduced to the Pickwickians his country cousin, one Serge Diaghilev, who had just arrived in St Petersburg to study law. The hearty young provincial Diaghilev had no knowledge of art and was educated, in this respect, by Benois.

Thus was born the group of friends who transformed the artistic environment of St Petersburg. Their aims were both nationalist and internationalist; they wanted to promote a Russian art which would, for the first time, contribute to the mainstream of Western culture. There were painters, composers, writers, actors, dancers. Diaghilev, who was none of these things, turned out to be a brilliant manager, connoisseur and talent spotter. His first important initiatives involved organising exhibitions and launching the magazine *Mir Iskusstva*, or 'World of Art'. Benois later explained that *Mir Iskusstva* was actually a society, an exhibiting organisation and a magazine:

> I consider that *Mir Iskusstva* should not be understood as any one of these three things separately, but all in one; more accurately as a kind of community which lived its own life, with its own peculiar interests and problems and which tried in a number of ways to influence society and to inspire in it a desirable attitude to art – art understood in its broadest sense, that is to say including literature and music.

The magazine itself ran from 1898 to 1904, a beautiful production comparable to the *Studio* in England, laying special stress on typography and design; several of the group were interested in fine book illustration and found an outlet for this with the magazine. They included Benois whose illustrations to Pushkin's poem *The Bronze Horseman*, which were published in the magazine in 1904, won international fame – adding yet another layer to the artistic impact of Falconet's great sculpture. The group held their first exhibition in 1899, which included embroidery from the artists' community at Abramtsevo, Tiffany and Lalique glass, and paintings by Puvis de Chavannes, Degas and Monet, as well as work by young Russian artists. Diaghilev organised eleven exhibitions between 1897 and 1906, presenting modern European art in Russia and, in 1906, Russian art in Paris.

In 1899 Diaghilev was appointed a junior assistant to Prince Sergey Volkonsky, director of the Imperial Theatres, and Filosofov got a job at the Dramatic Theatre. It was enough to turn the attention of the whole group to theatre, ballet and opera – designing, composing, writing, choreographing. Benois and Bakst, who went on to design productions for all the world's great theatres, each did their first show at the Hermitage Theatre. Diaghilev was sacked in 1901 and subsequently developed his talents as an impresario in Paris, rather than St Petersburg, ably abetted by Benois. But he remained active in other spheres in St Petersburg.

This ferment of artistic activity affected the Hermitage in numerous ways. One feature of the new art of St Petersburg was its antiquarianism. Benois produced many watercolours depicting eighteenth-century St Petersburg and often visited the Hermitage for inspiration. He was the most popular art writer of his day, running a magazine called *Artistic Treasures of Russia* (*Khudozhestvennyya sokrovishcha Rossii*) from 1901 to 1907 which profiled many of the great private art collections. Among the contributors were Ernest Liphart and James Schmidt, who had charge of the Hermitage picture gallery, and Stepan Yaremich, an artist and collector of drawings, who joined the staff after the Revolution. This meant that the Hermitage employees were in touch with private collectors and received gifts and benefactions as a result.

Benois's most enduring love was the city of St Petersburg itself. 'I sensed the beauty of my town, I liked everything in it, and later I realised its importance too,' he wrote in his memoirs. 'The Germans are patriots of their country as a whole: *Deutschland über alles*. I was moved – and still am – by one compelling emotion: *Petersburg über alles*.' This led him, from the position of influence he had achieved in the early years of the century, to do all he could for the Hermitage. He personally researched and published a guide book to the museum collection which was published in 1913.

Another of Benois's friends and exact contemporaries – they were born in the same year – was Sergey Troinitsky, who became director of the Hermitage after the Revolution. He came from a noble family and, like Benois, had studied law at university, taking up art as a hobby. His special enthusiasm was for the applied arts of which he developed a wide-ranging knowledge, becoming an acknowledged expert on porcelain, silver, *objets de vertu* and heraldry. In 1905 he founded the Sirius printing house which published two art magazines that attempted to take over the role of *Mir Iskusstva* after the latter's closure in 1904:

Starye Gody (Past Years) and *Apollon*. The first magazine, as its name implies, had an antiquarian orientation, while the second focused more closely on modern art.

Troinitsky remained in charge of artistic matters at the Sirius Press up to 1917 but from 1908 also worked at the Hermitage. His first job was in the medieval and Renaissance section where he was given charge of the Basilewski collection. In 1913 he moved across to become keeper of the section of *objets de vertu* and, when Tolstoy left Russia in 1918, he was unanimously elected director of the Hermitage, a post he retained until 1927.

The idea of magazines organising exhibitions, which was pioneered by *Mir Iskusstva*, was carried on by its successors. *Starye Gody* organised an important exhibition of paintings from private Russian collections in 1908, the first time that many of the works were seen in public, while *Apollon* held an exhibition of modern European art in 1912. It was in the context of the 1908 exhibition that the *Benois Madonna* was 'rediscovered'.

The painting of the Virgin dandling her baby on her knee in a lightly sketched interior had always been known as a Leonardo in the Benois family. According to family tradition, it had been bought in Astrakhan by Mrs Benois's maternal grandfather, a merchant called Sapozhnikov, from some Italian travelling musicians. The attribution had, however, never been tested in the fire of public opinion. In the exhibition catalogue the painting was described as 'Leonardo da Vinci?' It was Ernest Liphart, keeper of paintings at the Hermitage, who launched the argument in favour of this attribution in an article in *Starye Gody* in 1908.

'I have the courage of my conviction,' he wrote, 'despite the outcry that this attribution will give rise to. The painting is not pleasing at first sight, I agree; but study it and you will find yourself, little by little, discovering the mysterious charm of this modest, early work by the artist who later became the great, the unique Leonardo.' The attribution was accepted by most contemporary scholars without serious argument though one or two suggested that it might be by one of Andrea del Verrocchio's pupils. It is now firmly enshrined in the Leonardo *oeuvre*.

After the sensation the painting caused at the exhibition, the Benois family decided to sell it and, in 1913, asked the English dealer Joseph Duveen who was already making a name as *the* man for selling expensive paintings to American millionaires to handle the sale. Its export caused an outcry in Russia. Duveen had offered 500,000 francs but the Benois family now changed the deal. Ownership of the painting would not be transferred to Duveen until 1 January 1914, at the earliest, and only then if the Hermitage did not want it. In the event the painting, one of only two Leonardo oils to have come on the market in the twentieth century, was sold to the Hermitage for 150,000 roubles, to be paid in instalments.

7

The Shchukins and the Morozovs

here has always been a vivid rivalry between Russia's two capitals, Moscow and St Petersburg, and it is a curious twist of fate that Moscow should have supplied the Hermitage with the paintings for which it is now best known abroad, the superb Impressionist and Post-Impressionist works from the collections of Sergey Shchukin and Ivan Morozov. The two men were Moscow merchants and their collections, formed at the turn of the nineteenth and twentieth centuries, were confiscated after the Revolution. Initially their large family homes in Moscow were opened to the public as museums. Then, in 1927–8, the paintings were combined in the Morozov home which was renamed the Museum of Modern Western Art. In the 1930s there was further shuffling of art between Russian museums, for ideological and administrative reasons, and the Hermitage got a first instalment of pictures from Moscow; the rest came in 1948.

As Communism began to require conformity in aesthetic as well as other fields, Impressionist and Post-Impressionist paintings were branded decadent and exhibitions of them were gradually reduced, then banned. The Shchukin and Morozov pictures had a temporary reprieve during World War II when, along with the contents of other Moscow museums, they were shipped to Siberia for safe keeping, but after their return to Moscow the Museum of Modern Western Art never reopened. In 1948 its contents were split between the Hermitage and Moscow's Pushkin Museum. The Hermitage got the larger pictures – most of the Picassos and the best Matisses since it had more space – while the Pushkin focused on the Impressionists.

The first instalment of over one hundred paintings arrived at the Hermitage between 1930 and 1934. The Hermitage had just been forced to contribute some 400 Old Masters to the Pushkin Museum to enable Moscow, as the new capital, to boast a 'national gallery' of its own, and the modern pictures were secured as a modest compensation. They got another 200 or so in 1948, making around 300 in all. Some paintings were exhibited in the 1930s but most of them could not be displayed after World War II when modern Western art was branded decadent and corrupting by Stalin's apparatchiks.

The first post-war showings at the Hermitage were disguised among other exhibits. The curators slipped a few Impressionists into a 1955 exhibition of 'French Painting from the twelfth to the twentieth century'; in 1956 there was a Cézanne exhibition combining paintings from Moscow and Leningrad; in 1959 there was an exhibition of French landscapes in which Matisse and Derain were daringly included. The Shchukin and Morozov paintings were only put on show as a group in the 1960s. As I write, they are still hung in the former quarters of the ladies-in-waiting on the second floor of the Winter Palace, where they look wonderful but are extremely hard to find. Exhibitions drawn from the two collections have travelled all over the world, repeatedly to America and Japan, and to several European locations, culminating in a 'Morozov and Shchukin' exhibition in Essen in 1993 where paintings from Moscow and St Petersburg were shown and Morozov's frescoed music room was reconstructed.

It was no coincidence that the great pre-revolutionary collections of avant-garde art should have been formed in Moscow rather than St Petersburg. In the last decades of the nineteenth century St Petersburg society, which revolved, as always, around the court, was aristocratic and conservative; new art, as we have seen, took an antiquarian route. Moscow, meanwhile, was the base of the new merchant class and artists were reaching forward towards abstraction. It was a period in which the traditional differences between the two cities were sharply highlighted.

The grand medieval traditions of Muscovy lingered on in Moscow after Peter the Great removed the government to St Petersburg in the early years of the eighteenth century. Initially, Moscow remained inward-looking and Russian, while St Petersburg embraced European influence, most especially the sophisticated culture of France. Then, in the nineteenth century, many new merchant families – entrepreneurs who had climbed to impressive wealth on the back of the industrialisation of Russia and the new rail links which facilitated national and international trade – found Moscow a more convenient trading base than the northern capital.

As the later generations of merchant families sought distractions outside their counting houses, Moscow too became the setting for a vivid flowering of the arts. Pavel Tretyakov, heir to a textile empire, became the patron of the Wanderers (*Peredvizhniki*), the first home-grown, Russian artistic movement of any major significance. A loosely linked group of realists who painted contemporary life, landscape and scenes from Russian history, they were linked by the Society of Travelling Exhibitions, founded in 1863, which exhibited their work all over Russia – hence the name 'Wanderers'. The group included Ilya Repin among its portrait and genre painters, Vasily Surikov among its history painters and Isaak Levitan among its landscapists. In 1874 Tretyakov opened his gallery as a museum and by 1890 it attracted 50,000 visitors a year, the same number as the Hermitage.

In 1883 theatre, ballet and opera were released from state control and two years later Savva Mamontov, a railway tycoon, opened the *Opéra Privé* in Moscow, effectively the precursor of Diaghilev's travelling company. Mamontov had been obsessed with theatre since childhood. On his country estate at Abramtsevo he created an artistic colony which drew together the talents of the leading artists of his day, painters such as Valentin Serov and Mikhail Vrubel, the legendary theatre director Stanislavsky, the composer Mussorgsky and the singer Chaliapin. He presided over an extraordinary explosion of creativity.

Shchukin and Morozov made their own contribution to this environment by recognising the importance of the French avant-garde ahead of their contemporaries and buying in bulk. They started collecting French Impressionists only a little after the Havemeyers in America, well before most Europeans had recognised these artists' significance. More importantly, they collected Gauguin, Van Gogh, Picasso and Matisse on a massive scale almost before their work was saleable elsewhere. This meant that they had first choice. Shchukin's collection of pre-1914 Picassos, more than fifty canvases in all, is now recognised as the most important holding anywhere in the world. The collections the two men brought home to Moscow, before World War I and the Revolution closed down such bourgeois activity, were sensational.

The Shchukin and Morozov families were surprisingly similar. In both cases, the family fortune was based on the textile industry; in both cases, enterprising ancestors had found a hungry market for their wares in Moscow, after the city had been sacked by Napoleon, and stayed to make a fortune. There were several art collectors in subsequent generations of both families.

The Morozovs originally came from the village of Zuevo, some fifty miles east of Moscow. Savva Morozov, a serf, obtained permission to open a small ribbon factory there in 1797. After Moscow had been wrecked in 1812, he travelled there with a pack of textiles and ribbons on his back. The Muscovites were enthusiastic buyers and by 1837 he had 200 workers in his factory and had bought his family's freedom from serfdom. His youngest son Timofey proved an outstandingly acute businessman, becoming one of Russia's most powerful industrialists, a shareholder and director of both the Merchants' Society and the Commercial Bank. By the 1880s the Morozov factories at Zuevo spread over two- and a-half square miles and employed a workforce of 8,000. An eleven day workers' strike in 1885, which involved rioting and damage to machinery, had to be put down by the police with the help of a Cossack regiment.

The first Morozov art patrons belonged to the third generation. Timofey had two sons, Sergey who built and endowed the Moscow Museum of Handicrafts, an ambitious palace of folk art, and Savva who was the principal backer of the Moscow Art Theatre where Stanislavsky launched his theatre of realism. Savva built the company a new theatre with a plain white auditorium – in sharp contrast to the Baroque interiors of traditional theatres – a massively expensive revolving stage and comfortable dressing rooms for the actors. Stanislavsky commented: 'All for art and the actor, that was the motto that controlled his actions.'

Savva Morozov was a friend of the revolutionary writer Maxim Gorky, and had a strong social conscience. He did all he could to improve conditions in the family factories. But when he suggested a scheme for sharing profits with the workers to his widowed mother, the principal shareholder, she removed him from control of the company and sent him packing to the South of France. A month after his arrival there in 1905, he committed suicide.

Such was the sad fate of Timofey's branch of the family, but the descendants of his brother Avram, who had run the family's industrial complex at Tver, were to prove even more significant art patrons. The three brothers, Mikhail, Ivan and Arseny, grandsons of Avram, had been brought up by their widowed mother Varvara Morozova, a powerful and forward-looking woman. She supported equal education for women, founded trade schools for workers, endowed the first public library in Moscow and ran a brilliant salon attended by the likes of Tolstoy and Chekhov. She employed Konstantin Korovin, one of Mamontov's best theatre designers, to teach her children to paint. Her sons reacted to their enlightened upbringing in very different ways. Mikhail and Arseny refused to have anything to do with the family business. Arseny gave himself over to parties and pleasure. He built himself a Moorish castle in the centre of Moscow. When his chosen architect, Fedor Shekhtel, asked him in what style he wanted it built, Arseny replied: 'In all styles, I have the money.' The revelry ended in 1908 when he died of blood poisoning.

Mikhail shared his brother's taste for gambling and wild parties but he also lectured at the university, wrote books and formed the first great Morozov picture collection. He started with French landscapes of the Barbizon school, moved on to Degas, Monet and Renoir, and rounded the collection off with Gauguin and Van Gogh. He died at the age of only thirty-three in 1903 and his widow gave a group of his paintings to the Tretyakov Gallery. They were later moved to other museums and some of the best landed in the Hermitage: Renoir's full-length portrait of *Jeanne Samary* (1878), Degas's pastel, *After the Bath*, and Monet's dazzling *Poppy Field* (1887) among them.

The third brother, Ivan, was the collector who earned his family lasting fame. He was the only one who was interested in business and is said to have been the epitome of a Victorian tycoon: reserved, perfectly tailored and a little haughty. Where Shchukin welcomed visitors to his home, Morozov's collection was only shown to artists and friends. The conventional exterior hid warm feelings, however. Matisse's daughter remembered him as 'bluff, genial and kindly – rather like an explosive child'.

Ivan Morozov studied engineering in Switzerland, learned his trade by running the family textile mills at Tver, and in 1900 took over the head office in Moscow. To accord with his new social eminence he bought a large, eighteenth-century mansion on Prechistenka Street which had formerly belonged to a nephew of Catherine the Great's favourite, Prince Grigory Potemkin. The interior had been reworked in the 1840s in Neo-Gothic style and Morozov ripped this out to restore clean white walls. He had a leading architect redesign the interior as a background for his pictures. The building works lasted for two years, from 1904 to 1906; it is no coincidence that 1907 saw an explosion in Morozov's picture buying. After the Revolution, his home became the Museum of Modern Western Art.

Until Mikhail's death in 1903, Ivan Morozov appears to have regarded French painting as his brother's domain and concentrated almost exclusively on collecting contemporary Russian art. He contin- ued to buy Russian work, in parallel with French masters, throughout his life and by 1913 could boast of owning 430 Russian works – which are now mostly in the Tretyakov Gallery, Moscow. As a young man he had made a sketching trip to the Caucasus with his teacher Korovin and started the collection by buying Korovin's landscapes. He moved on to lakes and forests by Levitan, then to Vrubel's Symbolism and more Romantic, theatrical works by Mikhail Larionov and Natalya Gonchar- ova – a blaze of Russian colour. He also became a keen patron of a little-known artist from Vitebsk called Marc Chagall.

The Russian works reveal the keynote of Morozov's collecting, an abiding love of the decorative. Surviving records suggest that Morozov's first French painting was an Alfred Sisley landscape purchased in 1903, *A Frosty Day in Louveciennes*. He started to internationalise his collection in that year by buying the work of the Spanish painters Joaquin Sorolla and Ignacio Zuloaga, both at the height of fashion in France, who borrowed the Impressionists' approximative brushwork but applied it to more conventional subject matter. Still feeling his way in 1904, Morozov bought Sisley and Pissarro landscapes and a Renoir portrait of the actress Jeanne Samary. He may have bought the Renoir in memory of his brother Mikhail who had owned the highly finished, Salon portrait of Jeanne Samary now in the Hermitage; Ivan's purchase was a more intimate, impressionistic rendering and now hangs in the Pushkin.

Morozov came of age on the Paris scene in 1906. He helped Diaghilev to organise the ground-breaking *Exposition de l'Art Russe* at the Salon d'Automne – which had a catalogue by Benois – lending extensively from his own collection. He was rewarded with the Legion of Honour and election to honorary membership of the Salon d'Automne. He also bought his first two Bonnards – he became enthusiastically addicted to Nabis and Intimiste paintings – and his first Monet, a view of Waterloo Bridge, romantically depicted as a shadow in the mist.

The following year, 1907, saw him making vast purchases for his newly completed Moscow home. He bought his first Gauguins – the rich colour of the primitive Polynesian scenes probably reminded him of Russian folk art – and his first Cézannes, initially favouring landscapes in the manner of Pissarro whom he already admired. He went on to develop a particular enthusiasm for Cézanne, buying many of his late, more difficult pictures. Cézanne was the only artist with whom Morozov seemed happy to go beyond the decorative. He searched for a late landscape for many years, leaving a blank space over his fireplace to accommodate it, and finally found the Hermitage's famous *Blue Landscape* of 1904–6 in the storeroom of Ambroise Vollard, the French art dealer, in 1912.

Felix Fenéon, the French art critic, who ran the Bernheim-Jeune Gallery, which specialised in the avant-garde, has left a splendid description of Morozov's visits to Paris:

> Almost as soon as he gets off the train, he is to be found in a shop which sells paintings, settled into an armchair that is particularly deep and comfortable and which the art lover cannot easily haul himself out of, while pictures are presented to him like episodes from a film. By evening, Mr Morisov [*sic*], who looks at pictures with unusual care, is too tired to go to the theatre. After a few days spent in this way, he goes back to Moscow, having seen nothing except paintings; many he takes with him, the ultimate choice from what he has seen.

Not content with mere buying, Morozov also commissioned decorations for his Moscow mansion. The most ambitious was the scheme of wall paintings executed by Maurice Denis for his White Salon, or Music Room, a vast Neoclassical chamber, already supplied with pillars, frieze and a vaulted ceiling by its original architect. Denis was a central figure in the Symbolist movement and his paintings of the more affecting moments of history and myth look rather old-fashioned to the modern eye. His work was, however, the height of fashion in Paris – Morozov bought his *Sacred Spring in Guidel* from the Salon des Indépendants in 1906 – and Denis became the Russian patron's close friend and adviser. In 1907 Morozov commissioned him to paint five panels depicting *The Story of Psyche* for the Music Room and, after he arrived to hang them in 1909, he was commissioned to paint another eight panels to fill the rest of the walls.

The naked nymphs and cherubs disporting themselves among pink clouds, verdant gardens and palaces seem a strange accompaniment to Morozov's Van Goghs, Cézannes and Matisses. Yet they serve to underline both the decorative nature of the patron's taste and the wide range of artistic endeavour in France in the years which saw the birth of Modernism.

In 1911 Bonnard was commissioned by Morozov to execute a second decorative scheme in the space at the top of the grand entrance staircase. The mural entitled *On the Mediterranean* invited the visitor to enter a summer garden on the Riviera, with trees, roses, a stone balustrade, a few seated figures and the sparkle of blue sea in the distance. It was a vast triptych, the allotted space being divided into three parts by two massive Corinthian pillars.

The difference between Morozov and Shchukin as patrons of contemporary art is underlined by the paintings that the two men commissioned to greet their guests at the top of the formal entrance staircase. Shchukin commissioned two vast canvases from Matisse, titled *Music* and *Dance*, each a grouping of childishly naked figures on a bright blue ground. They are not pretty, 'easy' works like the artist's much loved nudes and flowers, or Bonnard's *Mediterranean*. Matisse used the simplified figures to make abstract patterns of colour; the two paintings look forward to the purely abstract, cut paper works he made in his later years and are now amongst the most highly regarded paintings in the Hermitage. Shchukin was determined to patronise the most important new developments in contemporary art, even if it meant buying art that was ahead of his own taste. Matisse recognised this when he wrote an account of their relationship:

One day he [Shchukin] dropped by at the Quai St Michel to see my pictures. He noticed a still life hanging on the wall and said 'I like it but I'll have to keep it at home for several days, and if I can bear it, and stay interested in it, I'll keep it.' I was lucky enough that he was able to bear this first ordeal easily, and that my still-life didn't fatigue him too much. So he came back and commissioned a series of large paintings to decorate the living room of his Moscow house . . . After this he asked me to do two decorations for the palace staircase, and it was then I painted *Music* and *Dance*.

Shchukin's friend Prince Sergey Shcherbatov, who wrote a lively account of the Moscow art scene of his day, recorded Shchukin's agony of misgiving over one of his Matisse purchases. 'You know, I privately hate this picture myself,' he told Shcherbatov, 'have been fighting with it for weeks, curse myself and almost cry that I bought it. But lately I feel that it has begun to overpower me.' These are not the doubts of a diffident ingenue, rather of a man used to relying on his own judgement in business, who knew that keeping ahead of the game was no easy matter. He had cornered the textile market at rock bottom prices during the 1905 Revolution and made a vast fortune on the speculation when order was restored. He tried to do the same again in 1917 but this time the textiles rotted in their warehouses and his fortune was confiscated by the Bolsheviks. You can't win every time.

The Shchukins were Old Believers, a fundamentalist sect that split off from the Orthodox Church in the seventeenth century; they had been involved in the textile business since the eighteenth century but they had never been serfs. Their modest Moscow shop was burned down in 1812 and Vasily, the Shchukin of the day, had to rebuild his business from scratch. His son Ivan – Sergey's father – was an assertive, bombastic figure who took over the firm in 1836 and turned it into a thriving business. When he changed its name to 'I. W. Shchukin and Sons' in 1878 the capital value of the company was four million gold roubles. Sergey improved on this; the firm was reputedly worth thirty million roubles by 1917.

An interest in the arts was introduced into the Shchukin clan by Ivan's wife, Ekaterina, who came from a distinguished family of tea merchants called Botkin. Their caravans had travelled between China and Russia since around 1800 and a branch of Botkin and Son was opened in London in 1852. Ekaterina's three brothers were all collectors. Dmitry Botkin collected drawings, rare books and modern French paintings – modern, in this context, meant Courbet, Corot, Théodore Rousseau and Charles-François Daubigny. Mikhail was a history painter and collected the kind of props he used in his paintings: medieval Limoges enamels, fifteenth-century Italian majolica, Roman terracottas, old Russian enamels, as well as paintings by his Russian contemporaries. Some of his collection ended up in the Hermitage after his death, but the curators having discovered that many of his treasures were fakes allowed Antiquariat, the State organisation for selling art abroad, to sell them off in the 1930s. Vasily was a famous writer and critic with advanced views, a friend of Turgenev and Tolstoy, and collected modern European paintings.

Ivan and Ekaterina Shchukin had eleven children, five daughters and six sons. The latter, in order of birth, were Nikolay, Petr, Sergey, Dmitry, Ivan and Vladimir. Their father expected all of them to enter the business in the true merchant tradition – but he was to be disappointed. Only Sergey, the future collector, inherited his father's business genius. Nikolay turned into an amiable sybarite. He played cards and collected English silver, rather than attend to business, though nominally employed by the family firm. Petr longed for the academic life and, when denied it by his father, combined his business trips with collecting prints, rare books, Oriental art and Russian folk art.

His visits to the annual Russian trading fair at Nizhny Novgorod on the Volga turned Petr's interests towards Russian antiquities. His Moscow home became an overflowing treasure house, beloved of scholars who came to study and catalogue but could not keep up with Petr's purchases. In 1892, at the age of thirty-nine, he decided to build a museum and, in keeping with his antiquarian interests, ordained that it should be built in seventeenth-century style. Three interlinked buildings in Old Russian style duly rose on Gruzinskaya Street in the centre of Moscow. There were vaulted ceilings, carved and gilded pillars, and a hall painted in imitation of the decorations on an eighteenth-century Russian charter.

In 1905 Petr gave his museum to the State and was rewarded with a civil service title equivalent to the grade of general in the army which allowed him to wear a white and gold uniform while he guided visitors around his collections. The picture gallery was largely devoted to the eighteenth- and nineteenth-century Russian school but two of his brothers lived in Paris and he could not resist the temptation of Impressionism. Finding himself short of money in 1912, he sold the stars of his collection to his brother Sergey. Monet's *Woman in a Garden*, painted in St Addresse in 1867, which he bought in Paris in 1899, is now in the Hermitage and is possibly the finest Impressionist painting in the whole collection. A woman in white with a parasol is walking in a sun-drenched rose garden with a bed of bright red, miniature roses in the foreground. With Victorian prurience Petr hung his best nudes in his private apartments, rather than the museum: a Degas pastel of a girl towelling herself called *After the Bath*, which is now in the Hermitage, and a Renoir study of a seated nude dating from 1876 – the artist's best period – called *La Belle Anne*, which is now in the Pushkin Museum in Moscow. Petr got the latter thrown in as a free gift when he was buying a Japanese screen painting.

Petr's brother, Dmitry Shchukin, became a passionate collector of Old Master paintings, notably Italian, Dutch and German. He had already declared in 1914 that he intended turning his home into a museum, but the Bolsheviks forced his hand. In 1918 it was nationalised and opened to the public as the 'First Museum of Old Western Painting', then in 1924 the 146 paintings and drawings were transferred to the Fine Arts Museum, later renamed the Pushkin, where Dmitry became the curator of the collection.

While he bought many notable paintings, Dmitry is particularly remembered for the story of the Vermeer that got away. On a trip to Germany he bought an allegorical painting of a woman sitting on a globe which bore the signature of the minor seventeenth-century Dutch master Caspar Netscher. When he got it back to Moscow, none of his friends liked it and he himself ended up disliking it intensely. The Berlin dealer he had bought it from kindly took it back, giving Dmitry a small profit on the deal. He was delighted with this transaction, until he read in a magazine that Dr Abraham Bredius, the director of the Hague Museum, had bought the painting and found, under the false Netscher signature, the name of Vermeer van Delft.

Ivan Shchukin, the fifth of the brothers, was also a collector of Old Masters, but a spendthrift whose costly liaisons and art purchases brought him to ruin. He and his younger brother Vladimir were the only two of the six sons who were permitted a university education by their father. Both attended Moscow University and, after their father's death in 1890, they moved to Paris together. Vladimir, who had always been sickly, died in France in 1895. Ivan, however, set himself up with a smart apartment on the Avenue Wagram where he dabbled in philosophy and established a famous salon which was attended by many leading painters – Degas, Renoir, Odilon Redon – and every colour of visiting Russian, from princes of the blood to Vladimir Ulyanov, otherwise known as Lenin. On occasion, Ivan was denied entry to Russia on account of his association with revolutionaries.

But it was his connections with the leading artists of the day which proved Ivan's downfall. He travelled across Spain with the Spanish artist Ignacio Zuloaga and the French sculptor Auguste Rodin in search of paintings for his collection, buying a notable group of El Grecos. When his debts became too pressing in 1907 he sold his Old Master collection – all but the El Grecos – at the Berlin auction house, Keller and Rainer. The auction prices were inexplicably low and it was clear that the El Grecos would have to go too; but the experts who came to assess them said they were fakes. On 2 January 1908 Ivan committed suicide, which is doubly tragic in that the El Grecos are now considered to have been perfectly genuine.

Sergey Shchukin, the great collector of Impressionist and modern paintings, was the third brother in order of seniority. While Nikolay and Petr had been sent to boarding school, Sergey was considered too delicate – he grew up with a severe stutter – and was kept at home with private tutors. Occasionally he escaped to St Petersburg to stay with his artist uncle, Mikhail Botkin, where he could wander at will through the big art collection – undoubtedly an influential experience. Another was into rthe business trip to Egypt he made as a young man. The stylisation of Egyptian art and its rich colour made a lasting impression on him – he later haunted the Egyptian section of the Louvre. The experience seems to have unlocked for him the doors to understanding the geometric structures of Cézanne and Picasso and the richly coloured primitivism of Gauguin.

In 1873 a visit to a doctor in Munster, Germany, substantially improved his speech and in 1878 he entered the family firm. It quickly became clear that the sickly child with a stutter had transformed himself into the business brains of the family. The loneliness of his childhood appears to have taught him self-reliance and a determination to beat the system which had initially seemed loaded against him. He drove himself to the limit to achieve the best, first in business, then in collecting. Even in his sociable later years, he retained a puritanical self-discipline. He slept with a window open all year round, ate only vegetarian food and walked, or took a cab, in preference to using his personal carriage.

The beautiful wife Sergey married in 1883 had luxurious tastes, however. Lidiya Koreneva came from a rich coal-mining family and loved social life. Shortly before the death of Sergey's father Ivan in 1890, the latter gave his son his eighteenth-century palace in the centre of Moscow. It had formerly belonged to the princely Trubetskoy family and Lidiya's lavish entertaining turned it into a meeting place for the liveliest minds in Russia – Diaghilev, Stanislavsky, Chaliapin and Rachmaninov all came there at one time or another. Even Lunacharsky, the future Soviet Commissar for Education, featured among Lidiya's guests.

Initially Sergey left the interior decoration of the Trubetskoy Palace to his wife. Indeed, he never interfered with the furnishings, but from around 1895 he began to claim the walls. His first purchases were pleasant, unremarkable landscapes in the French Barbizon-ish style in fashion at the time. He bought several by the Norwegian artist Fritz Thaulow and others by French contemporaries who were then enjoying a modest success but have now been thoroughly forgotten – Firmin Maglin, Charles Guilloux and Charles Cottet, for instance. Like everyone else he bought a Zuloaga and in 1897 he commissioned a Burne-Jones tapestry from the William Morris workshop – a copy of the *Adoration of the Kings* tapestry he had admired in Exeter College Chapel in Oxford in 1890.

The Burne-Jones tapestry was hung at the end of his dining-room where it was subsequently joined by sixteen Gauguins, hung edge to edge in the spirit of a Russian icon screen or iconostasis. The juxtaposition underlines a shift in Shchukin's perspective as a picture buyer which must have taken place somewhere between 1897 and 1900. He had begun by buying for amusement to decorate his walls, then the idea began to crystallise of bringing to Moscow the most important, pioneering, modern art of the French school; it has been argued that he refrained for so long from buying Picasso because he was a Spanish artist, rather than French. By 1907 the collector knew that he was creating a gallery of modern art for the instruction and enjoyment of his compatriots. In that year, following the death of Lidiya, he made a will leaving his entire collection to the city of Moscow.

Sergey Shchukin's buying can be divided broadly into three periods. From 1898 to 1904 he pursued Impressionism, but most importantly Claude Monet, whom he saw as the leader and creator of the school; from 1904 to 1910 he was mainly interested in Post-Impressionism, busily buying Cézannes, Gauguins and Van Goghs; from 1910 to 1914 he was almost exclusively concerned with Matisse, André Derain and Picasso.

Shchukin loved to give guided tours of his collection and an early glimpse of this is provided by a rather condescending entry in the day book of one Margarita Sabashnikova:

> 12 February 1903. Yesterday evening we went to the Shchukins to look at their picture collection. I saw Monet's *Rouen Cathedral*, his *Sea* and other things – Lobre, Brangwyn, Cézanne, Renoir, Ménard, Degas, Cottet, Carrière, Whistler – and finally Puvis de Chavannes, his *Poor Fishermen*. Our host was polite, switching on one light, then another and explaining the subjects of the paintings. He had the appearance of a cunning steward, his grey hair was combed over his forehead, his eyes looked out like mice from their holes . . . There was a complete mis-match between his acute aesthetic understanding, his clever choice of paintings and his low class, peasant appearance.

Shchukin's appearance cannot have been impressive. Picasso's mistress, Fernande Olivier, also wrote an unflattering account of their first meeting:

> One day Matisse brought an important collector from Moscow to see

him [Picasso]. Chukin [*sin*] was a Russian Jew, very rich, and a lover of modern art. He was a small, pale, wan man with an enormous head like the mask of a pig. Afflicted with a horrible stutter, he had great difficulty expressing himself and that embarrassed him and made him look more pathetic than ever. Picasso's technique was a revelation to the Russian. He bought two canvases, paying what were very high prices for the time – one of them was the beautiful *Woman with a Fan*, and from then on he became quite a faithful client.

Shchukin was a haunted man at the time of this meeting. A period of tragedy opened in his life in 1905 when his seventeen-year-old son, Sergey, killed himself by jumping into the Moscow river. Then his wife Lidiya died in January 1907, after only a week's illness; in January 1908 his brother Ivan poisoned himself and in 1910 his second son Grigory, who was almost completely deaf, committed suicide.

In an attempt to find some relief Shchukin embarked on a journey to the Holy Land in the autumn of 1907, confiding to his diary: 'In a short time I have suffered a great deal and borne irreplaceable losses. I felt I didn't have the strength to begin a new life. My religious feelings were weak. I dashed from one thing to another in the attempt to fill my life with something. For a time I plunged into private philanthropy . . . then I became passionately involved in my business . . . For a while this filled my life, but only for a while.'

In the ancient monastery of St Catherine's at Wadi el Der in Sinai he encountered a healing experience. A young monk had pinned a copy of a Matisse to the wall and was trying to teach himself to paint like the Fauves, the famous 'wild beasts' of Paris who had shocked the art world in 1905 with canvases ablaze with primary colours – Matisse among them. Shchukin spent many hours with the monk, discussing art and religion, and on his return to Paris he sent a large supply of paint and brushes to Sinai.

Shchukin had bought his first Matisse in 1905 but a few months after his visit to the Holy Land he commissioned Matisse to paint a large canvas for his dining room, the holy of holies where his sixteen Gauguins hung. A commission is, of course, a more trusting and personal affair than a purchase since the commissioner doesn't know in advance how the work will turn out. Then in 1912, his eyes finally opened by pain, Shchukin began to buy Picassos – not easy Pink or Blue Period romance, but early Cubism and works full of harsh distortion inspired by primitive African sculptures.

Shchukin understood that with Picasso he was not buying decoration and excluded from his Picasso room the Baroque ornamentation that filled the rest of the house. There were plain walls, straight-back chairs, some African sculptures. The effect on his Moscow contemporaries was explosive. One Petr Pertsov recorded his experience:

> It is theoretically inconceivable that a simple *Still Life*, a bottle, a vase with fruits, a pharmaceutical vessel – could be saturated with a feeling of world denial and immeasurable hopelessness. But go into the Picasso Room and you will see this miracle, there you will find a whole series of canvases that depict only these harmless objects and that breathe through their outlines such an unbearable depression, such a 'grief of the last days' that you will be seized by an involuntary horror.

The following year, pushing his new-found profundity to its limits, Shchukin commissioned *Dance* and *Music* from Matisse. He already knew the Matisse painting *Joie de Vivre* of 1906 which belonged to his American friends and fellow patrons, Leo and Gertrude Stein. In the back of it is glimpsed a tiny bacchanalian ring of dancers – the inspiration for *Dance*. The Steins also owned an oil sketch of *Music* which Matisse had exhibited at the Salon d'Automne in 1907. Early in 1909 Shchukin commissioned Matisse to paint the companion paintings on a monumental scale to decorate the staircase of the Trubetskoy Palace. Then he started to get cold feet. On 16 March he wrote to Matisse: 'I have taken three young girls (8, 9 and 10 years old) into my house – and here in Russia (we are somewhat Oriental here) one cannot show nudes to young girls. Make the same circle but with girls in dresses. And the same with *Composition II*.' Matisse refused. Instead he sent his patron the completed panel of *Dance*. The strategy worked. On 31 March Shchukin wrote to him: 'I find your panel the *Dance* of such nobility that I have decided to defy our bourgeois opinion and to place on my staircase a subject with nudes.'

But that was not the end of it. Before finally shipping the two completed panels to Moscow, Matisse exhibited them at the 1910 Salon d'Automne and sparked an explosion of abuse. One newspaper cartoon showed a horrified mother gathering up her children and hurrying them out of the Salon. Shchukin was in Paris for the opening of the exhibition and experienced the furore. He lost his nerve again and bought a huge allegorical work by Puvis de Chavannes, *Genius Instructing the Muses*, from the Bernheim-Jeune Gallery to substitute for the Matisses on the staircase. But on the long train journey back to Moscow he changed his mind one final, and historic, time and wrote to Matisse:

> While travelling (two days and two nights) I pondered a great deal and came to feel ashamed of my weakness and lack of courage. One should not quit the field of battle without attempting combat. For this reason I have decided to exhibit your panels. People will make a clamour and laugh, but since I am convinced that you are on the right path, time will perhaps be on my side, and in the end I shall emerge victorious.

When the panels arrived he still had misgivings about the flautist's private parts, as displayed in *Music*, and supplied a remedy by painting them out with his own hand. When Matisse came to Moscow in 1911 to help rehang his paintings, Shchukin was overcome with trepidation. According to an account given by his son Ivan in 1974 to Beverly Whitney Kean, author of *French Painters, Russian Collectors*, a study of Shchukin and Morozov, Shchukin greeted Matisse in the hall, then watched anxiously while he looked at the panels. After a long silence the artist shrugged and said, 'It doesn't change anything.' So that was that. Nothing, indeed, was changed until 1988 when the Hermitage curator Albert Kostanevich was invited to a Matisse symposium in Chicago. While preparing his account of the museum's Matisses he asked the restoration department to take a look at what Shchukin had done to *Music*, and see if his interference could be reversed. It turned out that the offending area had been painted over with water-soluble gouache on top of the varnish. They took a sponge and cleaned it off.

In 1911 the Matisse paintings were gathered from all over the house and hung together in the drawing-room with the artist's help and advice. The Derains were hung in the former nursery, the Gauguins in the dining room, and the Monets in the music room. Shchukin ended up owning thirteen Monets, thirty-seven Matisses, sixteen Gauguins, five Degas, sixteen Derains, nine Marquets, four Van Goghs, eight Cézannes and fifty Picassos. From 1909 onwards he opened his house to the public every Sunday and a wealth of accounts testify to the impact it had on the young Russian artists of his day. Teachers from the Academy accused Shchukin of 'corrupting' youth but the artists, including Kandinsky and Malevich, who absorbed and adapted the lessons of

Shchukin's pictures, are now regarded as being among the pioneers of Modernism.

Shchukin remarried in 1915 and in 1917 sent his wife and baby daughter, illegally, to Weimar where they set up house and awaited events. He himself remained in Moscow where he was arrested in January 1918 and spent a few nights in a police cell. He moved briefly into the caretaker's cottage in the grounds of his home, where he lived with his daughter Ekaterina, her husband and child. Under Decree Number 851 of 15 November 1918 the Trubetskoy Palace and its contents became 'The First Museum of Modern Western Painting'. It was, in fact, the first museum in the world exclusively devoted to modern art. On 19 December the Morozov house became the 'Second Museum of Modern Western Art'. Ivan Morozov was appointed assistant curator of his former collection.

Shchukin left Russia in August 1918 and, after living for a while in Weimar, made a home for his new family in Paris. He had kept some money abroad for buying paintings and the doll that his little daughter Irina had clutched on her way to Weimar was stuffed with the family jewels. They had enough to live on but not enough to buy art in any serious way. Denied his role as a patron, Shchukin shied away from the company of artists though he bought a few cheaper works by newcomers such as Le Fauconnier and Raoul Dufy. Ivan Morozov, who left Russia in 1919, was one of the first visitors to the Shchukins' modest Paris apartment. Already a sick man when he left Russia, he died in 1921. Shchukin, who managed to make a happier life for himself, did not die until 1936.

Shchukin made a French will in 1926, leaving 'all his belongings' to his three children. The Russian government was sharply reminded of this in 1954 when thirty-four of his Picassos were exhibited in Paris at the House of French Thought, a Communist Party institute. Irina Shchukina, who lived in France, went to court to claim them. The exhibition was closed and the paintings rushed to the Soviet embassy where they were protected by diplomatic privilege and could not be seized by the French police. They were secretly returned to Russia before the affair could develop into an international incident.

In June 1965, recognising the opportunities for *détente* offered by Krushchev's conciliatory approaches to the West, Irina wrote to General de Gaulle, then President of France, to say that she had no further intention of claiming the paintings though she was not 'renouncing her rights as heir'. After that, the Shchukin and Morozov paintings began to travel the world, gracing exhibitions all over Europe, America and Japan.

Political changes brought about by perestroika in Russia spurred Irina to further effort. On the eve of the great Matisse exhibition in Paris in 1993 she wrote to Boris Yeltsin to demand justice for her family. 'My father desired to turn the Trubetskoy Palace into a museum,' she told him, 'which would belong to his beloved Moscow'. She went on:

As the prosperous head of the famous trading house 'I. V. Shchukin and Sons' he had no idea that he would be forced to flee from Russia, taking with him only the family valuables stitched into the stomach of my doll Tamara. He could also not foresee that after his death in exile in 1936, as a result of the division of the collection between the Hermitage and Pushkin Museums in 1948, the logic of his collection would be destroyed. He did not expect his collection to be shown to the public without any mention of its origins or that a visitor, marvelling at what he had seen, would have no way of discovering how it had reached Russia . . .

As the only one of the three heirs left living, I, without touching on the rights of the descendants of my late sister, am obliged to deal, as best I can, with the bequest of my father – both moral and material – and to try to decide what he would have wanted to happen at this time.

My heart dictates this reply: to preserve the collection as the cultural heritage of my country, Russia, but on the understanding that Sergey Shchukin and his heirs should no longer be humiliated and insulted. For that to be achieved, it is absolutely necessary that the criminal decree of 1918 should be annulled and that the Shchukin family should voluntarily present the collection to the city of Moscow, as its creator wished, observing all the reasonable conditions which I set out today to Maître Bernard Jouanneau, advocate of the Supreme Court of Paris, who is defending my interests.

M. Jouanneau 'reasonably' requested that the family should receive one per cent of the insurance value of the collection from the Russian government, a little matter of £10 million or so, and that their copyright in the reproduction of the paintings in all publications, worldwide, should be recognised – another nice little earner. They have not succeeded on either count – yet. In 1993 the French court ruled that ownership in this case must be determined by the law of the country in which the property is located, namely Russia. Irina appealed against the decision but died in 1995 before the appeal reached court. Neither the Shchukin or Morozov families have renounced their rights and the potential for future litigation remains. Whenever the Hermitage lends pictures to exhibitions abroad, a special clause is inserted in the contract insisting that the borrower will pay all legal costs if the ownership of the paintings is challenged.

Meanwhile the paintings have achieved the very impact that Shchukin originally desired for them. His collection powerfully influenced the Russian avant-garde artists of the early twentieth century; it went on to influence the dissident artists of the 1950s and 1960s and its existence helps to explain why there were so many good artists in Russia in the 1970s and 1980s – most of whom moved to the West after perestroika made it easier for them to leave Russia.

8

The Revolution

*I*n 1917 the Russian calendar was thirteen days behind the rest of Europe. On Lenin's instructions February 1918 was reduced to fifteen days in order to catch up. So the 'February Revolution' of 1917 in fact took place in March. The Hermitage was closed early in the month because of shooting in the streets and the keepers organised a rota so that one of them should always spend the night in the museum. When required, he could call in Count Dmitry Tolstoy, the director, at short notice since the latter had an apartment in the Small Hermitage, just below the Pavilion Room, looking out over the river.

On Wednesday 14 March, the day before the Emperor finally abdicated, it was the turn of Yakov Smirnov to keep watch from a small room leading off the vestibule, used by the *Hofführer*, or museum manager, during the day. Smirnov was a keeper in the Medieval Department, a professor at the university, author of a classic work on Oriental silver and an authority on the relations between the Sassanian empire in Persia and the ancient Greeks. Tolstoy records in his memoirs that he was impulsive, obstinate and loved to criticise everyone, including himself, which on this occasion nearly proved his undoing. As Tolstoy tells it:

around 10 p.m. a worried security guard ran in from the Palace to say that the Preobrazhensky Guards [whose barracks faced the Raphael loggia of the Old Hermitage across the Winter Canal] had rung to say that they would fire on the Hermitage and flatten it if the machine guns were not immediately taken off the roof. The roof was the responsibility of the Palace Administration and I was not answerable for what happened there, though the *Hofführer* had a key. All the same, I was certain there were no weapons up there. The security guards refused to go up and look as they were frightened that the soldiers in the barracks might kill them . . . So we decided to tell the Preobrazhensky to send representatives to go up and search for themselves.

Only after midnight, after we had heard firing at the Millionaya Street entrance, did twenty or so drunk and excited soldiers break into the entrance and demand with curses that they should be taken upstairs. Smirnov, however, refused to take them up, saying that they might do damage with their rifles and a colourful argument ensued. One soldier pushed Smirnov over onto the marble floor and began to beat him with his rifle. I threw myself at the other soldiers and begged them to restrain him. They pulled him off and ordered Smirnov to get up, sticking a rifle under his nose.

In a move which foreshadowed the future balance of power in the museum, the uneducated gallery guards, or 'attendants', who had gathered to watch this brawl now advised Tolstoy and Smirnov to leave the situation in their hands. They 'persuaded us to leave them alone to talk to the soldiers, stating that the latter would be more likely to listen to their "brothers", and this indeed succeeded. The soldiers began to drift away, at first leaving two guards – who quite soon, however, preferred to leave themselves.'

By this time, virtually every barracks in the city had mutinied and the common soldiers were running their own affairs in defiance of their officers, with a minimum of direction from two new organs of government which had come into existence forty-eight hours before. The Revolution, it should be remembered, was initially an undirected popular movement. Nicholas II, and his personally appointed ministers, had been sending thousands of Russian citizens to their death in a war with Germany that was extravagantly mishandled. Neither the soldiers themselves, nor their relations and friends – Russia's workers and peasants – could finally tolerate the waste of so many Russian lives.

Crowds of demonstrators made up of industrial workers, their families and non-commissioned soldiers, began to surge through the streets of St Petersburg in the early days of March. The police, fearing violence, mounted machine guns on the roofs of strategic buildings and on Sunday, 11 March they began to fire on the crowds. A particularly vivid description of the horror that ensued has been left by a British diplomat, Bertie Stopford, who was staying at the Hotel Europe in Mikhailovskaya Street, just off Nevsky Prospect, the main artery of the city. He was changing for dinner when he heard a sound he 'knew but couldn't recall'.

> I opened my window wide and realised that it was the chatter of a machine-gun; then I saw an indescribable sight – all the well dressed Nevsky crowd running for their lives down the Mikhailovskaya Street, and a stampede of motor cars and sledges – to escape from the machine-guns which never stopped firing. I saw a well dressed lady run over by an automobile, a sledge turn over and the driver thrown in the air and killed. The poorer looking people crouched against the walls; many others, principally men, lay flat in the snow. Lots of children were trampled on, and people knocked down by the sledges or the rush of the crowd.

Similar scenes were repeated all over the city and on Monday 12 March the crowds fought back. They set fire to police stations and prisons, releasing thousands of political prisoners, as well as ordinary malefactors. By around midnight on 12 March, a new political order was born. The setting was the Tauride Palace, the imposing Neoclassical home built by Catherine the Great's favourite, Prince Grigory Potemkin, which was currently used as the seat of the elected parliament, or Duma.

Since its inauguration in April 1906, the Duma had become the chief critic of imperial policy and earlier on the 12th the Emperor issued a decree dissolving it which was duly ignored. Just before midnight, a parliamentary committee, composed of representatives from all parties, decided to assume power as a Provisional Government to rule Russia until democratic elections could be organised. The palace was full of a surging crowd of workers and soldiers and at the other end of it an even more momentous meeting was taking place. Representatives of the main workers' organisation, who had been released from the Kresty Prison earlier in the day, had met to organise the formation of the Council of Workers' and Soldiers' Deputies. The Russian word for 'council' is 'soviet' and it was in the name of this soviet in particular that the Bolsheviks were to seize power six months later, thus laying the foundations of the future Soviet Union.

At this stage, neither the Hermitage Museum nor the Winter Palace was a particular focus of attention for revolutionaries. The imperial family had not used the Winter Palace for a few years, preferring to live in less formal surroundings at the Alexander Palace at Tsarskoe Selo. The Empress Alexandra, however, had helped organise a hospital in the Winter Palace to accommodate the vast influx of wounded soldiers sent home from the front. It occupied the first-floor rooms overlooking the Neva and a section of the second floor. 'All was beds, screens and tables with medicines,' according to an account left by Alexandre Benois who saw it in 1916, 'and between them the pitiful shadows in their hospital clothes wandered silently. Many of them lay under their grey blankets attended by snow white nurses in caps. Everything was very dimly lit . . . by a few bulbs in the huge chandeliers, or by night lights.'

It is characteristic of the unreality reigning in imperial circles that General Volkov, head of His Imperial Majesty's Cabinet (or private office) should have invited Benois to look over the Winter Palace in 1916 – Benois had wanted to do this for many years. Volkov explained to him that he wanted to raise the artistic standard of the Winter Palace, something which, he said, no one had had time to attend to since the fire of 1837! It is incredible to conceive of Volkov deciding to get down to this on the eve of revolution and in the middle of a devastating war.

Benois was not impressed by the aesthetics of the palace. Moving on from the hospital, 'no more joyful impression was created by the personal rooms of His and Her Majesties. These are dominated by an outstanding lack of taste.' The rooms were overloaded with furniture, he said, evidence of the poor guidance their favourite architect, Robert Friedrich Meltzer, had given them. He described it as mainly 'heavy furniture', not the Art Nouveau which the imperial couple favoured at the Alexander Palace:

> I thought that we could save the impression of the palace by giving back the heavy rooms along Palace Square their former Rastrelli look. However, we should leave the old study of Nicholas I in the entresol looking over the Admiralty untouched. The furniture is severe but not without taste . . . Also of great historical significance is the study of Alexander II on the second floor. The decoration of the walls here has the character of the Catherine era, for it was also the study of Catherine's grandson Alexander Pavlovich.

Benois records that 'this all survived when I made a similar trip round the Palace in March 1917 but much was destroyed after the Bolshevik uprising when the soldiers had the free run of the palace for three days'.

It is important to remember that there were two revolutions in St Petersburg in 1917. First came what the Soviets liked to call the 'bourgeois revolution' in March and then, as the Provisional Government proved unable to control the newly enfranchised workers, soldiers and sailors, Lenin's 'October Revolution' which, of course, took place in November. The second posed a much greater threat to the museum complex since the Provisional Government had by then established its headquarters in the Winter Palace and the Bolsheviks were required to 'storm' it.

In Benois's estimation, however, the destruction on that occasion was no great loss to posterity. His disparaging view of imperial taste is echoed by a twenty-two-year-old art historian, Larisa Reisner, who worked as secretary to the Bolshevik Commissar of Enlightenment, Anatoly Lunacharsky – Tolstoy recalls that the Bolsheviks' cultural supremo had an eye for a pretty girl. She inspected the Winter Palace in November 1917 and left a vivid account:

> There, where the Tsar lived for the last fifty years, there is a very difficult and unpleasant feeling. Some tasteless watercolours, portraits done God knows when and by whom, the modern Art Nouveau style for furniture – it is painful to see such things in this accommodation built for demi-gods. What sideboards and desks and wardrobes – Oh my God! The taste of a trader on the stock exchange – the kind who has five good rooms with soft furniture and a photograph album of pictures of his parents. How you want to gather it all together, all this vulgar human rubbish and throw it into the royal stove and burn it to the glory and beauty of art – setting fire to it with a wonderful old Florentine candelabra.

The Provisional Government was the offspring of the duly elected Duma and took power after the Emperor abdicated. It was all, more or less, within the framework of the law and the Court Ministry, which included the Hermitage, had little difficulty in working with it. On 17 March the chief clerk of the Hermitage administration came to see Tolstoy to tell him that 'all institutions were sending the Duma papers recognising the new government and the attendants were worried that we hadn't done it. So we drew up a declaration and I signed it and this was given to an attendant who flagged down a car on Millionaya and took it to the Duma.'

In the first few days after the coup, there was a universal sense of a heavy yoke having been lifted from society and an utopia opening ahead. The educated bourgeoisie were taking over from the tsar's lieutenants in every sphere and the art lovers of the capital saw their first duty as ensuring the protection of the nation's artistic heritage in the aftermath of revolution. Benois's diary calls March 17 'an outstanding day in my personal life'. He confided to the diary that 'much of what can now be done in the special field of the arts can be done only with my close involvement, if not with me in charge. So I have taken up the standard.'

Maxim Gorky, the most famous writer in Russia, felt the same way. He had a natural affinity with the oppressed who were now throwing off the tsarist yoke. He had been brought up in abject poverty by his grandfather, a dyer, and achieved international fame in the early years of the century with novels and plays which presented an authentic picture of working-class life – the first time this had been attempted in literature. His famous play *The Lower Depths* is still performed, though his novels have become somewhat dated. He was naturally in favour of revolution and was to play a very active role in the cultural sphere in the early days of Bolshevik rule.

On 17 March Gorky organised a meeting for artists 'to come together to discuss their common cause', Benois recalled, 'and – what amazing speed and attention to detail – to put forward a candidate for Minister of the Arts. Everyone agreed that Diaghilev should be the Minister.' Benois went round to Gorky's early and they worked out a basic plan before the others arrived, which was lucky since 'everyone who had been invited came, but so did those who hadn't been invited and also those whom nobody knew at all. Altogether there were over forty people in Alexey Maximovich's small parlour which was full to bursting.' (Alexey Maximovich Peshkov was Gorky's real name, though he is better known under his writer's pseudonym.)

A delegation took their plans for protecting artistic treasures to the Duma in the Tauride Palace, where it was duly signed by the new prime minister, Prince Georgy Lvov. Indeed he gave them extra powers they hadn't asked for, 'the right to form a special militia to protect art and museums and the right to give orders necessary for this end'. Out of this initiative was born the Council for the Protection of Cultural Treasures of the Provisional Government, under the direction of the Commissar of the former Imperial Court, one Fedor Golovin, who was previously one of the Duma's leading deputies. Everyone who mattered in Russian cultural life was initially a member of this Council, including Benois, Count Tolstoy, the archaeologist Mikhail Rostovtsev, the artist and art historian Igor Grabar, and Count Valentin Zubov who founded St Petersburg's first Institute of Art History. Benois was its chief activist in St Petersburg and Grabar in Moscow. It was subsequently taken over by the Bolsheviks and renamed the Collegium for the Preservation of Monuments and Museum Affairs.

Protection was necessary because the old palaces now began to be turned over to new uses. The suite of rooms overlooking the river in Velten's Old Hermitage was taken over by the so-called Extraordinary Investigating Commission on the Former Imperial Ministers and Employees – the very rooms where Nicholas I had interrogated the Decembrists. Their ghosts must have watched with a wan smile as the officers of the regime they had sought to overturn a hundred years before were sternly interrogated by the revolutionaries. Catherine the Great had built these rooms to display her pictures, but the pictures had been removed to the New Hermitage in the 1850s and the rooms were subsequently used to accommodate visitors, becoming known as the 'Seventh Spare Part'. A request from the museum staff that they should be turned back into galleries had recently been turned down on the grounds that the Preobrazhensky Guards needed to walk through them on the way from their barracks to guard duty in the Winter Palace.

The government's failure to bring the war to a rapid and just conclusion led to new discontent among the workers and soldiers who had delivered power into its hands. Meanwhile the Germans, with exceptional perspicacity, had provided a special sealed train to take Lenin and his fellow revolutionaries from their exile in Switzerland to St Petersburg – they were not allowed out of the train on German territory. Lenin arrived on 16 April and began to fan the flames of discontent. He offered the people, in the name of his Bolshevik party, an 'immediate proposal of a democratic peace, the abolition of the landlords' ownership of land, workers' control over production and the creation of a Soviet Government'.

In the early days of July an attempted Bolshevik coup led by Trotsky and Lenin nearly succeeded, the soldiers in several barracks, including the Peter and Paul Fortress, went over to their side and there was rioting in the streets. After the suppression of the attempted coup, Alexander Kerensky, a brilliant young lawyer and one of the original leaders of the

Workers and Soldiers Soviet, became prime minister – he had been a highly influential justice minister in the earlier government.

It was Kerensky who decided to turn the Winter Palace into the seat of government. Its offices occupied the rooms on the first floor where the imperial family had previously lived, starting with the Malachite Room and continuing down the western side of the palace overlooking the garden and the Admiralty. Kerensky turned the library into his office and Alexander III's study, on the second floor, into his bedroom. The chancellery moved into the first-floor rooms overlooking the courtyard, where the museum now has a memorial display of Peter the Great's lathes and the items he made with them. Kerensky's secretary and other support staff moved into the rooms formerly used by the ladies-in-waiting on the second floor.

In such troubled times the government required a military guard and the state rooms on the first floor were turned into their barracks. As the situation worsened, more and more loyal soldiers were recruited to guard the palace, prominent among them the so-called *yunkers*, or students from the military academy – it was hard to find older soldiers who had not switched their loyalty to the Bolsheviks. The soldiers gradually extended their territory until beds and straw mattresses filled the Gold Drawing-Room on the corner of Palace Square, the Raspberry Drawing-Room and the White Hall.

According to Alfred Knox, the military attaché at the British embassy, writing on the eve of the October Revolution, 'the garrison of the Palace originally consisted of about 2,000 all told, including detachments from yunker and ensign schools, three squadrons of Cossacks, a company of volunteers and a company from the Women's Battalion. It had six guns and one armoured car.'

The influx of government officials and soldiers made the protection of palace treasures an immediate priority. In July, just before the move, a new commission known as the Artistic Historical Commission began work on an inventory of the art treasures in the imperial palaces. It was headed by the former Winter Palace Hofmeister (the executive manager of the palace) Vasily Vereshchagin who was also an art historian and had collaborated on the production of the magazine *Starye Gody*. The Commission's report for 7 August lists the contents of the main rooms of the Winter Palace but protests that their work has been ruined by the soldiers moving in – there were wet towels hanging up on marble statues and straw on the parquet floors.

Meanwhile Tolstoy and his staff were worrying about the advance of the Germans – who occupied Riga on 2 September – and the threat they posed to the Hermitage treasures. A particular focus of their anxiety was the group of paintings which Alexander I had bought from the heirs of the Empress Josephine in 1814 and which she, in turn, had received as the spoils of war from the collection of the Landgrave of Hesse-Kassel. Tolstoy and his associates feared that the Landgrave's descendants would reclaim the paintings – a *Descent from the Cross* by Rembrandt, four Claude Lorrains, a *Holy Family* by Andrea del Sarto and many other major masterpieces. Their fears were, in fact, shown to be justified after the Bolshevik Revolution, when the Germans inserted a clause claiming the paintings in the treaty of Brest-Litovsk. James Schmidt, keeper of the picture gallery, penned a well argued memorandum refuting the claim for Trotsky, who handled the peace negotiations; the pictures and the memorandum are still in the Hermitage.

At the keepers' meeting of 9 September it was decided to recommend evacuation of the museum's art treasures to Moscow. Tolstoy passed on the decision to Fedor Golovin, the Commissar in charge of the former Ministry of the Imperial Court, and on 31 August money was made available to begin packing. Carpenters were sent over from the Winter Palace to make crates – they ended up making 833 of them. Tolstoy writes:

> With terror I asked myself – when and in what state will these precious things again see the light of day? The Hermitage was living in a feverish, difficult time; it seemed as though we were caught in a nightmare, or burying someone very near and dear. The whole of the curatorial staff were working very intensely, our scholars themselves wrapping up and packing the objects they were responsible for . . . Igor Grabar and other artistic figures came up from Moscow to talk to us about where they should put the objects being taken from St Petersburg; we decided on the Armoury, the Great Kremlin Palace, the History Museum and the Museum of Alexander III [today's Pushkin Museum was then known as the Museum of Alexander III].

The first train load of crates left for Moscow on the night of 29–30 September. It had taken all day to load, with careful lists being double checked at the station to ensure that nothing had gone missing. Yakov Smirnov, the expert on Sassanian silver, accompanied the train to Moscow and reported back that 320 crates had been stored in the Great Kremlin Palace, 227 in the Armoury and sixty-seven in the History

Museum. In the second train which left on 19–20 October the Hermitage was only allowed five carriages since a large amount of material was being sent from the Winter Palace, including the finest items from the imperial wine cellar, disguised as archives – 100-year-old cognac, Madeira and Hungarian wines. The entrancing smell which broken bottles spread in the Kremlin Palace later led to repeated break-ins and put the Hermitage treasures in considerable danger. This time, the medieval works of art and the coin collection were stored in the Armoury while Houdon's life-size statue of the seated Voltaire – dismissed by Nicholas I as 'that old monkey' – was set up in the vestibule of the Annunciation Entrance of the Great Kremlin Palace.

The keepers continued packing but the third train was delayed for too long and had to be scrapped. It was supposed to leave on 7–8 November, the momentous twenty-four hours which saw the storming of the Winter Palace and the seizure of power by the Bolshevik revolutionaries. The timing of the coup was carefully planned by Lenin and Trotsky. The Second All-Russian Congress of Soviets was due to open on 7 November; this was an assembly of delegates from all over Russia who would have the right to dissolve the Provisional Government and hand over power – but the less extreme parties, the Mensheviks and the Socialist Revolutionaries, were going to be in the majority. The Bolsheviks therefore seized power in the name of the Petrograd Workers' and Soldiers' Soviet a matter of hours before the opening of the Congress.

In August the Soviet had moved its headquarters from the Tauride Palace to the Smolny Institute, a handsome yellow and white building constructed in 1806–8 to house a boarding school for young noble-women. The Congress assembled in the Lecture Hall but the 5 p.m. opening was delayed while the Bolsheviks seized power. By noon their supporters had surrounded the Winter Palace where the Provisional Government was meeting, though Kerensky had slipped out in the course of the morning to try and get reinforcements from front-line troops. The Bolsheviks' Military Revolutionary Committee demanded the unconditional surrender of the palace and when they received no answer, in the words of Sir George Buchanan, the British ambassador:

the signal for attack was given by the firing at 9 p.m. of a few blank rounds by the guns of the Fortress and the cruiser *Aurora*. The bombardment which followed was kept up continually till ten o'clock, when there was a lull for about an hour. At eleven o'clock it began again, while all the time, as we watched it from the embassy windows, the trams were running as usual over the Troitsky bridge [the bridge which links the mainland to the Petrograd Side 500 yards east of the Winter Palace].

The Congress belatedly opened its proceedings at around 10.40 p.m. but shortly afterwards 'a new sound made itself heard, deeper than the tumult of the crowd, persistent, disquieting – the dull shock of guns', as the American journalist John Reed reported. There were outraged protests from Mensheviks and Social Revolutionaries at the unsanctioned use of force and most of the delegates of these two parties walked out of the Congress. At 5 a.m. the rump of the delegates, now mainly Bolsheviks, approved a manifesto drafted by Lenin on the transfer of power. 'The Provisional Government is deposed,' he wrote. 'State power has passed into the hands of the organ of the Petrograd Soviet of Workers' and Soldiers' Deputies, the Military Revolutionary Committee, which stands at the head of the Petrograd proletariat and garrison.'

Meanwhile at the Winter Palace 'the garrison had dwindled owing to desertions' according to Alfred Knox.

No one had any stomach for fighting; and some of the ensigns even borrowed great coats of soldier pattern from the women to enable them to escape unobserved.

The greater part of the yunkers of the Mikhail Artillery School returned to their school, taking with them four out of their six guns. Then the Cossacks left, declaring themselves opposed to bloodshed! At 10 p.m. a large part of the ensigns left, leaving few defenders except the ensigns of the Engineering School and the company of women . . .

The defence was unorganised and only three of the many entrances were guarded. Parties of the attackers penetrated by side entrances in search of loot. At first these parties were small and were disarmed by the garrison, but they were succeeded by larger bands of sailors and of the Pavlovsky Regiment, in addition to armed workmen, and these turned the tables by disarming the garrison. This was, however, carried out, as an officer of the garrison afterwards stated, 'in a domestic manner', with little bloodshed. The garrison fired little and is said to have only lost three yunkers wounded . . . At 2.30 a.m. on the 8th the Palace was 'taken'.

Count Tolstoy lived through these events in the relative seclusion of the Hermitage Museum. At that time the museum was quite separate from the Winter Palace, with only one interconnecting door at the south end of the Small Hermitage. 'Things didn't look too good on the morning of the 7th', according to Tolstoy's memoirs:

> At first the Neva bridges were up to prevent the Bolsheviks and soldiers reaching the palaces and government buildings. But they were soon put down and not allowed up again from which we understood that things were not going too well for the Provisional Government. Once again lorries filled with workers and soldiers flew to and fro along the embankment, as they had in the first days of the revolution.

He was in his apartment in the Small Hermitage at 5 p.m. when he received a phone call from the museum to say that the revolutionary headquarters had rung and they were sending new guards to replace the *yunkers* then in charge of the museum.

> I summoned the senior soldier on watch and asked him what we were supposed to do. He said he was going to see the head of the watch in the Winter Palace and having got instructions would come back. On his return he told me that the *yunkers* wouldn't leave their posts. They would not give up the watch to anyone else and would defend to the last the institution they had been asked to protect.
>
> A keeper called Struve was supposed to be on night duty but he had not arrived and his wife rang up worried because of the shooting in the streets. Soon afterwards, Struve himself phoned. He was on his way but there had been a lot of rifle firing. I told him to return home and I would spend the night myself in the Hofführer's chair.
>
> Around 9 p.m. there was a loud knock on the door and about 30 members of the Preobrazhensky Guard came in with a low ranking officer. They demanded that the *yunkers* hand over their weapons and said that they would replace them. There was a lively discussion. I didn't manage to hear everything as it was so noisy. In the end the old watch gave in and had its weapons removed. The senior *yunker* came to me and apologised and explained that they could not defend the Hermitage against this larger group of soldiers. I confessed that I thought a peaceful conclusion was the best . . . The young lads were pleased and hoped to go back peacefully to their college or homes but

they were taken as prisoners of war to the Pavlovsk Barracks and who knows what happened to them. We only know that a large number of *yunkers* died that night.

The new guards moved heavy furniture, boxes and sofas to barricade the entrance to the Hermitage and all the passages between the Hermitage and the Winter Palace. They established military posts at the entrance and in all the galleries overlooking Millionaya Street or the Winter Canal – each guard had to take charge of several rooms. Tolstoy spent the night in the *Hofführer's* office where he got a little sleep despite his worries and 'the sound of the canons of the *Aurora* shooting at the Palace'. But at 6 a.m. he was woken by an attendant who had gone out and seen the lights on in his apartment.

I had ordered that the lights should never be put on without closing the curtains so as not to attract attention. After several unsuccessful attempts to get through on the phone, I managed to speak to a terrified servant who said that they were robbing my flat. The mob had broken into the flat through the Romanov Gallery and the internal staircase from the Winter Palace. They had broken cupboards, commodes, chests and tables and since 6 a.m. they had been carrying out as much as they could.

One of the night watch said he would go to my flat and, if possible, take me there with two of my relatives from Petrograd Side who had arrived to find out what was happening to me. He soon returned with two passes from the new commandant of the Palace and explained with great concern that he had taken my gramophone with its horn away from a sailor in the door of my flat. He was very worried about the theft of an item which was clearly of great interest to him. We set off along the embankment to my flat where we found only one sailor – he was wandering around the rooms waving an antique sabre he had requisitioned. The state of the flat was terrible, the furniture overturned and mess everywhere . . . straw, papers, the cupboards and commodes were all open . . . In places there were piles of dirty rags, the clothes and shoes that the thieves had thrown off, replacing them with clothes from our cupboards.

Revolution was clearly an unnerving business. Like Tolstoy, most of the keepers spent the night when the Winter Palace was stormed in the museum, partly because it was too dangerous to go home and partly out of loyalty to its treasures. On the preceding morning they had been summoned to a meeting in the Raphael Loggia at 11 a.m. to plan that night's evacuation of the collection – which, of course, never took place. Tolstoy himself did not turn up for the meeting as he had decided to try to see the British ambassador, Sir George Buchanan, and ask for his help; he took his deputy, Eduard Lenz, with him but the ambassador would not see them – jealously guarding his neutrality.

The rest of the keepers waited all day in the Raphael Loggia from whose windows they could see the Preobrazhensky Guards in their barracks on the other side of the Winter Canal, rushing to and fro and shouting out of the windows to revolutionaries in the street. At lunch time, the keeper of *objets de vertu*, Sergey Troinitsky left them, since he was staying down the street with Prince Lobanov-Rostovsky. He returned in a state of extreme agitation to say that the anti-government forces had almost completely taken over Palace Square and were trying to seize the palace itself. He brought with him a proclamation he had picked up in the street with an alarming message:

> Pogrom organisers may try to create confusion and bloodshed on the streets of Petrograd. The Petrograd Soviet of Workers' and Soldiers' Deputies takes responsibility for the maintenance of revolutionary order against counter-revolutionary and pogrom attacks. The Petrograd garrison will not allow any violence or disturbances. We call on the population to detain hooligans and Black Hundred agitators and deliver them to the commissars of the Soviet in the nearest military barracks. At the first attempt of dark elements to create disturbances, looting, knife attacks, or shooting on the streets of Petrograd, the criminals shall be wiped off the face of the earth. Citizens! We call on you to remain totally calm and keep control of yourselves. Order and the revolution are in strong hands.

As it began to get dark, the keepers heard machine-gun fire down the street. Tolstoy and Lenz still had not returned and Yakov Smirnov, the next most senior, announced that he was taking charge. He said that everyone who wanted to should go home but he himself intended to spend the night in the museum. Most of the other keepers decided to do the same, including Troinitsky, James Schmidt from the picture department, and Oskar Waldhauer, keeper of Classical antiquities. They encountered the new guards and helped them barricade the museum, then retired to the Italian picture gallery where they moved the velvet

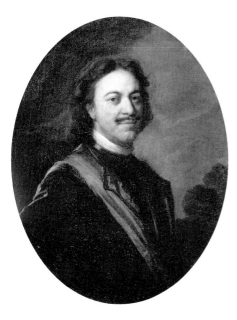

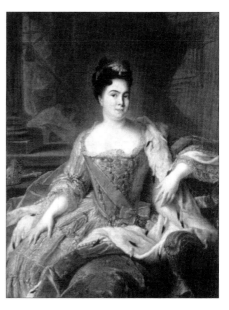

Peter I, known as Peter the Great
(reigned 1682-1725)
by Andrey Matveev.

Peter's wife *Catherine I*
(reigned 1725-1727)
by Jean-Marc Nattier.

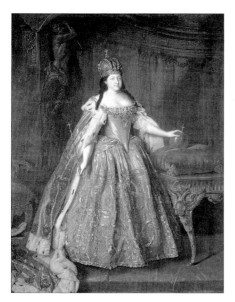

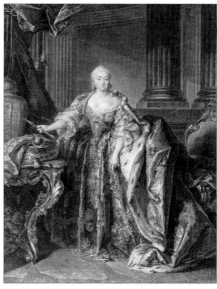

Empress Anna Ivanovna
(reigned 1730-1740)
by Louis Caravaque.

Empress Elizabeth
(reigned 1741-1761)
an engraving by Georg Friedrich
Schmidt after an oil painting
by Louis Tocque.

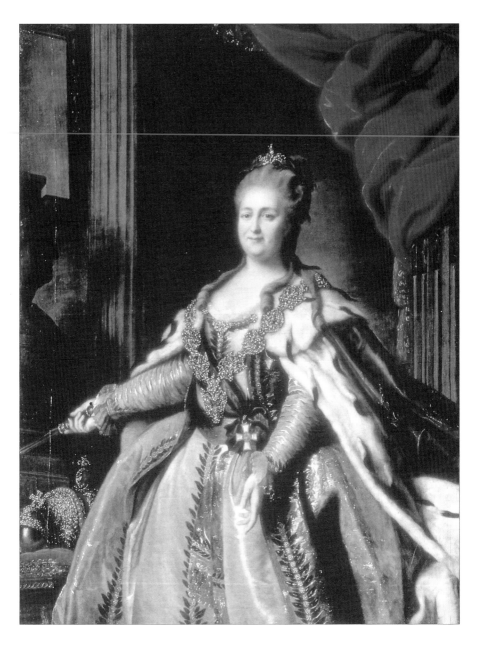

Catherine II, known as Catherine the Great (reigned 1762–1796).
One of several contemporary copies made for diplomatic purposes after a state
portrait of 1777-78 by the Swedish artist Alexander Roslin. Catherine complained
that he had given her 'a face as common as a Swedish pastry cook'.

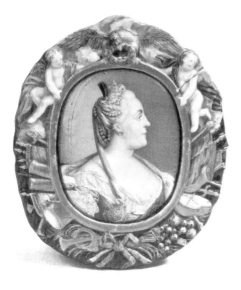

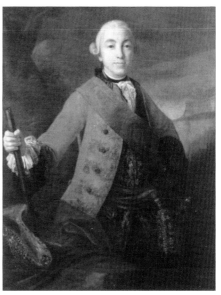

A miniature of *Catherine II*, painted on
porcelain by Andrey Ivanovich Chernyl,
a serf who worked at the Imperial
Porcelain Factory.

Peter III, Catherine's husband,
while still only Grand Duke,
after Pietro Antonio Rotari.

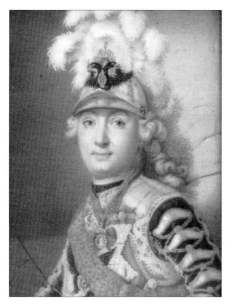

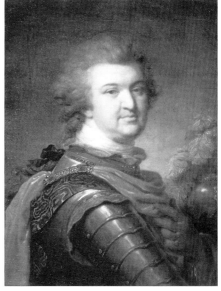

A miniature of *Grigory Orlov*,
Catherine the Great's lover for eleven
years, in masquerade costume, painted in
enamels on copper by Andrey Ivanovich
Chernyl in the late 1760s.

Prince Grigory Potemkin, around 1790,
by Giovanni Battista Lampi the Elder.
Potemkin was the most important of all
Catherine's lovers and may have been
secretly married to her.

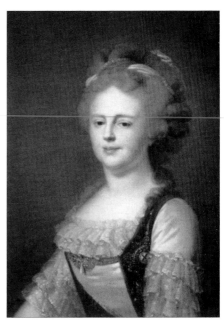

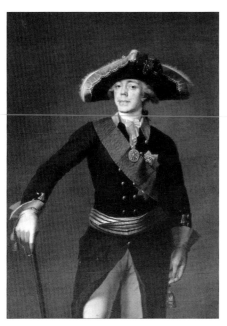

Paul I (reigned 1796–1801), the son of Catherine the Great, painted in 1796–7 by Stepan Semeonovich Shchukin.

Paul I's wife, *Maria Fedorovna*, the replica of a late-18th-century painting by Giovanni Battista Lampi.

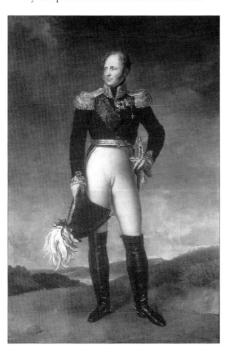

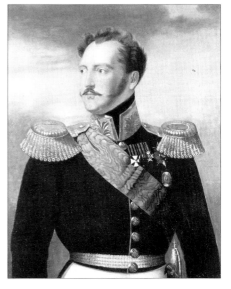

An anonymous portrait of *Nicholas I*, (reigned 1825–1854), now in a private collection. Nicholas, who built the New Hermitage, was the last Tsar who had an important influence on the evolution of the museum.

Alexander I (reigned 1801–1825), the 'Liberator of Europe', a portrait by Baron François Gérard in the Wellington collection at Apsley House, London.

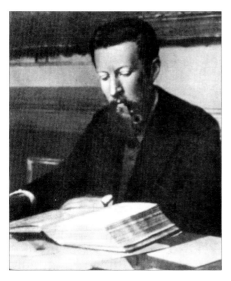

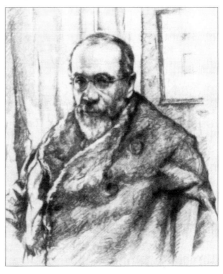

Sergey Nikolaevich Troinitsky, director of the Hermitage from 1918 to 1927.

Alexandre Benois, artist, theatrical designer, art historian and curator of paintings at the Hermitage from 1918 to 1926.

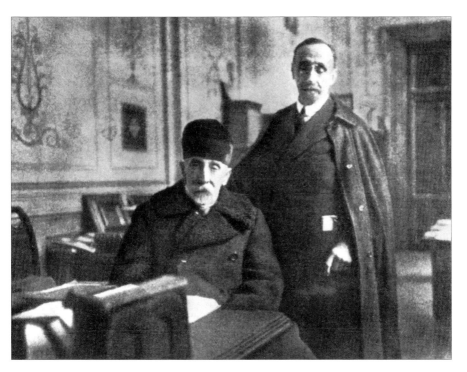

Ernst Liphart, seated, the curator of paintings, with Count Dmitry Tolstoy, standing, the director of the Hermitage from 1909 to 1918. The photograph was taken in early 1918, shortly before the Count left Russia.

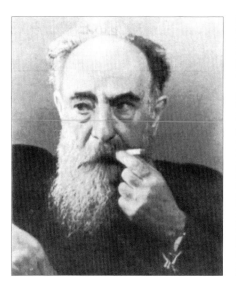

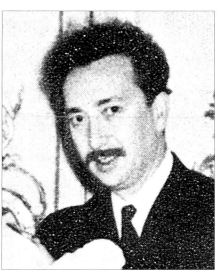

Iosif Orbeli, director of the Hermitage from 1934 to 1951.

Leonid Tarassuk, the curator of arms and armour who was sacked by the Hermitage in 1972 when he applied for a visa to leave Russia for Israel.

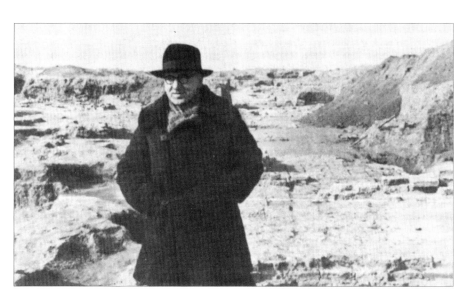

Mikhail Artomonov, director of the Hermitage from 1951 to 1964, with the excavations of the Khazar fortress at Sarkel in the background.

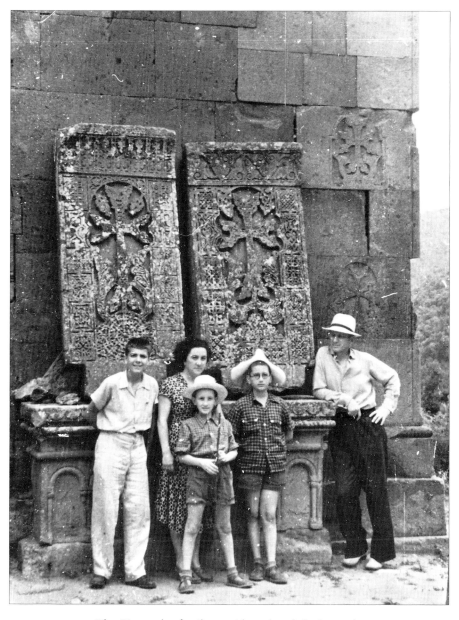

The Piotrovsky family outside a church in Armenia.
From right to left: Boris Borisovich Piotrovsky, director of the museum from
1964 to 1990, his son Mikhail Borisovich, the present director, his younger brother
Levon Borisovich, their mother Ripsime Djanpolodyan, and their cousin
Alexander Tamanyan.

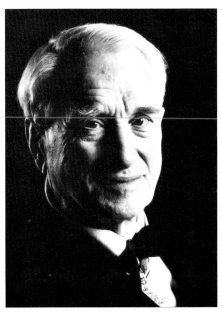

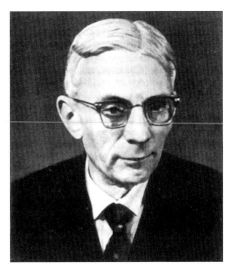

Vladimir Levinson-Lessing,
curator of paintings, author of a history
of the Hermitage collection, and deputy
director until shortly before his
death in 1972.

Boris Borisovich Piotrovsky, director of
the Hermitage from 1964 to 1990.

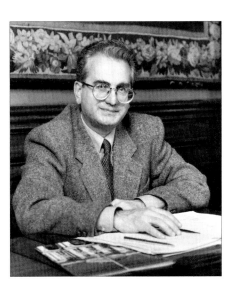

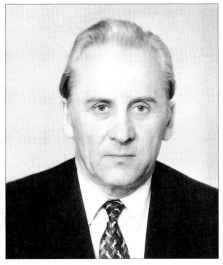

Mikhail Borisovich Piotrovsky, the
present director of the museum,
appointed in 1992.

Vitaly Alexandrovich Suslov, deputy
director of the museum from 1967 to
1990, director from 1990 to 1992.

chairs into a semicircle and sat and dozed in the dark. In the early hours of the morning one of the guards looked in to tell them that the Winter Palace had been taken.

The treasures of the Hermitage thus came through the Revolution virtually unscathed, some stored in Moscow and the rest still in place in St Petersburg. The same could not be said of the works of art in the Winter Palace – which was to be handed over to the museum in stages over the following decades. In his classic account of the Revolution, *Ten Days that Shook the World*, John Reed, the American journalist, gives a highly evocative account of the Winter Palace's fate – though it should be born in mind that Reed was seeing the event through the rose-tinted spectacles of a Bolshevik sympathiser:

> Carried along by the eager wave of men we were swept into the right-hand entrance, opening into a great bare vaulted room, the cellar of the east wing, from which issued a maze of corridors and staircases. A number of huge packing cases stood about, and upon these the Red Guards and soldiers fell furiously, battering them open with the butts of their rifles, and pulling out carpets, curtains, linen, porcelain, plates, glassware . . . One man went strutting around with a bronze clock perched on his shoulder; another found a plume of ostrich feathers, which he stuck in his hat. The looting was just beginning when somebody cried, 'Comrades! Don't take anything. This is the property of the People!' Immediately twenty voices were crying, 'Stop! Put everything back! Don't take anything! Property of the People!' Many hands dragged the spoilers down. Damask and tapestry were snatched from the arms of those who had them; two men took away the bronze clock. Roughly and hastily the things were crammed back in their cases, and self-appointed sentinels stood guard. It was all utterly spontaneous. Through corridors and up staircases the cry could be heard growing fainter and fainter in the distance, 'Revolutionary discipline! Property of the People!' . . .
>
> We crossed back over to the left entrance, in the west wing. There order was also being established. 'Clear the Palace!', bawled a Red Guard, sticking his head through an inner door. 'Come comrades lets show that we're not thieves and bandits. Everybody out of the Palace except the Commissars until we get sentries posted.'
>
> Two Red Guards, a soldier and an officer, stood with revolvers in their hands. Another soldier sat at a table behind them, with pen and paper. Shouts of 'All out! All out!' were heard far and near within,

and the Army began to pour through the door, jostling, expostulating, arguing. As each man appeared he was seized by the self-appointed committee, who went through his pockets and looked under his coat. Everything that was plainly not his property was taken away, the man at the table noted it on his paper, and it was carried into a little room. The most amazing assortment of objects were thus confiscated; statuettes, bottles of ink, bed-spreads worked with the Imperial monogram, candles, a small oil painting, desk blotters, gold-handled swords, cakes of soap, clothes of every description, blankets.

The organisation of the uprising was not as spontaneous as Reed would have us believe. It was being directed by the Military Revolutionary Committee in the Smolny and the fact that they had sent a group of Preobrazhensky Guards to look after the Hermitage before the storming of the Winter Palace indicates their forethought. On the following day, 8 November, Lenin announced his government which included as Commissar for Enlightenment Anatoly Lunacharsky, a forty-two-year-old writer and political activist who had studied philosophy in Switzerland and lived in Florence and Paris – as well as spending years in prison and exile. His job was a combination of minister of culture and education and he had two important qualifications for it, enthusiasm and understanding. He was well educated and personally acquainted with many of the country's leading cultural figures, Shchukin and Benois among them.

Besides Lunacharsky, two special Commissars were appointed for the protection of museums and palaces, Grigory Yatmanov, who remained in charge for almost twenty years, and a Pole called Berngard Mandelbaum, who only lasted two months. A third figure who had some influence over the fate of the Hermitage was pretty, young Larisa Reisner, who became the Secretary of Narkompros (the Ministry of Enlightenment). On Lunacharsky's advice, Yatmanov and Mandelbaum visited Benois on the morning of 8 November before they went to introduce themselves to the Hermitage staff. 'For a whole hour I sought to hammer into the wooden-headed representative of Lunacharsky, Yatmanov, my ideas and elementary demands, without success', Benois writes. He describes the Commissar not wholly unsympathetically, however: 'Yatmanov is rude only because of his stupidity and lack of education (and even then only moderately) and at least he is probably an honest man.'

Despite the difficulty of communicating it to Yatmanov, Benois's advice prevailed. On 9 November, only two days after the Revolution, the head of the old Inventorisation Commission, Vasily Vereshchagin, was asked to check what was missing from the palace. He had been stopped by soldiers when he tried to get into the Winter Palace to make an inspection on his own account the day before but when he was asked to do it on behalf of the Bolshevik authorities he refused – Benois had to go round and persuade him. On 10 November four members of the Commission accompanied by Yatmanov, Mandelbaum and Benois inspected roughly one hundred rooms. Vereshchagin dictated a report to the librarian V. Gelmerson as they moved from room to room:

There are traces of fierce battle in all the State Rooms of the First Spare Part, which housed the guards of the Provisional Government. The windows are shattered by bullets, scattered on the floor are dozens of mattresses on which the guards slept, some of them torn, the straw scattered, the furniture turned topsy-turvy in piles, having clearly served as barricades . . . In the reception room of Emperor Alexander II, used as the private chancellery of A. F. Kerensky, the drawers have been pulled out of the desks, the cupboards of paperwork have been smashed, all the papers thrown all over the place . . . In the personal apartments of the Emperor Nicholas II and the Empress Alexandra Fedorovna, used by the Provisional Government, the tables and cupboards have been smashed, the floor covered with torn up and crumpled files of the Provisional Government. In the reception room a painting depicting the coronation of Alexander III has been defaced. A bayonet has been used to tear a portrait of the parents of the Empress . . . in the adjutant's room, the study of Emperor Nicholas I, everything is turned over. Everything is tossed onto the floor . . . In the rooms of the ladies-in-waiting corridor, the court and ball dresses are thrown all over the floor . . . The study of Alexander III, turned by Chairman-Minister Kerensky into a bedroom, is scattered with papers of important state significance.

The report went to Lunacharsky and on 13 November he issued a decree on the protection and use of the palace:

1 The rooms of the Winter Palace of no serious artistic significance shall be given over to social needs with regard to which an order shall be given in due time. The rest of the Winter Palace is declared a state museum on an equal footing with the Hermitage.

2 The Palace administration is to continue to carry out its duties.

3 The military command is given to Cornet Pokrovsky and the general oversight of the Winter Palace is entrusted to Colonel Ratiev (the former administrator), whose orders must be counter-signed by the government commissar attached to the Winter Palace for the protection of its artistic treasures.

4 The Artistic-Historical Commission, under the chairmanship of V. A. Vereshchagin, is invited to continue its work on receiving and inventorising the property of the former palace administration.

5 The regimental committees are requested to help to search for and return objects which disappeared from the palace during the disorder of the night when the palace was taken.

6 It is to be explained through publications that those individuals who voluntarily return such objects to the People, their sole owner and master, should have no fear of being held responsible for having stolen objects in their possession.

Naturally enough, the treasures did not come back of their own accord. On 18 November the Military Revolutionary Committee gave Vereshchagin's commission the right to conduct searches. They didn't do it themselves but concentrated on drawing up as complete a list as they could manage of the items that were missing, identifying any special characteristics that would make them easy to search for. On 24 November several army battalions (1,000 soldiers) were sent to search the Alexandrovsky Market, the main place where you would have expected to find stolen goods for sale. The soldiers were not just looking for stolen treasures but also for food which had been hidden from the central authorities – which they confiscated and gave to the Central Food Administration – and for weapons. According to John Reed, about half the objects which had disappeared were found, some in the market and some in the baggage of foreigners leaving Russia.

Then came a flurry of hysteria over the fate of the Hermitage treasures which had been sent to Moscow for safekeeping. The Bolsheviks' battle for ascendancy was more fiercely contested in Moscow than St Petersburg. Fighting between Bolshevik forces and moderates, organised around the Committee of Public Safety, lasted a week and cost more than a thousand lives. The fighting was particularly fierce around the Great Kremlin Palace and on 15 November it was erroneously reported in St Petersburg that the Hermitage treasures had been destroyed.

Lunacharsky reacted with vivid emotion, instantly handing in his resignation. He issued a public statement on the evening of 15 November:

> I have just been informed, by people arriving from Moscow, what has happened there. The Cathedral of St Basil the Blessed, the Cathedral of the Assumption, are being bombarded. The Kremlin, where are now gathered the most important art treasures of Petrograd and Moscow, is under artillery fire. There are thousands of victims. The fearful struggle there has reached a pitch of bestial ferocity. What is left? What more can happen? I cannot bear this. My cup is full. I am unable to endure these horrors. It is impossible to work under the pressure of thoughts which drive me mad! That is why I am leaving the Council of People's Commissars.

In the same period Count Tolstoy gave an interview to a French journalist from the newspaper *Le Petit Parisien* and said: 'Tell the civilised world that Russia no longer has the Hermitage.' But the reports from Moscow were conflicting and it was decided that the museum must send one of its own staff to find out the truth of what had happened. Yakov Smirnov, who had accompanied the treasures to Moscow and knew where they were stored, insisted that he should undertake this task. Getting there wasn't easy – with no seats on the train and drunk revolutionaries sitting singing on its roof.

However, the elderly scholar reached his destination. He visited the History Museum first where Prince Shcherbatov took him into the Novgorod Hall piled with boxes of paintings, drawings and engravings from the Hermitage. There were eight or nine bullet holes in the windows but the attackers had been shooting upwards and the bullets ricocheted off the ceiling without doing any damage. He went on to the Kremlin where the Hermitage treasures had also sustained no damage. His attempt to enter the Armoury was thwarted by new revolutionary bureaucracy – he was not allowed a pass. Colleagues who had been inside, however, assured him that all was well.

He despatched a telegram to St Petersburg saying 'All safe' but the telegraph office considered it of such low priority that it remained in a pile on the office desk and was never sent. Smirnov got back to the Hermitage in person on 24 November and the ten-day drama over the 'destruction' of the Hermitage treasures was put to rest. Lenin had already persuaded Lunacharsky to rescind his resignation.

Another fantastic drama also ensued and, for a few days, put the future of the great museum at risk. The imperial wine cellar was located underneath the Hermitage and, although the finest liquors had been removed to Moscow, the stock that remained was vast. According to Larisa Reisner, 'first of all, they blockaded it with piles of wood, then they walled it up with a single line of bricks, then two layers of bricks. Nothing helped. Every night somewhere a hole would be made and people would suck out, lick out and draw out everything they could. Some mad, bare faced passion for the sweet would attract to this forbidden wall one crowd after another. After that, they tried putting a machine gun in every hole that was made.'

Count Tolstoy was well aware of the danger and 'many times drew the attention of the powers that be' to it. According to his memoirs there were tens of thousands of bottles of wine stored there. Wine merchants had offered eighteen million roubles for the cache, he said, but it was impossible to get the wine out safely. One day, coming in to work, he found the Hermitage 'surrounded by armed sailors. Then I saw that from the gates of the Hermitage side of the Winter Canal they were carrying out a soldier who seemed to have drowned in wine. Broken bottles were lying on the frozen canal and puddles of wine that looked like blood stains on the snow. Thanks to my pass from the Commandant I could go through the sailors' cordon and I heard that during the night the Preobrazhensky Guards had broken down the doors of the wine cellar, taken bottles out into the street and broken them there. The guards who were called also began to break bottles and the wine spilt in the cellar was more than two foot deep . . . All night long, they drank, drank, drank on the embankment, firing in the air. When it was possible to surround them, they lowered pipes from fire engine pumps and started to pump it out into the river.'

Naturally enough in the circumstances, published accounts of what happened do not exactly coincide – apart from confirming, in every version, that a lot of soldiers, sailors and ordinary citizens managed to get very drunk indeed.

With hindsight, we would expect revolution to involve high drama and it is perhaps most surprising to find so much continuing as it was before. On the morning after the storming of the Winter Palace, the museum keepers and attendants reported for duty as usual – it takes time for a new regime to affect the minutiae of daily life. Then, on 23 November, Tolstoy and his staff decided to join the boycott of the Bolshevik authorities which had been launched by the civil servants in all government offices. Lunacharsky treated the boycott with forbearance and none of the existing staff was sacked. After a few weeks, it fizzled out and the Hermitage staff began, unwillingly, to work with the new Bolshevik authorities.

The correct balance of power between the attendants, as representatives of the proletariat, and the bourgeois, scholarly keepers was a problem that vexed all minds from March 1917 onwards. Yatmanov, the Commissar appointed by Lunacharsky, repeatedly urged the attendants to take over the museum. 'Workers' control' was one of the platforms of the Bolshevik party, and workers' councils (or soviets) were taking over the running of private enterprise all over the country. The Hermitage administration, in collaboration with that of the Russian Museum – of which Tolstoy was also the titular head – decided to send Lunacharsky a delegation. They argued that 'museums are not conventional administrative institutions since they deal with things of scholarly and artistic interest which demand very special training and a certain level of cultural development ... it would be very difficult to cut off administration from scholarship.'

Lunacharsky agreed that museums were a special case. 'He himself thought that there should be a kind of artistic parliament,' Tolstoy reports, 'with 400 elected members, half of which were scholars and half representatives of the proletariat.' In the event, nothing so ambitious came to pass. But three new bodies were set up within the museum: a Council, comprising the keepers and director, a General Meeting which included the same people plus 'all other educated service personnel and representatives of the young attendants', and an Executive Committee comprising the director, two people elected from the senior staff and three from the younger – which worked very well, according to Tolstoy, thanks to the participation of the doorkeeper, Shchastnev, who was expert at smoothing things over.

In June 1918 Yatmanov granted Tolstoy leave of absence to travel down to the Ukraine where he had an estate. 'I hoped I would return by autumn – I was not planning to resign. I could not hand my resignation to powers I did not want to recognise.' But while he was away Tolstoy received news of the death of the imperial family, which 'shocked me so much that I found that I didn't have the strength to have anything to do with the people responsible. Under the influence of these terrible events, I wrote to say that I would not return.'

9

The New State Hermitage

*I*t might be expected that a Communist state would feel bound to desecrate or destroy an elitist collection of art treasures put together by a hated imperial family that had just been overthrown. The very opposite happened in Russia. The Hermitage, from the first days of Soviet rule, was regarded as a precious repository of national culture which should be preserved for the enjoyment of the proletariat. 'Amongst the broad masses of the population,' Benois commented, 'and unexpectedly for many, there was revealed, if not genuine appreciation, then something like awe which saved our treasures.'

Among the avalanche of posters produced in the early days of Bolshevik rule, inciting the citizens to virtuous behaviour in every department of life, there was one which read:

> Comrades. The working people are now in full control of the country. The country is poor, financially devastated by the war, but this is only a passing phase, for our country has inexhaustible potential. It has great natural resources, but apart from them the working people have also inherited a huge cultural wealth, buildings of amazing beauty, museums full of rare and marvellous objects, libraries containing great resources of the spirit . . . Russian working people, be a careful master! Citizens, preserve our common wealth!

There was, of course, some looting after the Revolution but, in the circumstances, surprisingly little. Later, however, the government raided the nation's stocks of art treasures in order to earn foreign currency to pay for vital technologies and industrial equipment from abroad. There were two waves of selling, the first one in 1920–4, concentrated mainly on gold, silver and precious stones, and the second in 1928–31 which saw the dispersal of several thousand items from the Hermitage, including some of the greatest masterpieces of the paintings collection. On top of this the Hermitage was expected to supply the new Pushkin Museum in Moscow with a ready-made collection and the new republics began demanding the return of their heritage – the Ukraine alone prised tens of thousands of pieces out of the old imperial museum. And the 1921 peace treaty with Poland after the Civil War theoretically entailed the return of all works of art that had left Poland for Russia since 1772, whether they were in private or public collections.

The outflow of art could be described as a haemorrhage. The museum was compensated by a massive volume of new acquisitions – though nothing quite matched the quality of the paintings sold abroad or given to Moscow. The result was a radical change in the profile of the museum collection. On one hand, the Hermitage was given all the best art in public and private collections in St Petersburg, and only required to share a little of it with other Russian museums. This resulted in a major accretion of applied arts and the acquisition of some good pictures to compensate for devastating losses. On the other, the range of the collection was extended by opening three new departments devoted to Oriental art, Russian art and archaeology. Artefacts recovered from digs hugely swelled the size of the collection. By 1996 the museum owned three million objects compared to one million in 1916. The old, imperial Hermitage had focused almost exclusively on Old Master paintings and Classical antiquities; the new museum was a much larger institution with a broad, almost encyclopaedic, sweep of interests. It became the Soviet government's number one cultural showcase.

High visibility had its drawbacks. It meant that the museum was repeatedly tossed on waves of political cataclysm. At each stage in the great Communist experiment, life in the museum faithfully mirrored the political evolution of the country. It started with muddle and high ideals, suffered desperate shortages of food and fuel, struggled to cope with a collection hugely extended by nationalisation, was forcibly politicised from 1928–31, then robbed of many staff by groundless arrests and executions during Stalin's terror. One colourful product of the times was the museum's very own autocrat, Iosif Orbeli, director from 1934 to 1951, a mini-Stalin, though much less destructive. He was an archaeologist and specialist on the Middle East who had set up the museum's Oriental Department in the 1920s. Hugely able and hugely ambitious, Orbeli was emotionally unbalanced, often indulging in wild rages. But he also had brilliance and charm which resulted in romantic liaisons with a succession of female curators. He had five official wives but Camilla Trever, the curator of Sassanian and Graeco-Bactrian art – whom he never married – remained his faithful mistress and collaborator throughout his long and distinguished career. She is said to have been very beautiful but was a rather pedestrian scholar.

Some vivid vignettes of the struggles of museum life in the 1920s and early 1930s are provided by the memoirs of a curator from the Paintings Department called Tatiana Tchernavin, who fell foul of the Party and the police and made her escape to the West in 1932. While her account (published in 1933) is anti-Communist to an unbalanced degree, reflecting her own terrible experiences of mental and physical torture, she provides a perspective on the period that no one who remained in Russia would have dared to express. 'To understand what it meant to work in a museum in the U.S.S.R.,' she wrote, 'it must be remembered that on the one hand, the museums were so rich in art treasures and so interesting that it was impossible not to be enthusiastic about the wealth of new material and new avenues of work opening up before one at every step; on the other hand, the Soviet Government, though apparently anxious to preserve them, was really their chief enemy. It was ready at any moment to give away or sell everything they contained and to imprison or exile the curators for the least attempt to resist this.'

Despite the cataclysms that affected the lives of all Russian citizens, the period from 1917 to 1941 saw the establishment of the State Hermitage Museum, as we know it today – a mix of national gallery, museum of applied arts and archaeological museum housed in a series of magnificent palace buildings. On paper, the Winter Palace was handed over to the Hermitage in 1918 – though many other institutions moved temporarily into the palace and the museum did not get full use of it until 1958. A new Oriental Department was established in the 1920s, an Education Department in 1925, an Archaeological Department in 1931 and a Department of Russian Culture in 1941 – all of them grafted onto the existing picture gallery, antiquities collection, the Arsenal and Numismatics Departments. The process of change was evolutionary with no sudden breaks, though there were many painful periods for the staff of the museum. From 1917 onwards, the story of the Hermitage becomes, above all, the story of its curators, their trials and their achievements.

Before the Revolution curators were appointed by the Ministry of the Imperial Court which survived, almost untouched, through the six-month reign of the Provisional Government. Besides the Hermitage it ran the imperial theatres, the Archaeological Commission, the Academy of Arts, the former palace orchestras, the Kappelle – a chapel choir school attached to the palace – the stables, the library and the Winter Palace itself. Lunacharsky sent a twenty-two-year-old Bolshevik Commissar, Yury Flakserman, to take over the Ministry – he was initially simply ignored. 'In the Palace Ministry,' he later wrote, 'there was complete order. Everyone came punctually to work and scribbled away as if nothing had happened.'

The keepers were essentially a conservative bunch – the museum's reluctance to recruit young connoisseurs had been a source of much criticism before the war. Many scholars had come and worked for free – Benois had written a catalogue of the museum without being invited to join the staff. Oscar Waldhauer, the young scholar who had charge of the Classical antiquities, taught at the university during the day and worked at the museum in the evenings.

Waldhauer has gone down in museum history as the first promoter of a populist educational programme; education later became a major part of the museum's activities, with a department to itself from 1925. Waldhauer organised lectures for school children and workers after the Revolution, having agitated unsuccessfully for them to be introduced before 1917. Count Dimitry Tolstoy's memoirs, however, paint him in a less saintly light. He was the first person the attendants wanted to sack as they began to flex their muscles after the February revolution. 'He was still young,' Tolstoy tells us, 'a very serious scholar but liable to fire up, and very demanding of servants – which often gave rise to dissatisfaction.'

Tolstoy himself had come to the museum through the ranks of the civil service, at that time a highly structured organisation which employed virtually all the nobility. Born in 1860, he spent several years in the Ministry of Foreign Affairs and travelled widely before being recruited in 1901 by Grand Duke Georgy to help run the Russian Museum, of which the Grand Duke was director. Tolstoy was a friend of many artists and art historians and in 1909 became director of the Hermitage, while continuing to act as the Grand Duke's number two at the Russian Museum. He is regarded as having overseen a renaissance of activity at the Hermitage in the immediate pre-revolution years.

His deputy was Eduard Lenz, a knowledgeable but old-fashioned figure who had charge of the Medieval Department which also included the Arsenal. The picture gallery was in the hands of Ernst Liphart, already seventy but of high scholarly distinction. He is reputed to have been a brilliant mimic. Fluent in German, French, English, Italian and Spanish, his imitation of an international congress – which involved him leaving the room and returning in the character of a succession of delegates – was a famous party trick. Among the other important figures were Yakov Smirnov, the expert on Oriental silver, and Sergey Troinitsky, who was in charge of *objets de vertu*. Troinitsky was a chain smoker with encyclopaedic knowledge and a lively sense of humour, according to the affectionate memory of one of his students.

At the beginning of 1918 the keepers were relatively unemployed. They had a museum building but all the best of their collections were in Moscow and the Hermitage was closed to the public. They went to work on rescuing private collections, making inventories and using their expertise to identify what was of value and what was not. Initially their attention was claimed by the inventorisation of collections that Tolstoy had taken into the museum store for safekeeping, for instance the collection of Countess Sofya Panina, one of the leaders of the Kadet party who was arrested on 11 December as an 'enemy of the people'. The museum had charge of her Poussins, her Claude Lorrains, her Boucher, Ribera and Zurbaran. Until 1928 these, and other paintings and works of art from private collections, were listed on separate inventories. Thereafter, those that had not been removed for sale abroad were merged with the museum collection.

Meanwhile Lunacharsky's Commissariat of Enlightenment was setting up new structures for the administration of the arts from its offices in the former children's apartments of the Winter Palace. When Lenin moved the seat of government from St Petersburg to Moscow in March 1918, Lunacharsky chose to remain in St Petersburg where so many of his responsibilities were concentrated, pointing out to Lenin that he would need a reliable representative in the old capital. 'Things will be hard for St Petersburg,' Lunacharsky predicted. 'It will have to go through the agonising process of reducing its economic and political significance. Of course, the government will try to ease this painful process, but still Petersburg cannot be saved from a terrible food crisis or further growth of unemployment.'

The two years of civil war did, indeed, bring St Petersburg incredible sufferings. Yury Annenkov, the Constructivist painter and graphic artist who later emigrated to France, recalled: 'It was an era of endless hungry lines, queues in front of empty "produce distributors", an epic era of rotten, frozen offal, mouldy bread crusts and inedible substitutes. The French, who had lived through a four-year Nazi occupation, liked to talk of those years as years of hunger and severe shortages. I was in Paris then, too . . . No-one died of hunger on icy sidewalks, no-one tore apart fallen horses, no-one ate dogs, or cats, or rats.' Yakov Smirnov, the keeper who first published the Hermitage's incomparable collection of Sassanian silver, was among the museum employees who died of hunger.

Meanwhile, March 1918 saw two important innovations. On 25 March the special Commissar, Grigory Yatmanov announced at a General Meeting of the Hermitage staff that the government intended to hand the whole of the Winter Palace over to the museum – a decision which took forty years to implement. On 18 March, Lunacharsky set up a new Collegium for the Preservation of Monuments and Museum Affairs, recruiting Troinitsky and James Schmidt, from the picture department, to serve on the council as representatives of the Hermitage. The Collegium took over the role that Benois and Gorky's Commission had played under the Provisional Government – Benois and Gorky were also invited to join the board – and added to its portfolio responsibility for Vereshchagin's Artistic Historical Inventorisation Commission. Having nationalised the imperial collections, the new government urgently required to know what was in them.

The process of identifying and listing the nation's store of art works was extended in the course of 1918 by the nationalisation of great aristocratic collections, which meant further urgent calls on the expertise of the Hermitage staff. Then, on 5 October Lenin signed a decree on 'the registration, inventorisation and preservation of monuments of art and antiquity owned by private individuals, societies and organisations . . . with the purpose of preservation, study and the fuller acquaintance of the broad mass of the population with the treasures of art and antiquity in Russia'. This was a first step in the process of taking all private collections into public ownership; the decree required that they should all be registered and listed. The new law warned that objects could be forcibly alienated from their owners if 'their preservation is threatened by the carelessness of their owners, or as a result of their owners being unable to take the necessary measures for their preservation or in the case of the owners not observing the rules on their storage'. The formal nationalisation – or confiscation – of all private collections did not come into effect until 1923.

Art and antiques were pouring out of the country in the baggage of emigrating nobles and Maxim Gorky drew the new government's attention to this in May 1918. He wrote to Lenin quoting from the letter of a friend who had been in Stockholm where he said there were 'almost sixty antique shops trading in pictures, porcelain, bronze, silver, carpets and other objects of art exported from Russia. In Christiana I saw twelve such shops and there are many more in Göteborg and other towns in Sweden, Norway and Denmark.'

When it was discovered that the Princess Meshcherskaya was negotiating to export her family's Botticelli tondo, there was a crisis debate in the government's ruling Council of People's Deputies. Lunacharsky was told to 'develop in 3 days an outline of a decree forbidding the export beyond the borders of the RSFSR of pictures and all important artistic valuables'. It was drafted by the Collegium on Museum Affairs, with the help of Troinitsky and Schmidt, and required all shops, commission offices and individuals trading in art, including middlemen and experts, to register with the Collegium. The new regulations were signed into law by Lenin on 19 September 1918.

It was in his role as academic secretary to Lunacharsky's Collegium on Museum Affairs that Iosif Orbeli, the future director, first began to take an interest in how the Hermitage was run. It is probable that he got the job through the influence of the renowned linguist and archaeologist Nikolay Marr, whose organisational secretary and right-hand man Orbeli had become after graduating from the Oriental faculty of the university. Marr was much esteemed by the revolutionaries. The Archaeological Commission, whose offices were in the New Hermitage building, was converted into the Academy of the History of Material Culture under the directorship of Marr in 1919. When Orbeli attended his first meetings at the Hermitage, he is said to have sat next to Yakov Smirnov who had taught him at the university. Orbeli's contacts thus conveniently spanned the revolutionary and the conservative.

The body of keepers could not remain unchanged under these new conditions. In June they decided that it would be desirable to strengthen their hand by recruiting influential outsiders to their Council. At a meeting on 18 June they voted to invite three people to join, Mikhail Rostovtsev, an eminent archaeologist and expert on the Scythians (elected unanimously), Alexandre Benois (ten in favour, one against) and Sergey Zhebelev, the Professor of Archaeology at St Petersburg University and a Classical historian (eight in favour, three against).

Rostovtsev emigrated a matter of two weeks after his election – and was shortly followed by Tolstoy himself.

Tolstoy's departure left Eduard Lenz, the deputy director, in the hot seat when, to the horror of all concerned, the Futurist art historian and critic Nikolay Punin was appointed Commissar of the Hermitage on 1 August 1918; the Futurists were on record as favouring the destruction of all 'old' art. It was a bad month for Lenz. On 2 August the Collegium on Museum Affairs called for a radical reform of the Hermitage and on 15 August the museum received a telegram from Trotsky's wife saying that she intended giving the Hermitage collections to the Moscow Museum of Fine Arts. Lunacharsky had appointed Nataliya Trotskaya head of the Museums Department in the Commissariat of Enlightenment's Moscow office a few days before. Lenz endeavoured to orchestrate a mass resignation of keepers in protest at these moves but failed to carry his colleagues with him. On 23 August he resigned.

Troinitsky was now appointed acting director and, in order to satisfy the call for reform, it was decided to hold democratic elections for all curatorial posts. The electoral college was to comprise the existing keepers, as to one third of the vote, and delegates from St Petersburg's main academic institutions for the remaining two thirds. On 11 November the twenty-eight delegates duly convened at the Hermitage and elected Troinitsky director. At the same time Alexandre Benois was elected keeper of the picture gallery and formally joined the Hermitage staff. Ernst Liphart, the former picture expert, considered himself too old for the job and his assistant James Schmidt had nominated Benois.

It was specified that the appointments were for one year only, after which there would be another round of elections. The electoral college was an essentially conservative body and the Hermitage became a haven for leading scholars who had lost their role in society as a result of the Revolution. Fedor Notgaft had been a rich private collector and now joined the staff as Benois's principal assistant in the picture gallery. Alexey Ilyin, who had inherited his father's cartographic business and was a keen collector of coins, now joined the numismatic department, later becoming its keeper and the deputy director of the museum. Mikhail Dobroklonsky, a young lawyer who had reached the rank of 'privy councillor' before the Revolution, was taken on in the prints department; he subsequently became the museum's principal expert on Old Master drawings.

Orbeli himself was elected curator of art of the Muslim East in 1920, a post left vacant by the death of Yakov Smirnov. And his principal mistress, Camilla Trever, was recruited in 1919. Also a trained archaeologist, she had been working as registrar of the Imperial Archaeological Commission and was out of a job when the Commission was gobbled up by the new Academy of the History of Material Culture.

The appointment of new staff begged the question of what the museum was going to do in the aftermath of revolution. In August 1918 its future was threatened by the new ascendancy of the Futurists over arts policy, on one hand, and Mrs Trotsky's efforts to keep the collections in Moscow, on the other. These issues loomed large for about a year.

The Futurists effectively cashed in on a vacuum. Lunacharsky was still being cold-shouldered by the vast majority of the cultured intelligentsia and he welcomed the Futurists' desire to cooperate with the Bolsheviks, giving them charge of the Fine Art Section (IZO) of the Commissariat of Enlightenment. Punin later wrote: 'There are few people who knew and felt the loneliness of the Bolsheviks in the first few months.'

The Futurists' period of power was brief but wonderfully spectacular. Their poets and artists had already achieved a *succès de scandale* in 1913 by travelling round Russia on a 'Futurist Train' giving lectures and performances. They regarded themselves as 'revolutionaries' in the field of art; their credo embraced a passionate belief in technical progress and social change which they saw invigoratingly revealed by world war – the new, high technology of war, such as tanks and aeroplanes delighted them. In every field they tried to throw out old forms; poets rejected punctuation and grammar, painters embraced abstraction. Moreover, painting on canvas was old hat – they wanted it on the streets. On 1 May 1918 they literally 'painted' the city of St Petersburg to celebrate Labour Day. They decorated the most important buildings, bridges and embankments with red banners, multi-coloured proclamations, garlands of greenery and flags. Giant posters, painted in blazing colours, depicted noble soldiers and peasants.

Lunacharsky meditated: 'It's easy to celebrate when everything is going swimmingly and fortune pats us on the head. But the fact that we, hungry Petrograders, besieged with enemies within, bearing such a burden of unemployment and suffering on our shoulders, still are celebrating proudly and solemnly – this is our real achievement.' The celebrations included a performance of Mozart's *Requiem* in front of an audience of 7,000 at the Winter Palace, which Lunacharsky had recently renamed the 'Palace of the Arts'. Aeroplanes circled overhead. There were fireworks and a parade of the city's firemen wearing their brass helmets and carrying blazing torches.

In November, when the time came to celebrate the anniversary of the 'October Revolution', the artist Nathan Altman transformed Palace Square, decorating the central column with huge abstract sculptures and using 20,000 arshins (15,500 yards) of canvas to drape the Winter Palace and the other buildings with Cubist and Futurist designs. Meanwhile, inside the 'Palace of Arts' itself, Punin and the poet Vladimir Mayakovsky organised a conference for 'the wide working masses' on the theme 'A sanctuary or a factory?' Mayakovsky suggested that the Winter Palace should be turned into a macaroni factory. 'We do not need a dead mausoleum of art where dead works are worshipped,' he said, 'but a living factory of the human spirit – in the streets, in the tramways, in the factories, workshops and workers' homes.' He proclaimed a similar message in a poem titled 'Orders on the Army of Art' which was published in the November 1918 issue of the semi-official newspaper, *Art of the Commune*, edited by Punin. No wonder the staid museum curators shook in their shoes. Lenin, however, had also seen a copy of this publication and urged Lunacharsky to tone things down. And by 1920 Lunacharsky himself had lost heart with the Futurists. They had proved 'unacceptable to the masses', he wrote, 'although they showed much initiative during popular festivals, good humour and capacity for work of which the "old artists" would have been absolutely incapable'.

Punin's impact on the Hermitage turned out to be minimal – he gave up the role of Commissar in 1919. His best remembered initiative is the First (and last) Free Exhibition in the Winter Palace which opened on 13 April of that year. The idea was an exhibition without a jury or vetting committee – everyone was allowed to show what he or she liked. There were 2,000 works by 300 artists whom the catalogue listed in strict alphabetical order, making no distinction between them on grounds of fame. The nineteenth-century Wanderers were represented – there was even a work by Repin – alongside the Futurists and Cubists and the Hermitage Museum staff. Benois exhibited, as did two artists he had recruited to work in the picture department, Georgy Vereisky and Stepan Yaremich. Vereisky is famous for his portrait drawings of leading artistic figures of the 1920s, while Yaremich's lasting contribution to the Hermitage was a collection of Old Master drawings that he bought with an acutely discerning eye, mainly in Paris, before World War I. The artist who sent the most pictures to the Free Exhibition, however, was

Chagall with a total of twenty-four. He was also caught up in the Revolution, becoming Communist Commissar of art in the city of Vitebsk.

The Hermitage staff also managed to mount a major exhibition in their galleries before the collections returned. Its centrepiece was a group of pictures from the collection of Grand Duke Constantine whose family had lived in the Marble Palace up until the Revolution. At first uneasy about the ethics of working with confiscated property – in early 1918 Yatmanov told them they could take what they liked from the Marble Palace but they refused – Benois and Troinitsky had bowed to the realities of the new situation when they were told that the building was being handed over to the military. From that point onwards, they seem to have taken the view that moving art works from nationalised collections to the Hermitage was a valid means of ensuring their safety.

The exhibition, which opened on 22 April, six days after the Free Exhibition in the Winter Palace, contained pictures from various sources besides the Marble Palace: from Tsarskoe Selo, the country palaces of Gatchina and Peterhof, and from collections that Tolstoy had stored in the Hermitage for safekeeping. There were also some works of art recently purchased from collectors who were emigrating. Lunacharsky had managed to secure purchasing funds for the museum to use for this purpose – prices, of course, were rock bottom. The exhibition could be said to mark the beginning of the immensely complex transfer of private art collections to the Hermitage, and through the Hermitage to other museums and for sale abroad.

The Free Exhibition was only one of the many uses to which the state rooms of the Winter Palace were put during its period as Lunacharsky's 'Palace of Art'. Films were shown regularly in the Nicholas Hall and concerts were held in the Armorial Hall which had seating for 1,200 but could, at a pinch, accommodate 2,000. There were also lectures – the lecture on colour photography was so popular that it had to be repeated two weeks running. Yury Annenkov mounted a Futurist production of Leo Tolstoy's play, *The First Distiller*, in the Armorial Hall. 'The scenery was made up of multicoloured crisscrossing ropes,' he later remembered, 'slightly camouflaged trapezes, various swaying platforms suspended in space and other circus equipment, against a background of abstract blobs of colour, primarily in a fiery spectrum. The devils flew and tumbled in the air. The ropes, trapezes, and platforms were in constant movement. The action developed simultaneously on the stage and in the audience.'

In November 1918 the Palace was used as a dormitory for several thousand participants who came to St Petersburg for the Congress of Rural Poverty. It was discovered after the peasant delegates left that they had filled both the Palace bathtubs and many rare Sèvres, Meissen and Oriental vases with excrement. Maxim Gorky, despite his commitment to the Revolution, was among those shocked by this insult to the cultural heritage. 'This was not done out of need,' he wrote. 'The lavatories in the palace were fine and the plumbing worked. No, this hooliganism was an expression of the desire to break, destroy, mock and spoil beauty.'

In October 1919, as the Civil War raged within a few miles of the city, Yatmanov, the museums commissar, revealed to Troinitsky his plans for a Museum of the Revolution in the Winter Palace. This proved a more enduring obstacle to the Hermitage's takeover – it didn't move out until after World War II when changes in ideology, and the execution of many former leaders, had rendered its original displays unacceptable. Its first rooms were opened in 1920 on a very simple basis; the old apartments of Nicholas I, Alexander II and Nicholas II were opened, with their original furnishings, as an illustration of the regime which the Revolution had overthrown. Later there were rooms devoted to the Decembrists, to the revolutionary movements between 1840 and 1880, to the Shlisselburg prison, to Tsarist 'justice' and exile, to secret printing presses in Russia, and other vivid manifestations of the revolutionary process.

With so much activity in the old Winter Palace, the Hermitage staff were pressed throughout 1918 to reopen the museum. Lenz categorically refused, saying that the collections were in Moscow, but when Troinitsky took over he agreed to open the antiquities galleries, whose marble sculptures had been too heavy to move. The keeper of Classical art, Oscar Waldhauer, was anyway keen to have them open to show his students. Troinitsky's cooperative attitude was rewarded in September 1918 with an undertaking that the museum could take over the Small Hermitage, the riverside galleries of the Old Hermitage, known since the pictures moved out in 1852 as 'the Seventh Spare Part', and the Apollo Hall, which connected the Small Hermitage with the Winter Palace. Lunacharsky also backed Troinitsky in the battle with Mrs Trotsky, ruling that the Hermitage collections should return to St Petersburg, not stay in Moscow. Troinitsky's first victories soon proved pyrrhic, however – the First Free Exhibition was allowed to spill over into the Small Hermitage while the return of the collections from Moscow was again challenged in December 1918.

This time the keepers read in the newspaper that the Council of People's Commissars (Sovnarkom), Lenin's inner cabinet, had decided to open the crates of treasures from the Hermitage and other St Petersburg museums and put them on exhibition in Moscow. They rushed round to Gorky's flat on 5 December and with his help put together a telegram that was despatched to Lenin, with a copy to Lunacharsky, now also based in Moscow: 'Extremely concerned at the danger threatening the treasures of the Hermitage, Russian Museum and Academy of Arts in the Kremlin Palace,' it read, 'as a result of the exhibition idea which will mean the unpacking of the boxes without the observation of proper guarantees of safety. The council of the Hermitage has gathered in the home of Maxim Gorky and unanimously sends a plea that you prevent the organisation of the exhibition and do everything you can to achieve the return of the collections to Petrograd which is the sole means of saving the treasures.' It was signed by eleven senior keepers and Gorky himself.

The telegram did the trick, but moving the collection proved impossible owing to lack of transport or food for transport staff and in May 1919 Mrs Trotsky was at it again. This time the Hermitage Council discovered that she was planning to open a Museum of Western Art in Moscow based on the Hermitage collection. Troinitsky wrote a letter to the Moscow Collegium of Museum Affairs on 27 May conceding that some of the Hermitage collection might be shared with other museums but arguing that the whole of the collection must first be returned to St Petersburg and 'only after this can it be decided which parts of the collection are unsuitable to the Hermitage and can be transferred to other museums on the basis of an overall plan of museum construction'.

Troinitsky was summoned to Moscow to discuss the matter in person but was wily enough to know that his own class origins would tell against him. He asked Stepan Yaremich, the artist son of a peasant, and Vselovod Voinov, from the Engravings Department, who had been a lowly clerk before the Revolution, to go in his place – but the train was so full that only Voinov managed to climb aboard. He arrived in Moscow to find that a three-stage process had been determined on: first the controlled opening of the crates, second a Moscow exhibition and third a division of the spoils between Moscow and St Petersburg. He was shown the potential exhibition rooms and complained bitterly – the skylights were broken in the Museum of Fine Arts and rain could get in and damage the pictures. In any case, he said, the pictures could not be hung on its marble walls. Eventually Moscow seems to have realised that the exhibition could not be mounted without the collaboration of the Hermitage staff – which was not going to be forthcoming – and again the threat was lifted.

But the Civil War was raging and there was no way the collection could be safely moved. So in September 1919 James Schmidt was sent down to Moscow to check the condition of the pictures. It was on this occasion that Schmidt visited the Shchukin and Morozov collections and had the brainwave of asking for a share of them to compensate for any Old Masters that Moscow might demand from the Hermitage. He managed to get the official backing of Lunacharsky and five years later, in 1924, a swap was duly negotiated. On paper, of course, Moscow got a much better deal than St Petersburg but the principle of sharing the two great modern art collections was established which led, after the second division of the pictures in 1948, to the Hermitage gaining a superlative collection of turn of the century art.

The re-evacuation of the Hermitage collection finally took place in November 1920; it began on 17 November, the day the Civil War officially ended. Yatmanov had secured a special train with a battalion of guards – it was assumed that the train would have to stop from time to time to gather fuel, so the art works would have to be guarded from theft. Young keepers were sent down from St Petersburg to organise the packing, including Orbeli, but in a last-ditch stand Mrs Trotsky refused to supply lorries to move the crates from the Kremlin to the station. These had to be sent down from St Petersburg as well. They were filled by day but only driven to the station in the middle of the night, accompanied by an armed guard, to avoid robbery. The first cases arrived home on 19 November and a banquet was held in the Malachite Room to celebrate.

The Rembrandt room was opened on 27 November, the other Netherlandish paintings on 12 December and the Italian paintings on 19 December. On 26 December the pipes burst. Through the desperate fuel shortages of the previous two years, the palace had been unheated. In winter the temperature in the museum had been between minus two and minus eight degrees centigrade – the keepers had worn fur coats and gloves to work. But in preparation for the receipt of the paintings they had been allowed a special fuel supply so that the temperature of the galleries would not damage the art. The old pipes were not up to this unexpected warmth. The water which drenched the paintings in the

Italian room turned the varnish on the pictures milky but this proved easy to put right.

The Hermitage scholars were also busily involved with setting the newly nationalised palaces in order. Tsarskoe Selo, Gatchina, and Peterhof were the first to be opened to the public as artistic displays – the rarest, museum-quality works of art were subsequently transferred to the Hermitage. Pavlovsk was still lived in by the family of Grand Duke Constantine at the time of the Revolution and was only nationalised in 1918, at the same time as the great palaces of the old aristocracy. The palaces of the Stroganov, Yusupov, Shuvalov, Bobrinsky and Shereme- tev families, all with composite collections formed by several generations of art lovers, were converted into mini-museums. The Hermitage keepers were called on to arrange the collections for display but this was easily squared with their consciences since the works of art remained *in situ* and, should the political climate have changed and the former owners returned, they would have found their possessions intact. The keepers were also asked to sort the art collections found in private apartments abandoned after their owners' precipitate flight. A huge volume of material was brought to the Hermitage for storage and was inventoried there.

The Stroganov Palace was scheduled as a 'branch' of the Hermitage and Camilla Trever, the newly recruited archaeologist, was sent down the road to run it. In 1923 the Stieglitz Museum was also rescheduled as a 'branch' of the Hermitage – there was no place for rich private foundations in the new order – as was the Stables Museum which contained carriages used by the imperial family from the eighteenth century onwards. Between 1925 and 1930 the palace 'museums' were successively closed down and the collections passed to the administration of the so-called Museums Fund – as the Collegium on Museum Affairs had been renamed in 1921. The Hermitage and the Russian Museum were allowed to pick what they wanted and the rest went to the Museum Fund storage – they had two large storage depots, one of which was actually in the Hermitage.

The dismemberment of private collections was gradually followed by a parallel dismemberment of museum collections – the many specialist museums established with such idealistic intentions in the nineteenth century. The Stieglitz was closed and most of the contents transferred to the Hermitage between 1923 and 1942. The same happened to the museums attached to the Academy of Arts and the Academy of Science, the Society for the Encouragement of the Arts, and the Archaeological

Society. The collection successfully repatriated from the Russian Archaeological Institute in Constantinople – no mean feat at the time – was also dispersed. Between the mid-1920s and the mid-1930s almost all smaller institutions were closed down and their collections absorbed by the Hermitage, the Russian Museum and the Museums Fund – some items went first to the Museums Fund and were only passed to the Hermitage at a later date.

The maintenance and security of a multitude of small museums posed impossible administrative problems. Professor Mikhail Dobroklonsky, who was in charge of the museum in the former Bobrinsky palace before joining the Drawings Department of the Hermitage, used to tell his students horror stories about the uncontrolled thefts. On one occasion, when he was doing his rounds to check the collection, he actually found a thief hiding in a chimney.

The concentration of collections was also politically in tune with the times. Stalin was busy with his brutal collectivization of agriculture, whose advantage lay in replacing a multiplicity of small farms by large units responsive to directives from the centre. Clearly, the government's cultural policy could be more easily imposed on a few large museums than on quantities of quirky, individualistic institutions. And Stalin was looking everywhere for potential sources of foreign currency in order to pay for the industrial equipment that was vital to his 'five year plans' and the rapid industrialisation of the country. Works of art from the Museum Fund stores, and from the museums themselves, were sold on a massive scale between 1928 and 1932. The sales stopped when the Depression had effectively closed down the Western art market and there was no more demand for Russian treasures.

While the Hermitage gained a few church treasures and a large volume of art from private collections as a result of the Revolution there was a terrible outflow. The most damaging losses were the Old Master paintings ceded to Moscow which have turned the Pushkin Museum into a great picture gallery. The negotiations, as we have seen, began in 1918 and were not concluded until 1924. Between 1922 and 1924 Alexandre Benois and his colleagues in the Picture Department fought a rearguard action to avoid handing over major paintings. They managed to keep hold of the dazzling core of the collection but a total of seventy-eight paintings from the pre-Revolution Hermitage galleries were despatched to Moscow. Paintings from the old private collections of St Petersburg were also divided between the Hermitage and the Pushkin – notably the Yusupov collection. The Pushkin ended up with some 400

St Petersburg paintings. The Hermitage managed to argue that such generosity should be reciprocated and got around one hundred of the Shchukin and Morozov paintings from Moscow, including works by Sisley, Monet, Cézanne, Van Gogh and Gauguin.

Once Moscow's claims were satisfied it became the turn of Poland. Under the terms of the Russo-Polish peace treaty of 18 March 1921, a miscellany of Polish works of art which had been acquired by the Hermitage over the centuries were ceded to Warsaw. These included Bellotto's famous series of *Views of Warsaw*, with whose help the old city centre was reconstructed after World War II, a Rembrandt *Portrait of Martin Soolmans*, Salomon von Ruysdael's *Whitening Sheets Near Haarlem*, and the coronation sword of the Polish kings which had disappeared from the Wawel Palace in Cracow in 1795 and entered the Hermitage along with the Basilewski collection. The Poles also claimed Fragonard's *The Kiss* which the Hermitage had acquired in the eighteenth century with the collection of Catherine the Great's lover, Stanislaw Poniatowski. However, the Hermitage managed to retain it by offering the Poles a Watteau, *Polish Woman*, in its place.

Next, the various republics making up the Soviet Union wanted to develop their own museums and expected the Hermitage to supply them with exhibits. 'Beginning in 1932,' according to Mikhail Piotrovsky, the museum's present director, 'hundreds of paintings and objects of the decorative arts were transferred to picture galleries all over Russia, Ukraine, Belorussia, the Caucasus and other parts of the Union.' A particularly large volume of material was handed over to the Ukraine. Listed in the Acts of Transfer were 'tens of thousands of items – archaeological finds, gold and silver, paintings, Zaporozhian banners, documents, objects associated with the Ukraine and objects not associated with the Ukraine'. Most of them, Piotrovsky notes, were looted or destroyed during World War II.

The sufferings of the keepers were not confined to losing art works which they would have liked to believe inalienable Hermitage property. Political repression and the politicisation of art history began to invade the museum in the second half of the 1920s. Benois presumably saw it coming. He had been allowed extraordinary freedom to visit his family in Paris. In 1924 he duly returned from a long trip abroad but in 1926 he took leave of absence and never came back; he gave the key of his St Petersburg apartment to the curator Stepan Yaremich who visited him in Paris that summer and some of the papers which Yaremich rescued are now in the Hermitage archive.

In May 1927 Troinitsky was relieved of his duties as director as a result of a long and bitter struggle with Orbeli who was building his Oriental Department with single-minded determination and complete lack of consideration for the rights of other curators – but who managed nevertheless to keep on good terms with the authorities in Moscow. Troinitsky was subsequently arrested and sent into internal exile; the story of his tribulations will be told in a later chapter. From 1927 to 1931 he ran the Applied Arts Department and from 1931–5 he worked for Antiquariat, the iniquitous sales organisation which stripped the Hermitage of so many of its treasures. He was replaced as director, for a matter of nine months, by Oscar Waldhauer, the museum's specialist on Classical history. But Waldhauer was only classified as 'acting director' and was himself removed from power the following year, simultaneously resigning from the museum's ruling Council.

This was at the time when Stalin had been consolidating his power. In the spring of 1928 he staged the first of his 'show trials', charging fifty-three engineers from the Shakhty mining district in south Russia with economic sabotage of Soviet enterprises at the behest of foreign intelligence agencies and White émigré former owners. Despite obvious signs that several defendants had been tortured to extract 'confessions', they were found guilty and five of them were shot. Thereafter purges spread into every branch of society and most especially affected St Petersburg intellectuals. One group would denounce another, only to find themselves denounced by a new wave of activists.

After Waldhauer's resignation as 'acting' director in February 1928, five different directors were appointed in quick succession. None of them had anything to do with the museum – they were political activists and were presumably introduced in order to whip the old guard curators, with their dubious class origins, into shape. The speed at which they replaced each other reflects the ease with which party activists made and lost their reputations at this time. Some may have been repressed; the Hermitage has little or no information on their subsequent histories. 'The Marxist authorities did not last longer than six months,' Tatiana Tchernavin tells us in her memoirs. 'They were replaced by others of the same stamp; the learned experts who happened to come into conflict with them were dismissed from their posts or found themselves in prison.'

In the official history of the museum, the former director Boris Piotrovsky sets out some indications of where these men came from. German Lazaris, who was in charge from February to December 1928, was a non-party man from Moscow with no previous experience of museums, he says; he could have been one of the undercover police agents who were assigned specially sensitive tasks at this period, but not necessarily under their own names. He was replaced by Pavel Klark, who lasted exactly a year. Klark had exemplary qualifications as a revolutionary, having been sentenced to death by the imperial regime in 1906. The sentence was subsequently commuted to fifteen years' hard labour and Klark succeeded in running away to live in Japan and Australia before returning to Russia in 1917. In his memoirs, Piotrovsky unbuttons a little and adds that Klark was 'very ill, very short and unhealthily fat'.

Klark was ostensibly appointed with the job of injecting Communist ideology into the Hermitage display but he displeased somebody and was replaced by another outsider, Vladimir Zabrezhnev, who lasted just under two months. He in turn handed over in February 1930 to Leonid Obolensky, a literary publisher and party activist; the Hermitage archives contain a quantity of texts written to prove he had no connection whatever with the princely family of the same name. Obolensky had previously worked for the Ministry of Finance and is said to have been opposed to the sale of museum treasures which was going on at the time. He is the only one of the five short-lived directors whose subsequent fate is known. A sick man when he was appointed, he died in October 1930 and was replaced by his deputy, Boris Legran.

Legran was a military and political man who had played an important role in the Civil War. A member of the Collegium of the People's Commissariat for the Navy and of the Revolutionary Military Council on the Southern Front, he worked with the 10th Army on the defence of Tsaritsyn (now Volgograd) during 1918–19. In 1926 he was appointed ambassador to Armenia and took an active part in the Sovietisation of the republic. Piotrovsky clearly liked him. He describes Legran in his memoirs as highly educated, a wonderful organiser and very well dressed. Not so, according to Tatiana Tchernavin: 'A former Soviet diplomatist, who disgraced himself in the Far East by drunkenness and scandalous love affairs, he was made as a punishment, director of the Hermitage,' she writes. 'It certainly was a punishment for all the museum workers; he was very rude, and was hand in glove with the OGPU [the secret police].' Tchernavin's venom may reflect the fact that Legran refused to take her back on the Hermitage staff when she came out of prison.

When Legran was appointed deputy to Obolensky, it must have been on the understanding that he would subsequently take over from the sick director. And he proved to have exceptional staying power by the standards of the time – he remained director of the Hermitage for three years and ten months. It was during his term of office, in 1931, that the Workers' and Peasants' Commission of the Russian Federation arrived to check out the backgrounds of the Hermitage staff. Mass sackings were called for on the grounds of the curators' unacceptable class origins and contacts with foreigners. However, for some reason the authorities decided to be merciful and a good number were re-engaged.

The Hermitage still has a document listing the 'filth' of the museum: there were no White Army officers or imperial policemen, but there were seven officers of the old army, one factory owner (Alexei Ilyin, head of the Numismatic Department, whose family mapmaking firm was nationalised and transformed into the official State cartographers), five children of 'those who followed religious cults' (i.e. priests), four traders and merchants and fifty-five nobles. Piotrovsky records that the Hermitage staff were particularly angry about the dismissal of Ilyin who was 'old and very respected, partially paralysed, and stood holding up his head with his hand as he was attacked by young and energetic people'. He was eventually rehabilitated and returned to his post. All the accused were allowed to continue working in the museum until their appeals were heard

Tchernavin gives a vivid account of the Workers' and Peasants' Inspectorate's 'sifting' of the political acceptability of the Hermitage staff:

Factory hands were put on committees to investigate the 'trend' of the work and the suitability of the staff. Good old workmen who had been minding machines for the last 20 years, and uppish young men of the new type – machinists, electricians, stokers – were brought into laboratories and studies filled with books. They were shy, astonished, interested, and utterly at a loss what to believe. It all seemed to them rather like black magic. It was hard to decide whether all these books and those elderly, spectacled scholars were doing good or harm to the proletarian state.

It looked as though the sifting might prove a failure, and 'the class enemies' would not be detected. Then members of the OGPU and the Communist party confined the inquiry to the social origin of the intellectuals, their liking for the old regime and so on. So-and-so had once held a post in such-and-such a ministry, so perhaps he was a friend of the Minister. That man's wife was a countess or a princess by birth, or a general's daughter, or something of the sort. This one, though he was not a gentleman by birth, like the others, continued to write in the old spelling; and that man there said 'gentlemen' instead of 'citizens' or 'comrades'.

Such a method greatly simplified matters, and soon most of the experts and specialists received notices of dismissal 'in the 1st category' – ie, without the right to seek employment elsewhere . . . The sifting lasted for a couple of months. When it was over, the authorities, after bidding amiable goodbye to the bamboozled workmen, began to understand that the work of the learned institutions could not be carried on. There was no one to replace the highly-qualified specialists who had been dismissed, and so most of them were 'temporarily' left at their posts. But time had been lost, work interrupted, peoples' nerves wracked – all for the sake of a show of 'proletarian watchfulness'.

The 'sifting' of curators was accompanied by an ideological reorganisation of the museum exhibition on which Legran published a booklet in Russian and French in 1934 titled *The Marxist Reconstruction of the Hermitage*. The reorganisation was begun in the autumn of 1930 and drove Tatiana Tchernavin, and the more conservative curators, to despair. 'We were commanded in the shortest possible time to reorganise the whole of the Hermitage collection 'on the principle of sociological formations,' she writes.

No one knew what that meant; nevertheless, under the guidance of semi-illiterate half-baked 'Marxists', who could not tell faience from porcelain or Dutch masters from the French or Spanish, we had to set to work and pull to pieces a collection, which it had taken more than a hundred years to create . . . OGPU reigned supreme everywhere, either openly or through party committees interfering with all one did and striving to fit everything into the narrow and often senseless framework of party instructions enforced by utterly ignorant people. Everything had to be arranged on 'Marxist' lines. The way it was done can be judged from the following conversation between the members of our staff at the Hermitage.

'Do you know in what year feudalism came to an end?'

'In what year? What are you talking about?'

174

'We've just been to a committee meeting for furthering Marxism and have been informed that feudalism came to an end in 1495.'

'What nonsense is this?'

'Don't you see, it was the year of the discovery of America!'

'Is it supposed to have been the same in all countries, then?'

'The same everywhere. It was settled at the committee.'

'That's worth knowing!'

Another conversation, a month later.

'Have you heard the latest?'

'No, what?'

'Feudalism came to an end in 1848.'

'Another committee meeting?'

'Yes, and it's been settled for good. Keep it in mind.'

'And what about the discovery of America?'

'That's been cancelled. It's out of date, and to attach importance to it is "opportunism".'

'And how long will the decision of your committee be in force?'

'Till the next meeting, let us hope. Perhaps by then our Marxists will have read some other pamphlet.' This was how young Communists implanted Marxism, while old and intelligent experts helplessly watched them do it. Everyone who protested was immediately declared to be a class enemy and a 'wrecker'.

Tchernavin is, no doubt, unfair to those who were attempting to rewrite history at this time. What they were up to was very parallel to the more recent Western rewrites that have resulted from changed attitudes to the British empire or to race discrimination. But Russia's Marxist revision of history had special repercussions. James Schmidt, who had charge of the picture gallery, and Troinitsky, who was the head of applied arts, were both numbered among the 'class enemies'. The two departments were combined into a new 'Department of Western European Art' and a former guide from the Museum of Revolution, Tatyana Lilovaya, was put in charge of it.

In order to conform with the new Marxist approach to art, the galleries were rehung and a new display combining pictures and applied arts was opened. This proved a convenient way of masking the disappearance of several of the museum's best loved masterpieces which had been sold abroad. Even Hermitage habitués had no way of telling whether the paintings had left the museum or just been tucked into store.

Legran adopted a lofty tone in his 1934 pamphlet to describe how the Hermitage was brought into line with political orthodoxy. He calls the reconstruction of the museum 'an academic exercise based on dialectic materialism', and goes on to explain that 'the aim of the reconstruction of a Soviet museum is to present an exhibition whose themes are completely in tune with the ideology of the proletariat. Dialectical materialism, which uses Marx and Lenin's scientific methods to explain natural phenomena, society and their laws of evolution, reflects the ideology of the proletariat and exclusively determines the direction of academic studies in a Soviet museum.'

Since the picture galleries were the most important part of the museum, they were attacked first. French eighteenth-century art and artefacts were available in such abundance that it proved possible to put on a show that included every aspect of 'material culture' along with the pictures themselves. It opened in 1932 and was arranged in two sections, 'French art in the era of disintegration of feudal society and the bourgeois revolution' and 'French art in the era of industrial capitalism and imperialism'. Other new exhibitions included: 'Italian art in the era of disintegration of feudalism, 14th–15th centuries', 'German art at the time of the peasant war, 15th–16th centuries' and 'German art in the era of industrial capitalism'.

One positive feature of the 1932 exhibition was the showing of newly arrived pictures from the Shchukin and Morozov collections. Impressionist and Post-Impressionist painting was not yet considered too degenerate to show to the general public – that was a post-war phenomenon. Monet and Manet were shown as examples of 'art of the era of the highest development of pre-monopolist capitalism and the first attempt at a proletariat dictatorship', Van Gogh and Gauguin as 'art of the era of rotting capitalism' and Matisse and Picasso as 'art of the era of imperialism'.

Legran's pamphlet explained that the old keepers knew their subjects very well but had no understanding of 'history'. 'Most of them have now adopted the new ideology and the methodology of Marx and Lenin in their academic work', he wrote, but to achieve this it had been necessary to recruit new staff – Marxist historians, art historians and experts on literature – to work with the old guard and teach them new ways. The need for this was most 'urgent' in the department of Western European Art; 'the gallery of paintings and the applied arts section were the weakest parts of the old Hermitage in terms of academic understanding,' says Legran.

In contrast, Legran describes the Oriental Department as the most advanced: 'possibly the most remarkable department of the entire Hermitage'. He seems to have been overwhelmed by Orbeli's brilliance and to have adopted him as his scholarly mentor. Orbeli became his deputy in 1933 and when Legran left the Hermitage in 1934 to become director of the Academy of Arts – a demotion which was reputedly followed by a police investigation which led either to a heart attack or suicide (accounts vary) – he saw to it that Orbeli succeeded him as director. In *The Marxist Reconstruction of the Hermitage* Legran describes Orbeli's empire building with vivid enthusiasm.

In 1921, when Orbeli was a one-man department of Muslim art, there had been 7,000 Oriental items spread around various departments of the Hermitage. By 1934 there were 84,000 pieces; the new department had sought out Oriental treasures from the museum stores of St Petersburg and elsewhere in Russia. Legran lists the Institute of Archaeology, the Stroganov collection, the Bobrinsky collection, the Academy of Art, the Academy of Sciences, the Russian Museum. The academic studies of the Oriental Department, he says, were in advance of any other section of the museum and he remarks in a footnote that responsibility for this lay with 'I. Orbeli and the group of his students who were closest to him'.

Orbeli's achievement was, indeed, remarkable. The department he created had, within a decade, gained a worldwide reputation for its scholarship, despite the limited contacts between Russia and the rest of the world, and it still has curators with international reputations. In 1935 Orbeli played host to the Third International Congress on Persian Art. The Hermitage devoted eighty-four rooms to a dazzling exhibition drawn from its greatly expanded collections, as well as loans from museums in the Soviet republics of the Caucasus and Central Asia, from Iran itself, from the Louvre and from America. Orbeli and his beautiful curator of Sassanian silver, Camilla Trever, played host and hostess to a gathering of over 300 scholars drawn from eighteen countries.

Legran explains Orbeli's outstanding achievements on the grounds that the ideas of archaeologists are far in advance of those of art historians. 'The history of art,' he says, 'is particularly backward among bourgeois academic disciplines.' The reconstruction of the Hermitage thus came to put a special accent on archaeology. The Greek and Roman Department, where the presentation was previously almost exclusively 'artistic' was reorganised and, in 1931, a new department of 'primitive society' was established. 'The exhibition of primitive culture, stretching from the very origins of human life, to the beginning of property ownership, class structures and the nation state, must be one of the most essential features of the general structure of the Hermitage,' says Legran.

It is a curious fact of Soviet life that archaeology proved so much easier to analyse in terms of Marxist theory than art history. Nikolay Marr had shown the way in 1919 by persuading Lenin to back the establishment of an Academy of Material Culture to replace the imperial Archaeological Commission. 'Material Culture' is a perfect Marxist euphemism. In its name Orbeli was to launch the Hermitage's direct involvement in archaeological excavations, thus adding a new and important dimension to Hermitage activities. He took over from Legran as director of the Hermitage in 1934 and was to hold on to the job for almost two decades, notably defending the museum through the agony of World War II.

10

Art Sales

*I*n the spring of 1930 Tatiana Tchernavin received mysterious instructions from the short-lived Marxist director of the Hermitage, Leonid Obolensky. She was to stay behind in the museum after it closed at 6 p.m., take one of the masterpieces of the collection off the walls, Jan van Eyck's *Annunciation*, and hand it to an unnamed representative of the People's Commissariat for Foreign Affairs. She was then to rearrange the way the paintings were hung so that the public would not notice a gap. She was not permitted to ask for an explanation of what she did.

Negotiations for this painting's sale were already under way and the following June it was bought by Andrew Mellon, the United States Treasury Secretary, for $502,899. The *Annunciation* was one of the twenty-one paintings that he acquired from the Hermitage, including several of the stars of the museum collection. Mellon, a vastly wealthy banker, went on to found the National Gallery, Washington – he paid for the building himself and filled it with pictures. The Hermitage paintings have thus voyaged across the world to become the stars of America's national collection.

How much it matters whether great masterpieces of Western art are exhibited to the public in St Petersburg or Washington is open to debate. But the massive sales from the Hermitage collection that took place between 1928 and 1932 are still regarded at the Hermitage itself as a criminal act on the part of the Soviet government. It is an interesting reflection on Russian mentality that the senseless arrest of curators, followed by their execution or sentence to terms of hard labour, arouses less passionate comment. Such summary punishment, aimed at the protection of the State, has been part of the texture of Russian life for centuries and is, in some sense, regarded as 'normal' – while the art sales were definitely 'abnormal'.

In all, several thousand items were sold from the Hermitage collection, principally Western European works of art and coins. The collection of Classical antiquities was only marginally trimmed since there was little market for such works at the time, while most of the collection now curated by the Russian Department did not arrive at the Hermitage until 1941. The furnishings of the Winter Palace, which were not technically the property of the museum, were sold off in bulk since the Hermitage curators – shortsightedly – considered them of no historic interest. But it is the loss of great Old Master paintings that still rankles most. Roughly twenty-five world-class paintings were sold. The Hermitage collection was so rich that, without these paintings, it remains one of the two or three greatest collections in the world. To give some idea of the dent caused by the sales, one can look at the 1914 edition of Baedeker's *Russia*. The scholarly guidebook's introduction to the picture collection cites fifty-six major paintings by name, of which nine were sold.

The political background to the sales lies in Stalin's first Five Year Plan and the country's shortage of foreign currency. In his determination to build up Russia's industrial base and create the first economically viable Socialist state, Stalin was prepared to demand unlimited sacrifices from his people. Millions of *kulaks*, or prosperous peasants, were executed or shipped to Siberian labour camps for resisting collectivisation. So critical was the need for foreign currency that Stalin in 1929–30 chose to export grain and allow his own citizens to starve. Establishing new industries and buying new technologies took precedence over all other considerations. That he should not have spared the nation's museums is hardly surprising in these circumstances. It is almost more surprising that he should have ordered the cessation of sales from the Hermitage in 1932 just as he launched the second Five Year Plan.

The decision may have reflected a realistic appreciation of the diminishing returns of the art market, as much as sympathy for the museum. The Wall Street Crash in October 1929 led to the collapse of one major Western company after another and ushered in the Great Depression. The art market was not immediately affected by the crash, but as collectors became poorer its activity wound down until, some two years later, art became almost unsaleable. This meant that the Russians' auctions in the West of art treasures confiscated after the

Revolution became less and less successful. By 1932 their chief salesman was arguing against delay on the grounds that 'each extra day reduces the price of goods and makes a loss for the State'. The period 1928–33 was, therefore, an unfortunate one to choose for a major art sales campaign.

There was nothing new about the idea of selling art abroad to generate foreign currency – just the scale on which it was attempted during this period. Stalin's minions had long experience of selling confiscated treasures when they began to rob the Hermitage in 1928. Revolutions inevitably lead to the breakup of old collections, and the Russian one was no exception.

During the six-month reign of the Provisional Government in 1917, and the early months of Bolshevik rule, emigrating Russians sold art on a massive scale. In September 1917 the American who headed the Red Cross mission in St Petersburg wrote home to his wife:

Today I saw a beautiful Fragonard and some other pictures at the home of one of the princes, and I have appointments at several palaces shortly. Thus far I have purchased you a beautiful set of Dresden dishes . . . I expect to look at some Gobelins tomorrow, and will have an important collection of Russian pictures Wednesday, and it is possible that I shall find a French Gobelins set for you. Am only looking at the finest things.

Lenin quickly realised the possibilities offered by art and antiques and, after introducing export restrictions to stop private sales, began to sell confiscated art on behalf of the State. In the early years of the Civil War, when the Soviet government was not recognised by any of the Western nations, art, along with silver, gold and jewels, was bartered across the northern frontiers for tractors and guns. Since his trading partners would have been arrested had their governments realised what was going on, Lenin's art sales were treated as top secret. The first accounts of what happened were not published in Russia itself until the late 1980s. The art sales in the late 1920s were also surrounded by a wall of silence although they were legal in terms of international law. Lenin and his successors did not want their citizens to know that the nation's cultural heritage was being sacrificed.

The government's official position can be gauged from a publicity booklet of 1967: 'From the first days of the victory of the Great October Socialist Revolution, the Soviet state paid immense attention to the preservation of historic treasures,' it stated. In fact, the beginnings of Soviet art sales stretch back to 30 December 1918 when the Commissariat of Trade and Industry put Maxim Gorky in charge of an expert commission whose aim was to select and evaluate objects of artistic significance from the thirty-three depositories of nationalised objects in St Petersburg. These contained items collected from pawn shops, antique shops and the apartments of émigrés and Gorky was asked to create an Antique Export Fund from them. It is a curious task to have given to the nation's most famous author. His companion, the former actress Mariya Andreeva, also became an important player in the art trade. She was made a Commissar of Gorky's Expert Commission in July 1919 and in 1921 she was sent to Berlin to set up a sales organisation there. Their relationship was over by this time and she remained in Berlin for almost ten years.

By October 1920 Gorky's Commission had selected 120,000 items, including pictures, antique furniture, bronzes, European and Oriental porcelains and Antique glass, whose value he estimated at more than a billion roubles. Lenin needed the money badly and wrote to the Trade Commissariat to 'insist on the extreme speeding up of this matter'. At the time, Gorky had eighty people working for him and Lenin now increased the number to 200. 'I consider it absolutely necessary to increase the expert commission and give them a special ration on condition they finish the work soon,' he wrote. It is characteristic of the harsh realities of the time that Lenin hoped to increase the productivity of the Commission by increasing the staff's food ration.

In February 1920 a second organisation, called Gokhran, was set up under the auspices of the Finance Ministry – Gorky was working for Trade and Industry – to collect and curate the national stock of items made from gold, silver and precious stones, a role it plays to this day. Gokhran itself was not a trading organisation but government trading organisations were allowed to take stock from Gokhran for sale abroad. The scale of its activities soon eclipsed Gorky's; gold, silver and jewels were much easier to sell than pictures and antiques. A massive calling in of the nation's privately owned gold and jewels was launched in July 1920; individuals were required to hand in all gold, silver, platinum and precious stones above a set ration per head. Private individuals had to hand in '(a) gold and platinum objects weighing more than 18 zolotniki per person, (b) objects from silver weighing over 3 lbs per person, (c) diamonds and other precious stones of over 3 carats per person and pearls over 5 zolotniki per person'.

A Latvian businessman who was employed as a consultant by the Moscow Currency Administration, Moisey Lazerson, has left a vivid description of what he found when first inspecting the Gokhran stores in 1923: 'Confiscated silver, gold, precious stones and pearls and sequestrated church property had been accumulated in the Gokhran in such enormous quantities as could hardly be conceived in Western Europe. I passed through the vast halls crammed on both sides up to the ceiling with all sorts of luggage-cases (trunks, baskets, boxes, satchels and so on).'

Lazerson also wrote about the mass destruction of confiscated church silver:

I came to a hall where I found a man engaged on the task of hammering off the silver binding from an old service book. I examined the book and found it to be a work of the seventeenth century. To my question how he came to be removing the binding from the book, he replied that he was doing it at the express command of the chief of Gokhran. He had been engaged on this task for months. Considering the very large size of the books and the fact that he had already hammered off a respectable number of them, a good deal of silver had thus been gained, in spite of the thinness of the bindings.

The sequestration of church art – monasteries had been closed in 1918 and other churches in 1929 – should also have been a source of enrichment of the Hermitage but, in fact, very little church silver was saved from Gokhran's melting pot. And icons only began to be rescued from closed churches on a substantial scale in the 1950s. Lazerson comments that 'The Administration of the Museums did everything in its power to sift from the huge mass of silver all that was most valuable from the antiquarian, artistic or purely historical point of view. The director of the Hermitage, Professor S. Troinitsky, arranged in the rooms of the museum an excellent exhibition of the confiscated Church silver which was qualitatively of a high level.'

Virtually everything in Troinitsky's exhibition was subsequently sold abroad but his initiative had one, small bonus for posterity – it was sold as antiquarian silver and not melted down. One exceptional piece remains in the Hermitage to bear witness to his battle with the authorities, a huge silver monument known as the Sarcophagus of Alexander Nevsky which came from the monastery church dedicated to the saint. Alexander Nevsky was a prince of Novgorod who won the territory around St Petersburg from the Swedes in the thirteenth century and died in 1263. He was declared a Russian saint in 1549 and Peter the Great had the idea of making him the patron saint of the Petersburg area, commissioning the construction of the Alexander Nevsky Monastery at the other end of Nevsky Prospect from the Admiralty. The saint's relics were brought from Vladimir and installed in the monastery in 1724.

It was Peter's daughter, the Empress Elizabeth, who commissioned the spectacular, pyramid-shaped sarcophagus, the largest silver monument in the world. It is made up of several pieces, a central pyramid-shaped construction some sixteen feet high, topped by angels holding inscribed shields, two pedestals to each side supporting arms and banners, two massive candelabras and a box-shaped sarcophagus ornamented with battle scenes in high relief and surmounted by a crown and a broken sword. A silver sarcophagus made in 1695, in which the saint's remains had been brought from Vladimir, was placed inside the new one. The monument is a magnificent example of Russian rococo and was designed by the court portrait painter Georg Christoph Grooth – not Carlo Bartolomeo Rastrelli, as Troinitsky was later to argue. It is made from sheet silver spread over a wooden carcase but, all told, contains one and a half tons of silver. Despite the discovery of new silver mines at Kolyvan, the treasury could not come up with enough silver for its construction for several years. Commissioned in 1746, it was not completed until 1753.

Gokhran's eyes grew very large when they lighted on it and St Petersburg connoisseurs had to battle to save it. The Hermitage archives contain a telegram sent on 10 May 1922 to Mikhail Kalinin, the nominal head of State (chairman of the All-Russian Central Executive Committee), with a copy to Mrs Trotsky at Narkompros. 'The State Hermitage and Russian Museum request urgent order stop destruction of iconostasis Kazan Cathedral and shrine Nevsky Monastery – monuments of world artistic significance.' It was signed by Troinitsky, Benois and Ivan Sychov, the director of the Russian Museum. The solid silver iconostasis designed by Andrey Voronikhin for the Kazan Cathedral was melted down but the telegram saved the sarcophagus.

At the height of the museum sales, the idea of melting the sarcophagus was raised again. By this time Troinitsky had been demoted from the directorship and headed the department of applied art – but he went back into battle, sending the following letter to the new director:

As it has been suggested that the Sarcophagus of Alexander Nevsky be melted down, I consider it my duty to express the following:

1 The Sarcophagus of Alexander Nevsky is an outstanding work of art of the middle of the eighteenth century and at the present time is almost the only monument of its kind in the world. It was made by a Russian master to a design undoubtedly from the hand of the famous architect Rastrelli.
2 On one hand, the Sarcophagus is a cultural historical monument of outstanding significance and, on the other, it is an effective tool for anti-religious propaganda.
3 In monetary terms it is not as valuable as is generally believed since most of the structure is made from thin sheets of silver laid over an oak carcase.

Thus, the financial return gained from destroying a unique work of art, which has become an integral part of our museum, could be a comparatively modest sum and, as such, can hardly be considered worthwhile.

The argument that this magnificent creation was 'an effective tool for anti-religious propaganda' was a wily move on Troinitsky's part in an era when Christianity was regarded as dangerous superstition and was being actively suppressed. The archives also contain the resolution of Comrade Saakov – whoever he may have been – dated 20 September 1930: 'Leave it in the State Hermitage.' The Hermitage, however, was required to supply other silver to be melted in its place; large quantities of coins and domestic silver were sacrificed.

In the early 1920s, trading organisations came and went, mostly in line with particular deals, but in 1925 the government decided to set up a central organisation through which all art exports would be channelled. It was called the Central Office for State Trading of the USSR for the Purchase and Sale of Antique Objects, or Antiquariat for short, and came under the People's Commissariat for Foreign Trade (Narkomvneshtorg). The key figure behind the museum sales was thus Stalin's Armenian friend, Anastas Mikoyan, who was Commissar for Foreign Trade from 1926 to 1930. The government also maintained foreign trade delegations in New York, Berlin, Paris and London which sometimes took a hand in selling, notably the New York agency known as Amtorg.

Since Germany was the first country to recognise the Soviet government, under the Rapallo Treaty of April 1922, Berlin became a particularly important conduit and Gorky's mistress, Mariya Andreeva, who had been sent there in 1921, played a key role in arranging art sales. Britain recognised the USSR in February 1924 and the other great powers followed in the course of the same year with the exception of America which stuck it out until 1933. Thus Andrew Mellon, the supreme guardian of the US economy, in his role as First Secretary to the Treasury, paid for his art purchases in pounds sterling in Berlin. Not surprisingly, he tried to keep them secret.

Major art sales began in 1928. In January Sovnarkom, Stalin's inner cabinet, issued a document titled 'Measures to increase the export and sale abroad of objects of art and antiquity'. The following year Trotsky was exiled and his wife lost her job as head of the Narkompros Museums Department. In the same year Lunacharsky himself was sacked as Commissar for Culture. Yatmanov, who still had charge of the Leningrad museums, was discredited. Effectively, all those in prominent positions who opposed the sales were removed.

The Hermitage did not go down without a fight. Reacting to Sovnarkom's demand that thirty million roubles be raised through the sale of works of art, Troinitsky launched into a new letter of protest:

> The very fact of mass sales, all of top quality objects, creates the impression that the country is in a catastrophic state and will lead to a desire to make use of this.
>
> The truth of this is shown by the offer from Mr Gulbenkian who wishes to purchase pictures for ten million roubles and put forward a list of eighteen of the best pictures in the Hermitage, worth on the most modest assessment no less than twenty-five to thirty million roubles. The open sale of some of them, such as Raphael's *Alba Madonna*, Giorgione's *Judith* and Rembrant's *Prodigal Son*, would undoubtedly lead in some countries to national subscriptions for their purchase, and would well exceed the sum of ten million roubles.
>
> Of the sum of thirty million, it is suggested that twenty-five million should be from the allocation of one hundred objects of a value of no less than 100,000 each, i.e. an average of 250,000 each. In Moscow and provincial museums only a few such objects can be found and thus the whole burden of this operation will be placed on the Hermitage, above all on its picture gallery.
>
> At the same time a reasonably precise assessment has shown that

the Hermitage has only around 115 pictures of a value of over 100,000 roubles and between twenty-five and thirty other objects of such value.

Thus the realisation of one hundred objects of such quality will result in the destruction of the Hermitage and reduce it from its place as the first museum in the world to the status of a store of second and third rate objects.

When he received no answer, Troinitsky recruited other, more powerful voices to fight for the cause. Among those who struggled to persuade the government against the sale were Sergey Oldenburg, the Secretary of the Academy of Sciences of the Soviet Union, and Nikolay Marr, the linguist, archaeologist and philologist who was given charge of the new Institute of Material Culture in 1919. Both of them were members of the Hermitage Council and had the museum's interests close to their hearts. Oldenburg's wife kept a diary which describes a visit they made to Moscow around this time:

Worst of all is the question of the sale of museum objects. Literally an orgy of selling, at the head of it all the Commissar for Trade, Mikoyan. On the first day he arrived in Moscow, Sergey had a phone call from Vladimir Ivanovich Nevsky who asked Sergey and Marr to come and see him in the Lenin Library [Nevsky was director]. He told them of the catastrophic state of affairs with the sale of valuables from the Hermitage, showing them in confidence the lists of objects intended for sale: five Rembrandts, Raphael, Correggio, and various other objects which Sergey could not remember. We must hurry and save them from this despoliation . . . From Nevsky, Sergey went with Marr to Litvinov, who is deputising for Chicherin. He is upset by the sales, but says that he can do nothing. From him Sergey went on the same matter to Enukidze, then to Kalinin. Kalinin is terribly against it, he knew nothing, this was done in his absence. He told Sergey roughly this: 'People who have wormed their way in are trying to make money out of this. We will get only kopeks from all these millions, compared to what we need.' He promised to do everything which depended on him. Lunacharsky is also against, although, of course, he has far too little influence.

By 1928 Lunacharsky's star had waned and in 1929, as Stalin began to purge the intelligentsia whom Lunacharsky had always supported, he resigned from Narkompros. But it is interesting that Mikhail Kalinin, who survived as head of State up to his death in 1946, did not have the power to dissuade Stalin and Mikoyan from selling off the Hermitage treasures – though maybe he helped delay the sale of major pictures. In October 1928 Oldenburg attempted a blitz on Party leaders, explaining to them the shame for the Soviet Union if the rest of the world knew they were selling their museum collections and the very modest financial returns that such sales could achieve. He wrote to Kalinin, to Alexey Rykov, chairman of the Central Executive Committee, to Nikolay Bukharin, chairman of Comintern and to Stalin's friend Avel Enukidze, then chairman of the Commission for the Support of the Academy of Science.

But it was to no avail. Antiquariat dispatched teams of 'experts' to pick out exhibits from the museum collection which they considered suitable for sale abroad. At the urging of the Hermitage staff, they concentrated first on the selection of duplicates and items whose sale would not substantially damage the collection. Karl Maison, the Berlin dealer in Old Master drawings, remembered working through the Hermitage collection making balanced piles of drawings – four Fragonards on the export pile, for instance, had to be balanced by four Fragonards on the pile that was to remain in the museum. Within the restrictions of the existing political situation, the staff seem to have fought to retain their collection as fiercely as they dared.

The Hermitage archives contain two letters of complaint of April 1929, marked '*Top Secret*', from Troinitsky, then head of applied arts, to Pavel Klark, the Party activist who was director of the museum from December 1928 to December 1929. Troinitsky says that the commission selecting objects for sale was only giving the keepers twenty to thirty seconds to explain why an object was necessary to the museum collection and continues:

(2) Since not one member of the commission is able to judge the necessity of any object for the Hermitage, and moreover none of them have the knowledge required to qualify the objects being looked at, to determine their date and place of origin, I am essentially the only expert in this matter and thus the presence of two to five members of the commission, of whom only one writes down what I dictate, is an inefficient waste of working time.

(3) At the present speed, which is the maximum possible, looking at up to 500 objects a day, bearing in mind that the Department of

Applied Arts has over 50,000 objects, we will spend around 120 working days on this matter, i.e. around four months, in addition to the two already past. And at the same time the result of this work will simply be to establish what, from all the objects included in the Section's inventories, might possibly be allocated for export.

In view of the above, I consider the haste of the transferral not only to be without good foundation, but also threatening to bring direct harm to the interests of the state, and of this I feel it my duty to inform you.

The battle between museum curators and Antiquariat was not restricted to the Hermitage. A 1929 letter from Viktor Lazarev, keeper of the Moscow Museum of Fine Arts – now the Pushkin Museum – to the head of Glavnauka, the section of Narkompros that dealt with educational institutions and museums, suggested 'the radical reorganisation of the staff of Antiquariat through the replacement of those employees who comprehend nothing of antiques and carry out one act of sabotage after another with those party comrades who would feel the deep and principled difference between trading in pickled cucumbers and Rembrandts'.

In the 1990 official history of the Hermitage Boris Piotrovsky, the former director, quotes from a letter the museum received from Antiquariat in January 1930 in which they demanded ' "superfluous" gold and platinum objects, 250 paintings with an average value of not less than 5,000 roubles each, weapons from the Arsenal to the sum of 500,000 roubles, Scythian gold "to a sum to be agreed with the administration of the Hermitage" and duplicate engravings'. Only the Scythian gold was denied them.

Almost every department still mourns losses from its collection. A two-volume book on the Hermitage silver collection was published by the keeper, Baron Ariny Foelkersam, just before the Revolution from which Antiquariat selected the material it wanted for sale – the lost pieces are neatly identified. For instance, only forty-six items from the famous Orlov Service – ordered from Roettiers in Paris by Catherine the Great for her lover Count Grigory Orlov – are left in the Hermitage collection. There were over 1,000 pieces before the Revolution.

The duplicates sold from the Print Department included the original set of Piranesi engravings which Count Ivan Shuvalov sent Catherine the Great from Rome and about which she wrote with such enthusiasm to her confidant Melchior Grimm. There are still plenty of Piranesis in the collection but Catherine's historic folios have been lost. Or again, most of the battle paintings commissioned by Nicholas I from contemporary Russian artists were sold off. Nineteenth-century painting was out of fashion at the time and the Hermitage curators, no doubt, felt that such paintings were easier to part with than earlier and more distinguished works – but a whole, historic unit has disappeared for good.

Now that they were preparing to sell on a massive scale, the Soviets turned to auctions rather than private dealers. The first two sales took place at the end of 1928, one at Rudolf Lepke's auction house in Berlin and the other at the Dorotheum in Vienna, both devoted mainly to applied arts and furnishings with only a smattering of minor pictures. The Lepke catalogue was a very grand affair, with many illustrations and an introduction by Wilhelm von Bode, director of the Kaiser Friedrich Museum in Berlin and one of the great connoisseurs of his day. It contained more than 400 items from the Hermitage and confiscated aristocratic collections. Local émigrés made a small splash by trying to stop the sale and some items were withdrawn on the orders of a Berlin court – but the ruling was subsequently cancelled by a higher court in Leipzig.

Despite the 'legality' of the sales, the prices were low. The Russians responded by pouring more and more material onto the market, sometimes identifying their ownership in catalogues and sometimes not. Lepke's auction house was the most favoured outlet – the firm had been working with Gorky's mistress Mariya Andreeva, since 1922 – but the Russians also sold through dealers such as Hugo Helbig in Munich, Gilhofer and Rauschburg in Lucerne, Boerner in Leipzig, Hase in Berlin and Kende in Vienna. Boerner sold the best of the Hermitage drawings and prints in lavish, carefully researched catalogues – frequently quoting from the compendium of Hermitage drawings, *Dessins des Maitres Anciens*, which the keeper Mikhail Dobroklonsky had published in 1927.

The contents of the Stroganov Palace, a 'branch' of the Hermitage from 1918 to 1928, were also sold at Lepke in Berlin on 12 and 13 May 1931. The Hermitage had been allowed to retain some special items but the sale was sensational – and the prices abysmal. Rembrandt's *Christ and the Samaritan at the Well* made $49,980, an *Adam and Eve* by Cranach the Elder $11,186, a Houdon bust of Diderot $6,188; the top price was $157,080 for a pair of Van Dyck portraits. The 256 lots, including fine French furniture, bronzes and sculpture, made only $613,326. Then the

Princess Stroganov in Paris claimed ownership of the collection and her nephew George Shcherbatov requested the US customs to seize any of the 'stolen property' that was shipped to America. The legality of the sale was, however, upheld. The customs wrote back to Shcherbatov to say that 'the Bureau is unaware of any provision of the law which would warrant the detention of the merchandise referred to unless it is brought into the US illegally. Your request, therefore, must be denied.'

Although they were prepared to sell the Stroganov collection for rock-bottom prices, Antiquariat held back from offering the great masterpieces of the Hermitage at auction. According to Oldenburg they were already slated for sale in 1928 when he attempted, unsuccessfully, to lobby the government against such a move. Indeed, the list of paintings with which he was provided included several masterpieces that have remained in the Hermitage, such as Rembrandt's *Flora* and Giorgione's *Judith*. Antiquariat had apparently realised that selling paintings of this importance required long and careful negotiations.

Armand Hammer, later chairman of Occidental Petroleum, and his brother Victor were the first Americans to go after the paintings. Neither had yet achieved fame or fortune but their father, Julius Hammer, who ran a small chain of drug stores, was a committed Communist and worked for one of the first Soviet trading organisations in New York, the Ludwig Martens Bureau, from 1919–20. When Julius became ill, the mantle descended on Armand's shoulders and he travelled to Russia where he set up a series of trading deals. In the later 1920s and 1930s, the Hammers secretly became the American agents for the sale of the Soviet government's stock of Fabergé jewels and other precious Russian baubles.

Towards the end of 1928, Armand and Victor received a mysterious letter from a leading New York lawyer called Max Steuer asking them to find out whether paintings from the Hermitage were for sale and, if so, to act as agents in purchasing them. They went to see the head of Antiquariat, a man called Shapiro, who pretended to be enraged at the proposal, according to the account they gave John Walker, director of the National Gallery, Washington. 'What!' he said to Victor, 'Sell treasures from our great Hermitage – ridiculous!' But then, he added, 'If your friends in America want to make offers we are obliged to submit them to the proper authorities, and then whatever happens, happens.' The Hammers understood the hint.

It turned out that Steuer was representing Joseph Duveen, later Lord

Duveen of Millbank, the most famous art dealer of his day – he had the simple insight that there was a lot of art in Europe and a lot of money in America and the two could profitably be put together. When Shapiro's promising hint was passed back to him, the Hammers received a cable asking them to negotiate the purchase of forty itemised masterpieces, including works by Leonardo da Vinci, Raphael, Van Eyck and Rubens, and offering a flat five million dollars.

This time Hammer took the offer to Anastas Mikoyan himself. And, according to his autobiography, 'Mikoyan, who knew the price of a button let alone a Leonardo, dismissed the bid out of hand, calling it ridiculous. "The Leonardo alone is worth two and a half million dollars," he said.' It was the Benois *Madonna* that was in play at this point. Hammer inaccurately describes it as 'even finer than the Mona Lisa hanging in the Louvre' but correctly notes that there was no Leonardo in the United States at that time, so 'the offer of the *Madonna* aroused huge excitement.'

Informed of Mikoyan's reaction, Steuer and Duveen apparently felt the picture was already within their grasp. Hammer received the following cable: 'Concrete offer on Leonardo da Vinci $2,000,000. If offer accepted will arrange irrevocable letter of credit and ask Bernard Berenson to go to Leningrad to seal up the picture.' Berenson was a distinguished American art historian and specialist on Italian painting who made a tidy income on the side by authenticating pictures for Duveen. But the Russians did not allow themselves to be parted from their Leonardo that easily. Nothing came of these negotiations. Quite why is unclear. It has been surmised that Antiquariat felt it could get better prices by dealing directly with collectors rather than dealers, but maybe Duveen's prices were just too low.

Next on the scene was Calouste Gulbenkian, an Armenian business-man who was a naturalised British citizen and head of the Iraq Petroleum Company. He is said to have helped the Soviets sell Baku oil on the Western market which would explain his friendship with Georgy Piatakov, Mikoyan's trade delegate in Paris. Gulbenkian was an avid art collector, with both knowledge and taste, who was interested as much in the applied arts as in painting. His private collection has now been turned into a museum and is one of the glories of Lisbon.

He bought four separate groups of art works from the Hermitage between 1928 and 1930. According to José de Azeredo Perdigao's book, *Calouste Gulbenkian, Collector*, the procedure that he followed was always more or less the same:

the negotiations took place in Paris between Gulbenkian and the representatives in that city of the Leningrad Head Bureau of the U.S.S.R. Gostorg, for the Purchase and Sale of Antiques – 'Antiquariat' – which had its headquarters in Moscow. From the legal point of view each sale was transacted in Leningrad and the works of art named in the contract were handed over through the Berlin Customs, on payment by means of bankers' drafts in sterling, made out to the U.S.S.R. Commercial Representative in France. Before the actual purchase Gulbenkian would send trustworthy experts to Russia, with instructions to go where the works of art were stored, to identify them, to examine their state of preservation, and finally to supervise the packing. When the objects arrived in Berlin to be handed over against the exchange of documents, they were again examined for identification and freedom from damage. Only then were they sent on to Paris.

On his first 'fishing trip' Gulbenkian acquired twenty-four pieces of fine French silver and gold tableware made by the top craftsmen of the late eighteenth and early nineteenth century: François-Thomas Germain, Jacques-Nicolas Roettiers, Jean-Baptiste-Claude Odiot, besides two pictures by Hubert Robert, both depicting the creation of the royal gardens at Versailles, a painting of the *Annunciation* by the rare fifteenth-century Flemish master Dieric Bouts and a Louis XVI writing table by Jean-Henri Riesener. On Sergey Ol'denburg's list of Hermitage paintings slated for sale, the Bouts alone had been valued at 500,000 roubles but Gulbenkian got the lot for £54,000.

The second purchase comprised another fifteen superb pieces of silver, valued at £100,000, and a Rubens *Portrait of Hélène Fourment* for £55,000. The silver included two tureens from the Paris Service, made by Germain for Empress Elizabeth, and Gulbenkian's contract stipulated: 'As there are eight equally fine tureens in the Hermitage Palace Collection, you have agreed to sell me the two most beautiful ones and the ones in the best condition as to gilding etc.'

Then came Gulbenkian's biggest snip, Houdon's marble statue of *Diana*, two paintings by Rembrandt: his *Portrait of Titus* and *Pallas Athene*, a Watteau, a Ter Borch and a Lancret, all in for £140,000. The Hermitage archives contain a delightfully illiterate telegram confirming this purchase: 'Convey information re Antiquariat decision pictures Rembrandt Pallass Rembrandt Tatus Watteau Musician picture glass of lemonade Vamdondiana.' The Russian alphabet does not contain an H, which clearly presented the Antiquariat clerk with insuperable difficulties over identifying Houdon's *Diana*.

Antiquariat, quite rightly, got cold feet over this purchase. Gulbenkian realised something was amiss after the expert that he had sent to Leningrad was kept waiting for two weeks without any communication from the Soviet authorities. He stayed at the Hotel Europe, the best in town, where 'he ate little but at great expense, saw nobody and was unable to buy any French or English books or newspapers'. Gulbenkian brought this ordeal to a close by sending a cable and a letter to his friend George Piatakov who was now the governor of the Soviet State Bank, Gosbank, in Moscow and a very important person. In a letter dated 22 June 1930 the governor replied that the order to suspend the sale contract had been cancelled and that the agreement would be implemented although the Russian authorities believed the prices were too low. Gulbenkian wrote back:

You have been told that I have obtained the objects in question at ridiculously low prices. In virtue of the mutual and friendly trust which exists between us and of our past relations, I would never dream of imposing either upon you or your friends in such a manner.

The trouble is due to the fact that several of your Departments, who regard these works of art from the point of view of the 'savant' or custodian, are very reluctant that they should be sold. I heartily approve of their feelings and I have no doubt that a great many of these people are attaching to these works of art a value which, from a commercial point of view, is quite absurd. 'The proof of the pudding' as the saying goes, 'is in the eating'. Your friends, when you were in Paris, asked tremendous prices, but they afterwards discovered that they could not get a quarter of what they asked for many of the objects.

The Russians clearly suspected that they were being cheated by Western dealers and collectors – probably rightly so. The director of the Lenin Library in Moscow wrote Lunacharsky a 'Top Secret' letter towards the end of 1928, protesting at the planned sales, in which he points out: 'In March of this year museum objects to the sum of around 700,000 roubles were sent abroad. Of these only pieces to the sum of around 10,000 roubles were sold. This reveals that (1) the market in the West has limited capacity for works of art, and (2) that Western European antiquarians have agreed among themselves, coming together also possibly with Russian speculators, with the aim of lowering the prices of the pieces exported by us onto the market.'

Gulbenkian only managed to squeeze one more bargain Old Master out of the Hermitage, Rembrandt's *Portrait of an Old Man*, which he acquired for £30,000 in October 1930. However, the careful documentation of his purchases at the Gulbenkian Foundation in Lisbon throws interesting light on the secret despatch of art works from the museum. An expert he sent to St Petersburg to supervise the collection of one group of acquisitions submitted a report which contains this passage: 'As for the packing, it was quite a difficult and delicate work for we lacked tools and the men were not very expert. The workers used small hatchets with, I must say, great skill, but it was not easy for me as it was not possible to work during the day. The packing took place at night, by the light of ordinary candles.'

Gulbenkian's star waned in Moscow when Antiquariat discovered a new, more profitable, sales channel – leading indirectly to Andrew Mellon, First Secretary of the US Treasury. It is unclear whether Mikoyan and his associates knew where the paintings were going since Mellon did not personally intervene in the negotiations as Gulbenkian had done. He bought from the Knoedler Gallery in New York, which, in turn, was working with Colnaghi's in London and the Matthiesen Gallery in Berlin, with the latter handling the negotiations with Antiquariat. The Matthiesen Gallery was run by a brilliant and scholarly German art dealer called Franz Zatzenstein – he changed his name to Francis Matthiesen when he moved to London in the 1940s.

Matthiesen's gallery was in the Victoria Strasse and he rented rooms on the first floor to Karl Maison, the young drawings dealer who helped sort out which of the Hermitage drawings should be sold; Maison and Matthiesen later became partners. When he discovered the Hermitage paintings were for sale, Matthiesen had to find capital to buy them and turned to his friend Otto Gutekunst, who owned Colnaghi's, a Bond Street firm of Old Master dealers, for help. Gutekunst approached Charles Henschel who ran Knoedler's in New York. Henschel turned out to have a client with an unlimited bank roll – Andrew Mellon. The Mellon Bank had a stake in many of the largest corporations in America and Mellon himself was one of the richest men in the world. He was also a passionate art collector. He had begun collecting Old Masters in the early 1920s under the guidance of Henry Clay Frick, founder of New York's Frick Collection.

Henschel's reaction to Gutekunst's suggestion is recorded in a letter he wrote in January 1930 to his own European representative, one George Davey:

> I told him [Gutekunst] that we were prepared to buy a number of these pictures for a good round sum, provided that we got the pictures that we wanted and not necessarily the pictures that they wanted to sell. My idea was that if we purchased about £500,000 worth, it would tempt them, and we could then get some other pictures on consignment from them. Zatzenstein has apparently put this matter up to Gutekunst.

By April 1930 the deal was beginning to bear fruit. Henschel had already taken delivery of Franz Hals's *Portrait of a Young Man* and two Rembrandts, *A Girl with a Broom* and *A Polish Nobleman* now in the National Gallery, Washington – for an outlay of $559,190 and the ongoing agreement with Mellon had been finalised. He was to act as financier for Knoedler's purchases from the Soviets and take first pick among the paintings for himself. A letter from Knoedler's confirmed the arrangement:

> It is understood that you have authorised us to purchase for you certain paintings from the Hermitage Collection in Petrograd, and that if you decide to retain them you will pay us a commission of 25 per cent of the cost price. In the event you do not wish to keep any of them, it is understood that we will sell them for your account, and pay 25 per cent of the profit on the price we receive for them. We have shown you reproductions of the paintings which we decided to purchase from the above Collection, and it is understood that we will acquire them at a price at which we consider they can be disposed of, should you not care to retain them, of approximately 50 per cent profit.

Henschel was excited and decided to visit St Petersburg himself. On board ship – he travelled on the *Olympic* – he received one of the first ever shore-to-ship, radio telephone calls. It was from Matthiesen's Moscow representative, Mansfeld, to tell him that the Soviets were prepared to sell Van Eyck's *Annunciation* for $500,000. Once arrived in Europe, Henschel travelled on to St Petersburg with his nephew, Gus Mayer, from Colnaghi's and Mansfeld from Matthiesen's. Like Gulbenkian's experts, they found themselves spending long hours in their hotel waiting for a communication from Antiquariat. Only Mansfeld could speak Russian and all he could find for them to eat was sturgeon, caviar and vodka.

A chink of light is thrown on the condition of life at the Hermitage by a story told by Henschel of how he offered a cigarette to one of the museum officials and was wistfully turned down. The official explained that unless Henschel was prepared to give a cigarette to everyone at the Hermitage, including labourers and guards, the acceptance of such a gift might very well cost him his job. Nevertheless, Henschel's team pulled off the deal of the century, obtaining an agreement for the purchase of twenty-five paintings for something over seven million dollars, twenty-one of them for Mellon.

It took another year to get the pictures out of Russia after a series of setbacks and delays. It had taken all of Matthiesen's wiles to make Antiquariat honour its undertakings and he clearly considered Henschel ungrateful. In a letter of early 1931 he told Henschel in his appealingly broken English: 'I quite agree that it is a tremendous sum you paid out, but you must not forget that you would have lost this business entirely not having your European partners and you also do not give care enough to the fact that this business is giving us such a lot of work, that we are more or less since we started it a branch of Knoedler's, eagerly proceeding in the art to perform and exquisitely display how to be successful in social communication with the Bolsheviki.'

A few of Henschel's paintings ended up in the Metropolitan Museum, New York, while the Philadelphia Museum managed, in 1932, to buy Poussin's *Birth of Venus* for $50,000 through Amtorg, and a few other museums successfully negotiated purchases. However, most of the major masterpieces from the Hermitage ended up with Andrew Mellon. As Treasury Secretary he had overall control of America's economic policy and it is not surprising that he kept his very controversial purchases secret. Not only was the Soviet government not recognised by America but 1930, the year he negotiated his purchases, saw fierce lobbying from the business community for legislation to prevent the Soviet Union dumping goods on the US market at bargain prices. The Smoot-Hawley Tariff Act of June 1930 imposed import duties on Russian goods and only by a paper fiction did Mellon purchase his paintings in April and May 1930, thus avoiding customs duty – most of them were actually delivered several months later.

Public knowledge of the Mellon purchases had to wait for a sensational court case brought against him by the Internal Revenue

Service for allegedly cheating on his tax returns. He had taken a tax deduction of over three million dollars in 1931 when he passed ownership of several Hermitage paintings to the A. W. Mellon Educational and Charitable Trust through which he intended to pay for the new National Gallery, but he had overlooked some of the necessary paperwork that would ensure this was classified as a charitable donation. Mellon had been forced to resign as Treasury Secretary in 1932 after the Democrats ousted the Republicans from the White House – he had served under three Republican presidents. He was compensated by being appointed British ambassador and retired to London where he hung his pictures in the embassy there. Then, in 1935, came the challenge from the Internal Revenue service.

Leading museum curators and dealers were summoned to give evidence on Mellon's behalf. William Valentiner, director of the Detroit Art Institute, characterised the Hermitage's *Alba Madonna* as 'one of the greatest pictures of Raphael' and Botticelli's *Adoration of the Magi* as 'one of the greatest masterpieces of the world'. Duveen told the court that Van Eyck's *Annunciation* was a bargain at $503,000. 'If Mr Mellon would like to dispose of it,' he offered, 'I will give him $750,000 for the picture.' He added: 'The Hermitage is no more the greatest collection in the world, it has gone to pieces. I do not see how a nation could sell their great pictures of that kind.'

In this Valentiner was coincidentally echoing Viktor Lazarev's January 1929 letter to the head of Glavnauka. After expressing his distress at the sale of eight pictures of major importance, including Van Dyck's *Suzanna Fourment* and Franz Hals's *Portrait of a Man*, both of which went to Mellon, Lazarev said: 'It is sufficient to sell another fifteen to twenty pieces of similar quality, for the Hermitage – which could be the central attraction for foreign tourists – to cease to exist as a collection of world importance. For it is clear that the significance of the Hermitage is based not on the quantity of paintings but on the quality of two or three dozen world masterpieces, of which eight have already been sold by Antiquariat.'

The sales did not, in fact, destroy the Hermitage but it was a close-run thing. In the event, neither of the Leonardos was sold, nor Giorgione's *Judith*, nor the two great Rembrandts, *The Return of the Prodigal* and *Flora*, all of which had been on the list of potential sales handed to Sergey Oldenburg. The Hermitage may have been demoted from 'the greatest collection in the world' to 'one of the greatest', but no more than that.

The bitter struggles within the museum which the sales generated are still treated as confidential. They set curator against curator, as some gave in and collaborated easily, and some did not. To save their skins and stay out of prison, curators were forced to help Antiquariat on the selection and cataloguing of items for sale. But few did it willingly. Troinitsky, who had struggled so long and relentlessly to protect the collection, actually worked for Antiquariat after he was sacked by the museum in 1931. His attitude appears to have been that he was better qualified than most to decide what could be sold and what couldn't. Vladimir Levinson-Lessing, the picture curator responsible for the present hang and one of the best loved scholars working in the museum from the 1920s to 1960s, is listed as a member of the Expert Assessment Committee of Antiquariat from 1928 to 1933. Grigory Borovka, a keeper in the Antique Department before he was arrested and shot, used the sales as a means of visiting his family in Berlin and explained to them that the items sent for auction were purposely miscatalogued in the hope that they would not sell and be returned to the museum.

Quite a lot of material failed to sell at the various German auctions and was returned to Russia. Sometimes Antiquariat gave it back to the Hermitage. On other occasions it was given to provincial museums. For instance, some of the 500 drawings from the collection formed before the Revolution by the artist-curator Stepan Yaremich, which he gave or sold to the Hermitage in the 1920s and 1930s, can now be found not only in Amsterdam and Stockholm but also in provincial Russian collections.

The sticking point came with Iosif Orbeli's new Oriental Department. Having spent a decade building up this collection by ardently searching every major or minor institution in Russia for hidden treasures, or even wrongly attributed pieces, Orbeli was not going to lightly hand over his trove to Antiquariat. According to a story told within the Hermitage, when the Commission came to select Sassanian silver for sale, Orbeli personally blocked the door to the storeroom and, holding up the key, threatened to swallow it if they attempted to enter.

Boris Legran, the Communist apparatchik who was then director of the museum, clearly fell wholeheartedly under the influence of Orbeli's fiery charm and supported his campaign with notable courage. An undated letter from Legran to Ivan Luppol, the head of Glavnauka, reads in part:

> I did not allow Antiquariat to draw up lists until I could clarify with Narkompros the basic question as to whether the extension of

Antiquariat's export operations at the cost of valuables from the Oriental Department – which alone confirms the world reputation of the Hermitage as a whole – is permissible at all.

I beg that you urgently put this question to Narkompros and the further bodies and achieve the necessary limit to the expansion of Antiquariat.

Until I receive your instructions, I shall continue to strictly follow the line I have already set, despite the fact that it threatens new complications with Antiquariat and perhaps another approach by them to the Regional Party Committee, this time with a complaint against me rather than Kapman, but I have no other line of behaviour at my command.

Legran's opposition to Antiquariat clearly went further than just protecting Orbeli's department. A letter, dated 14 February 1932, that he received from the chairman of Antiquariat contains an undercurrent of threat. 'With regard to the essence of your letter stating that the Hermitage does not accept Antiquariat's "ultimatum" I would like to say that no ultimatum has been or is being presented,' he begins and, after some argument, finishes:

It is totally understandable that the pace of work seen in resolving the question of letting us into the Hermitage stores to look at bronzes for allocation should not suit us at all and cannot suit us. We desire that the work on allocation should go quickly, energetically and with a full consciousness that each extra day reduces the price of the goods and makes a loss for the State.

If this our desire – in our opinion a totally valid desire – is qualified by you as an 'ultimatum' then we, as Bolsheviks, do not understand and cannot find an explanation of your attitude.

We feel it would be useful that the competent party organs should look at this question and establish whether or not our demand that the lists should be studied within five days is an 'ultimatum' or the most urgent necessity and part of the battle which the whole party is fighting for hard currency.

The final lifting of the threat to the Hermitage collection was engineered by Legran and Orbeli acting in unison. The idea was to convey a personal letter to Stalin, playing on the fact that he was a Georgian and pointing out that the treasures of southern Russia and the

Caucasus were under threat – his own heritage. Rather than writing to Stalin directly, as had been done by other friends of the Hermitage anxious to protect its collection, they had the idea of passing Orbeli's letter through the hands of a close associate of Stalin who also had roots in the south. Stalin's Georgian intimate, Avel Enukidze, who was an old friend of Legran's from his days as a Party activist, was chosen as the most promising carrier for the letter. And the strategy worked.

Stalin's answer was brief but to the point: 'Respected Comrade Orbeli! I received your letter of 25 October 1932. An investigation has shown that Antiquariat's requests are not justified. In this connection, the Commissariat of Foreign Trade and its export bodies have been ordered by the respective agency not to touch the Oriental Department of the Hermitage. I think that should take care of the problem.' It was written in green ink on a sheet of jotting paper which was enclosed in a plain envelope and passed back to the Hermitage through the Commissariat of Internal Affairs. Over the following months any works of art demanded from the Hermitage by Antiquariat were found to be 'Oriental' – carpets, porcelain, paintings. After some fruitless skirmishes, Antiquariat threw in its hand and demanded nothing more from the museum.

11

Archaeology

*T*he way in which archaeology came to play a major role in the life of the Hermitage after the Revolution is one of the quirkiest features of the museum's evolution. One of the important factors that encouraged this orientation was the Communist Party's efforts to rewrite history in support of the theories of Marx, Lenin and Stalin. There wasn't much that could be done with the history of post-Renaissance European art, apart from reclassifying it as 'art in the era of disintegration of feudal society' or 'art in the era of industrial capitalism'. Archaeology, however, deals with the reconstruction, on the basis of newly discovered artefacts, of the lifestyle of forgotten peoples and its findings could be massaged by the Soviet authorities to show that the evolution of Marx's dialectical materialism was inevitable – the main preoccupation of the 1920s and early 1930s – or that the ethnic superiority of the Slavs was established in antiquity – a patriotic theme brought to the fore by the threat of war with Hitler. From the 1930s onwards, the Soviet government poured money into archaeological expeditions on a massive scale while the Party hierarchy dictated, broadly speaking, what results should be obtained.

The Hermitage gained many unexpected rewards from this orientation. On top of its traditional role as a repository of Western art and Classical antiquities, it became the most important archaeological museum in Russia and one of the most important in the world. The staff were allowed to conduct their own excavations across the whole territory of the Soviet Union, at sites ranging in date from Neolithic times to the Middle Ages, as well as helping with digs run by other institutions. The high standing of archaeology also helped in the development of three new departments, the Oriental Department which evolved under the direction of Iosif Orbeli from 1920 onwards, the Department of Archaeology of Eastern Europe and Siberia, founded in 1931, and the Department of the History of Russian Culture which opened in 1941, just before the museum was evacuated to escape Hitler's invasion.

Another result of this orientation has been the preference for archaeologist-directors. After the turbulent succession of Party apparatchiks who directed the museum between 1928 and 1934, it was a relief for all concerned to have scholars in charge. For, despite the glow of official approbation in which archaeology basked, many good scholars chose to become archaeologists in the Soviet period because it was a field where genuine research could be undertaken without serious political interference.

Since the day that Iosif Orbeli took over in 1934, the museum has been run almost exclusively by practising archaeologists; the exception is the brief directorship of Vitaly Suslov, an expert on Russian painting of the Soviet period. Suslov was only allowed a twenty-one month interregnum between the death of Boris Piotrovsky in October 1990 and the appointment of his son Mikhail Piotrovsky, the present director, in July 1992. Orbeli, who was an expert on Sassanian art and excavated in the Caucasus, was succeeded in 1951 by Mikhail Artamonov, an expert on the Khazar and Scythian cultures. He was followed in 1964 by Boris Piotrovsky, who specialised in Urartu and Egypt, while his son is an Islamic scholar who has conducted his own excavations in the Yemen. The Hermitage was the Soviet government's cultural flagship and only archaeologists were considered reliable enough to run it.

The patron saint of Russian archaeology in the pre-war period was a crazy genius called Nikolay Marr, who was a member of the Hermitage Council and had a very direct influence on the museum's development. It was the Soviet habit to create heroes whose example could be held up to the nation. There were war heroes, heroes of labour – factory workers, farm workers – and in a similar spirit, Marr was built up by the press and radio as a hero of scholarship.

He was born in Georgia in 1864, the son of an eighty-year-old Scottish gardener and a young Georgian peasant woman. According to his biographer, B. M. Alpatov, Marr's father, who died when he was ten, could not speak a word of Georgian, while his mother could not speak English, and their lack of communication stimulated in their son a passion for languages, ancient and modern. He studied linguistics in the department of Eastern Languages of the University of St Petersburg, where he graduated effortlessly from student, to researcher, to professor and finally to director of the faculty. In addition to work of lasting significance on the grammar of Georgian, Armenian and other languages of the Caucasus, Marr gradually developed lofty theories on the interaction of language, culture and archaeology, most of which are now dismissed as bunkum.

It was his invention of the 'Japhetic' family of languages that led to his involvement with Soviet archaeology. Starting from the erroneous assumption that the languages of the Caucasus were not Indo-European in origin, Marr postulated a second family of languages with a common root in antiquity which he called Japhetic – after Noah's third son Japhet. This linguistic family grew steadily in size and cultural significance; Marr claimed the Basque language of northern Spain had a Japhetic origin, along with Etruscan and several of the languages of Southern India. He then needed to find a common origin for them in the dead languages of the ancient Caucasus, which led him to study Urartian inscriptions and attempt to decipher them; Urartu was a mysterious empire that flourished in Turkey, Armenia and the Caucasus around the eighth century BC. It was a short step from the study of inscriptions to the study of ancient cultures and archaeological remains. In the words of Boris Piotrovsky, the Japhetic theory 'was full of contradictions and totally brilliant guesses; it was essentially a hotchpotch of ideas, often incorrectly presented'.

Marr does not appear to have had any pronounced political views and was equally happy that his studies should be supported by the imperial academic establishment or the Bolsheviks. During the six-month rule of the Provisional Government in 1917, he and a group of colleagues drew up plans for a new archaeological academy which, after the Bolsheviks seized power, they presented to Lenin. Most of the intelligentsia were boycotting the Bolsheviks at the time and Lenin seems to have seen Marr's project as an opportunity to create a great new academic institution to serve as a flagship for the new era. By a decree of 18 April 1919 he launched the Academy of the History of Material Culture, which took over the role of the old Imperial Archaeological Commission and extended it. Marr was made its first director and, in 1924, was given the Marble Palace that Catherine the Great had built for Grigory Orlov as a headquarters.

The country's most distinguished archaeologists shifted across from the Imperial Commission to the new Academy which became an important institution with wide-ranging international contacts – until Stalin began to impose strict Party discipline on all walks of life in the late 1920s. Marr belonged to the old guard of pre-revolutionary scholars but he joined the Communist Party in 1919 and came up with a theory of cultural and linguistic development in pre-history which appeared to accord perfectly with Marxism. In essence, he claimed that peoples evolved from one stage of technological and cultural development to the next according to an inevitable process of revolutionary phase transitions which was not affected by migrations and cross-cultural influences. His postulation that the evolutionary process was the same for all the peoples of the world accorded neatly with the Marxist view of history and the internationalism of the Bolsheviks who, at the time, regarded world revolution as the next, inevitable development on the political stage.

From its inception, the Academy of the History of Material Culture worked closely with the museum. Initially it had its offices – those of the old Imperial Archaeological Commission – inside the New Hermitage building and later the two institutions shared many staff. Three directors of the Hermitage, Iosif Orbeli, Mikhail Artamonov and Boris Piotrovsky, were Marr's pupils and all three worked for both institutions. Orbeli was the first to be recruited by the museum – partly as a result of Marr's influence – but he continued to work at the Academy and, after the Academy's name was changed to 'Institute of the History of Material Culture' in 1937, was simultaneously director of the Institute and the museum for a period of two years (1937–9). Artamonov succeeded him at the Institute, directing it from 1939 to 1943, and Piotrovsky was director of the Institute from 1953 to 1964.

Artamonov and Piotrovsky belonged to the new generation of scholars who acquired their education after the Revolution. Their characters contrasted sharply with each other and with the flamboyant brilliance and aggression of Orbeli. Artamonov was the son of a peasant, and served the Revolution as a young man. He took part in the Soviet of Soldiers' Deputies during World War I and was sent to run a bank when its staff boycotted the new Bolshevik government. He began his archaeological studies as an adult student in the 1920s. Older Hermitage staff remember him as a great director who had the courage to ignore Party directives and who created an atmosphere of scholarship in the museum – a quiet man, a poet and a notable administrator who never lost his regional accent. Piotrovsky, in contrast, came from a family of soldiers and educators which had belonged to the minor nobility – his younger brother was denied an university education by the Bolsheviks on account of his class origins. As director of the museum he was open and friendly, more careful than Artamonov to retain good relations with the Party bureaucracy, but acknowledged throughout the length and breadth of the country as a great scholar and Academician. His good looks and eloquence, despite a pronounced stutter, made him a hit on TV.

In the early days of Bolshevik rule, Marr was constantly in and out of the museum. He was voted on to the Hermitage Council where, together with Sergey Oldenburg, the eminent Orientalist, he backed the appointment of Iosif Orbeli to the museum staff in the hope of strengthening its commitment to his beloved Caucasus. Orbeli joined the museum in 1920 to run a new 'Section of the Muslim Medieval Period', which changed its name in 1921 to the 'Section of the Caucasus, Iran and Central Asia' and, in 1926, became a fully fledged 'Oriental Department', in its own right.

Orbeli had studied under Marr at the University and became his close assistant in the years immediately preceding the Revolution when they worked together on a big excavation at Ani, in present-day Turkey. They made a strong team, with Marr playing the role of vague professor and Orbeli that of efficient organiser. They ran the only Russian archaeological expedition mounted in the course of World War I, following the Russian troops who had penetrated into Asia Minor and excavating at the site of the former Urartian capital, Toprakkale, on Lake Van in present-day Turkey. The hunt was on for the 'source' of Japhetic languages and Orbeli contributed by finding a stone stele with a lengthy inscription recording events in the reign of the Urartian King Sarduri II, dating from the mid-eighth century BC.

Another St Petersburg archaeologist came on the Toprakkale expedition: Alexander Miller, who was to run the Archaeology Department of Leningrad University after the Revolution and was also, briefly, a member of the Hermitage Council – he taught both Artamonov and Piotrovsky. Miller was one of the many archaeologists who suffered under Stalin's purge of the St Petersburg intelligentsia in the 1930s – almost all the archaeologists of the older generation were arrested at this time. Some were shot, others exiled or sent to the camps. Miller was arrested in 1933 and died in exile in Siberia a few years later. His crime was 'writing long drawn-out reports on things he had excavated', otherwise known as 'empiricism'. According to his accuser: 'empiricism is a convenient screen behind which you can hide whilst deviating from Marxism'.

His archaeologist brother, Mikhail Miller, escaped to the West where he set about publicising the sufferings of his colleagues. His book *Archaeology in the USSR*, published in 1956, paints a vivid picture of what was happening. He explains how the trouble began in the late 1920s:

> At numerous meetings young students who were members of the Komsomol, at the prompting of their Party cells, criticised from a Party viewpoint the concepts and individual works of the older archaeological scholars. The criticism consisted of direct attacks and overt accusations of being anti-Marxist and anti-Soviet. At lectures given in the university archaeological departments, Komsomol members among the students used to cry out, 'Take off the mask!' 'Show your true face!' 'What is your attitude to Marxism?' and so forth. The older professors and scholars were required to renounce publicly their old views, confess their errors and declare their loyalty to Marxism and the Soviet regime.

A turning point came in late 1929 when Professor Vladislav Ravdonikas, a local historian from Lake Ladoga who was well in with the Party, gave a report to the assembled members of Marr's Academy titled 'For a Soviet History of Material Culture' which, for the first time, criticised other archaeologists by name and attempted to set out how archaeological studies should be conducted in future. The term 'archaeology' was to be replaced with 'Marxist history of material culture', and 'bourgeois' classifications, such as Stone Age or Bronze Age, were banned. His published report set the tone for archaeology across the length and breadth of the Soviet Union. As a Party 'trusty' he was given charge of the department of Archaeology at the Hermitage – then known as the 'Department of Pre-Class Society' – from 1932 to 1935. The Department had been set up in 1931 by Marr's chief disciple, Ivan Meshchaninov, who was also well in with the Party and a 'Hero of Socialist Labour'.

In 1931 an All-Russian Conference for Archaeology and Ethnography was held at the Academy of the History of Material Culture and the Party workers took it upon themselves to organise an exhibition of Soviet archaeological literature. Mikhail Miller says that this was the beginning of the end for the old guard:

> Separate exhibits were set up for each of the principal non-Marxist

schools and trends in archaeology; over every exhibit there was a sign indicating the trend represented, such as 'creeping empiricism', 'bourgeois nationalism', 'formalism' and so forth. It was obvious to everyone that the authors of works so exhibited were doomed. And, indeed, arrests began, the consequence of which was the liquidation of almost all the old archaeologists and a great many young ones who were not able to or did not want to adjust themselves to the new requirements and failed to convince everyone of their devotion to the Party and government.

Boris Piotrovsky was arrested at a party thrown by fellow archaeologists in February 1935 and spent forty days in prison; he notes in his memoirs that the Hermitage took him straight back after this experience, while he had to take the Academy to court in order to get reinstated there. But he himself considered that he had had it easy: 'Conditions were much better than they were later on. We still got food, and notes from home, and cultural activists in the detention centre brought in bundles of books, fiction and a wide selection of other things, which they distributed round the cells.' The story of other members of the Hermitage staff who lost their jobs or their lives during the Stalinist purges will be told in the next chapter.

Together with the purges came a new scheme for the socio-economic periodisation of history which all historians and archaeologists were thereafter expected to use in their writings; it also provided the basis for Legran's *Marxist Reconstruction of the Hermitage*. Miller lays it out thus:

    I Pre-class society: (a) formation of human society; (b) pre-clan era; (c) clan matriarchal society; (d) clan patriarchal society; (e) stage of decomposition of the clan (transition of the clan to the village community).

    II Class society, slave-holding formation: (a) oriental, primitive slave-holding society; (b) developed, ancient slave-holding society.

    III Feudal system: (a) early feudalism; (b) developed or later feudalism.

    IV Capitalist society.

    V Classless society: (a) socialism; (b) communism. Communist society is the final stage of development and is not subject to further changes.

Very little field work or scientific publication was undertaken during the period 1930–4, when every surviving archaeologist was busily reinterpreting his previous work in terms of the new formation. Articles in learned journals were all devoted to the new orientation under titles such as 'Marx-Engels and the Basic Problems of Pre-Class Society' or 'Engels' Theory of the Origin of Man and the Morphological Peculiarities of the Skeletal Remains of Sinanthropus'. The Academy of the History of Material Culture published a volume entitled *Marx, Engels, Lenin and Stalin on Primitive Society*. Miller lists those archaeologists whose scientific papers were never subsequently accepted for publication. They include Sergey Oldenburg, the Orientalist and champion of the integrity of the Hermitage collections, and Oskar Waldhauer, the indefatigable curator of Classical antiquities who had defended his collection through the Revolution and briefly succeeded Troinitsky as acting director of the museum.

Nikolay Marr, whose principal theories coincided so neatly with Marxism, remained unmoved by the storms around him, though Piotrovsky records that a group of Communists in the Academy set up an organisation called the Linguistic Front which attempted to criticise him. It may perhaps be regarded as good fortune for the distinguished old man that he suffered a haemorrhage of the brain in October 1933 and died the following year. He was accorded a hero's funeral. His coffin lay in state in the Marble Palace and was carried to its permanent resting place in the Communist Square of the Alexander Nevsky monastery's cemetery – the place of honour at the time – on a catafalque draped in red flags, attended by a military guard and representatives of the government.

Relative peace broke out in the archaeological establishment in 1935. Stalin who had finally achieved the power of an absolute dictator, announced that during 1930–4 the Soviet Union had 'changed at the roots, casting off the guise of backwardness and medievalism . . . From a dark, illiterate and uncultured country, she became, or more correctly, is becoming a literate and cultured country.' And, as Miller explains: 'under these conditions a demand arose for the continuous growth and raising of the general level of education and science. The works of scholars were expected not only to be on a high ideological level but also to show a profound knowledge and use of factual scientific material. Learned degrees and the defence of dissertations, which had been abolished at the beginning of the Revolution, were reintroduced.' In this more scholarly atmosphere, the terms 'archaeology', 'Stone Age',

'Bronze Age', 'Paleolithic', 'Neolithic' etc. were allowed back into circulation.

The period from 1935 to 1950, despite Hitler's intervention in their lives, was something of a golden age for Soviet archaeologists. Finance for archaeological excavations and research was liberally available, especially for those whose work served a patriotic purpose by illuminating the illustrious past of the Russian people. The Party called for special efforts in the study of the genesis of the Eastern Slavs so as to prove by archaeological means that the historical Slavs, as well as their prehistoric ancestors, were from time immemorial the inhabitants and masters of the territory of the European part of the Soviet Union. But, as Miller points out, 'the task was difficult, not to say impossible, since this historical concept, dictated by political demands, did not find confirmation in the data of archaeology'.

Broadly speaking, archaeologists were prepared to adjust their findings to coincide with political requirements – in most cases it meant fairly minor compromises. But in 1950 Stalin suddenly upset the apple cart by personally attacking 'Marrism', the archaeological orientation that had previously been considered sacrosanct. There was a new flood of dismissals and arrests and archaeologists, who had been rigorously toeing the Marrist line, hurried to reconstruct their previous theses in the light of Stalin's 'brilliant' contribution.

Stalin himself contributed two long articles to *Pravda* on 'Marxism and the Problems of Linguistics' which excoriated Marr and all of Marr's disciples. He had made no public statements for the previous five years – on any subject – and his signed articles were greeted with an explosion of fervour out of proportion to their content. His biographer Isaac Deutscher notes that:

> Stalin, uninhibited by the scantiness of his own knowledge – he had only the rudiments of one foreign language – expatiated on the philosophy of linguistics, the relationship between language, slang and dialect, the thought processes of the deaf and dumb, and the single world language that would come into being in a remote future, when mankind would be united in Communism. Sprinkling his Epistle with a little rose water of liberalism, he berated the monopoly the Marr school had established in Soviet linguistics and protested against the suppression of the views of its opponents. Such practices, he declared, were worthy of the age of Arakcheev, the ill-famed police-chief of Alexander I.

Stalin's intervention was followed by a witch-hunt of 'Marrists' which inevitably affected the Hermitage – where Orbeli and Piotrovski, who had become Orbeli's deputy in 1949, were both Marr pupils. In 1951 Orbeli, now a seasoned autocrat who brooked no contradiction in the running of his museum, even from the Party, chose to tender his resignation over a minor dispute – a strategy for getting his own way that he had often used before. On this occasion, to his outrage, the resignation was accepted. Artamonov, then pro-rector of Leningrad University, was appointed to replace him, despite the fact that he, also, had studied with Marr and introduced 'Marrist' ideas into his writings. Artamonov's star was riding high at the time as a result of his important work on the Khazars, a forgotten people whose emperors, he demonstrated, had ranked in importance with those of Byzantium and the Holy Roman Empire in the seventh to tenth centuries and whom he presented as an important influence on the Russian state.

But he, too, was brought down to earth within a year of his appointment. In January 1952 *Pravda* thundered a denunciation of his work; it appears that the powers that be had suddenly discovered that the Khazars were Jews. 'The Khazar kingdom, far from promoting the development of the ancient Russian State, retarded the progress of the eastern Slav tribes,' said *Pravda*. 'The materials obtained by our archaeologists indicate the high level of culture in ancient Russia. Only by flouting the historical truth and neglecting the facts can one speak of the superiority of the Khazar culture. The idealization of the Khazar kingdom reflects a manifest survival of the defective views of the bourgeois historians who belittled the indigenous development of the Russian people. The erroneousness of this concept is evident. Such a conception cannot be accepted by Soviet historiography.'

In order to survive as director of the Hermitage, Artamonov had to grovel and admit to making terrible mistakes. A surviving letter to the secretary of the Leningrad Regional Party Committee makes this pathetically clear:

Having lost hope of speaking to you personally I want to explain my position in writing. I have heard that in the local Party conference you accused me not only of contributing to the diseased book of Professor Bernshtam [an eminent specialist on Central Asia], which is quite true and for which I am completely to blame, but that I am also at fault as a Marrist. It is about this second accusation that I want to beg you for clarification . . . When the work of I. V. Stalin over the question of Marxism in linguistics appeared, my mistakes immediately became clear to me and in my book on the genesis of the Slavs which was published in 1951, I tried to present the genesis and early history of the Slavic peoples in the manner I. V. Stalin had indicated.

Piotrovsky was also under fire. After Orbeli's departure, Artamonov had kept him on as deputy director but he was regularly accused of defending Marr and supporting out-of-date theories alien to Marxism. By diligently defending himself against attack, however, he managed to turn the tables and come out of the imbroglio holding a winning card. To understand what happened one needs to appreciate that the anti-Marrist witch-hunt was caught up with the rivalry between the Leningrad and Moscow branches of the Institute of the History of Material Culture. During the years of Marr's ascendancy, that is from 1917 until Stalin's articles in 1950, Leningrad archaeologists, who were mostly Marr's pupils, were undisputed masters in the field. Now Moscow was taking its revenge. Leningrad was demoted to the status of a branch of the Moscow Institute in 1951 and Moscow became the publishing base for the Institute's learned journals and the source of funds for excavations.

When Piotrovsky was called to the regional Party headquarters in the Smolny in 1953 and offered the job of director of the Leningrad branch of the Institute, his first thought was that this was a subtle plot by Moscow to get the branch closed down. 'I said that this would lead to increased criticism against me. They would close the section altogether, which was what the Moscow archaeologists were dreaming of,' he writes in his memoirs. 'But the Party secretary said that they would not be allowed to do that since the Leningrad Party organisation would not permit it and announced that from 1 May I must move to the Institute. The City Committee was not against my working at the Hermitage in parallel.'

Later, when Artamonov had offended the Party establishment by ignoring their dictats, Piotrovsky was, in his turn, appointed director of the Hermitage. His attitude to the Party bosses was more conciliatory and he managed to remain director from 1964 to his death in 1990 – though he came within a hair's breadth of enforced resignation in the early 1980s. His long reign naturally reinforced the importance of archaeology within the museum structure. And, despite all the political shenanigans, the museum's involvement with archaeology has produced results of lasting importance to world culture.

Piotrovsky himself brought to light the character and history of the ancient civilisation of Urartu whose remains had previously been ignored or misinterpreted. As he wrote himself in 1969:

> Time has dealt in different ways with the kingdoms of the past. The fame of some of them has resounded through the ages; the memory of men has preserved the names of their kings, their triumphs and achievements . . . But elsewhere the situation was very different. A kingdom which had known its period of greatness and then declined would sink into total oblivion; the achievements of its rulers, such of its buildings as were spared by the passage of time, and even its oral traditions would be ascribed to other nations, often enough to the very nations that had been its enemies; and it would disappear for many centuries from human consciousness. This was the fate of Urartu, a kingdom which developed in the mountainous area around Lake Van, on the territory of present-day Turkey, and became a powerful force in Western Asia between the ninth and seventh centuries BC. Then, early in the sixth century, the kingdom of Urartu was overthrown and soon afterwards forgotten, in the turmoil which accompanied the formation of new nations and new kingdoms in the territory which it had controlled.

Urartu's rediscovery can be counted the happiest consequence of Nikolay Marr's determination to find an origin for his spurious Japhetic theory of language. He and Orbeli had already excavated on Lake Van before the Revolution, searching for hieroglyphic remains of its language. Marr set his disciple Ivan Meshchaninov the job of compiling an Urartian grammar and he set his bright young student, Boris Piotrovsky, the task of studying its history. Piotrovsky's first love was Egyptology but in March 1930, he tells us in his memoirs, Marr came to him and said: 'Egypt was a long way off and there was no knowing when it would be possible for me to go there, but in the Caucasus, in Armenia, there was a whole unrevealed culture of one of the peoples of the ancient state, the Urartians. We knew of inscriptions on rock faces in Soviet Armenia. He said I should start seeking monuments of this culture in the Transcaucasus.' This brought Piotrovsky into the orbit of Orbeli, who was head of the sector of the Academy where those studying the Urartian language worked.

When Meshchaninov set up the Department of 'Pre-Class Society' at the Hermitage in 1931, Piotrovsky went with him as a junior researcher.

But he was soon transferred, at Orbeli's insistence, to the museum's Department of Antiquities to look after the miscellaneous collection of artefacts from Urartu and the Transcaucasus – there were some notable bronzes that had been bought from clandestine diggers in the nineteenth century. Through the 1930s Piotrovsky explored Armenia on summer expeditions searching for a site that offered opportunities for a major excavation. He finally settled on the mound of Karmir-Blur on the outskirts of Yerevan and the excavation was launched in a most promising manner by Orbeli's scholarly girlfriend and fellow curator, Camilla Trever.

In the summer of 1939, as Piotrovsky gathered his team to commence digging, Orbeli visited the site with Trever and the head of the Armenian Branch of the Soviet Academy of Sciences. The latter, gesticulating excitedly with a cigarette, inadvertently burned Trever's hand. She screamed, dropped her handbag and as she bent to pick it up noticed a broken stone with a cuneiform inscription. It fitted into a second fragment, found by Piotrovsky on an earlier visit, to make the name of King Rusa of Urartu, the son of Argishti, who reigned in the seventh century BC.

Piotrovsky was to excavate at Karmir-Blur for almost thirty years and the site, which turned out to be an important border fortress, gradually revealed its secrets. In 1945 an inscription was found on the hinge of a storeroom door which told him the settlement's name: 'The fortress of the city of Teishebaini, belonging to King Rusa, son of Argishti,' it read. Even then the excavators could not be certain that the old bronze latch had not come from another site. But in 1962 they found the foundations of a temple with two long cuneiform inscriptions. King Rusa, it was written, had built this temple in the city of Teishebaini, which had been a desert before he began his building. The inscriptions also recorded what sacrifices had been made to the Urartian gods and goddesses in honour of the building work – bulls, kids and sheep had been sacrificed to the gods and cows to the goddesses.

The excavations provided an extraordinary insight into the daily life of Urartu. The fortress had been abandoned in the sixth century BC after a successful night attack by the Scythians, following which they had set the settlement on fire. The surprise element of the attack meant that the burned remains of life had been buried without any previous tidying up. There was sesame oil cake on the floor of the oil press, traces of malted barley in a stone vat where beer was brewed, sawn-off pieces of horn –

and saws – in a room used for working stagshorn. There were traces of pests – weevils and ants – in the grain store.

There were also jewellers' and metal workers' workshops; the remains of plums, grapes, quinces, cherries and pomegranates; 400 vast pottery wine jars – sufficient to store 9,000 gallons of wine; 1,036 polished red pottery jugs to pour it out and hundreds of bronze cups to drink from. In a formerly dank storeroom there was a wasps' nest and the skeleton of a frog. And in an accidentally formed vacuum a flower that had fallen from a pomegranate tree was perfectly preserved – the petals had fallen but the rest was intact.

Thus Piotrovsky rediscovered Urartu and pieced its history together. The first tentative suggestion that such a civilisation had flourished had been made by a French scholar in 1871; in the 1890s the Russian historian Mikhail Nikolsky had travelled round the Transcaucasus collecting inscriptions; in the late nineteenth century treasure hunters had raided Urartian sites and sold their unidentified finds to the British Museum, the Hermitage and the Louvre; in the early twentieth century, Marr, Miller and Orbeli – and other teams – had excavated at Lake Van. Putting these, previously unconnected, elements together, Piotrovsky wrote the first history of Urartu in the cellars of the Hermitage, by candlelight, during Hitler's siege of Leningrad in 1941–2.

The most important discoveries at Karmir-Blur, however, were made after the war and Piotrovsky subsequently revised and extended his book. Most of his finds are now displayed in the Historical Museum of Armenia in Yerevan but one room in the archaeological section of the Hermitage is also devoted to artefacts from Urartu, including shields, swords, wine vessels, jugs and a remarkable bronze, half woman, half beast, which formed part of a throne dismantled by treasure hunters in the nineteenth century.

As museum exhibits, however, they are outshone by the remains of other civilisations. The most extraordinary, and visually exciting, archaeology galleries of the Hermitage contain the tomb furnishings buried with nomadic chieftains, priests and other high-ranking individuals in the valley of Pazyryk, in the high Altai mountains, between the fifth and third centuries BC – and some of the mummified chieftains themselves. The richly coloured textiles, felt, leather, furs, elegantly carved wooden artefacts and even tattooed human skin from these tombs had been frozen for over 2,000 years. It is a unique survival; elsewhere articles made in antiquity from such organic materials have crumbled into dust. Like a giant deep freeze, the permafrost at these high altitudes preserved them. The pieces, moreover, display great artistry and technical skill. They include a pile carpet which the tribal chief in whose grave it lay, neatly folded, must have obtained from Persia. It predates all other known carpets by more than 1,000 years but its artistry is as sophisticated as sixteenth-century survivals. The red, velvety carpet – 3,600 knots per $1\frac{1}{2}$ square inches – is framed by a file of grazing deer and a procession of horsemen.

It shares the honours in visual terms with a huge thirty-five square yards felt wall hanging of appliqué work made by the tribe itself and, no doubt, carried around to keep the draughts from the chieftain's tent. This depicts a female figure seated on a throne holding a flowering branch while a male rider approaches her; they are surrounded by lotus flowers, foliage and the stylised antlers of deer, all in rich colours. There are also wonderfully lifelike stuffed felt swans which some experts think were originally associated with the wall hanging, but others prefer to see as ornaments for a wooden carriage found nearby. The carriage is also a unique survival, a complex structure of wooden poles and leather straps – not a single nail was used – which was drawn by four stocky Mongolian horses that lay, preserved in the permafrost, nearby.

The nomadic tribes of southern Siberia, closely related to the Scythians who made their way westward to the Black Sea area, chose to bury their dead in the high mountains surrounding their summer pastures. The first attempt to excavate a frozen tomb was made in the 1870s but a serious study of them – and all the great discoveries – belong to the Soviet era. The first exploratory investigations were made in 1924–6 by Sergey Rudenko, who worked simultaneously for the Academy of the History of Material Culture and the Ethnography Department of Leningrad's Russian Museum but, at the time, he did not have enough money to open a frozen barrow. In 1929 he went back with his pupil Mikhail Gryaznov to explore the hilly Gorno-Altai region, where he had previously found a valley with a whole row of barrows, known to the locals as Pazyryk.

Rudenko, Gryaznov and a team of fifteen workers proceeded to open the first frozen barrow in the Pazyryk valley. It was virgin territory with grass up to their heads; there were no roads, so they travelled up there on horses, and there was no nearby village, so they had to carry their own food supply. When they started digging they found that the barrow was covered with large boulders which the horses had to drag off. The soil underneath was rock hard with permafrost. They boiled water at the edge of the site, threw it on the earth and dug as it melted.

Beneath they found huge timbers forming a room-sized wooden box for the burial. Clearly those who built the barrows foresaw the danger of robbery and attempted to make their tombs impenetrable.

They were right to fear that this would happen. All the Pazyryk tombs turned out to have been robbed in antiquity – before they were fully frozen. Greedy for gold, silver and jewels, the looters carried off the ceremonial weapons of the dead and, taking bodies from the half-frozen coffins, cut off a hand for a bracelet, a finger for a ring or a head for its torque. But clothing, cloth, leather, wooden artefacts and anything made from humble materials were left behind beside the desecrated corpses. The wooden tombs, it was found, were always surrounded by sacrificed horses which the robbers had not touched – chestnut horses, still completely frozen, wearing richly ornamental harness, carved from wood in swirling animal forms and plated in gold.

The process of archaeological discovery was then rudely interrupted by the political witch-hunt in progress in Leningrad. Rudenko was arrested in 1933 and sent as forced labour to help build the White Sea Canal – he didn't return until 1939. Gryaznov was arrested one year later and charged with being an Ukrainian nationalist. As he had never even visited the Ukraine, he was returned to circulation quite rapidly. However, Hitler's war was approaching and Rudenko and Gryaznov did not resume the excavations at Pazyryk until 1947. Rudenko, by that time, was working at the Institute of the History of Material Culture, while Gryaznov divided his time between the Institute and the Hermitage. He and the Pazyryk finds had been transferred from the Russian Museum to the Hermitage in 1941 when the new Russian Department opened. The two archaeologists excavated four more barrows between 1947 and 1949 and made discoveries which were to stir the imagination of the whole world.

During the 1940s and 1950s, however, the main thrust of Soviet archaeology was directed towards the study of ethnogenesis and aimed at a patriotic enhancement of the ancient peoples who had fathered the latter-day Soviet Union. This meant, on one hand, a determined and unsuccessful effort to link the Scythians to the Eastern Slavs and, on the other, extensive study of medieval sites in Russia and the autonomous republics. Far more archaeological effort has been devoted to the medieval period in Russia than in the West, where sites of this period only began to be excavated in the 1960s. The most remarkable medieval excavation run by the Hermitage, in collaboration with local archaeologists, is that of the city of Pendjikent in Tadjikistan. Situated on the border with Uzbekistan, some forty miles from Samarkand, the city flourished from the fifth to the eight century AD, after which its population was forcibly moved elsewhere.

The rediscovery of Pendjikent is the result of a romantic accident. In 1932 a shepherd grazing his sheep on the heights of the nearby Mug Mountain came across a basket of manuscripts. They turned out to be written in the language of Sogdiana, the civilisation which flourished in the area around AD 500 to 700. Leningrad archaeologists dug on the site of this discovery and unearthed a fortress and more manuscripts – which they identified as the archives of Dewastich, the last king of Pendjikent. He must have taken the manuscripts with him on his flight from the capital before being defeated and crucified by the Arabs in AD 722. This turned attention to the city of Pendjikent itself.

Joint excavations run by the Hermitage, the Institute of the History of Material Culture and the Tadjikistan Academy began in 1946 and are still continuing as I write, fifty years later. The city extends across the plain and includes a citadel, palaces, dwelling houses, temples, work-shops of many trades and shops. But its great glory is its murals. Each aristocratic house had a huge reception hall, measuring up to ninety-five square yards, whose walls were painted from top to bottom. The murals depict, on the one hand, aristocratic life in Pendjikent – banquets, apparently restricted to men, libations to the family deity, concerts, recitals – and, on the other, local legends and epic sagas hitherto only known from fragmentary allusions in Persian texts of the Islamic period.

The discovery of the murals has called into being a new Hermitage Restoration Department which specialises in the preservation of wall paintings. Some of the murals have been treated on site and others, brought back for painstaking attention in St Petersburg, are now on display in the Hermitage galleries. The expertise of these restorers has been equally useful in preserving the medieval murals that decorated the churches of the old city of Pskov in northern Russia. Hermitage archaeologists worked there over a forty-year period, in collaboration with local experts, to reopen the site of the so-called Dovmont City, in the centre of town, investigating its architecture and tracing the development of its streets. The excavation site has been turned into an open-air museum and fragments of its medieval murals are now displayed in the Hermitage galleries.

Artamonov, who became director of the Hermitage in 1951, had also begun his career by studying the medieval period. He worked on the frescoes of Staraya Ladoga, a medieval village some fifty miles east of St

Petersburg, close to the vast Lake Ladoga, out of which the River Neva flows down to the sea. Then he joined his professor, Alexander Miller's, excavations of Scythian sites on the estuary of the Don and acquired an expertise on the Lower Don, the Caucasus and the Steppes which stretched from the Bronze Age to the Middle Ages.

While Artamonov swung in and out of favour with the authorities like other archaeologists – he was demoted from director of the Institute of the History of Material Culture to head of the Bronze and Early Iron Age sector of the Institute in the mid-1940s – he remained one the grandees of the archaeological establishment. It was natural therefore that he should have been recruited to direct the most ambitious archaeological undertaking of the whole Soviet era – the investigation of the territory which was to be flooded by the building of the Volga–Don Canal.

The excavation's main focus of attention was the Khazar fortress of Sarkel on the lower reaches of the Don. In around 833 the Khazar king had sent an embassy to the Byzantine Emperor Theophilus asking him for architects and craftsmen to help build the fortress to protect his empire from invasion by the Norsemen, or 'Rus', as they were called in the East. The excavation yielded the first full story of the daily life of the Khazars, innumerable artefacts, and the remains of sixth-century Byzantine marble columns – useful building materials that had presumably been contributed by Theophilus himself.

This massive excavation was supported by the allocation of prisoners from the local prison camp to handle the heavy digging and earth movements – 600,000 prisoners worked on the Volga–Don canal. The atmosphere was unusually grim for an archaeological expedition. In the first year there were still houses for the visitors to live in; after that the houses had been cleared and the archaeologists lived in tents surrounded by control towers that watched for runaway prisoners. The main prison was some eleven miles away from the site but the prisoners helping with the dig lived in a barbed wire encampment next door – which they were marched into and out of in columns, night and morning. They were mostly 'politicals', a lot of them women who had been arrested for such crimes as holding back two pounds of grain from harvest fields so as to feed their own families.

The archaeologists and other specialists from Leningrad – there was a team of over one hundred – made friends with the prisoners and worked a nine-hour day beside them, starting at 4 a.m. in the morning and breaking at midday to avoid the extreme heat. For a couple of decades, whenever the museum's Archaeology Department threw a really good party, it would end with everyone drunkenly singing songs of the Gulag of the 1940s that they had learned on the Volga–Don expedition. When Artamonov compiled his curriculum vitae in 1953, he listed his two most important publications as *The History of the USSR from the Ancient Times to the Beginning of the Old Russian State*, vols 1–2, 1939 and *The History of Old Russian Culture: Works of the Volga–Don Expedition* (1958, 1959 and 1963).

Since pre-perestroika days, the artefacts recovered from Sarkel by the Volga–Don exhibition have been locked away in the Hermitage storerooms, mostly in a series of vast basement rooms on the Admiralty side of the Winter Palace. There are only two vitrines of Sarkel items in the public exhibition. No one wished to draw attention to this particular civilisation. The Khazars spoke Turkish while extracting tribute money from the Russians and – worst of all – converted to Judaism in AD 740. Moreover, Artamonov himself fell foul of the Communist Party establishment in 1964 and was sacked from the museum.

12

'Enemies of the People'

*D*uring the post-war years Sergey Troinitsky's role in Hermitage history was consistently underplayed. A pair of scissors was used to snip his image out of a group photograph of senior staff in the museum history by Sergey Varshavsky and Boris Rest published in 1978. Snipping people out of photographs was a standard Soviet technique for editing history. Troinitsky was the only director of the Hermitage to be arrested and prosecuted by the security police. He was found to be a 'socially dangerous element' and sent into internal exile in 1935.

He had been demoted from the directorship in 1927 following a ferocious battle with his successor Iosif Orbeli – Orbeli fought with most of the older staff of the museum on his way to the top. Troinitsky then spent four years in charge of the Applied Arts Department before being sacked by order of the Workers' and Peasants' Commission in 1931 and banned from holding any administrative post for the next three years. He was given a lowly job by Antiquariat, the government sales organisation that stripped the Hermitage of so much art in the 1920s and 1930s. Thereafter Orbeli blamed Troinitsky for the Hermitage sales – which, as we have seen, he actually fought relentlessly. Since many Hermitage staff owed their careers, or even their lives, to Orbeli, Troinitsky's reputation suffered.

In contrast, Orbeli's memory has been hallowed within the museum. He plays a heroic role in everything that has been written about its twentieth-century history, most especially on account of his defence of the Hermitage in the first terrible year of World War II when Leningrad was under siege. This is also somewhat misleading. Orbeli's fiery temper did much damage despite his many positive achievements and the brilliance of his scholarship. He caused chaos within the museum when he was building up the new Oriental Department in the 1920s and, in consequence, it was a deeply unhappy institution that was handed over to the sequence of Soviet apparatchiks who were appointed to run it – and impose Marxist attitudes – between the departure of Troinitsky and Orbeli's own appointment as director in 1934.

The battle between the two men helps to underline the confusion of right and wrong which is inevitable for those who try to live normal lives within a police state. In the extraordinary atmosphere of the late 1920s and 1930s in Russia, as Stalin launched his reign of terror, even playing office politics was dangerous for all concerned. And Orbeli played office politics with a single-minded passion in order to get his own way that accepted no restraint. On occasion, he played in the same spirit in the national cultural arena. And a number of those who got in his way ended up in prison or worse. When his protégés or friends were arrested, however, he did everything in his power to rescue them, repeatedly risking his own skin. Black and white, good and bad, are not applicable in these conditions. Troinitsky and Orbeli were both great men, great achievers on behalf of the museum which they both loved. Both were good scholars – but rivals.

Their fight was mostly to do with their contrasting characters rather than issues. In fact, there was only one issue – whether Orbeli's Oriental Department deserved to expand at the expense of other sections of the museum. Luckily for Troinitsky, the battle took place in the mid- to late 1920s, before Stalin's terror had really begun. Orbeli had nothing to do with Troinitsky's arrest in 1935 which, according to the latter's daughter, was merely on account of his noble birth. He was sentenced to three years internal exile in Ufa, an easy option. In the 1940s he lived in Moscow, where he had considerable difficulty finding work – his former qualifications did not count under Soviet rules – but eventually had a brief spell as chief curator of the Pushkin Museum where he built a new Applied Arts Department.

Troinitsky, born in 1882, was only five years older than Orbeli. He was thirty-five at the time of the Revolution while Orbeli was thirty. At that stage Troinitsky was the more obvious achiever. A man of means as well as noble birth, he had studied law and read lectures at Munich University while still in his twenties. In 1905 he founded the Sirius printing house which was to publish the two most important art journals of the period, *Apollon* and *Starye Gody*. He was caught up with all the leading figures of the Russian Silver Age and the renaissance of interest in the visual arts which they cultivated. He began work at the Hermitage in 1908 in the Medieval and Renaissance Section, moving over to *objets de vertu* in 1911. He ended up with an encyclopaedic knowledge of porcelain, silver and the other applied arts as well as being an expert on heraldry. Charming and popular, his election as director of the Hermitage in 1918 seems to have been a foregone conclusion.

All accounts are agreed that Troinitsky's perfectly tailored elegance was an important part of his image, along with the red hair and beard and the pipe which he smoked continuously – though he switched to chain-smoking cigarettes after he lost a lung to tuberculosis during his exile. His daughter Elena remembers how his elegant figure in a well-made grey suit fitted harmoniously into the rich, old-fashioned decoration of the Antiquariat building in 1934. Troinitsky himself enjoyed this fitness, she says, taking an aesthetic pleasure in it.

Like Orbeli, Troinitsky seems to have been dangerously attractive to women. Elena, born in 1913, and her elder sister Nataliya were his only official children. He left their mother, Varvara Timrot, directly after Elena's birth and she did not meet her father until 1934. His second wife Marfa was previously married to Stepan Yaremich, the artist and collector who became a keeper of drawings at the Hermitage after the Revolution. The two men were old friends – Yaremich had worked with *Starye Gody* – and his demotion to the Restoration Department in 1927 may have been a result of Troinitsky's disgrace. Even in the post-war years, colleagues remembered with affectionate amazement how Yaremich had loved his ex-wife so much that he would gather wood and carry it round to Troinitsky's apartment to make sure she kept warm.

By 1934 Troinitsky was married to his third wife Marianna, the daughter of the famous artist Viktor Borisov-Musatov. According to Elena, Borisov-Musatov was 'an outrageous hunchback and his daughter was an ugly person too. She had no children and a terrible character . . . She was significantly younger than Troinitsky.' Nevertheless, she followed him faithfully to Ufa and back to Moscow where they were not allowed official residence and slept on various floors – for a time they were allowed to camp in some outhouses of the Kuskovo Ceramic Museum. Mrs Troinitsky got a job stencilling script on shop windows while her husband taught at the Moscow Arts Theatre School where he had an affair and a child with the head of the Art Department, Alexandra Hohlova. He died in Moscow in 1948 and is buried in the corner of a cemetery reserved for the use of Hohlova's family – even finding burial space was difficult for him.

Orbeli's noble blood was even more ancient than Troinitsky's. The Orbeliani had been one of the pre-eminent families of Armenia since the twelfth century. But his style was more suited to a revolutionary age. He had a shock of untidy dark hair, a flowing beard and was habitually shabbily dressed. According to the memoirs of the weapons curator Mikhail Kosynsky, he used to make malicious jokes about anyone with pretensions to elegance. Friends remember the holes in his shoes during the war and the unconcerned way he marched around the Hermitage with wood shavings in his beard while its treasures were packed for evacuation in 1941. He is universally credited with a brilliant 'eye' for artistic quality but his scholarly interest lay in cultural history rather than aesthetics. Epigraphy was one of his central interests and he was even criticised by his admirer, Boris Legran, director of the Hermitage from 1930 to 1934, for laying too much stress on the history of language in the displays he created.

Orbeli, like Troinitsky, was a liberal who sympathised with the Revolution and wanted to play a role in shaping the cultural policies of the new regime. In 1919 he became the academic secretary of the Museums Department of the Commissariat of Enlightenment – the Bolshevik equivalent of the Ministry of Culture. But like Troinitsky, he never joined the Communist Party.

When Orbeli came to the Hermitage in 1920 to run a new department of the 'Muslim East', he had the personal backing of the two most important scholars in the new Soviet hierarchy, Nikolay Marr, director of the Academy of the History of Material Culture, and Sergey Ol'denburg, secretary of the Soviet Academy of Sciences. Both were members of the Hermitage Council and the new department was their idea – as was the choice of its first director. Ol'denburg himself was an Orientalist of exceptional distinction and was anxious to see the cultures of the East properly represented in the museum. In imperial times there had only been a section of the 'Classical East' in the Antiquities Department and Iosif Orbeli, then an ambitious young man, was given the task of building something bigger and better.

Orbeli's ambition took the form of an assumption that what he was interested in was more important than anything else in the world. With his fiery temper, he blasted those who stood in his way and ignored accepted norms of polite behaviour; there was soon pandemonium in the Hermitage. He sought out Oriental artefacts in every section of the museum and demanded, with threats if necessary, that they be handed over to him. With Oldenburg's loyal backing his fiefdom was extended in 1921 to the Caucasus, Iran and Central Asia and in 1926 was renamed the 'Oriental Department', thus taking in China, Japan and the great civilisations of the Far East. His patrons also got him appointed deputy director of the museum in 1924, from which position he could coerce reluctant curators to hand over their collections more effectively. It must be said, of course, that once the Oriental Department was established, it was only proper for Orbeli to take over responsibility for the Oriental possessions of the Hermitage – it was, rather, his manner of doing it that was at fault.

Orbeli's papers, now in the Academy of Sciences archives, paint a vivid picture of the chaos he caused while building the department. There is a letter of complaint from other members of the staff dated 28 April 1925:

> In recent times, the Director's Assistant I. A. Orbeli has increasingly frequently used a manner of address towards employees of the State Hermitage which is impermissible in a State Scholarly Institution. Such a form of address is not only insulting to the staff, but also extremely harmful to work, creating a nervous atmosphere which totally precludes the ability to work calmly. In view of this we most strongly request that you protect the staff of the Hermitage from such a manner of address and thus create the conditions necessary for normal productive work.

The twelve signatories included the Egyptologists Nataliya Flittner, Boris Piotrovsky's friend and mentor, and Militsa Matthieu, a committed Communist who was to become deputy director of the museum under Orbeli in 1941.

Grigory Borovka, the keeper of Helleno-Scythian antiquities, also signed the letter. He was to fight long and hard with Orbeli, who wanted Borovka's collection for the Oriental Department. In 1927 Borovka resigned from the staff claiming that Orbeli had manufactured complaints against him in order to remove 'a certain object' from his care to the Oriental Department. He was criticised for launching an 'unfair' attack on Orbeli and persuaded to withdraw his resignation. He continued to have charge of the museum's incomparable collection of Scythian gold until his arrest in 1930 – of which more later.

There were more complaints in 1926 that Orbeli was not scholarly and that he was always interfering in other people's work. So clamorous were they, that he resigned from the administration in protest – or maybe in order to position himself better for attack. Resignation was one of his favourite levers for getting his own way throughout his career. He also liked a show of heavy formality, pressing his interest at meetings of the Hermitage Council in measured periods: 'I addressed the Council's attention at a sitting on 21 January of this year [1927] to the fact that I did not want to deviate from the narrow framework I had set over the issue of the essential requirements of the Oriental Department, which I was raising not for the first time, and pointing out the department's difficult situation while it remains cut off from the very valuable and wide collections which should be under its control.'

He was asked to put his complaints in writing and penned a lengthy paper on 'The Unscholarly Structure of the Museum'. His argument was that the organisation of the museum should not be divided by countries or periods but by cultures. And, of course, everything relevant to Oriental cultures should be handed over to his department: the Medieval Department should hand over Mauritanian faience, the Armoury Oriental weapons, the Classical East scarabs and carved gems . . . The latter point was treated at particular length since the keeper had lent Orbeli a group of gems in 1923 which Orbeli had refused to sign for, and had then published as part of the Oriental Department collection, refusing to hand them back.

So important was his paper considered that a commission was set up to reconsider the structure of the museum. Its members included, among others, Marr, Oldenburg, Troinitsky and Orbeli himself. Troinitsky was quickly established as the 'enemy' of progress. In early February Orbeli wrote a letter in which he accused Troinitsky of deliberately setting a meeting to discuss the matter on dates when people from the commission, including himself, could not be present as they were at a conference in Moscow.

Around April Orbeli seems to have moved in for the kill. He adopted the simple strategy of sending a letter of resignation to the head of Glavnauka, the museum and university section of the Ministry of Culture in Moscow, rather than to the Hermitage administration, thus drawing the higher authority into the fight. He explained his action by saying that when he previously resigned in January 1926, Troinitsky tore his letter to pieces and threw it on the floor in front of his eyes. Troinitsky went to Moscow to try and make his peace, in which he appeared to have been successful. There followed a stormy meeting of the Hermitage Council at which Troinitsky called for a vote of confidence. But, as Orbeli thundered in yet another letter of resignation, Troinitsky would not leave the room and insisted on chairing the confidence debate himself. 'If S. N. Troinitski is not removed as director, and overall as head of the institution,' Orbeli wrote, 'I wholeheartedly request that you allow me not to be a witness of the disgraceful things taking place in the Hermitage, since as an employee I am in effect a participant in behaviour with which I am totally unable to come to terms.'

Troinitsky was duly demoted to director of the Applied Arts Department, and Oskar Waldhauer, the head of Antiquities, was made acting director of the museum. Orbeli's actions, however, caused such a storm of resentment among the staff that the following year a special commission had to be set up 'for Resolving the Conflict between the Scholarly Personnel of the Hermitage and I. A. Orbeli'. Letters poured in to the commissioners: 'Orbeli is personally arbitrary, although he has the habit of covering his form of behaviour with the appearance of formal justification', 'Orbeli who usually claims for himself the merit of strict observation of museum discipline, in reality is demanding and strict only with regard to others, and is himself a disrupter of the main rules of museum work', 'the vast majority of employees seek to reduce to a minimum even the most necessary official contacts with I. A. Orbeli and there is no chance whatever of regarding him as a comrade,' and so on. The members of the commission wisely decided that resolving the conflict was beyond them. Their findings conclude by expressing the conviction that 'the heavy atmosphere of work and relations created within the Hermitage has already improved and, if mutually desired, will disappear altogether'.

The destructive power of Orbeli's rage is interestingly analysed in a diary kept by Sergey Oldenburg's wife. As the helpmate of Russia's leading scholar, she was drawn into Orbeli's highly successful battle to discredit the archaeologist Sergey Zhebelev in 1928; Zhebelev was professor of archaeology at Leningrad University, had been the first chairman of the Hermitage Council in 1918, and had recently been elected an Academician. 'At the height of his unbridled anger,' Mrs Oldenburg writes of Orbeli, 'when he is mastered only by anger and hatred, his good sense is silent. Like the most primitive person, he can blindly and cruelly bring harm to other people. But when the storm has passed, his inherent sense of kindness takes control and his common sense speaks once more. But often his earlier outburst of anger and hatred has already spoiled things too much.'

This was the case in the Zhebelev affair which snowballed into a national scandal, with both the Moscow and Leningrad branches of the Academy of Science formally voting to rescind the title of Academician which they had granted Zhebelev the year before. And then the security police began to take an interest. 'Because of him, they have arrested three other people, Sivers, Waldenburg and now Benistevich,' Mrs Oldenburg laments. Alexander Sivers was a curator in the Numismatics Department of the Hermitage and recent signatory to a letter of complaint about Orbeli.

By 1928 Stalin's reign of terror was beginning and academic squabbles were no longer a matter merely of scholarly reputation. Over the following ten years the Leningrad intelligentsia was decimated and repression took a remorseless toll of Hermitage staff. More than fifty curators were arrested and sentenced to internal exile, prison, labour camps or execution. A bewildering variety of trumped-up charges was used – twelve of the staff were executed as spies. There were Japanese spies in the Oriental Department, German spies in the Coins and Antiquities Departments – fields where German scholarship had played a dominant role since the nineteenth century. There were Armenian terrorists plotting to overthrow the constitution and Ukrainian national-ists with the same end in view. Those who published articles in foreign scholarly journals were, of course, foreign spies, while at home, noble birth was enough to convert the most harmless scholar into a 'socially dangerous element'.

None of this had anything to do with the museum *per se*. It was a reflection of the madness that held the whole nation in thrall and can only be understood in the context of national history. The machinery of terror used by the government against its citizenry, which was not dissimilar to that previously used by the tsarist police, grew out of institutions established during the Revolution and Civil War when there was logic to hounding class enemies. A secret police reporting directly to the cabinet (Sovnarkom), and with extraordinary powers to interrogate and punish, was established in December 1917. Initially known as the *Cheka* – the Extraordinary Commission for Struggle with Counterrevolution and Sabotage – its name was changed several times over the years: to OGPU in 1922, NKVD in 1934, NKGB in 1943, MGB in 1946, and finally KGB in 1953; its role, however, did not change.

Legislation to establish concentration camps was passed in April 1919 and official figures show that by 1922 there were 190 camps containing 85,000 prisoners. The scale on which the machinery of terror was used between 1920 and 1925 was relatively modest but it remained in place. Then, following Lenin's death in January 1924, Stalin moved cautiously to usurp absolute power. He managed to rid himself of the Left Opposition – Trotsky, Zinoviev, Kamenev – in 1927, and the Right Opposition – Bukharin, Rykov, Tomsky – in 1929. He contented himself at this time with their expulsion from the leadership – their trials came later.

The reign of terror began in earnest in 1928 with the show trial of fifty-three engineers from the Shakhty mining district in Southern Russia who were charged with economic 'wrecking' of Soviet enterprises at the behest of foreign intelligence agencies and White émigré former owners. As was to become the general rule, the case rested on confessions obtained through physical and psychological torture. Most were found guilty and five were shot. The horrifying process had begun of denunciation, arrest, torture, further denunciations and further arrests, which was to sweep a large proportion of the population into custody over the next decade. Honest men denounced their colleagues to save their own wives and children, signing crazy confessions which could lead to their own deaths.

The murder of Sergey Kirov, first secretary of the Leningrad Communist Party, on 1 December 1934, was a turning point. He was shot in the Party headquarters in the Smolny by Leonid Nikolaev, an embittered and deranged Young Communist. It is now believed that the murder was arranged by Stalin and the NKVD but, at the time, it was presented as part of a conspiracy that embraced half the population of Leningrad – including everyone Stalin wanted to get rid of. On the day of the murder Stalin issued a decree to speed up the investigation of 'terrorist organisations or acts'; they were to take no longer than ten days and be presented to a military court which allowed no appeals and could order an immediate death sentence. This decree was to structure criminal justice for the next twenty years, until Stalin's death in 1953.

There followed three show trials of party leaders. In August 1936 Grigory Zinoviev, Lev Kamenev and others confessed to having arranged Kirov's murder and to being part of a 'Trotskyist-Zinovievite Centre' which had plotted the death of Stalin himself. In early 1937 a group including Karl Radek and Grigory Pyatakov confessed to spying, plotting assassinations and industrial 'wrecking'. A similar string of offences were confessed by Nikolay Bukharin, Alexey Rykov, Nikolay Krestinsky and Genrikh Yagoda in March 1938. Most of the accused were executed. A crescendo of arrests among the population at large for related conspiracies followed in 1938–9. Finally Stalin realised that the scale of the operation was undermining the national economy – so much of the productive labour force was in custody – and brought the terror to a close in 1939. In the late 1940s, however, shortly before his death, he launched a new campaign against 'cosmopolitans' and Jews.

It is against this background that the hounding of 'enemies of the people' on the Hermitage staff must be seen. They were particularly vulnerable since so many of them were of noble birth. Most of the St Petersburg intelligentsia had belonged to the nobility before the Revolution and it was natural that the scholar-curators at the Hermitage should have been drawn from this class. As every child of a hereditary noble automatically belonged to the nobility, the class was large and not especially élitist – more like the British 'gentry'. There were also scholars who were made honorary nobles. Tatyana Tchernavin, for instance, was the daughter of a university professor who had had nobility conferred on him on receiving his degree although he was the son of a peasant. When she explained to her prison examiner that nobility conferred on individuals was not hereditary, she was accused of hiding her social origins and being a typical class enemy. As a result she was prosecuted for 'furthering economic counter-revolution'.

'There was no point in speaking about the accusation, which I simply did not understand,' she wrote; 'neither of the OGPU officers who examined me ever asked a single question relating to it . . . I could not have explained what "economic counter-revolution" meant, to say nothing of my "furthering" it; history, literature and art were the subjects at which I had worked all my life. But charges against other prisoners were just as senseless, so that I was no exception.'

Arguments concerning 'history, literature and art' could, however, easily be twisted into political issues in such an environment. Tchernavin was arrested, more on account of her husband, a zoologist who was already in prison, than in her own right. Grigory Borovka, however, who was one of the first Hermitage staff to be repressed, was accused of being a German spy because of his involvement with plans for a joint Russo-German archaeological expedition to the Crimea. He was one of some one hundred scholars to be arrested in this connection in Leningrad and Moscow, the most prominent being Academician

Sergey Platonov; the event has come to be known as 'the Academicians' affair'.

The affair had its origin in the collaboration between Russian archaeologists who had emigrated at the time of the Revolution and those who had stayed in Russia. The two groups had worked together before 1917 and continued to collaborate at long distance in the 1920s. This was particularly important to Borovka since Academician Mikhail Rostovtsev, who emigrated first to Oxford, then to Princeton, was the accepted world expert on the Scythians, his own area of study. Borovka worked with a group of other scholars, under Rostovtsev's direction, to compile an anthology of studies of the archaeological monuments of Southern Russia. In this connection Rostovtsev's book *Sarmatia, Scythia and the Bosphorus* was translated into German by the Hermitage curator Yevgeny Pridik; Borovka took Pridik's manuscript to Berlin and was handed payment to take back to him in Leningrad. It is quite easy to see how this transaction came to be interpreted as espionage.

It was actually Orbeli who first interrupted the peaceful international collaboration of archaeologists with his campaign against Zhebelev. The scandal grew out of a volume of papers published in Prague in memory of the Hermitage scholar Yakov Smirnov, the great expert on Sassanian silver who had been Orbeli's teacher. Zhebelev had contributed an obituary in which he wrote that 'Yakov Ivanovich died on 10 October 1918, just when the terrible time of troubles was beginning.' Smirnov had, in fact, died of hunger and Zhebelev's words would have seemed fairly innocuous, had it not been for a paper by Rostovtsev published in the same volume which expanded and dramatised the issue. 'It is painful to think,' he wrote, 'that if it had not been for the uprising, and everything connected with the uprising, hunger, despair, disillusion with both the present and future, Yakov Ivanovich would be with us still and we would be writing articles in his honour and not in his memory.'

Mrs Oldenburg's diary explains what happened. Orbeli 'was angry with Zhebelev for having referred several times in his article to unpublished material by Y. I. Smirnov which was in the possession of I. A. Orbeli. By these words, in Orbeli's opinion, Zhebelev threw a shadow on his reputation (i.e. suggested plagiarism). Orbeli began to shout about the article everywhere, pointing out its non-Soviet tone, interpreting the unfortunate expressions and so on. By his shouts he attracted the attention of the Communists in the Hermitage to this article . . . and they were off.' As we have seen, the Zhebelev affair snowballed into a national scandal. The result was a ban on the publication of studies by Soviet scholars in émigré journals and a sharp cutback on their publication in any foreign periodicals.

The Zhebelev affair began in 1928 and rumbled into 1929 when it merged with the furore over Academician Platonov's arrest for creating a counter-revolutionary monarchical organisation with links to the German spy system. Among those prosecuted as a result of the 'Academicians' affair' were Alexander Miller, the professor of archaeology who taught two future directors of the Hermitage, Mikhail Artamonov and Boris Piotrovsky; Miller subsequently died in custody. And, of course, there was Grigory Borovka who was sentenced to ten years in the camps. He was let out in September 1940 but restricted to living in the Komi Autonomous Republic. At the outbreak of the war with Germany he was rearrested and shot.

Borovka's story can be taken as an example of the human realities of repression. His family was of German origin – they had moved to Russia during the reign of Peter the Great's daughter, the Empress Elizabeth. Thereafter they were mainly involved with theatre, music and art. His father was a professor of music at the Conservatoire and ran his own music school. Scared by the Revolution, the rest of the family moved back to Germany in 1918 where they no longer had any connections and lived in reduced circumstances. Grigory seems to have remained in St Petersburg for two reasons, the fascination of the work he was doing under Waldhauer at the Hermitage and the charm of his girlfriend, Katya Malkina, with whom he lived. She was also a curator in the Hermitage Antiquities Department but resigned in protest after Borovka's arrest. A poet and a romantic, she later became a significant literary figure in her own right. She worked at the Pushkin House where, among other things, she compiled a bibliography of Nikolay Gumilev, the famous poet who was executed in 1921.

Borovka's family still retain some moving memorials of his life, notably his letters to his mother and the postcards that Katya sent to keep the family informed about what was happening to Grigory after his arrest. In the 1920s he had taken advantage of every opportunity to visit his family in Berlin. In 1927 he was elected a corresponding member of the German Archaeological Institute and in 1928 he organised an exhibition in Berlin of artefacts from the Noin-Ula burial barrows. He also helped with the sale of Hermitage antiquities at the Lepke auction house, confiding in his family that he had miscatalogued the pieces in the hope they would not sell.

He was arrested on 21 September 1930, and remained in prison for over a year without trial while the OGPU gathered evidence on the 'Academicians' affair'; but they failed to turn it into the major conspiracy they had hoped for. Borovka was finally prosecuted as a German spy and sentenced on 7 October 1931, to ten years in the camps. He was sent to Ukhta, in the far north, where he studied palaeontology and set up a geological museum. Katya devotedly visited him in prison, sent him food packs and books and travelled to Ukhta on her summer vacations whenever she could manage.

On 30 September 1931 Katya writes to Borovka's brother:

Gory sends you his greetings. He's in good health – I've seen him three times. He's now perfectly well nourished – much better than he would be if he was living with us; for the last two months I've been able to take him additional food (before that it was not allowed) . . . He has the following request for you: if you have got the money from his book *Scythian Art* [published in London, 1928] stored up, could you buy two German books for him and send them to me – the third volume of Marx's *Kapital* and the *Dialektik der Natur* by Friedrich Engels. If there is any money left over, could you send that too and I'll buy him some food.

By 1934 Katya's hopes were withering away. In April she wrote: 'I don't know whether it will be possible for me to visit Gory this summer. I am afraid that I won't get enough holiday – it is such an endless journey. I can't travel without getting news of Gory, but staying in touch by post is very difficult as letters take weeks on the way. Life in this world is often so terribly sad.' In November: 'Bad news from Gory; his health is not very good and he's terribly depressed . . . I help him as much as I can and send him parcels every month. His letters are rare and irregular.' The postcards stopped in 1936 when Katya no longer had the opportunity to organise foreign correspondence. And the family knew nothing more of Grigory's fate until 1994 when, at their request, the St Petersburg archaeologist Vadim Zuev found out what had happened to him.

Besides Borovka, two other Hermitage curators were arrested in 1930, Olga Fe, a noblewoman who worked in the Drawings Department, who was sentenced to three years in a concentration camp for spying – the sentence was later commuted to five years' exile in Ufa – and the Orientalist Alexander Strelkov who was arrested as an agitator and spent two years in prison before the case against him was dropped. Like, Borovka, Strelkov was later rearrested and shot as a German spy.

The next 'plot', which culled a swathe of Hermitage curators, was known as 'the affair of the Russian National Party' or the 'Slavists' Affair' and erupted in 1933–4. The party was supposedly organised from abroad by the émigré fascist leader, Prince N. M. Trubetskoy, who argued the primacy of nations over class and publicly advocated an end to Communism and the establishment of a national government. The 'plot' was initially uncovered in the Ukraine but collaborators were subsequently found in Moscow and Leningrad. Two specialists from the Hermitage Armoury were among those caught up by it. The Kharkov Museum in the Ukraine had requested the loan of antique weapons for an exhibition and thirty-one pieces were duly despatched in June 1933 by the curators Alexander Avtomonov and Emile Lindroz. On 29 November and 1 December respectively, Avtomonov and Lindroz were arrested and accused of supplying arms to Ukrainian nationalists. Lindroz also had a private collection of antique weapons which was interpreted as 'storing of weapons with the aim of using them in the organisation of an armed uprising' – although he had written authorisation from the Hermitage for his collection.

Both of them were sentenced to ten years in the camps. In the case of Avtomonov, a second hearing took place in 1938 after which he was shot. Lindroz remained in the camps until 1945 and then became a watchman with the forestry commission in the Pestovo region, near Novgorod. He was still living there in 1956 when he was rehabilitated and the prosecution was expunged from his records as incorrect. There was a big campaign of rehabilitation of wrongly accused former prisoners three years after Stalin's death.

An explosion of arrests at the Hermitage followed in the wake of Sergey Kirov's murder. Vera Nikolaeva, an Egyptologist and art historian who worked in the 'Classical East' section of the Antiquities Department, was the first to go. She and her brother were arrested within days of the murder for the simple reason that they had the same surname as Kirov's murderer – though there was no family connection. Accused of plotting to overthrow the constitution, her case was heard in June 1935 and she was sentenced to ten years in prison; the sentence was changed to execution on 4 November 1937, and she was shot on 17 November.

In February and March 1935 nearly all the former nobility who lived in Leningrad were arrested. There was a theory that Kirov's murder was part of a counter-revolutionary plot in which many of them had collaborated. Alexey Bykov from the Coin Department, who had received his initial education at the college of the imperial *Corps de Pages*, was arrested as a former noble on 20 March and sentenced to five years' exile in Samara. His exile was annulled in April 1936 and he returned to the Hermitage where he later became head of the Coin Department. Similarly Vera Gerts, a specialist on Poussin and French seventeenth-century painting, was arrested on 4 March and sentenced to five years' 'social defence' in Astrakhan. She was freed on 25 April 1936, on reconsideration of her case. There were many others.

Troinitsky was one of those arrested on account of their noble birth. On 4 March a military court sentenced him to three years' exile in Ufa and, according to the KGB records, he was not freed until 8 December 1938, rather more than three years later. According to his daughter Elena, however, a deputation of influential friends approached Stalin on Troinitsky's behalf and obtained his early release. They included Alexey Shchusev, the architect who designed Lenin's mausoleum, Vladimir Shchuko, one of the architects who designed the famous 'Palace of Soviets', and the mural painter Evgeny Lansere. 'If he is not so dangerous he can return home,' Stalin told them, according to Elena. 'And Troinitsky was swiftly freed. But he did not return to Leningrad. It was too painful for him to do this. That is why he decided to live in Moscow.'

It was also at this time that Boris Piotrovsky, the future director of the museum, was arrested at a Shrove Tuesday pancake party thrown by a fellow archaeologist. His memoirs suggest that there were some real political activists at the party and that he and two other archaeologists, Andrey Kruglov and Georgy Podgaetsky, were arrested with them by mistake – they were accused of belonging to a terrorist organisation. Piotrovsky describes the room in the police station where he was taken which was divided from the corridor by a grille:

It was very, very full and people were sleeping on mattresses on the floor under the beds. When I went in many woke up and began asking with interest where I had come from and why I had been arrested. I couldn't guess what I'd been arrested for. I had to occupy the last place which meant on the floor, under a bed, right up by the grille. As people were let out, the queue moved up and people occupied the places of those who'd left, so there was some hope that you would get a bed eventually. It was very uncomfortable. There were rats running up and down the corridor next to me and the guards threw their bunches of keys at them.

Kruglov and Podgaetsky were released on 10 April and Piotrovsky on 19 April, after forty days' incarceration. The Hermitage took Piotrovsky straight back but he found that he and Podgaetsky had been sacked, *in absentia*, from the Institute of the History of Material Culture where both also worked. They took their hard luck story to the trade union which decided, on 1 July, that the Commission of the Institute had been wrong and advised the two young archaeologists to take the Institute to court. They followed this advice and were duly vindicated and taken back, an extraordinarily 'fair' result by the standards of the time. It has been suggested that the successful court action protected Piotrovsky for many years to come; it would have been taken to mean that he had influence in high places and was therefore untouchable.

The story of the Japanese spies unearthed in the Hermitage in 1937 is almost unbelievable. Dmitry Zhukov, who had worked for the Russian government in Japan and joined the Hermitage Oriental Department in 1935, was arrested on 29 May 1937. Under torture he 'confessed' to having been lured into the service of the Japanese and having run a Trotskyite spy and terrorist group which included the poets Nikolay Oleinikov and Wolf Ehrlich, the writer V. Matveev and numerous Orientalists. Zhukov was shot on 24 November.

Among those he denounced under interrogation was Nikolay Nevsky, a Russian scholar who lived from 1915–29 in Japan where he is considered one of the founding fathers of ethnography. While in Japan he began to study the Tangut scripts that Kozlov had found at Khara-Khoto and was urged by Russian Orientalists to return to Leningrad and work on them there. He began to work at the Institute of Oriental Studies at the invitation of Sergei Oldenburg in 1930 and in 1934 joined the staff of the Hermitage. His Japanese wife and daughter joined him in Russia in 1933. After his arrest in 1937, Nevsky's first priority was to defend them and it was for their sake that, after severe torture, he 'confessed' to working for the Japanese intelligence service and setting up a network of spies in Leningrad to gather information on military sites, aerodromes, factories, etc.

He did not know that his wife, who spoke no Russian, had been arrested four days after him and that his confession could not help her. Husband and wife were both executed on 24 November 1937, along with Zhukov. Nevsky was rehabilitated in 1957 and his Tangut studies, published in 1960, were hailed worldwide as one of the most important philological discoveries of the twentieth century. He was awarded a posthumous Lenin Prize in 1962.

In 1937–8 the conspiracies confessed to at Stalin's show trials were found, with the help of torture, to involve an ever-widening circle of citizens across the whole Soviet Union. In the autumn of 1937 almost the entire leadership of Armenia's Central Party Committee and Council of People's Commissars was arrested. On the last day of the year eight of them were executed. The purge then spread to the Armenians living elsewhere. In February 1938 virtually every Armenian in Leningrad was arrested. The job was simplified for the NKVD by the fact that most Armenian surnames end in the letters 'an'. On the night of 4–5 February – most arrests were made in the early hours of the morning – three Armenians from the Hermitage Oriental Department were arrested: Anton Adzhan, Leon Gyuzalyan, and Gaik Gyulamiryan. Only Gyuzalyan survived; Adzhan and Gyulamiryan were both shot the following October.

Orbeli was also Armenian by birth but he used the Georgian version of his surname, Orbeli, rather than the Armenian Orbelian and it is seriously suggested that this is one of the reasons he was not prosecuted. The three curators from the Oriental Department were all his ex-students and special protégés. Adzhan, a specialist on Turkish art, had succeeded him as head of the Oriental Department when Orbeli became director of the museum in 1934. Orbeli leapt to Adzhan's defence. He took a train to Moscow the moment he heard of the arrest and sought out Anastas Mikoyan, the man to whom Stalin had given charge of the Armenian purge. He was not in his office and Orbeli announced that he would wait for his return. It was 2 a.m. when Mikoyan finally turned up and told Orbeli that he had come too late. Anton Adzhan, he said, had already been executed. Curiously, the papers on Adzhan's arrest that have emerged from the KGB since perestroika show that he was, in fact, still alive at this point and was not executed for another nine months. Mikoyan had lied to get Orbeli out of his office.

It has also emerged that Orbeli himself was in grave danger at this time. Gyuzalyan, who returned to the Hermitage after the war, was pressured for many weeks by the NKVD to denounce Orbeli. The same happened to Alexander Strelkov, another employee of the Oriental Department – an expert on pre-Islamic Central Asia, Iran and India – who was arrested in February 1938 and executed the following September.

Gyuzalyan was eventually sentenced to five years' corrective labour but was not, in fact, let out of the camps until after the war. He amazed his colleagues at the Hermitage by telling them that he had not known there was a war on. 'There were some rumours about some trouble but we but didn't know what,' he told his close associate Adele Adamova – Gyuzalyan was an expert on Persian literature and Adamova on Persian painting. Like many other prisoners, he was banned from living in a large city after his release and only got back to Leningrad with Orbeli's help. Though officially exiled 'beyond the 100th kilometre', Orbeli allowed him to work in the Hermitage from 1947 onwards. He was, no doubt, aware that he owed his own life to Gyuzalyan's dogged refusal to sign a denunciation. In 1955, after Stalin's death, Gyuzalyan was formally rehabilitated and officially re-recruited to the Hermitage staff.

Gyuzalyan and Adzhan had been student friends and collaborators of Boris Piotrovsky. All three had worked on Urartu in the early 1930s though Adzhan had then moved over to study Turkish art and Gyuzalyan Persian epigraphy. It was Piotrovsky who secured the posthumous rehabilitation of Adzhan in 1956 and it was Piotrovsky whom Gyuzalyan first sought out in Leningrad after his release from the camps – still wearing the padded cotton jacket that was standard issue in the Gulag. The jacket ended up as a gift to the present director of the Hermitage, Mikhail Piotrovsky, for whom Gyuzalyan became a friendly, uncle figure. 'He gave it to me when I went to do my agricultural labour as a first year university student, saying it would keep me warm.'

Gyuzalyan was loved and respected on his return to the Hermitage but the Gulag had robbed him of his best years and – cruelly – the NKVD had destroyed all his papers in 1938, including his laboriously compiled card file. He never had the heart to reconstruct it. 'He would have been a very good scholar if he hadn't lost all those years,' comments his fellow Orientalist, Igor Diakonoff. 'When he came back, he was already old and weak. It was a wonder that he survived.' In fact, he was in his nineties when he died in 1994.

Orbeli's courage and determination in defending his curators was also demonstrated in the case of Pavel Derviz, a silver specialist and former baron, who took over the *objets de vertu* department from Troinitsky. Arrested, like other nobles after Kirov's murder in 1934, he was already on the train which would take him into exile when Orbeli arrived at Leningrad's Moscow Station with papers for his release and took him off it. Rearrested in November 1938, probably on account of his family's

German origin, Derviz was charged with participation in a counter-revolutionary plot. This case was also dropped and he was released in April 1939, but he had been beaten so severely in prison that his lungs were permanently damaged. He was an invalid from then on. In 1941, when the Hermitage treasures were being packed for evacuation, he was very ill but insisted on being taken to the museum to see the Alexander Nevsky sarcophagus, the world's grandest silver monument, for one last time. He died in 1942 during the siege.

The war brought Stalin's purges to a temporary close and they never regained the universal character of the 1930s. Nevertheless, the post-war years saw a paranoid tightening of ideology in every field and persecution of deviant artists, writers and scholars. Stalin had always feared the independence of the people of Leningrad and in 1948 he launched a savage purge of the Leningrad Party organisation. All the leading officials in the Leningrad region were arrested and executed as were several hundred of their subordinates. A mass arrest of the Leningrad intelligentsia, particularly university staff, followed. This time most of the 'enemies of the people' were categorised as cosmopolitans and Jews.

Matvey Gukovsky, a professor of Renaissance history at the university, an expert on Leonardo and a deputy director of the Hermitage, qualified on both counts. He was arrested while on holiday with friends in the Caucasus. As visitors, they were required to register with the police. Gukovsky was arrested and his friends released. In August 1950 he was sentenced to ten years in the camps for 'counter-revolutionary propaganda'. Luckily for him, Stalin died in March 1953 and shortly afterwards all sentences were reduced by half. He was released on 11 January 1955 and started writing angry letters to the prosecutor's office asking what he had been accused of. In November 1956 he was told that the charges against him had been dropped for lack of evidence. His rehabilitation followed, after which he became director of the Hermitage library.

Lev Gumilev, a brilliant geographer and historian, joined the staff of the library in the same year. Artamonov, who was by then director of the museum, went out of his way to recruit scholars who had suffered at the hands of the KGB and took on Gumilev to help with his research on the Khazars.

Gumilev was an extreme case. He was the son of two of Russia's best loved poets. His father Nikolay Gumilev was executed in 1921. His mother Anna Akhmatova survived, though her lyrical poetry was hardly published in the 1930s and fell under Stalin's particular disfavour in the post-war years. It was criticised as 'imbued with the spirit of pessimism, decadence . . . and bourgeois-aristocratic aestheticism'.

Lev Gumilev was under a shadow from the start. He was not allowed into the university on account of his social origin. This ban was lifted in 1934 but he was arrested in 1935 – and not allowed back into the university when he got out of prison. Rearrested in 1938, he spent five years in custody, coming out just in time to join the army and fight in Germany. After the war, when he could have hoped for a period of peace, his mother's political disgrace was extended to include him. In 1949 he was rearrested and sentenced to ten years in the camps. Then, like Gukovsky, he was let out after serving five years and came to work for the Hermitage. Artamonov and the Hermitage launched his new career. He became one of Russia's most popular scholars with an array of published works. He had a vast TV and radio audience hanging on his words after perestroika and died a natural death in 1994.

13

The Siege of Leningrad

*F*rom 8 September 1941 to 27 January 1944 – some 900 days – Leningrad was under siege from Hitler's forces. It is almost incredible that any city could withstand the technology of twentieth-century warfare for so long a period. One third of the population died, more than half of them from hunger, but the city survived. Then Stalin completed the tragedy that Hitler had begun by arresting and executing the Party workers who led the struggle for survival. Hundreds of minor officials, writers and artists, were also arrested.

The museum's magnificent architectural complex was hit by thirty-two shells and two bombs, but it remained standing with all its windows, some five acres of glass, shattered and boarded up with plywood. The cream of the collection spent the war years at Sverdlovsk in the Urals, better known by its pre-revolutionary name of Ekaterinburg. It was there that Nicholas II and his family had been held by the Bolsheviks in 1918, and then executed and secretly buried. The house where the imperial family had lived spent World War II as one of the Hermitage storerooms.

The great museum on the Neva came back to life on 8 November 1944 with an exhibition of art works that had not been evacuated. And on 4 November 1945, the first sixty-eight rooms of the museum, restored to their former glory and filled with their former collections, were opened to the public. Despite the dangers associated with packing over a million objects and sending them 1,500 miles by train in wartime, despite the bombs, shells, ice and floods that threatened the works of art that were left behind, very little of the collection was lost. And the building was patched and painted until it looked like new. No one today could guess at the ordeal it went through. In bad weather, however, the building still springs leaks where the shells hit it, according to the present director, like an old soldier troubled by his war wounds.

It is impossible to write about Leningrad during World War II except in terms of heroism. Those who lived through it and, indeed, those who died, may not have chosen the hero or heroine's role but it was thrust upon them. The first winter, from October 1941 to March 1942, was the period of fiercest suffering. The food ration would not sustain life; people ate dogs and cats and any food substitute that came to hand. Many died of hunger in the street. The survivors did not have the strength to break the frozen earth and bury them; on the outskirts of the city, piles of corpses lined the roadway. After March 1942 the rail link to the rest of Russia was secure enough for a mass evacuation of the city and there was more food for those who remained. But the links were tenuous and the Germans continued to pound the city with shells and bombs until January 1944. Contemplating the stories of the siege, as recorded by its poets and intelligentsia, one is filled with awe at the resilience of the human spirit. Lidiya Ginzburg's *Blockade Diary* conveys something of the feel of it:

> Whoever had energy enough to read, used to read *War and Peace* avidly in besieged Leningrad. Tolstoy had said the last word as regards courage, about people doing their bit in a people's war. He also spoke of how those caught up in this common round continued playing their part involuntarily, while ostensibly busy solving problems affecting their own lives. The people of besieged Leningrad worked (while they could) and saved (if they could) both themselves and their loved ones from dying of hunger. And in the final reckoning, that was also essential to the war effort, because a living city barred the path of an enemy who wanted to kill it.

It all began in the early hours of the morning of 22 June 1941 when Hitler's forces invaded Russia simultaneously from the north, the west and the south. Most people only discovered this at midday when Vyacheslav Molotov, the foreign minister, broadcast over the radio. There were loudspeakers mounted in all city streets in Soviet times and people gathered round them to hear Molotov speak:

> Men and women, citizens of the Soviet Union, the Soviet

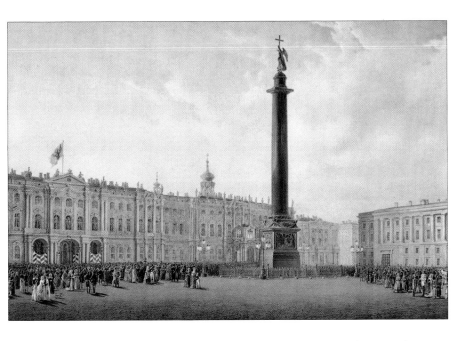

A watercolour view of Palace Square, with the Alexander Column in the foreground and the Winter Palace behind, by Vasily Semenovich Sadovnikov.

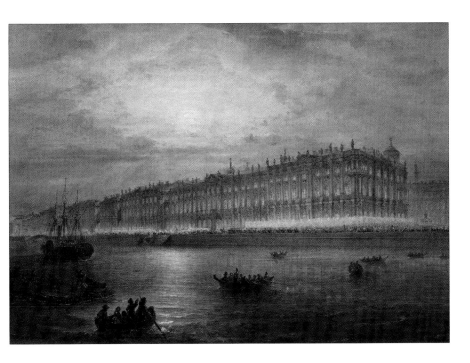

The Winter Palace illuminated on a feast day evening with the River Neva in the foreground. A moody watercolour of 1851 by Vasily Semenovich Sadovnikov.

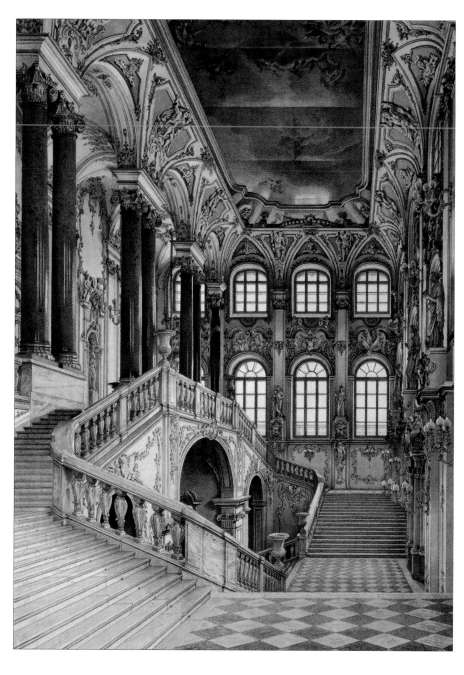

The Jordan Staircase, also known as the Ambassadors' Staircase,
painted by Konstantin Andreevich Ukhtomsky after its complete restoration
by Stasov following the 1837 fire in the Winter Palace. Bartolomeo Rastrelli's
exuberant Baroque design was retained with a few restraining touches – the
pillars turned from pink to grey.

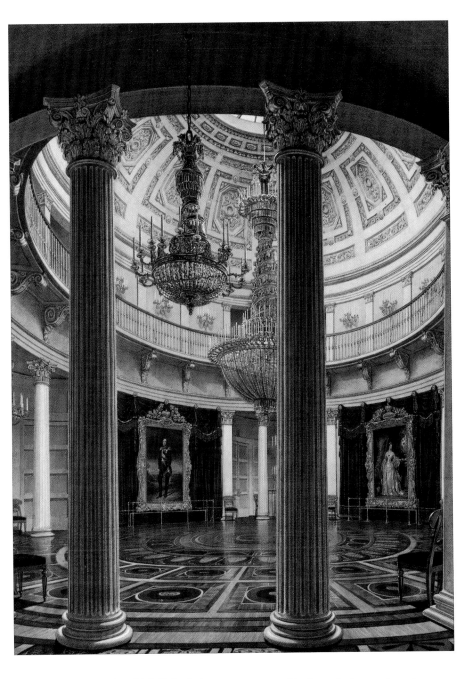

The Rotunda which linked the state rooms with the private apartments of the imperial family, depicted in 1862 by Eduard Petrovich Hau. It was in this Rotunda that Boris Borisovich Piotrovsky used to meet a colleague by night during the siege of Leningrad to exchange knowledge that both believed might be lost to humanity if they starved to death.

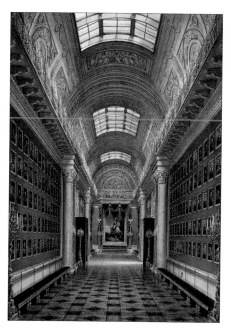

The Gallery of 1812, containing 332
portraits of generals who fought
Napoleon. A watercolour of 1862 by
Eduard Petrovich Hau.

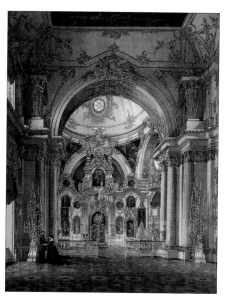

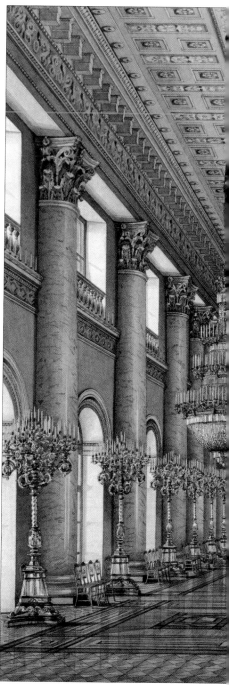

The Great Church of the Winter Palace,
first consecrated in 1762 and elevated
to the rank of cathedral in 1807, in
an 1866 watercolour by Eduard
Petrovich Hau.

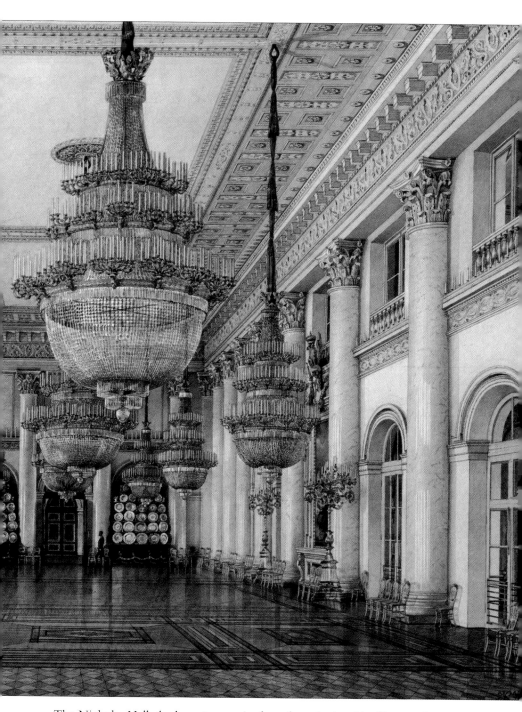

The Nicholas Hall, the largest room in the palace, depicted by Konstantin Andreevich Ukhtomsky in 1866. It was also known as the Great Hall and had a floor space of 1103 square metres. In 1855 an immense equestrian portrait of Nicholas I by Franz Krüger was hung in the centre and the room was renamed in memory of the recently deceased Tsar.

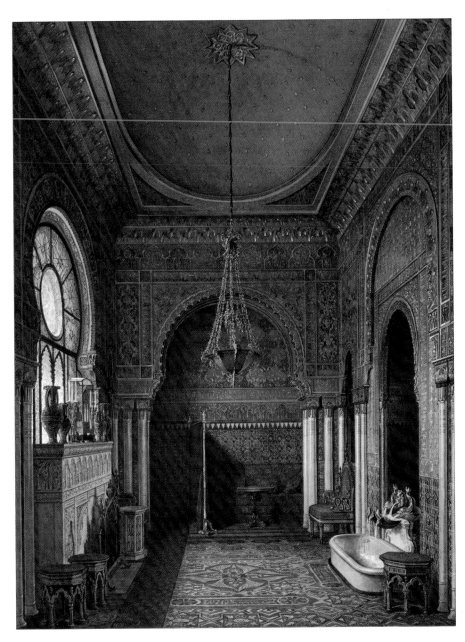

The bathroom of Empress Alexandra Federovna designed in Moorish style by Auguste Montferrand and faithfully restored after the 1837 fire, depicted here in a watercolour of 1870 by Eduard Petrovich Hau.

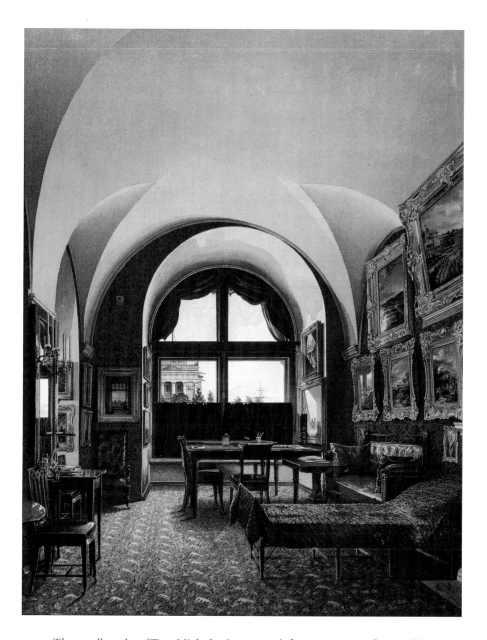

The small study of Tsar Nicholas I, a ground-floor apartment favoured by
the Tsar who set great store by simplicity. He died on the iron camp bed shown
in the foreground on March 2, 1855 and the room was left untouched as a
memorial until the Revolution. It is seen here in a watercolour by
Konstantin Andreevich Ukhtomsky.

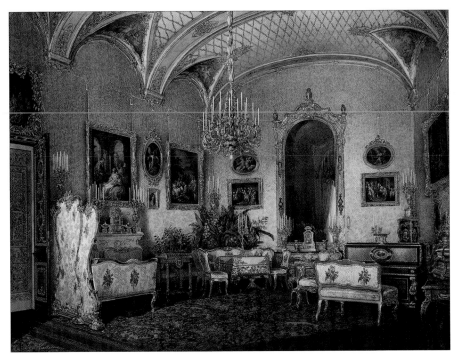

The White Drawing Room, designed by Stakenschneider, depicted by
Eduard Petrovich Hau in 1860.

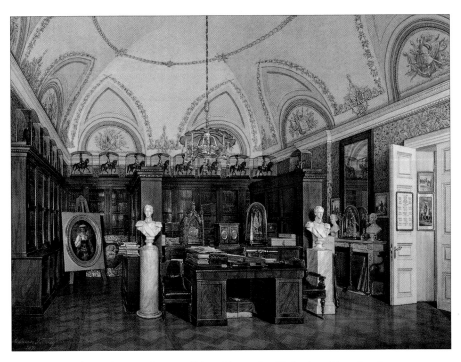

The Military Library of Tsar Alexander II depicted in 1871 by
Eduard Petrovich Hau.

Government and its head, Comrade Stalin, have instructed me to make the following announcement: at 4 a.m., without declaration of war and without any claims being made on the Soviet Union, German troops attacked our country, attacked our frontier in many places and bombed from the air Zhitomir, Kiev, Sevastopol, Kaunas and other cities . . . This attack has been made despite the fact that there was a non-aggression pact between the Soviet Union and Germany, a pact the terms of which were scrupulously observed by the Soviet Union . . . The government calls upon you, men and women citizens of the Soviet Union, to rally even more closely around the glorious Bolshevik Party, around the Soviet Government and our great leader, Comrade Stalin. Our cause is just. The enemy will be crushed. Victory will be ours.

Stalin had obstinately refused to see the war coming, despite intelligence reports and the massing of German troops on the frontier. He is reputed to have suffered a nervous breakdown after the invasion, which put him out of action for many weeks. Preparations for war had been generally forbidden in case the Germans interpreted them as aggression, but Iosif Orbeli had been secretly stockpiling the packing materials that would be needed to evacuate the Hermitage collection.

At 11 a.m. on Sunday 22 June, the Hermitage doors had opened as usual and a large crowd poured in to admire the collection; guided tours had begun their slow progress around the galleries. After the noon announcement the museum emptied. Orbeli ordered that the forty most important paintings be taken down and stored in the special, steel-clad, windowless galleries on the ground floor which housed the jewellery and Scythian gold – where they would be most likely to survive a bombing raid. At this time, Russians expected something like the London Blitz to be repeated in Leningrad.

In faraway Armenia, Boris Piotrovsky had just begun his summer excavations of the Urartian fortress at Karmir-Blur. Since the excavations were within sight of the Turkish border, he was ordered to continue his work there for several days after the invasion so that the enemy should see that Russia was unperturbed by Hitler's challenge. He travelled back to Leningrad in the early days of July in a train that was already observing the blackout – the guard had only candles and lamps in the corridors. Piotrovsky was to live in the Hermitage through the cruel winter of 1941–2 and became its principal chronicler.

On 23 June, the day after the invasion, Orbeli ordered the

preparation of the Hermitage treasures for evacuation, a fantastic packing marathon which continued without pause for six days and nights. Nature was on their side. During the famous 'white nights' of St Petersburg the sun never completely sets. The longest day, 21 June, had only just passed and the packers could see what they were doing throughout the night.

'It was as if we had all been confined to barracks,' the Byzantinist Alisa Bank wrote.

> The work went on twenty-four hours a day. In the pre-war years, there was no artificial light in the exhibition rooms but the 'white nights' meant that we didn't have to stop packing even for an hour. The box in which we placed the objects stood on the floor and we had to work bent over all the time. Soon many of us developed a kind of professional illness – nose bleeds. In a nearby room there were some folding beds. You would lie down and rock your head until the bleeding stopped and then rush back to the boxes. We didn't stop for days. But how many days can you go without sleep? You're finally exhausted and just before morning you collapse for half an hour wherever you can – on the same folding bed or on a sofa, on the box you've just packed or on chairs placed in a row in the chancellery. You lose consciousness immediately. You fall into emptiness and half an hour or an hour later some inner spring, some nervous impulse, switches on your consciousness once more. You jump up, shake yourself off and back to work.

The head of the picture gallery, Vladimir Levinson-Lessing, was more interested in the technicalities:

> Pictures of small and medium format were stacked away in crates fitted with cloth-padded parallel dividers, in between which they neatly fitted and were held in place by wooden blocks. One such case could hold between twenty and sixty paintings. Larger pictures were removed from their stretchers and put on rollers, with each roller taking from ten to fifteen canvases with layers of tissue paper between them. After that the rollers were placed in oil-cloth casings, deposited in long, flat boxes and lashed tight. Because of the length of the process of removing large pictures from their stretchers and the inevitability of a certain amount of damage to the canvas – and the possibility of cracking – this method was only used when it was

strictly necessary, only for those pictures which were too large to get into a railway carriage without the removal of the stretcher.

With thousands of paintings to pack, the staff of the Hermitage was not sufficient to get the work done in time. Art historians and artists poured in to help from all over the city, including a team of students from the Academy of Arts who had copied paintings in the Hermitage before the war. Only one painting got a crate to itself, Rembrandt's *Prodigal Son*, which was considered too fragile to roll up – but there was great anxiety over whether the crate that Orbeli had ordered for it was too large to get into a railway truck. Rembrandt's *Descent from the Cross* is an even larger painting and throughout the six days, scholars and restorers debated whether it was better to risk damaging the surface by rolling it up or to leave it in Leningrad at Hitler's mercy. It was eventually decided to roll it.

Only the two Leonardos, Raphael's *Connestabile Madonna* and the Italian primitives, painted on panel, were packed with their frames. Under Orbeli's instructions the rest of the frames were left hanging in their original positions on the walls. This, he thought, would facilitate the laborious process of matching each picture with its frame when they returned and speed up the reopening of the museum.

Each different material posed different packing problems. Experts from the Lomonosov Porcelain Factory came in to help pack the porcelain. The large, silver wine ewer of the fourth century BC, embossed with ornamental birds and scenes from Scythian life, which had been found in the Chertomlyk burial mound, was so fragile that it was decided to fill it with crumbled cork. However, the wine strainer soldered across its neck prevented access and two devoted ladies spent days feeding cork into the vase with teaspoons through a crack in its lip.

Carlo Rastrelli's waxwork figure of Peter the Great had to be dismantled. First his clothes were removed – blue caftan, waistcoat, shirt of fine holland and the actual breeches Peter had worn at his wife Catherine's coronation. Then the figure was taken to pieces and the wooden body, arms and legs packed separately from the wax head, feet and hands. Houdon's marble statue of the seated Voltaire was the last to leave. The naval ratings who had been called in to help pack the lorries for the journey to the station placed runners under Voltaire's chair and rolled the statue up to the top of the New Hermitage's ceremonial staircase. Having covered all three flights of marble steps with planks, they used a system of ropes and pulleys to allow the statue to roll slowly down them and into the massive crate which awaited him in the vestibule.

Igor Diakonoff, a young Orientalist, stood beside the Atlantes at the main entrance with a list of the boxes and their numbers. He had to check which boxes went into a lorry and get the driver to sign for them. 'I stood there for more than 24 hours, repeating the same formula, lorry after lorry. After that I would wake up in the night muttering "the accompanying personnel to sign for the contents". There were more than a thousand boxes.' After it was finished, he went upstairs with some friends to the galleries where the pictures used to hang: 'We saw only shavings and empty frames and we wept.'

The train which pulled out of the Leningrad goods yard at dawn on 1 July had been intended for the evacuation of the Kirov armaments factory. It was Orbeli's luck that the factory's move was delayed. First a pilot locomotive went ahead to clear the tracks. Then came the train: two engines, an armoured car carrying the most valuable items, four linked Pullmans for other special treasures, a flat car with an anti-aircraft battery, twenty-two freight cars filled with art, a passenger car filled with Hermitage staff, a passenger car containing a military guard and, finally, a second flat car with a second anti-aircraft battery. Orbeli was at the station to watch it leave. Even those on board did not know where they were going.

The first train contained most of the works of art generally on display in the museum, some half a million items. A second train left on 20 July containing the next echelon of art owned by the Hermitage – just short of a million pieces packed into twenty-three freight cars. By this time able-bodied staff were being recruited for the People's Volunteers, the scratch army that the city threw against the Germans with savage losses. They were trained on Palace Square, outside the Hermitage windows, as a motley team of architects, professors and students replaced them as packers. Other members of the Hermitage staff spent their days helping to dig the circle of trenches around the city which finally stopped the German tanks.

At this point the packing materials that Orbeli had secretly ordered before the war ran out. Militsa Matthieu, a noted scholarly expert on ancient Egypt, was made deputy director and given the responsibility of finding packaging material. Indefatigably, she rang shops and warehouses around the city, begging for anything from carpenters to egg boxes, and a third train load was packed and made ready. But with too great a delay. On 30 August the Germans cut off Leningrad's railway connections with the rest of the Soviet Union and the evacuation of treasures was cancelled. The 351 crates that Matthieu had prepared were never moved from the long pillared corridor of the Rastrelli Gallery on the ground floor of the Winter Palace.

The cream of the Hermitage collections thus spent the war at Sverdlovsk with the much-loved director of the Western European Department, Vladimir Levinson-Lessing, in charge of them. The small, spectacled expert on Rembrandt and the Netherlandish school, a passionate collector of antiquarian books, was faced with the problem of storing securely one and a half million art treasures in a town of half a million residents, to which a series of armaments factories were also being evacuated – he had to fight for buildings, transport lorries, fuel.

The first trainload filled the local museum, whose own displays were packed away into the cellar. Voltaire, as usual, caused problems. His crate would not go through the door and had to be swung into the gallery through a first-floor window. The crate containing Alexander Nevsky's silver sarcophagus wouldn't even go through the window. It had to be unpacked, the sarcophagus carried in on its own and the crate reassembled inside. The treasures were hardly installed before the second train arrived under the care of Mikhail Gryaznov, the keeper of Siberian antiquities who had helped open the famous tombs of Pazyryk. It was pouring with rain the night the train reached Sverdlovsk and the police guards summoned Levinson-Lessing to meet a soaked professor who was beating suspiciously on the door.

There was now no more room in the museum and they had to search the town for other buildings, eventually obtaining the use of the single-storey Anti-Religious Museum and a church. The former had tiled stoves which would keep the exhibits too hot while the church had no heating at all. After a careful assessment, the Hermitage treasures were divided up into those which could best survive cold or heat and distributed accordingly. They were also assigned the house where Nicholas II's family had died, though this particular storeroom is not mentioned in any of the Soviet histories of the Hermitage on account of its imperial associations. Boris Yeltsin had the house pulled down when he was Party Secretary for the Sverdlovsk region so that it could not become a monarchist shrine.

Levinson-Lessing's team was desperately anxious about fire risks. The museum was surrounded by wooden sheds and warehouses which would inevitably cause a great conflagration if bombed. They managed to have the nearest warehouse taken down and the staff themselves

painted the museum's beams with fire-resistant fluid. They all participated in guarding the buildings twenty-four hours a day, one staff
member per building by day and two by night.

The fire hazard was also in the forefront of the minds of those who
stayed in Leningrad. A barge containing hundreds of tons of sand was
moored outside the back entrance of the Winter Canal, and an army of
young people – students from the Conservatoire and the Academy of
Art, and enthusiastic members of the Komsomol – carried it to every
gallery in the Hermitage and Winter Palace. In drawings and
photographs of the Hermitage interior during the war the pile of sand
with a spade stuck in it is a recurring feature. A particularly important
sand castle was created in the cellar below the Athena gallery where the
porcelain figures, vases and dinner services which had not been sent to
Sverdlovsk were half buried in sand – the top half of each piece was
allowed to protrude. On the night of 18 September an artillery shell
burst outside the museum entrance, chipping the Atlantes and blasting
the windows of the Athena gallery to smithereens – but the Meissen
shepherds and shepherdesses and the rest of the elegant company in the
cellar were unmoved.

Everyone who was not already in the People's Volunteers was
conscripted to the firefighters. Boris Piotrovsky, who had started
training with the Volunteers, was one of a group of Hermitage
researchers sent back to the museum – they turned out to be hopeless
riflemen. Piotrovsky now became Orbeli's assistant and deputy head of
the fire team. Two lookout posts were established on the roof to watch
for fires, one above the Armorial Hall of the Winter Palace and the
other beside the great skylight of the Italian picture gallery. Igor
Diakonoff recalls sharing his duty watch with Antonina Izergina, the
beautiful expert on modern painting who was to become Orbeli's last
wife and the mother of his only son. A keen mountain climber, she
suggested they should have a rope with them for escape. 'I told her it
would be no use to us. If a bomb hit, we'd go down with it. If it didn't,
we wouldn't need a rope.'

The huge cellars lying below the Winter Palace and the Hermitage
buildings were converted into bomb shelters in which the remaining
museum staff, their families and other people involved in the arts from
all over the city lived through the first winter of the war – there were
some 2,000 of them in all. 'The bomb shelters during the siege looked
most peculiar,' Piotrovsky wrote. 'The low basement windows were
filled with bricks and iron doors were put in. Next to the crudely made

plank beds was gilded furniture from the museum. Whenever electricity was cut off, candles and oil lamps would be lit on the tables. I remember that there were even wedding candles. Before the war many women employees had them hidden behind icons at home. They were thick with golden bands. But what was most important, they burned for a long time.'

One of the city's young architects, Alexander Nikolsky, was living in Bomb Shelter No. 3 and made sketches of the scene – he actually held an exhibition of the drawings in the shelter in December 1941. His drawings have assumed particular importance for posterity since all private cameras were confiscated at the beginning of the war and official photographers seldom visited the Hermitage.

Nikolsky's diary describes the difficulty of finding your way to the shelter. 'At night this route, from the doors of the Hermitage through its halls and passageways to the shelter itself, was fantastic to the point of terror. The enormous museum windows were not blacked out and of course no lamps could be lit, except for the tiny guide bulbs on the floor at each end of the Hall of Twenty Columns that were fed by the storage batteries standing there. Everything around was as black as soot.'

Piotrovsky also wrote of the museum at night:

During the autumn and winter of 1941–2 there used to be as many as ten to twelve air-raid alerts sounded daily. At night we were obliged to run to our posts through the pitch-dark rooms and halls of the Hermitage and Winter Palace. However, we grew so used to these routes, which at times were as much as three-quarters of a kilometre long, that we could have done it blindfolded . . . It was extremely cold in the halls and rooms. On my tours of inspection I used to bring to my colleagues, manning the posts, mugs of what we called tea, but which was actually no more than tepid water.

An unexpected visit from a submarine commander and 'Hero of the Soviet Union', A. V. Tripolsky, restored a measure of electricity to the museum. Orbeli took him through the pitch-black Hall of Twenty Columns to the wartime office he had established beside Bomb Shelter No. 3, where he lit a candle in a medieval silver candlestick. The battle with darkness reminded Tripolsky that the *Polar Star*, former pleasure yacht of the imperial family which was now an auxiliary vessel for the submarine squadron he commanded, was anchored in the frozen Neva outside the museum. He arranged that an electricity cable should be strung across the road to the Hermitage. 'The ship fed electricity to several of the Hermitage rooms,' Nikolsky wrote in his diary. 'It was light now where it had been dark before and this was of priceless value.'

The greatest struggle in the Hermitage, and throughout Leningrad, was with hunger. The inadequacy of the city's food reserves began to be realised at the end of August and bread rations were cut on 2 September to 600 grams a day for workers, 400 grams for office workers and 300 grams for dependants and children. But on 8 September the Germans bombed the city's largest food store; the stench of burning meat, sugar, oil and flour blew over the city. After that, the ration was cut over and over again. From 20 November to Christmas it was 250 grams for factory workers and 125 grams (two slices) for everyone else; front-line troops got 500 grams and rear echelons 300 grams. That was the lowest point. Afterwards the ration began to creep up again but many people were already so debilitated that it made little difference.

Bread was the staple diet – there was very little of anything else. The whole population of the city turned to a search for food and the invention of substitutes. Mothers would trudge into the country with what treasures they could muster to barter for vegetables, meat or eggs. The exchange rate between jewels, clothes or furniture and food was at an all-time low. Pets and pigeons disappeared. A stock of cottonseed cake, designed as fuel for shipping, was commandeered by the city government and, after the poisons were extracted, used for baking the daily bread. People remembered that wallpaper was attached by using flour paste. The paste was eaten – and also the paper. Shoes and leather bags were boiled for soup.

There was no distinction in the size of the ration between men and women or between young children and teenagers. This meant that it was men and teenagers who tended to die first. In November 1941 11,085 people died of hunger, in December 52,881 and in January and February 1942 combined – only 60 days – 199,187. Lidiya Ginzburg's *Blockade Diary* describes what was happening to them:

During the period of greatest exhaustion everything became clear: the mind was hauling the body along with it. The automatism of movement, its reflex nature, its age-old correlation with the mental impulse – all that was gone. It turned out, for example, that the vertical posture was by no means inherent in the body; the conscious will had to hold the body under control, otherwise it would slither away as if it were falling down a cliff. The will had to lift it up and sit it down or lead it from object to object. On the worst days it was not only difficult climbing stairs, it was very hard to walk on level ground.

Or again:

Genuine hunger, as is well known, is not like the desire to eat. It has its masks. It used to display the face of misery, indifference, an insane urgency, cruelty. It most resembled a chronic disease, and as with any disease, the mind played a most important role. The doomed were not those with the blackest features, or those most emaciated or distended. They were the ones with the strange expressions, looks of weird concentration, the ones who started trembling in front of a plate of soup.

Boris Piotrovsky records having a birthday feast on 14 February 1942. His brother came back from the front bringing with him a slice of bread which had turned to crumbs in the frost. Orbeli gave him a small bottle of eau de cologne (100 per cent proof) with which to wash it down and allowed him a ration of furniture glue which the Hermitage staff had learned to serve up as jelly – the large stock of glue laid in by the restorers just before the war was one of the principal reasons why any of the Hermitage staff survived. The restorers' drying oil was also used for frying appetizing morsels like potato peelings.

The snow had come early that year. The first flakes fell on 14 October and by 31 October the city was blanketed in snow at least four inches deep. 'There was no running water, no electricity and no heat,' wrote Piotrovsky. 'People were using furniture and parquet floors for firewood. The situation in the Hermitage was a little better, because the supplies of wood in the carpenter's shop from before the war and old display screens were used for heating.' Their water supply came from the Neva – the staff made a hole in the ice which froze again every night and had to be rebroken.

The busy life of the museum, however, continued. 'The Hermitage employees were working and living according to the regulations of military discipline, although when not engaged in their defence duties they would continue with their research work,' Piotrovsky wrote. 'There were orders pertaining to the defence of the Hermitage, sending employees to build fortifications or to fight at the front, promoting or demoting them, messages of appreciation, and even reprimands for being overly late for work (a few minutes did not count, of course). The only thing that testifies to the tragic situation are the long lists of employees "missing due to death".'

In the pre-war years Orbeli had loved to celebrate jubilees and anniversaries at the Hermitage and he was determined to continue this tradition despite the dangers and difficulties introduced by the German blockade. Plans were already afoot for the celebration of the 800th anniversary of the birth of the Azerbaijani poet Nizami Gandzhevi on 19 October 1941 before the German invasion. Orbeli applied to the Party administration in the Smolny for permission to go ahead, and it was reluctantly granted. The meeting started at two in the afternoon and closed just minutes before the first air raid.

With even madder courage, Orbeli insisted on celebrating the 500th anniversary of the birth of the Uzbek poet Alisher Navoi on 10 December, when the siege had moved into its harshest period. Piotrovsky has left a description of the occasion:

> The introductory speeches were read by our director, Iosif Orbeli, Prof. Alexander Boldyrev and myself. The poet Vsevolod Rozhdest-vensky, who had come back from the front, and Nikolay Lebedev, an employee of the Hermitage, recited translations of Navoi's poetry. In the showcases porcelain, glasses and boxes painted with subjects from Navoi's poems were displayed.
>
> The next day the jubilee meeting was continued with Lebedev's recital. He was so weak that he had to recite while seated. A few days later he died. There he was lying on the bed in the shelter covered with a coloured Turkmenian rug, and it seemed that he was still whispering his poems.
>
> The city which Hitler had pronounced dead was celebrating the birth of a poet and enlightener from the fifteenth century. It did not matter that among the audience there was not a single person who had an Azerbaijani or Uzbek background. It was a challenge to the enemy. Light was fighting darkness.

In fact, the Hermitage was the only institution in the Soviet Union that celebrated Nizami's birth, though major exhibitions and meetings had originally been planned in Moscow and Baku. Piotrovsky's account of the Hermitage during the siege continues with a moving description of how the staff handled the mental challenge that accompanied their physical suffering:

The siege became a test of the human spirit and even a test of human relations, for it really revealed a person's worth. I am more pleased with the articles I wrote by the light of an oil lamp than with some I wrote in times of peace. This is understandable. That winter one could either not write at all or write with great enthusiasm. Each scholar retained his strong desire to understand the world, and this was stronger than hunger or physical weakness. We were afraid that our knowledge might perish with us. I was not the only one who thought that. I was on duty in one of the halls and my friend Andrey Borisov, an expert Orientalist, in another. Our posts were separated by the famous Rotunda. We would meet there between bombings and read courses of lectures to each other. Iosif Orbeli used to get very angry with his employees for having their gas-mask bags filled with books.

Yet we had to do something not to think just about ourselves. We were worried that we would not be able to pass on our knowledge if we died and that then someone would have to start everything all over from the beginning.

Caring for the physical condition of the collection also remained a challenge. The Stieglitz Museum in Solyanoi Lane was named an outstation of the Hermitage after the Revolution and, though most of the collection had been removed in the mid-1920s, material was stored there on behalf of the 'History of Everyday Life' Department of the Russian Museum, responsibility for which was transferred to the Hermitage in 1941 when its Russian Department was opened. The Stieglitz building was bombed in the early autumn. The glass dome of the central hall was smashed to smithereens and porcelain and furniture were blown to pieces, but no lives were lost. It was decided to remove what remained of the collections stored there to the Hermitage, but this was no easy matter since no lorries or cars were available for so frivolous an undertaking. The Hermitage staff began to move the collection with handcarts. After the snow fell they used sledges, harnessing themselves to them to pull the larger objects across town. Smaller, more easily transportable pieces came in rucksacks. Exposed to rain and snow, some of the items were already mouldy or corroded before they could be removed from the half-demolished building.

On 24 January the city administration announced that a small convalescent centre was to be established at the Hermitage. It was set up in the ground-floor rooms of the Small Hermitage overlooking the

Neva – where the director, Dmitry Tolstoy, had his private apartment before the Revolution – and was to serve staff from the Hermitage and four other city museums. There were one hundred beds and it had a throughput of 400 patients before closing down again in May – many of them were so emaciated that neither increased rations nor intravenous shots of glucose could save them from death. The cellar under the library at the Millionaya Street end of the Small Hermitage was turned into a mortuary. When the burial squad reached the Hermitage in early April 1942, forty-six frozen corpses were lifted into its lorry.

There were almost no air raids in the early months of 1942, though the Germans continued to shell the city. But the water and sewage pipes froze. In these circumstances those who had been living in the Hermitage cellars chose to move home again. By February the air raid shelters were empty. Moreover, the 'road of life' across the frozen Lake Ladoga, which had brought food into the city from November onwards, was greatly improved by the laying of a new road connecting Leningrad with the south-east bank of the lake. The lorries that now brought food into the city carried out evacuees. The whole of the university was evacuated and the history faculty, which was most closely linked to the Hermitage, reopened in Saratov. On a visit to Leningrad Alexey Kosygin, deputy chairman of the Sovnarkom, inspected the Hermitage and having seen its condition ordered that it should be reduced to the status of a 'conserved' institution – which meant merely keeping the building intact – and that the staff should be evacuated. Curiously enough, despite their sufferings, few of them wanted to leave.

Orbeli himself had been appointed director of the Academy of Science of Armenia and left for Yerevan on 30 March – where he spent the rest of the war. He took a motley collection of associates with him: his former wife, Mariya, his new wife, Elizaveta, Elizaveta's mother, Vladimir Vasiliev – secretary of the museum's Party organisation, the Hermitage Chief Architect – Andrey Sivkov, and Boris Piotrovsky – who had developed an inflammation of the lung in January and had been faithfully nursed by his old teacher, the Egyptologist Nataliya Flittner. Piotrovsky records that when the lorry that took them out of the city reached the railway line he was given a bowl of soup and was immediately sick. His body could not digest such rich food.

The journey south was enlivened by a stop in Stalingrad where the city administration and a delegation of doctors turned out to greet Academician Orbeli. Unfortunately the advance warning they had received of Orbeli's arrival had not indicated which Academician Orbeli was on the train. The Stalingraders had turned out under the impression that they were honouring Levon Orbeli, Iosif's brother and a great physiologist who had inherited the mantle of Ivan Pavlov, the Nobel prize winner famous the world over for his work on the conditioned reflexes of dogs. The delegation retired in confusion when the bearded Orientalist alighted from the train.

Orbeli and his retinue did not allow the war to hinder their enjoyment of the south, according to Piotrovsky's account. Having travelled to Yerevan with two of his wives, Orbeli was soon trying to persuade his devoted mistress, Camilla Trever, to join them from Tashkent where she was then at work. The whole party travelled from Yerevan to Tashkent to visit her. It was Trever who ended up typesetting the history of Urartu that Piotrovsky had written in the Hermitage air-raid shelter – omitting the inscriptions on the margin of the manuscript which read 'terribly cold', 'it's hard to write, it's so cold' and so on. Orbeli had run the publishing house at the Academy of the History of Material Culture after the Revolution and set great store by his own ability to typeset. He had persuaded many of his associates to learn in the pre-war years. It was the only way to ensure that quotations from Oriental languages, using script unfamiliar to an ordinary typesetter, were correctly reproduced.

The history of Urartu was published in Yerevan in 1944. Since Karmir-Blur, the Urartian fortress which Piotrovsky had begun to excavate before the war, was only a few miles from Yerevan, he was able to continue his work – with the aid of a young Armenian archaeologist, Ripsime Mikhailovna Djanpolodyan, to whom he became engaged in 1943 and whom he married in February 1944. In April 1944 Piotrovsky paid a return visit to Leningrad to pick up some books but caught typhoid and got stuck there for several months. His memoirs record that Orbeli was a frequent visitor to Leningrad at this time, his romance with Antonina Izergina, the Hermitage expert on modern paintings, having just begun.

When Orbeli left for the south in March 1942, he appointed Professor Mikhail Dobroklonsky as acting director of the Hermitage. A former imperial civil servant, Dobroklonsky had always dreamed of becoming director of the Hermitage, according to his adopted granddaughter who works there today. He had trained as a lawyer and spent 1910–15 visiting the great museums of Europe to study how they ran their exhibitions and scholarly work in preparation for his future role. But the likelihood of realising his dream appeared to go out of the window when the Bolsheviks took over. Nevertheless, he was one of the many members of the old nobility given jobs by the museum after the Revolution, working in the Drawings Department under Benois. His scholarly catalogue of the Hermitage drawings is still the last word on the collection.

The war tested Dobroklonsky almost beyond endurance. Both his sons were killed. The eldest, Login, died in his arms in the military hospital while the younger, Dmitry, who was really too young for the army, but lied about his age because it was hoped there would be more to eat at the front, disappeared without trace. And his home was destroyed by a bomb. In March 1942, however, he realised – temporarily – his youthful dream, becoming acting director of the Hermitage. In June 1943 he drew up a report on the activities of the Hermitage staff:

Our main tasks were to restore the building and do everything we could to ensure the preservation of the collection in our care. As a result of the shelling, most of the windows and the hanging lights were broken in all the buildings and many of the rooms were full of broken glass, snow and ice. All of us worked on cleaning out these rooms, regardless of our age or status in the museum. Everyone, workers, security guards, professors and scholars, helped to sweep up the glass and snow and carry buckets of sand. Using only our own staff, we cleaned a surface of over 2,000 square metres and carried out around thirty-six tonnes of broken glass, building rubbish, snow and ice. We also had to try to prevent glass from being rebroken by covering it with wood; we had to repair the rooves, pump water out of the cellars, repair the water system and, to date, we have covered 6,000 metres [of glass] with hardboard. As it became clear which storerooms were in better condition than others, we moved furniture and other exhibits into those rooms. It was necessary to dry out and air all the furniture and fabrics.

Most of the staff Dobroklonsky directed were women, the able-bodied men having gone to war, but they included a former museum guide and lecturer, Pavel Gubchevsky, who had been rejected by the army on account of a serious cardiac defect. He was appointed chief of the museum security guard. Writing in 1942, he left his own account of the problems:

On the guard payroll are sixty-four people of whom only forty-six report for duty (before the war there were 650). Guards are posted outside and inside the building on day and night shifts. They watch over some one million cubic metres of space, a display area fifteen kilometres long and 1,057 rooms in the Winter Palace alone. Guarding of the interior is currently especially difficult because the damage caused by shelling means that a number of premises may be easily infiltrated . . . My mighty troop is composed mostly of elderly ladies of fifty-five years of age or more, including some who are seventy. Many are cripples who before the war served as museum room attendants, as a limp or some other disablement did not then interfere with their job of seeing that proper order was maintained . . . as a rule at least a third are in hospital.

As the spring weather began after the long, harsh winter of 1941–2, the water pipes burst and melting snow gushed into the museum through holes in the roof caused by the German attack. The 'mighty troop' of old ladies had to rescue the collections in the basement and ground floor from the ensuing floods. The porcelain figures and vases which had been half buried in sand in the cellar under the Athena gallery had survived bombs and shells but were now in even greater danger. One of those who helped with the rescue was Olga Mikhailova, an art historian and critic.

I saw with horror that all the porcelain was drowned in water. 'We ran for rubber waders and descended into the dark cellar. The water reached our knees. Each movement created waves which raised it even higher. Placing each foot down carefully, so as not to tread on the fragile porcelain, we felt around to pluck out piece after piece. Some of the porcelain vessels were floating on the surface. Here and there the necks of some of the taller vases jutted out above the water, but most of the items had filled up with sand and filth and settled on the floor. Much later, recalling these searches in the darkness, the wading through the water, and how we, loaded down with porcelain, climbed the dark steep staircase, not seeing the steps but feeling them with our feet only, it was all unbelievable, as if we had pulled off some incredible acrobatic stunt, and we were amazed that we broke nothing.

Having removed the porcelain from the cellar, we set to to clean off all the dirt. Though they were not the gems of the Hermitage collection, still every piece before us was a work of art . . . It was easy enough to wipe the glazed items clean. But as for the biscuit pieces, their unglazed white porcelain had absorbed the water and had yellowed. Some of the items that had previously been restored had come unstuck. Many objects had lost their inventory numbers, which could lead to head-spinning confusion in museum inventorisation; hundreds of soaked paper labels were floating around in the cellar . . . We had to do everything at once – wash, wipe clean and restore the number. We dried the porcelain out in the yard in the spring sunshine, on top of sacking or right out on the greening grass.

The Hermitage courtyards did not only sprout porcelain. Furniture was also carried there to dry out. 'We made use of every sunny day,' wrote another member of the troop, Alexandra Anosova, 'to drag all the upholstered furniture out into the courtyard. The upholstery on the sofas and chairs was covered with a thick, furry layer of mildew, as if these pieces of furniture had been upholstered not in velvet and silk but in some revolting, hideous yellow-green sheepskin. The sun-dried mildew was brushed off and all day long clouds of dust and the acrid fumes of sulphide filled the air, so much so that towards evening our clothes reeked of it, while the dust choked eyes, ears and nose and rasped the throat.'

There were other uses for the courtyards too. The city was still under siege and food supplies were pathetically small and deficient in vitamins. Vegetable gardens began to spring up in all the city squares – and, of course, the palace courtyards. But the museum's principal vegetable supply came from the Hanging Garden that Catherine the Great had built on the first floor of the Small Hermitage. It was planted with carrots, beet, dill, spinach, cabbage – in place of the ornamental shrubbery favoured by the Romanovs. 'We ripped out the bushes of lilac and honeysuckle to make way for our vegetable garden,' Olga Mikhailova recalled. 'As, day after day, we dug the earth and planted the vegetables, the torn-out bushes lay by the wall, with clods of earth still clinging to their roots, and slowly withered. During that blockade spring we witnessed many deaths. The lilacs of the Hermitage also died a long and tortured death.'

German bombing and shelling continued and new wounds were constantly inflicted on the Hermitage. On 18 June a shell broke into the carriage store, blasting to smithereens seven carriages and two palanquins used by the imperial family in the eighteenth century. On 25 January

1943 a one-ton bomb exploded in Palace Square, causing the Winter Palace to 'rock like a cockle-shell on a storm-ridden, choppy sea', in the words of Pavel Gubchevsky. In May a second bomb was dropped on the Winter Palace itself but did not explode – an almost miraculous escape. The gardeners working in the Hanging Garden gave the alarm after seeing what they took to be smoke billowing out of the Kitchen Yard.

'What we feared most of all was fire', wrote Pavel Gubchevsky:

By the time I reached the Kitchen Yard the clouds of smoke had dispersed. A few minutes later the municipal fire chiefs arrived. We examined the spot carefully, but did not see anything burning. Nor could we smell fire. The firemen left but I still felt worried. Once again we looked around carefully and I suddenly noticed a broken window on the ground floor . . . Dragging a stepladder to the spot, I climbed up and peered inside. You can imagine how startled I was to see a quarter-ton bomb lying amidst the scattered paintings on a bed of torn canvases and shattered stretchers. Only later did I realise what had actually happened. It appeared that the bomb dropped by a Nazi plane had hit the eaves of the building across the yard, not, however, with its detonator but with its casing. Under the impact, the hundred-year-old masonry had crumbled into dust and raised a thick cloud. Meanwhile the bomb itself had ricocheted and fallen into the window, but again sideways, and then came to rest, without exploding, on a disarrayed stack of paintings.

The very last German shell struck the Hermitage in December 1943. Professor Dobroklonsky immediately reported the damage to the city administration. 'An enemy shell that exploded in the courtyard of the Winter Palace on 16 December blew out up to 750 metres of glass, including windows in the Armorial Hall, the Fieldmarshals Hall, the Peter the Great Hall and other premises with richly decorated interiors. The State Hermitage requests assistance in the procurement of 5.5 cubic metres of plywood.'

On 27 January 1944 the blockade of Leningrad was finally lifted. According to the radio announcement that sounded from the loud-speakers throughout the city that day: 'after twelve days of fierce fighting the troops of the Leningrad front have hurled the enemy back across its entire length to distances of between sixty-five and one hundred kilometres from the city. Our forces are continuing to thrust forward.' That night a victory salute of twenty-four salvoes was fired from 324 guns on the battered battleships anchored in the Neva. A flaming stream of red, white and blue rockets lit up the skies above the city.

Once it was known that Leningrad was saved, the fate of the Hermitage immediately became a topic of vivid interest to the culture-loving population of the Soviet Union. The government newspaper *Izvestiya* sent a reporter up from Moscow to investigate its condition. 'At the door was a gray-haired elderly lady who looked more like a music teacher,' wrote Tatyana Tess.

> The old lady sat in a warm sheepskin and with a warm hood on her head. A rifle was propped by her side. As she examined my identity card, a stream of bluish vapour issued from her mouth. It was so bitterly cold in there that it seemed to me as though the cold had been gathered from all over the city and had been packed and locked in this place. Right in front of the door two medieval knights stood as sentinels, stripped of their armour – two dummies, no more than faded trunks on skinny legs stuffed with sawdust. By their side were crates of sand, axes, crowbars and a pair of enormous pincers.

Orbeli was put back in charge of the museum in June 1944. Summoned to Moscow from Armenia, he was ordered to draw up a list of the building materials that would be needed to start the restoration work on the Hermitage. His list included sixty-five tons of gypsum plaster, eighty tons of alabaster, one hundred tons of cement, two tons of joiner's glue, 4,000 metres of Bohemian glass of triple strength plus 2,000 metres of extra fine glass, 2,000 metres of assorted canvas, 30,000 metres of decorative fabrics, two tons of casting bronze, two tons of sheet bronze and six kilograms of gold leaf. The Germans surrendered on 9 May 1945 and the ordeal was over.

14

Trophy Art

he term 'Second World War' is seldom used in Russian publications. It is referred to instead as the 'Great Patriotic War', an emotive reminder of the struggle and sacrifice involved in driving Hitler's forces out of Russia and assuring his ultimate defeat. Over twenty million Soviet citizens died in the war and this horrifying statistic means that most Russian families lost some close relation or friend. The ferocity of Hitler's onslaught even turned many victims of Stalin's purges into patriots, and victory converted Stalin's image – temporarily – into that of the country's saviour. None of this has been forgotten in Russia.

In the last months of the war and the first years of peace the Russian army removed more than two million works of art from Germany and sent them by air and train to Russia, mostly to the Pushkin Museum in Moscow or the Hermitage in Leningrad. They seized the finest museum masterpieces, crate loads of secondary exhibits and any private collections that crossed their paths. At the time the operation was regarded as fully justified reparation. In the 1990s, however, when memories of the war had faded elsewhere, the continuing presence of German 'trophy art' in Russian museums aroused sharp controversy.

Most of the art removed by the Russians from East Germany and Poland was returned in the 1950s as a fraternal gesture to fellow Socialist states. But a miscellany of art works from West Germany and other sources remained hidden in Russian museums. The very existence of these stores is still officially a state secret but the secret was blown, as far as the West is concerned, in 1991 when the American magazine *Artnews* published a carefully researched article on 'trophy art' by two Russians,

Konstantin Akinsha and Grigory Kozlov, both formerly museum curators.

The two men had been collecting documents and combing archives since 1987 and their book *Stolen Treasure*, published in 1995, remains the chief source of information on this curious page of Russian history. Both felt it necessary to leave Russia to avoid harassment by the angry authorities and settled in Germany to write their book. As a result, they are criticised back home for telling the story with an anti-Russian bias. Their researches have, however, shaped the international attitude to this topic.

It is not a story of looting. The removal of art works was ordered by the Central Committee of the Communist Party of the Soviet Union and organised by art historians and other arts professionals who were given temporary military rank and dressed up in uniform. The art itself was consigned for safekeeping to the great national museums. But the government's ambivalent attitude to the ethics of the project is reflected in the degree of secrecy with which the removal and storage of the trophy art has always been surrounded. A train full of treasures from Berlin arrived at the Hermitage in October 1945, six days after the museum's evacuated collection came back from Sverdlovsk. While the arrival of the Sverdlovsk train, and the drama associated with transporting the collection back from the station to the Hermitage, was trumpeted in the press, the arrival of the treasure train from Berlin went unremarked.

The Minister of Culture, Nikolay Gubenko, admitted the presence of trophy art in Russia in June 1991, in response to Akinsha and Kozlov's articles. But what trophy art remains hidden in Russian stores is only gradually being revealed. In 1994 it was admitted, after rumours and denials had filled the press for three years, that Schliemann's gold was in Moscow – the famous golden jewellery found at the site of ancient Troy by the archaeologist Heinrich Schliemann in 1873, and donated to the German nation in 1881. A major exhibition of the Trojan gold was mounted by the Pushkin Museum in 1996. In 1992 the Hermitage had led the way by exhibiting Old Master drawings taken from the Bremen Kunsthalle, following up, in 1995, with seventy-four Impressionist and Post-Impressionist paintings from German private collections. The 1995 exhibition, titled, *Hidden Treasures* attracted massive press coverage and visitors from all over the world. After twice extending the closing date of the exhibition, the museum decided to mount a permanent display of the pictures in exhibition format – the Pushkin, in contrast, has chosen to hang its trophy pictures alongside its own collection, as if they already belonged to the museum.

The revelation of the secret stores was one of the major art sensations of the 1990s and controversy raged over whether all or some of the pieces should be given back to their former owners.

In 1995 the Russian parliament, known as the Duma, drafted a law that would nationalise the treasures and keep most of them in Russia. Passed by the lower house, it was defeated in the Legislative Council, or upper house, in the summer of 1996 and sent back for redrafting. A slightly amended draft was passed by both houses in 1997, but vetoed by Yeltsin. As I write, the trophy treasures still in Russia have no defined legal status and it looks as if Russian decision-making on the issue will be a long drawn-out affair. If the nation's attitude to returning the remaining art were to be tested by a referendum, however, the Russian people's answer would, undoubtedly, be 'no'. The memory of the war is still too vividly alive.

The idea of removing art from Germany and its allies in compensation for the cultural treasures the Nazis had stolen or destroyed in Russia was first raised in 1943 by the artist and art historian Igor Grabar, editor of the official thirteen-volume *History of Russian Art* and veteran of the campaign to protect Russia's own artistic monuments in the wake of the Revolution. While Benois and Gorky were fighting to preserve the treasures of St Petersburg in 1917, Grabar was doing the same for Moscow. In 1943 he approached the newly instituted – and ponderously named – Extraordinary State Commission on the Registration and Investigation of the Crimes of the German Fascist Occupiers and their Accomplices and the Damage Done by them to the Citizens, Collective Farms, Public Organisations, State Enterprises and Institutions of the USSR – with a new idea.

Grabar's suggestion was to compile a list of art works 'equivalent' to those stolen or destroyed by the Nazis which could be confiscated from museums in Germany and allied countries after Hitler's defeat. The historic palaces of Tsarskoe Selo and Peterhof, outside St Petersburg, had already been reduced to ruins by the German invaders, as had the churches of Novgorod and Pskov. The major cities of the Ukraine and Belorussia had been devastated. Thousands of paintings and other art works had been taken from Kiev; the picture gallery in Kharkov had been looted and burned; the Minsk museum had been emptied. Grabar suggested that the Extraordinary State Commission should establish a special division 'to make up lists of objects in the museum collections of

Germany, Austria, Italy, Hungary, Romania and Finland that could be named as eventual equivalents. Business trips abroad would not be necessary for the conduct of this work because complete sets of the catalogues of all European museums are in the libraries of some Soviet art historians, and their own notes contain complete information about these museums.'

Grabar suggested that the nation's three top experts should compile the lists of equivalents: he named himself, Sergey Troinitsky, former director of the Hermitage and a specialist on the applied arts, and Viktor Lazarev, former curator of paintings at the Pushkin Museum. Troinitsky had, by this time, returned from exile and was working as a consultant to the Kuskovo Museum of Ceramics in Moscow.

The idea of equivalents was enthusiastically received and the most ambitious lists compiled. Grabar's team intended taking 179 paintings from Berlin's Kaiser Friedrich Museum (which became Berlin-Dahlem after the war), including Van Eyck's *The Virgin in a Church*, Giotto's *Entombment of Mary* and Raphael's *Colonna Madonna*; they listed another 125 pictures from Munich's Alte Pinakothek, comparable numbers from Dresden and Leipzig and a whole range of masterpieces from Italy – Botticelli's *Madonna with a Pomegranate* from the Uffizi and Tintoretto's *Portrait of Two Senators* from the Doge's Palace in Venice. Six works by Breughel and four by Velazquez were among those to be confiscated from the Kunsthistorischesmuseum in Vienna; fifty-two paintings were to be taken from the National Gallery of Budapest and El Greco's *Adoration of the Magi* from the private collection of the king of Romania.

The list of paintings, sculpture and Byzantine art handed to the government's Arts Committee on 26 February 1945 had, in the event, been compiled by Viktor Lazarev from the Pushkin, Nikolay Vlasov from the sales organisation Antiquariat, and Vladimir Levinson-Lessing, keeper of Western European art at the Hermitage. Since Levinson-Lessing had worked with Antiquariat on the art sales of the 1930s, he and Vlasov were thought to understand the monetary value of art which was so important for estimating the equivalents correctly – the same, of course, applied to Troinitsky.

Similar lists of drawings, applied art and antiquities were also drawn up. The compilers were particularly anxious to acquire monuments of Slavic culture. This was the time when the government propaganda machine was demanding embellishments to the history of the Slavs for patriotic reasons. 'It is very important to nominate Slavic archaeological objects, which are exceptionally well represented in German collections, as equivalents,' wrote Sergey Tolstov, the director of the Institute for the History of Material Culture. The total value of equivalents was calculated at $70,587,200. The most expensive item on the list was the Pergamum altar frieze valued at $7.5m. Carved in high relief in the second century BC to decorate the altar of Zeus at Pergamum, the marble frieze depicts the battle of the gods and the giants and is 2.3 metres high and 120 metres long. The Pergamum Museum in Berlin, built specially to accommodate it, was opened in 1930, but from 1945 to 1958 the frieze was held at the Hermitage.

Summing up the work of selection at a meeting of architects on 14 January 1944 Grabar concluded: 'It seems that in Moscow there will be a museum whose equal never existed in the world.' The sculptor Sergey Merkurov, then director of the Pushkin Museum, seized on this idea and wrote to the head of the Arts Committee of the Council of People's Commissars two months later:

> The German-Fascist barbarians, who tried to annihilate Russian culture and destroyed many famous examples of Russian art, must be held responsible for all their crimes. The museums of the Axis countries are full of wonderful masterpieces, which must be given to the Soviet Union as compensation. All valuables received from the Axis countries must be concentrated in one place and can play the role of a perfect memorial dedicated to the glory of Russian arms.

Hitler had dreamed of raising the greatest museum in the world in Linz, his birthplace, by removing the art treasures of conquered nations, and now the Russians were dreaming of doing the same in Moscow. But neither dream was destined for fulfilment.

The collection of trophy art turned out to be a more pragmatic affair. The decision to divide Germany into occupation zones was taken at the Yalta conference which ended on 12 February 1945. Stalin won the Allies' grudging approval for a $10 billion compensation scheme and on 25 February a Special Committee on Germany was established, headed by Georgy Malenkov, to oversee the confiscation of valuables in the occupied territories. It was a huge undertaking with whole factories being dismantled and shipped east, besides trainloads of industrial products and consumer goods which were in such short supply in Russia. In all, 90,000 train carriages were filled with confiscated material and sent home. Most of the decisions on the removal of goods to the Soviet Union were signed personally by Stalin.

In this context, the removal of art objects was only a sideline, but in February 1945 the government Arts Committee began to recruit trophy brigades to select, pack and transport art back to Russia on a large scale. Andrey Belokopytov, manager of the Moscow Art Theatre, was given charge of the brigade on the Belorussian front, and ended up in Berlin, while Boris Filippov, director of the Moscow Drama Theatre, directed that on the Ukrainian front. For some reason, theatre managers seem to have been considered particularly suitable organisers.

During the war the contents of Germany's great museums had been evacuated for safekeeping to a variety of depositories around the country. The Russians never got their hands on the great Old Masters from Berlin's Kaiser Friedrich Museum, which were found hidden in a mine in the American occupation zone, but they found many others. Belokopytov's first successes involved locating art works from Polish and Baltic museums that had been stashed away by the Nazis. In March 1945, in tunnels leading off an underground aircraft factory at Hohenwalde, near Meseritz, he found the contents of the Poznan, Tallinn and Riga museums. He was allowed twenty-two railway carriages to send his trove back to Moscow.

Next Belokopytov took charge of the palaces of Potsdam. 'Summarising the results of the inspection,' he wrote in his official report, 'we can say that we have several thousand original pictures . . . of German, French and Italian masters and a large quantity of valuable copies of the works of world-famous artists, several hundred marble statues . . . a very large quantity of old palace furniture and *objets d'art*. There are several thousand miniatures. There are about 50,000 rare (some antique) editions of books . . . The value of all counted objets, which could be deconstructed and removed to the Soviet Union . . . is about 150,000 golden roubles.' Some of the paintings are still in the Hermitage.

But Belokopytov's greatest find in Potsdam was Dr Carl Justi, formerly director of the Berlin National Gallery, who provided him with detailed information on where museum treasures had been hidden in the capital. The Russians also found and arrested Hermann Voss, the head of the Dresden gallery who had been named by Hitler as the future director of the Führer Museum to be built at Linz. Voss explained to them where the famous Dresden pictures had been hidden, Augustus the Strong and other connoisseur rulers of Saxony having accumulated one of the world's greatest collections of Old Masters in their Dresden gallery.

One of the most bizarre features of the trophy story was the post-war argument over who found the Dresden pictures, and where. It has never been resolved. So many people wanted to claim responsibility for 'saving' Raphael's *Sistine Madonna*, which became one of the best known cultural icons in Russia, that each fictionalised his or her own account. The Dresden pictures were returned to East Germany in 1955 and in the barrage of publicity which surrounded the transfer a book written by an artist, Leonid Rabinovich, who worked with the trophy brigade attracted special attention. His book, *Seven Days*, written under the pseudonym Leonid Volinsky, gave a highly charged and entirely fictitious account of how he personally rescued the picture. Despite the protests of other brigade members, Rabinovich's book ran through two editions, was broadcast on the radio and turned into a film.

One of the Dresden pictures reached the Hermitage by mistake – a Van Eyck *Triptych* was found in a crate of swords and sabres from the Dresden Historical Museum and Orbeli put it in his safe – but it was mainly the treasures unearthed by Belokopytov's brigade in Berlin that came to fill the storerooms of the Hermitage. Some were sent direct to Leningrad while others went first to Moscow and were sent on by the government's Arts Committee which had charge of distributing trophy art around Russia's museums. The sheer volume of material, and the inadequacy of the documentation which accompanied it, meant that even the registration of what had been received took years of work.

Gathering up Berlin's treasures and despatching them to Russia was a complicated business. Before the war they had been proudly exhibited in a complex of major museums, most of them on the so-called Museum Island – literally an island in the river in Berlin where the National Gallery, the Alte Museum, the Neue Museum, the Bodemuseum and the Pergamonmuseum were located, the latter dedicated to the Pergamum altar and other major architectural complexes of Greek and Roman origin. In 1940 the most important treasures had been sent to the strong rooms of the Reichsbank and the New Mint or to two, virtually impregnable, anti-aircraft towers – their walls made of reinforced concrete two yards thick – which had been built, one in the Zoological Garden and one at Friedrichshain.

It was the anti-aircraft tower in the Zoological Garden that was found to contain the greatest treasures. It was forty-four yards high with a platform on the roof for anti-aircraft guns, the gunners' barracks on the floor below, then a hospital floor, two floors devoted to museum treasures, two floors containing kitchens, air-raid shelters and emergency quarters for the national broadcasting station and, below that, six underground levels for storing ammunition and equipment. The Trojan gold and the Pergamum altar frieze were stored there, together with a quantity of royal arms and armour from the Armoury, jewellery and sculpture from the Egyptian Museum, primitive carvings from the Ethnographic Museum, portfolios of drawings and prints, including Botticelli's illustrations for Dante's *Divine Comedy*, from the Kupfer-stichkabinett of the Alte Museum and a group of large paintings from the National Gallery.

The Soviets began their bombardment of the tower on 27 April but it was not taken until 1 May and fell into the hands of SMERSH, the military counter-intelligence service established by the NKVD – there had been rumours that high-ranking Nazi officers were hiding there. The evacuation of the treasures began on 13 May and continued for over two weeks.

The three crates of Trojan gold were removed on 26 May and airlifted to Moscow on 30 June, along with new microscopes destined for the Academy of Science, the collection of gems from the Alte Museum, and eighteen paintings from the Gerstenberg and Koehler collections – private collections that had been stored for safekeeping at the National Gallery and ended up among the *Hidden Treasures* exhibition of the Hermitage. When the aircraft was checked at Vnukovo airport in Moscow, however, it turned out that half the crates on board were not listed on the freight documents. Someone at the Berlin end had decided to take up smuggling. The unlisted crates contained shoes, raincoats and textiles and the whole cargo was seized by the military authorities. The museum treasures were only reluctantly yielded to the Pushkin Museum some days later.

The removal of the Pergamum altar from the Zoo tower was a more difficult and dangerous affair on account of its vast size. Belokopytov and the art historian Serafim Druzhinin had found the altar on 10 May, after being alerted that 'some ancient stones, apparently valuable' had been found there. Druzhinin's diary waxes lyrical: 'a giant, crying, screaming in torture, and the proud, victorious Athena are in front of me, on the left side of the entrance. Zeus, stormy and triumphant, is on the right. And so the "ancient stones" meant the frieze of the Pergamum Altar . . . The battle of the gods and the giants! The eternal subject – the fight of life and death, of light and darkness. I was frightened – the artist spoke two thousand years ago about the events of yesterday, the memories of which were alive for us that day . . . Victory and catastrophe, destruction and the passionate, ecstatic success of life.'

By the end of May there was fierce pressure on Belokopytov and his brigade to remove everything they could from those sectors of Berlin which were to be occupied by the Western Allies – which included the Zoo tower – but SMERSH would not let enough people into the building to move the massive sculptural reliefs. Trading on his old popularity as manager of the Moscow Art Theatre, when he had been able to provide bigwigs with scarce theatre tickets, Belokopytov wangled an interview with Marshal Zhukov, the commander of the Soviet Forces in Germany. 'If the Americans get this collection, you'll regret this mistake,' Belokopytov told him and Zhukov duly ordered SMERSH to yield up the altar.

Belokopytov has left an account of what happened. A unit of sappers under the command of one Major Kulakovsky was sent to the Zoo to help him.

> We looked at the friezes and sculptures that were stored on the third level. Our sappers were not very young; these were old men who had constructed the pontoon bridges on the Vistula and Oder. Kulakovsky asked them: 'How can we get this stuff out?' 'Very simple,' they answered. 'Let's smash one wall and put a crane there and we can fish them out.' They immediately began to cut down old trees in the park and make wooden frames three by two metres each. The hospital was quickly evacuated by SMERSH. We took mattresses and luxurious plush blankets from the hospital rooms. We put the mattresses on the frames; we put the reliefs packed in blankets on the mattresses and then let them down carefully through the hole in the wall our sappers had blown out. In a day and a half, everything was removed.

Transporting the frieze to Russia, however, was a chapter of accidents. A train containing sections of the Pergamum altar, distributed between forty carriages, left Berlin on 27 September under the escort of Serafim Druzhinin. The heavy reliefs were put on the floor of each carriage and lighter museum valuables from the Zoo tower were piled on top. Since the distance between the rails in Russia is wider than that in Europe the train had to be repacked at the Soviet border. Then it got lost. Druzhinin had been ordered to escort the train to Moscow but a few hours after he left Berlin a telegram arrived there requesting it be rerouted to Leningrad. It was not until 8 October that the authorities found the train and, when it finally arrived in Leningrad on 13 October, it turned out to be accompanied by fictional documents. The originals had been lost in Berlin and creating new ones would have required unloading the whole train. One of the officers had decided to make up an imaginary list instead.

The arrival of the train, six days after the return of the Hermitage's own collection from Sverdlovsk, was a nightmare for the museum. Orbeli's report recorded that 'the unloading of the first special train arriving in Leningrad took place on the day when the work of unloading the returned valuables of the Hermitage was finished. The unloading was very fast. The crates transported to the Hermitage blocked all the portals and the nearest halls. It was necessary to open the crates to understand to which department they belonged . . . The codes in most cases gave no information about the contents of the crates . . . many had no codes or numbers at all.'

Boris Piotrovsky, the future director of the museum, had the happy duty of unpacking the Egyptian art from the Neue Museum that had been stored in the Zoo tower – Piotrovsky had been fascinated by Egypt since childhood and the Neue Museum contained one of the greatest collections of Egyptian art in the world. He found himself unpacking crates of rich jewellery and sculpture, including the famous unfinished, yellow-brown quartzite head of Queen Nefertiti that dates back to around 1350 BC.

A group of papyri with middle-Persian inscriptions in Aramaic (middle-Persian script, Aramaic language) that belonged to the Austrian National Library was found among the Egyptian papyri, to the Hermitage curators' surprise. Only a handful of people in the world are capable of reading these inscriptions and the Austrians had apparently sent the papyri to the Egyptian Museum in Berlin in the hope that one of the scholars there could interpret them. Overtaken by the war, they were stored for safekeeping in the Zoo tower with the museum's own collection and thus arrived in Russia. Some of the Persian papyri were returned to Berlin in 1958, along with the Egyptian ones, and it took the Austrians years to get them back. Others, it is now revealed, remained in the Hermitage and the restitution battle has had to be started all over again.

Four trainloads of art were sent to Leningrad in the course of late 1945 and 1946. The Hermitage received most of the art works that had been stored in the second massive anti-aircraft tower in Friedrichshain – or rather such of the material as survived. Some of Berlin's most important museum treasures had been stored there, 411 large canvases from the National Gallery, 400 sculptures, 8,500 antiquities packed in boxes and 2,800 glass objects, according to surviving records. On 5 May 1945, only one day after Belokopytov had been authorised to start removing art from the Berlin repositories, a mysterious fire broke out in the tower. It was later blamed on fanatical SS officers who were determined to prevent Germany's heritage falling into Russian hands. Belokopytov's team literally excavated the surviving works of art from the ashes. Several dozen crates of burned, broken and damaged treasures eventually arrived at the Hermitage and were a nightmare to deal with since everything had to be identified and inventoried. A crate opened by the head of the Hermitage Sculpture Department, Zhanetta Matsulevich, in July 1946 illustrates the problem. She listed the contents as follows:

1 A relief of rectangular shape, made of marble. Half-figure of the Virgin and Child by Rossellino. Broken. Many of the parts are missing. 2 Bas-relief of rectangular shape made of marble. Half-figure of the Virgin and Child by Donatello. Broken in many pieces. The marble is burned on the surface. The right elbow of the Virgin is covered with soot. 3 Statuette of the Virgin and Child made of marble by Giovanni Pisano. The heads of both figures are broken off, all projecting parts are seriously damaged, sides are crumbling.

Not all the Hermitage trophy art was taken from Germany in the first flush of victory. The ninety-eight paintings from the private collection of Otto Krebs, a German industrialist, were not discovered and removed until 1948. The collection formed the backbone of the museum's *Hidden Treasures* exhibition in 1995. Krebs had stored the paintings, along with his collections of Oriental art and antiquities, in a specially equipped room in the cellar of his country estate, Gut Holzdorf, near Weimar. In 1941 he died of cancer and left all his property to a cancer research foundation. The house was occupied by the Americans from April to June 1945 but they didn't notice the iron door in the cellar. Nor did General Vasily Chuikov who turned Gut Holzdorf into the Soviet military headquarters for Thuringia in 1946.

In 1948 a German art historian told the Soviet authorities that an art collection was secretly stored in the basement of the castle. The iron door in the cellar was cut open and Krebs's treasures revealed. There were quantities of Impressionists, including two good portraits by Manet and works by Renoir and Pissarro; there were early still lifes by Gauguin and Tahitian scenes rich in colour and personality; there were late Van

Gogh landscapes, Cézannes, a Toulouse-Lautrec, a Picasso and even a Matisse *Ballerina* of 1927. These were all exhibited at the Hermitage in 1995. The following year fourteen watercolours by Paul Signac that had belonged to Krebs were shown in the museum's exhibition of trophy drawings. As I write, Krebs's German paintings of the same period, still at the Hermitage, have not yet been exhibited.

In the immediate post-war years the Pushkin and the Hermitage naturally expected to exhibit their new treasures. The Pushkin actually received permission to include the best of the Dresden pictures when they opened their new, post-war display in the autumn of 1946 but permission was cancelled on the eve of the opening and the 200 trophy pictures were hung postage-stamp fashion, floor to ceiling, in two closed galleries which it required special permission to visit. Goya's *Maypole* and Degas's *Place de la Concorde* were briefly shown at the Hermitage and the museum's chief architect, Alexander Sivkov, drew up plans to reconstruct and display the Pergamum altar – he estimated the cost at 369,630 roubles (about £50,000).

The *Hidden Treasures* catalogue explains that in 1995 there were:

> still visitors to the Hermitage old enough to remember a time when, alongside familiar Hermitage objects, there might appear unexpected antique statues, or a work by Goya, from Berlin. But such sightings were brief. As soon as Western newspapers printed a photograph of a very rare visit, in those Iron Curtain years, by an American delegation to the Hermitage, posing with Greek sculptures, there was the smell of scandal in the air, since one could glimpse a work from the Pergamum Museum, Berlin, among the other objects. Measures were quickly taken: the careless museum guide was fired (though soon reinstated) and works were sent to storage, where they remained until it was decided to return them to the German Democratic Republic.

In late 1948 or early 1949, according to Akinsha and Kozlov, tours of trophy stores in Russian museums were banned and total secrecy imposed. The Hermitage interpreted the ban quite freely at first; artists were allowed to see the pictures, and anyone else with a serious interest. The present exhibition designer, Viktor Pavlov, says he used to take his girlfriends from the Academy of Art. 'The curator would ask "is she a chatterer?" and if I said she wasn't, it'd be OK.' From about 1973 things got stricter, he says; it was only possible to sneak in at the weekend when the bosses weren't about.

The veil was temporarily lifted in 1955 with the return of the Dresden pictures. 'The Council of Ministers of the USSR,' ran a statement published by Soviet newspapers on 31 March, 'has decided to return to the government of the German Democratic Republic all paintings of the Dresden Gallery that are kept in the Soviet Union, for the purpose of further strengthening and developing friendly relations between Soviet and German people and because the government of the German Democratic Republic is loyal to the policy of peace and friendship . . . There are about 750 paintings belonging to the Dresden Gallery in the Soviet Union.'

The German museum treasures, previously regarded as fully justified 'reparations' now became 'cultural valuables of the GDR temporarily stored in the USSR.' Moreover, it was claimed, they had been 'saved and removed to the Soviet Union' by the Soviet army. The paintings were exhibited at the Pushkin Museum before they were despatched to Germany and in his speech opening the exhibition the Minister of Culture, Nikolay Mikhailov, referred to the paintings as 'twice saved', first from damp caves by the heroic Red Army and secondly by museum officials and restorers.

In 1956 the Pushkin Museum hosted a second exhibition devoted to paintings, drawings and engravings from Polish museums which had also been 'saved' by the Red Army and which, in their turn, were graciously returned to Poland. They included a much travelled Hans Memling – a *Last Judgement* (1473) from the Marienkirche in Danzig – which had been stored at the Hermitage. It was originally commissioned by Tommaso Portinari, the representative of the Medici bank in Bruges, but it was captured by pirates from the Hanseatic city of Danzig on its way to Italy and given to the church. Napoleon removed it to Paris and it spent a brief period in the Louvre before returning to Danzig. At the outbreak of war it was removed from the church and hidden but the Russians found it in April 1946 and took it to Leningrad.

In 1957 the governments of the Soviet Union and the GDR signed a protocol recognising East Germany's invaluable support over 'the suppression of counterrevolution' in Hungary and adding a number of friendly codicils which included one stating that: 'Both sides affirmed their readiness to discuss questions connected with the return on a mutual basis of cultural valuables (art works, archival materials etc.).' The Germans presented the Russians with a list of art works missing from the Dresden and Berlin museums and the Russians established a commission of museum curators and bureaucrats to prepare proposals for the return of trophy art. The first problem that faced them was to establish what they had. After inquiries had been made in all relevant institutions the Minister of Culture discovered that he had 2,614,874 objects and 534 crates of archaeological material. The Hermitage reported 829,561 works, including 2,724 paintings, 180 of them from private collections, and 26,214 objects of unknown origin. The struggle to identify the latter still continues in the 1990s.

To the Soviets' surprise, the GDR announced that it had no trophy art from Russia and the idea of returning art 'on a mutual basis' had to be scrapped. Museum curators advised against over-generosity. A letter to the Minister of Culture from Vladimir Levinson-Lessing, head of the Western Art Department, and two curators from the Pushkin argued that 'under these conditions the return to the GDR of all artistic and cultural valuables located in the Soviet Union would not be in the interests of the Soviet Union, just as it would not be without its dangers for the preservation of the very works of art. If nothing remains in the USSR, then in the future we shall have no means to provoke the other side to seek out and return our valuables (both in the GDR and the FRG, since the objects are being returned to the German people as a whole).' The letter went on to list 'top quality works' which the experts thought should be retained and which in their view were 'roughly equivalent to the artistic valuables removed from the USSR'. The idea of 'equivalents' had by no means died.

Nevertheless, most of the art from GDR museums was returned. Two massive exhibitions of the treasures that were being sent back to Germany were mounted in 1958 at the Pushkin and the Hermitage. Restoration posed a major problem since the proud Russians were determined to demonstrate how carefully they had looked after everything. The Central Restoration Workshop in Moscow was given charge of bringing the exhibits up to scratch and a team was sent to Leningrad to help the Hermitage restorers. A shed with huge tubs was set up in one of the courtyards to clean the burned sculptures from the Frierichshain tower. But despite their best efforts 561 objects were considered beyond restoration and unreturnable.

Another curiously nineteenth-century feature of the Hermitage preparations for the exhibition was the commissioning of copies to be retained in Leningrad. A cast of the vast Pergamum altar frieze was the most ambitious undertaking; after slumbering in the stables of the Winter Palace underneath Catherine's hanging garden for forty years, the plaster frieze was donated to the re-emerging Stieglitz Museum in

1996. The Hermitage also made plaster casts of thirty-seven Greek and Roman sculptures, eight from the ancient East, including the head of Queen Nefertiti, and twelve from India. They made reproductions of bronze fibulas and plaques. And, finding they had in their possession the original wood blocks carved by various fifteenth- and sixteenth-century German engravers, Artamonov, then director of the museum, ordered that new prints should be pulled from them, thus acquiring two Dürers, five Cranachs, five Albrecht Altdorfers, twenty-one Hans Shaüfeleins and sixty-seven other assorted prints.

The 1958 Hermitage exhibition contained 200,000 paintings, graphics, sculpture and works of applied art, together with 600,000 coins from Berlin's numismatic collection. It was a panorama of world culture. There were Egyptian stone carvings and Fayum portraits, Persian miniatures, Greek marbles, Roman bronzes, Renaissance sculptures in terracotta and plaster, German Gothic wood carvings, animalier sculptures by Antoine-Louis Barye and others. There were Old Master paintings as well as a smattering of moderns – Cézanne, Van Gogh – and a fine showing of the German nineteenth-century schools; the drawings included works by Rembrandt, Poussin, Henry Fuseli, Constantin Guys, Degas, Van Gogh, Käthe Kollwitz and Oskar Kokoschka. Among the highlights were the Pergamum altar, Nefertiti's head and Botticelli's drawings for the *Divine Comedy*. Contemporary press coverage records that 5,000 people visited the exhibition on the first day. In expectation of vast numbers of visitors the museum had installed artificial light in the galleries which were kept open until 10 p.m. at night. Mikhail Artamonov described the exhibition as 'evidence of the deep faith of the Soviet people and the ordinary people of Germany, on both sides of the border dividing them, who most of all want peace and friendship'.

The next Hermitage exhibition of trophy art did not take place until 1992. For thirty-three years the secret stores had slumbered undisturbed. In each department, one curator was given the responsibility of maintaining an inventory of the trophy art and regularly checking its condition. They were not supposed to speak to their colleagues about this duty. How strictly they interpreted this rule varied from curator to curator.

The 1992 exhibition was devoted to European drawings of the fifteenth to twentieth centuries from the Kunsthalle in Bremen, which had been recently transferred to the museum. In his introduction to the catalogue the Russian Federation Minister of Culture, Yevgeny Sidorov, described the exhibition as 'the first significant action of the new democratic Russia on the resurrection of the masterpieces of world art long considered to have been hopelessly lost, while the Moscow art historian Alexey Rastorguev called it 'a small opening into thousands of lost and hidden works of art'.

The first step down a new road is always the hardest and the story of the re-emergence of the Bremen drawings is no exception. They had been found in the cellars of Karnzow Castle, near Kiritz, north of Berlin. A young architectural student called Viktor Baldin, then a captain in the Red Army, chose the castle as suitable quarters for his brigade in May 1945. The castle's owner, Count Königsmark, after he had been informed of his fate, took a boat and rowed out to the middle of his lake where he and his mistress both slashed their wrists – she survived but he didn't. While the Russians were preparing to move out of the castle two months later a Russian labourer who had previously worked for Königsmark informed them that there was a false wall in the cellar with a secret room behind it.

This turned out to be one of the stores where the collection of the Bremen Kunsthalle had been hidden and is believed to have originally contained fifty paintings, 1,715 drawings and about 3,000 prints. Baldin first saw the store after the Russian soldiers had broken down the wall and begun looting. He gathered up the best of the drawings that were lying on the floor and later acquired others, mainly nudes, from soldiers who had helped themselves to them. He donated his 362 drawings and two paintings – one Dürer and one Goya – to the Shchusev Museum of Architecture in Moscow in 1947 (of which he himself later became director). He says that he tried to persuade the authorities to return the drawings to Bremen on many occasions but with no success. Then, following perestroika, he took the law into his own hands. On a visit to Germany in 1990 he contacted the director of the Kunsthalle and told him where the drawings were hidden. The director wrote to Mikhail Gorbachev, and the German Foreign Minister wrote to his Soviet counterpart.

The result, according to press reports, was not what they desired. The Soviet Minister of Culture, Nikolay Gubenko, accompanied by a group of KGB officers, turned up at the Shchusev Museum and confiscated the drawings. They were secretly handed to the Hermitage which was asked to prepare an exhibition catalogue; the Soviets, apparently, planned to 'rediscover' the drawings in a provincial museum and put them on show there – maybe as a preliminary to restitution. But by 1990 a new spirit of individual freedom and democracy was abroad and the Hermitage curators would not tolerate what they considered irresponsible treatment of masterpieces of Western art. A letter of protest was sent to the director of the museum by the 'scholarly staff of the Department of Western European Art'. Some forty signatures had been collected.

As Alexey Larionov, one of the prime movers, told me:

Two or three weeks after *Moscow News* had announced the removal of the Bremen drawings from the Shchusev museum by the KGB, something very strange was going on in our museum. Some of our colleagues were spending time in a secret room. The rest of us were not allowed in and there was a special form of knock. Slowly it became clear that the Bremen collection was here. In a month everyone knew ... 1991 was a very special time; everything was changing. The drawings were brought to the museum in May. In August came the putsch which brought Yeltsin to power. The exhibition was supposed to start in December 1991 or January 1992. By the end of December the catalogue was ready and, at this point, we decided to try and stop the drawings being sent away. We told *Moscow News* that the drawings were in the Hermitage and wrote a letter to the director.

Their letter pulled no punches:

The presence of the Bremen drawings in the Hermitage has been surrounded by a curtain of secrecy from the very beginning. Apart from three or four people, none of the specialists working in the museum were given access to the drawings; even the normal routine checks of their condition by restorers were not organised and the very fact of the drawings' presence in the museum was denied. All this time, a number of the sheets were being prepared for an exhibition in an unknown location: the catalogue was being prepared, mounts were being made ...

The curators pointed out that many drawings were in a very poor state and had old mounts whose destructive acidic effect was a proven scientific fact. They argued that it was irresponsible to send world class masterpieces, 'including famous pieces by Dürer, Rembrandt, Van Dyck, Van Gogh and other major masters', to a provincial museum for exhibition when the Hermitage itself had stopped lending art works inside Russia for security reasons. 'In this situation,' they concluded, 'we feel that the Hermitage administration should take the only intelligent and civilised position:

1 Place a veto on the dispatch of the Bremen drawings from the museum to other stores in our country.
2 Make public their presence in the Hermitage.
3 Until the further fate of these works has been decided, take upon ourselves the responsibility for their preservation and give restorers access to control their condition.
4 Give specialists access to the drawings whether they work within the museum or outside it.

We also feel that a similar model of events should be used with regard to all other closed storerooms and special collections existing in the Hermitage. We hope that the heads of the museum will pay attention to our point of view. We reserve the right to call upon public opinion.

It is a remarkable reflection on the new Russia – and on the new director of the Hermitage, Mikhail Piotrovsky, appointed in June 1992 – that their protest was wholly successful. Piotrovsky had been deputy director when the drawings arrived at the museum and was furious that he had not been officially informed – he only heard of their existence from the protest organisers. He saw to it that the Bremen drawings were kept at the Hermitage where they were subsequently restored, remounted and exhibited with a handsome exhibition catalogue (which only arrived from the printers after the exhibition had closed, due to the economic chaos in the country at the time). Piotrovsky has announced that it is his intention to exhibit all the trophy art the Hermitage has in store and make it available to the world's scholars. Whether or not the art works will eventually be returned to their former owners is a question which can only be resolved by the Russian government, he says. At present, their legal status in Russia remains undefined; either the President or the parliament must rectify this.

In 1995 the Hermitage started to put his policy into action with the exhibition of *Hidden Treasures*, a group of seventy-three Impressionist and Post-Impressionist paintings from private German collections, plus a Monet from the Bremen Kunsthalle – this painting, together with a substantial group of Bremen drawings, came to the Hermitage through various sources, quite separately from Viktor Baldin's initiative. The exhibition was an international sensation and was followed by an exhibition of drawings from the same collections in 1996. Since the paintings and drawings had been in private collections before the war, most of them were wholly unknown to the public – or only known through small, black and white photographs in old catalogues.

The exhibitions contained many masterpieces. First among them was Degas's *Place de la Concorde* of 1875, with his artist friend, Vicomte Lepic, his daughters and a dog in the foreground – a triumphant combination of intimacy and monumental space. Other oil paintings included two Gauguins dating from the artist's first visit to Tahiti, one of them, *Piti Teina* (The Two Sisters) being completely unrecorded, four Van Goghs, seven Cézannes, a host of Renoirs of varying quality, six Monets and a dazzling Seurat landscape. The drawings exhibition contained no fewer than thirty-five Goyas – a mix of scenes from daily life and imaginary horrors brilliantly worked with a greasy lithographic crayon – which emerged from the museum's closets as fresh as if he had made them yesterday. There was also a brightly coloured watercolour of boats by Van Gogh.

Roughly eighty-five per cent of the paintings came from the collection of Otto Krebs which had been discovered in the cellars of Gut Holzdorf in 1948 – including a number of fakes which were not put on show. The other main collections represented in the exhibitions were those of Otto Gerstenberg, an insurance magnate and collector of world repute, who had owned the Degas *Place de la Concorde* and the Goyas, and Bernhard Koehler, an industrialist closely connected with the Blaue Reiter artists. Gerstenberg's daughter had given his paintings and drawings to the Berlin National Gallery for safe-keeping before the war, as had the heirs of Bernhard Koehler. Gerstenberg's descendants have commissioned Sotheby's to try and negotiate the return of their pictures; the representatives of the Mannheim cancer charity to which Krebs left all his property have done the same with Wildenstein's, the major international dealers based in New York, while the Koehler heirs have handed responsibility over to the German government.

As I write, it is hard to forecast their chances of success. In 1992 President Yeltsin and Chancellor Kohl of Germany reaffirmed the 'Good-Neighbourliness' Treaty that Kohl and Gorbachev had signed two years before. It included an article stating that 'lost or unlawfully transferred art treasures which are located in the governments' territories will be returned to their owners or the owners' successors'. The Russians contend that the transfer of German art to Russia was conducted within the framework of Russian law and was thus perfectly 'lawful'. The two countries have also set up a joint government commission to advise on restitution. Piotrovsky and Werner Schmidt, director of the Dresden Museums, are members of the commission and joint chairmen of its museums subcommittee. But nothing is so far resolved and the commission's activity is on hold.

In his introduction to the 1992 Bremen catalogue of drawings from the Kunsthalle, the Minister of Culture, Yevgeny Sidorov, described the exhibition as 'an act of justice' because 'the unique drawings by Dürer, Rembrandt, Goya, Delacroix, Van Gogh are returning home, to the Kunsthalle Museum in Bremen'. In fact, he jumped the gun – they still repose in handsome portfolios in the Hermitage Drawings Department. From 1991 to 1994 there were negotiations over the return of many collections. In 1993 Piotrovsky and Gerstenberg's heirs negotiated a draft scheme whereby the collection would be split more or less 50–50, with the Hermitage retaining half and half going back to the family. It gained Sidorov's approval but he could not deliver a go-ahead.

Infuriated by Yeltsin taking a group of art works back to Hungary on a state visit without parliamentary approval, the Duma, in 1994, voted a moratorium on the return of cultural valuables pending the preparation of a new law. A draft law, effectively nationalising all trophy art, was circulated in 1995 and passed by the Duma but it was thrown out by the Legislative Council, or upper house, in June 1996. The German government considered the draft an insult and pressured Yeltsin to prevent it becoming law. A slightly amended draft was passed by the Duma and the Legislative Council in early 1997 but vetoed by Yeltsin. The draft law declared all trophy art Russian state property subject to a list of exceptions. The exceptions included art that had belonged to religious or charitable institutions and art that had belonged to private collectors who fought actively against Fascism or had suffered on account of their race, nationality or religion.

As I write, the contents of various storerooms, scattered around the old palace buildings that the Hermitage inhabits, wait patiently for the politicians to determine their fate. There are ceramics and bronzes unearthed by Schliemann at Troy – the gold jewellery was stored at the Pushkin but the Hermitage has the rest of Schliemann's material; there are Japanese sword fittings, Chinese lacquer boxes, Chinese bronzes and other Far-Eastern material from the Ostasiatische Museum in Berlin; there is a large quantity of European silver; there are German paintings and drawings from Krebs's and other private collections; there are Old

Masters from the palaces of Berlin and Potsdam; there is one of the oldest and finest German stained glass windows – a compendium of 111 individual scenes mainly from the life of St Anthony of Thebes and the Bible, removed from the Marienkirche in Frankfurt-am-Oder. Their ultimate fate is likely to depend on international politics and Russian pride.

15

The Post-War Years

*I*n the post-war years the Party was the central point of reference round which the intellectual and administrative decision-making of the nation revolved. At the Hermitage, as elsewhere, its influence was both coercive and permissive. It pointed out the directions in which the institution should evolve and saw that permitted activity was watered with cash. Before the war, Party power had been a new experiment, its mechanisms constantly changing and evolving. During the war years, patriotism and the battle for survival took over as the main directive forces of national life. Now physical reconstruction of the museum building went hand in hand with a reinforcement and bureaucratisation of Party control over its administration, internally through an elected Party Bureau and externally through the city, regional and Central (i.e. national) committees.

As elsewhere, the openly acknowledged machinery of the Party – some ten per cent of the staff were members – was reinforced by a KGB representative who had charge of either the personnel or foreign relations department. And he in turn was supported by a network of unofficial and unacknowledged informers. In this way the Party's influence structured the intellectual environment of the museum for nearly five decades after the war. Even its suppression in the early 1990s did not immediately change the psychological attitudes the structure had engendered.

The Party did not always have an easy ride, however. At the best of times, in the best of environments, scholars are an unruly and difficult lot and the staff of the Hermitage have never been exceptions to this rule.

Often brilliant and colourful, as well as bloody minded and contradictory, they were continually bumping up against the walls of intellectual conformity set by the Party machine. The two great directors of the immediate post-war years, Iosif Orbeli and Mikhail Artamonov, both fell foul of the Party and were dismissed, Orbeli in 1951 and Artamonov in 1964. Even Artamonov's successor, Boris Piotrovsky, who was particularly adept at avoiding confrontation with the Party, was driven to the point of resigning – though his resignation was not accepted.

It was against this background that the museum had to fulfil its day-to-day tasks. The extension of the Hermitage exhibitions into the Winter Palace, which had begun before the war, continued, stage by stage, in the post-war years. The Museum of the Revolution never reopened and the Hermitage obtained its extensive ground and first floor galleries along the Admiralty side of the building. In his director's report for 1957, Artamonov noted that the museum, which had had 200 exhibition rooms before the war, now had 320. In that year the restoration of the Nicholas Hall had been completed, along with the ornate reception rooms in the south-west corner of the palace. The Pushkin Memorial Museum was still occupying a substantial section of the second floor and there was an urgent need to find it a new home, he said. The Pushkin finally moved out in 1962, leaving the Hermitage in sole possession of the former palace building and a total of 345 rooms.

Artamonov, who had been Pro-Rector and acting head of Leningrad University for several years before being appointed director of the Hermitage in 1951, placed a special emphasis on raising the level of scholarship within the museum and went out of his way to encourage young scholars. He opened the museum's own publishing house which issued periodical collections of papers and books by the staff. This was particularly important at a time when state publishing houses were run for the benefit of Party-approved writers and independent scholars had great difficulty in getting their work into print.

Following the death of Stalin in 1953 and Krushchev's rise to power, the nation entered an era of reform. Intellectuals were released from concentration camps and allowed to return to society; those who had died were posthumously rehabilitated; criticism of Stalin was permitted; writers and artists were allowed new freedom; universities and museums were allowed to re-establish contacts with the West. Artamonov took immediate advantage of this situation, sending staff on study trips abroad whenever possible, learning from Western approaches to museology to improve the Hermitage exhibitions, and employing outstanding scholars who returned from the Gulag. A man who concealed strong emotions under a reserved exterior, Artamonov always went out of his way to help talented Jews and former political prisoners.

In 1945, however, the first priority was to restore the shattered building. And for this Orbeli was the ideal director. In the 1930s he had taken on the architectural challenge of converting a palace into a museum with vivid enthusiasm. In his memoirs Piotrovsky describes Orbeli and the chief architect, Andrey Sivkov, marching round the building thinking things out. The palace kitchens, originally located underneath the throne room, were converted into an exhibition hall for antiquities of the Bosphorus and Black Sea region with a connecting bridge to the Antique halls of the New Hermitage. They ripped an entresol out of the Rastrelli gallery and revealed the handsome capitals of its pillars which had not been seen since the fire of 1837. The Ministers' rooms, which had lined the corridor connecting the Pavilion Room with the Field Marshals' Hall, were thrown together to make a series of large galleries. In the process Orbeli threw out some 200 marble fireplaces and Alexander I's bath.

The Hermitage curators, who had turned their hands to any trade that was necessary during the war, began the restoration of the building themselves before hostilities were over. They cleaned and repainted the first floor galleries of the Small Hermitage in the course of 1944, reglazing the vast, eighteenth-century windows, as well as restoring and rehanging the chandeliers which had been stored in the cellars and fallen apart during the floods. It was in the Small Hermitage that the first, limited exhibition was held in November 1944. In Orbeli's own excited words 'the chamber beamed'.

After the Germans finally capitulated in May 1945 the government poured money and resources into the restoration of Leningrad. The city was one of six to be officially declared a 'Hero City' – there is still a neon sign announcing 'Leningrad Gorod Geroi' (Leningrad Hero City) on the roof of the hotel opposite the Moscow railway station. This meant also that special resources were made available for its reconstruction in recompense for the wartime sacrifices of the civilian population. Even more fantastic than the restoration of the Hermitage to pristine, palatial grandeur – with bronzes recast, stucco remoulded, wood and marble recarved and regilded – was the complete rebuilding of the imperial palaces on the outskirts of town, Tsarskoe Selo, Peterhof and Pavlovsk. The Communist government did not regard these palaces as symbols of a rotten imperial past, but as proud monuments of Russia's artistic creativity. Heroes deserved palaces and a school for restorers was set up in Leningrad to create the technicians required for this majestic undertaking. The rebuilding was a symbol of Russia's victory over the Germans.

The Party took a totally opposite attitude to the value of Impressionist and modern art. The Shchukin and Morozov collections, along with the contents of other Moscow museums, had been evacuated during the war and the Morozov mansion, then known as the Museum of Modern Western Art, where they hung, was in very bad condition by the end of it. The building was restored and the staff were ready to reopen the museum but permission was not forthcoming. Alexander Gerasimov, president of the Moscow Academy of Art, a Socialist Realist painter and one of the most influential figures in the artistic world of the time, wanted it closed. He disliked the 'bourgeois' art it contained and wanted the handsome building as a home for his own institution. He invited his father-in-law, Marshal Klementy Voroshilov, the Politbureau member whom Stalin trusted in matters of art, to come and look at the collection. Voroshilov was shown Matisse's *Music* and *Dance*, rolled out on the floor, and 'let out a short burst of laughter, Tee-hee-hee,' according to N. W. Yavorskaya, the museum director's wife and, briefly, successor. 'They all joined in. It was many years ago but I still have that laughter echoing in my ears.' The Academy of Art was given the building and, she continues, 'the Museum Department of the Committee for Artistic Affairs intended to spread the works among various provincial museums and destroy some of them altogether. Only the best were to be given to the Pushkin and the Hermitage. It is hard to describe the state the Museum staff were in at the time.'

The story reached the Hermitage where the specialist on nineteenth- and twentieth-century painting, Antonina Izergina, was now married to Orbeli. She saw to it that Orbeli went to Moscow without delay in order to save as much as he could for their museum. Orbeli's own interests were centred on archaeology but Izergina was the most strong-minded of his five official wives – clever, warm, with a strong sense of humour – and no doubt imparted her own enthusiasm to him. She had joined the Hermitage staff in 1929, when she was only twenty-three, and became curator of nineteenth-century art in 1937 – on grounds of merit, not her influence with Orbeli. There was nothing between them at this time. In the pre-war years she was herself busy with other men, including Nikolay Punin, under whom she had studied art history at the university. Izergina and Punin were both evacuated to Samarkand in

1942 but came back to Leningrad in 1944 where they split up. Five years later Punin was arrested for 'cosmopolitanism' and sent to Siberia where he died in the camps.

The affair between Izergina and Orbeli began after he returned to Leningrad from Armenia in June 1944. It ripened into marriage as a result of her pregnancy and the birth of their son, Dmitry, in 1946. Despite his many marriages and liaisons, this was Orbeli's first child. Moreover, it was a son, a matter of vast importance to a man proud of his ancient Armenian lineage. With considerable difficulty, he divorced his previous wife to marry Izergina. Whereas marriage had been disdained as a bourgeois irrelevance in the first decade after the Revolution, the Party began to encourage a return to family values in the mid-1930s and from 1944 onwards divorce became contingent on court proceedings.

The director of Moscow's Pushkin Museum, Sergey Merkurov, the leading Russian sculptor of the day and an accomplished Socialist Realist, together with Orbeli, who had no special interest in modern art, nobly divided the Shchukin and Morozov pictures between them and did it quickly, so that the paintings were not sent elsewhere or destroyed. Both of them were perfectly aware that they could not put such art, reviled by the Party, on exhibition, but they acknowledged that the pictures had a value which would eventually be recognised. Stories of how each got the best of the deal have entered into the mythologies of both institutions. Izergina, with the more advanced taste, had reputedly urged Orbeli to make for the Picassos and Matisses. He also got advice on what to pick from Yavorskaya, who became acting director of the Museum of Modern Western Art after her husband's death and who was outraged that Merkurov had not invited her to take part in the division.

The paintings curator at the Pushkin, Andrey Chegodaev, who died in 1994, was also convinced that he got the best pictures. In an interview he gave Konstantin Akinsha in May 1990 he claimed: 'I shared out the collection myself. And today, those paintings which you can see on the upper floor of the museum, beginning with Eduard Manet, reflect my taste and my selection. Izergina sent a short list with Orbeli, which included six paintings she wanted. I don't know why she selected four of them, but two paintings mentioned on the list I didn't want to give – *Girl at the Piano* by Cézanne and *Boulevard Montmartre* by Pissarro. But it was necessary to be polite, because I played for our own profit in all other cases.' In fact, the Pushkin got the best Impressionists while the Hermitage got the best twentieth-century paintings.

Just over 200 pictures were acquired by the Hermitage from the Shchukin and Morozov collections at this time. At first only the most conservative, realist paintings could be shown – an Albert Marquet view, for instance, and a *Rouen Cathedral* by Emile Othon Friesz. After Stalin's death things got easier. The museum mounted a major exhibition of French painting down the ages in 1956 and showed almost everything – though not the Cubist Picassos. Matisse's *Music* and *Dance* were hung on the stairs where it was hoped they might escape serious notice. The pictures stayed on display after the exhibition closed and gradually other pieces were added, including the Cubist Picassos around 1963. Georges Rouault's pastel of *Women*, offensive on account of his treatment of nudity, was the last to go up. The Education Department devised a new guided tour of French art, beginning with Neoclassicism and running up to Picasso – which initially received a rather shocked and puzzled reception.

Another new centre of attention was the Russian Department which had opened in April 1941, three months before Hitler's invasion, but only became an active part of the museum in the post-war years. It had arrived more or less ready-made, complete with curators, having previously belonged to a succession of other institutions.

In June 1918 Narkompros had encouraged the Russian Museum to open a new 'Historical Department of Everyday Life'. While the title of the department sounds proletarian, its curators, in fact, collected the finest silver, porcelain, marble, furniture and other applied arts from the imperial palaces and nationalised private collections – those of the Shuvalov, Stroganov, Yusupov and similar families. They soon required new space to display this extraordinarily rich collection and in 1922 were given the handsome Bobrinsky Mansion near St Isaac's Cathedral. For a period, the Department also had the Sheremetyev Fountain House, Peter the Great's Summer Palace and the Menshikov Palace. But around 1930, as museum outstations were closed and collections sold abroad, they were cut down to size. In 1934, by which time they had collected 200,000 objects, the display was closed and both the collection and the staff were transferred to the Museum of the Revolution, then housed in the Winter Palace.

It was soon realised that the transfer was a mistake, since the Museum of the Revolution had no space and little interest in the pieces or the curators. For the next seven years the collection was effectively homeless, as responsibility was transferred from one institution to another. The objects were packed up and stored in various locations around the city and the staff constantly pressed for a new home to be found. Finally Orbeli came to their rescue and agreed to incorporate the collection in the Hermitage.

There was, no doubt, a political edge to this decision, as well as a natural desire by Orbeli to extend his empire. He never joined the Communist Party and had already been in trouble with the authorities in the 1930s – several of the staff who had been arrested by the NKVD were pressured to denounce him. So in 1941, when patriotism was high on the Party agenda, Orbeli must have hoped that opening a Russian Department would bolster his standing with the Party while also protecting the Hermitage itself against the charge of containing only élitist foreign art.

The Party's lack of faith in Orbeli was, however, demonstrated by the appointment of one of their own apparatchiks as director of the new department, Vladimir Vasiliev. According to his museum colleagues, Vasiliev was also a KGB informer, responsible for keeping the authorities up to date on what was happening in the museum and recruiting other informers among the staff. The son of a sailor, he distinguished himself in Komsomol and Party activities before joining the Hermitage in 1939 as head of the Education Department. He moved across to the Russian Department in 1941 and was department head from 1942 to 1975, but was cordially disliked by a large proportion of the staff.

In a certain sense Vasiliev may be regarded as Orbeli's minder, the Party man who was given responsibility for keeping him in line. Relations between them were often difficult, according to Piotrovsky, who writes that Vasiliev 'was always careful and restrained so that things didn't get as far as open conflict. On one occasion I was present at a conversation between Vasiliev and Orbeli and saw for myself how a chair thrown by Orbeli splintered into pieces – but still no conflict came out of it.' When Orbeli and Piotrovsky were evacuated to Yerevan in 1942, after the first terrible winter of the war, Vasiliev went with them and shared a room with Piotrovsky in the Russian Pedagogical Institute.

The Russian Department now contains a wide-ranging collection: some 40,000 archaeological finds from ancient medieval cities such as Kiev, Novgorod and Pskov; silver, gold and enamelled objects dating from the fifteenth to the twentieth century, including work by Fabergé; over 11,000 porcelain items from the Imperial Manufactory and other firms; some 3,000 pieces of Russian glass; textiles ranging from fifteenth-century embroidery to the designer dresses of the last tsarinas and their daughters; over 12,000 items of Russian furniture, much of it designed by famous architects; some 300 of the 500 known items of steel furniture made by the arms manufacturers of Tula in the eighteenth and early nineteenth centuries; a huge collection of flags and banners, reflecting the tsars' love of military pomp; historical tools, including those used by Peter the Great; Russian portraits of the imperial family and the nobility; drawings; engravings and sculpture.

Ultimately, the existence of a Russian Department was not enough to protect Orbeli from the Party. Around 1950 Stalin purged most of the leaders and directors of institutions in Leningrad in the so-called 'Leningrad Affair', and Orbeli lost his job along with the rest of them. He was particularly under a cloud at the time as a prominent 'Marrist'. While he had always been prepared to make speeches in honour of Comrade Stalin, he was not prepared to take Stalin's posthumous witchhunt of his old professor Nikolay Marr sitting down. It was in 1950 that Stalin's article in *Pravda* unexpectedly blackening the name of Nikolay Marr, the linguist and first director of the Institute of the History of Material Culture, was published. Marr himself had died back in 1934. It was thus against his pupils and disciples that the article was directed, among whom Iosif Orbeli was one of the most prominent.

According to his fellow Orientalist, Igor Diakonoff, Orbeli made no attempt to toe Stalin's line. 'Of course, Marr went mad at the end of his life,' says Diakonoff. 'Orbeli went around saying that before he went mad, Marr was a genius and did a lot for Armenian and Georgian linguistics. He said it very emphatically, wherever he went. He wasn't afraid of anything.' Less independent archaeologists were beating their breasts at this time and admitting their errors in the light of Comrade Stalin's brilliant analysis. And it seems to have been the Marr issue that turned the Party definitively against Orbeli – though he was already unpopular on other grounds. His style of administration by confrontation, shouting and the despatch of missiles across rooms, which was not unusual for the 1930s, was out of fashion by the 1950s when conventional bureaucracy prevailed. On many previous occasions, he had threatened resignation when the Party wouldn't let him have his way – and achieved his aims. In 1951, to his astonishment, one of his letters of resignation was accepted. According to Piotrovsky, memoranda and reports on Orbeli's unsuitability for the directorship had been submitted to the Party some months before. The decision was well prepared. But having allowed him to hold so important a position, the Party could not now abandon him completely without losing face. Orbeli was appointed director of the Institute of Oriental Studies but he never entered the Hermitage again.

He was replaced by Mikhail Artamonov, a man of a very different stamp, who is remembered affectionately throughout the museum as a 'great director'. While he did not join the Party until 1940, by which time he had risen through the ranks to succeed Orbeli as director of the Institute of the History of Material Culture, Artamonov was well regarded by the authorities on account of his peasant origins. He was born in 1898 in the village of Vygolovo, in the Tverskaya region, and moved to St Petersburg at the age of nine because his father had got a job in a factory.

He left school at the age of sixteen to become a clerk but continued his studies in the evening. At the beginning of 1917 he was mobilised for military service and sent to the front where, following the February Revolution, he was elected a member of the Soviet of Soldiers' Deputies. The respect in which he was already held is reflected by the fact that, by the end of the year, he was sent to work in a Petrograd bank whose staff was refusing to collaborate with the Bolsheviks – he was only just nineteen. After these high dramas, and a period teaching in the country, he began to study archaeology in 1921. Never a narrow specialist, he also attended courses at the Academy of Art where he learned to paint. He mixed with the brightest young artists and poets of his generation, providing illustrations for a book of poems by Sergey Yesenin, the then husband of Isadora Duncan, as well as publishing a book of his own verse.

He began his graduate studies at the Institute of the History of Material Culture in 1925, ran his first expeditions to excavate the Khazar fortress of Sarkel on the River Don in 1934–6 and in 1939 was elected by his peers to replace Orbeli as director of the Institute. Orbeli, as usual, had got into fierce arguments with both the staff of the Institute and the local Party; Artamonov was elected to head the opposition, and, since his peasant origins endeared him to the Party, he was subsequently chosen to replace Orbeli. He quickly demonstrated his organisational capability. Evacuated with the Institute during the war, he was appointed Pro-Rector of Leningrad University in 1948 and appointed to the chair of archaeology in 1949. From that year he was acting head of the university and also began the three-year 'rescue' excavation of Sarkel which was about to be flooded by the construction of the

Volga–Don canal. It was the biggest archaeological expedition ever mounted in Russia.

When he was first asked to take over the Hermitage he is said to have refused and to have maintained his opposition for some months. But during the summer excavations at Sarkel in 1951 a telegram arrived summoning him to Moscow, signed by Stalin himself. The present head of the Archaeological Department, Galina Smirnova, was there and remembers the drama of the motorcycle arriving at their camp. On his return from Moscow, Artamonov bitterly told his team of his new appointment and drove them to unprecedented effort to complete the full investigation of the fortress by the end of the season. He became director of the Hermitage on 1 September 1951.

At first the reserved man who had taken over the museum was treated with suspicion by his staff. He liked to work at his desk, whereas Orbeli had prowled the corridors, and he still had a country accent. But his actions spoke louder than words. His declared aim was to render the scholarly activities of the museum worthy of the institution's great reputation. He didn't sack existing staff but recruited new ones, notably bright young graduates and scholars returning from the Gulag after the general amnesty of 1956. He found Lev Gumilev, the brilliant historian and geographer son of Russia's best-loved poet, Anna Akhmatova, a job in the library; here Gumilev worked on the history of the Khazars and helped Artamonov with his books. Gumilev had been sentenced three times to the prison camps: 'once on account of my father, once on account of my mother and once for myself,' he joked.

Orbeli had fancied himself as a typesetter and started a publishing house in the museum but let it die. Artamonov now revived it with the aim of publishing scholarly papers by museum staff and books about the collections. He introduced annual seminars in the theatre at which the scholarly work of the museum was reviewed. They lasted for several days and Artamonov attended every session, demanding that the best papers should be followed up and published. On occasion, he also fought the censor on the writer's behalf. He would not allow the Party to interfere with the scholarly running of the museum.

He also embarked on a running battle with the Ministry of Culture over staff pay. The Hermitage staff were categorised as 'cultural' workers, rather than academics and, at this time, the latter were much better paid – the balance of advantage has varied over the years. As a result, Hermitage staff got roughly five times less than their counterparts at the university. Orbeli seems to have regarded the sacrifice involved in working for the museum as morally desirable. 'Only idiots or fanatics work in the Hermitage,' he is recorded as telling Marshal Voroshilov when the latter visited the museum. 'Most of them are fanatics.'

Artamonov finally managed to get a decree raising museum pay but the Minister of Culture, Ekaterina Furtseva, scuppered it by adding a codicil to say that the new levels would only be put into effect if the ministry could afford it – and it couldn't. So Artamonov decided that the publishing house must pay its writers. Under the Soviet system, those working for scholarly institutions were not paid for their publications, which were regarded as part of their normal work, though other writers got fees. Artamonov set high levels of pay, to compensate for the low salaries, but the museum's auditing commission caught up with him, ordering him not to pay his writers and issuing a fine. The argument rested on whether the Hermitage staff were working for a scholarly institution or not. If they were, they could not be paid; if they were not, they could be. The auditing commission applied to the Ministry of Culture for a decision and the Ministry, according to museum legend, replied that the Hermitage was 'one of our theatrical and performance organisations and no scholarly work is done there' – having assumed that the query referred to the Hermitage theatre in Moscow. The Leningrad curators got their pay.

The creative interpretation of regulations to further one's own interest was one of the most important arts for those living under Soviet rule. Take for instance the bizarre story of the Jewish keeper of arms and armour, Leonid Tarassuk, who was arrested for the grave crime of stockpiling arms to use against the government. He got off with a three year prison sentence and was taken back onto the museum staff by Artamonov but ended up leaving Russia and working for the Metropolitan Museum in New York before being killed in a car accident in 1990.

No one who knew Tarassuk can hear his name without a nostalgic smile spreading over their face. He was the master of the practical joke, the slayer of every woman's heart with a flash from his bright eye, and clearly plain fun to be with. The legends that surround his memory are legion and it is now virtually impossible to distinguish fact from fiction. He is said to have demonstrated the administrative inadequacies of the scholarly deputy director Vladimir Levinson-Lessing by submitting two memoranda for his signature which directly contradicted each other. Levinson-Lessing duly signed them both. Another memorandum, requesting the central stores to supply embalming fluid for a recently deceased curator, was signed by Boris Piotrovsky himself – unread, of course. Tarassuk framed it and hung it on his office wall. Another good joke of his was slipping into the museum early in the morning to pin a black-edged sheet onto the noticeboard announcing his own death. The board was located beside the cloak room, halfway up a broad staircase. Tarassuk nipped upstairs and watched his colleagues' reactions over the stone balustrade. He kept a large sofa in the Arms and Armour Department for an afternoon nap – and maybe more nefarious purposes. He would also entertain friends there for target practice with imperial pistols – but only if they were good enough shots.

He became a fencing champion while studying history at Leningrad University and joined the staff of the Hermitage Arms and Armour Department at the age of twenty-seven in 1952 – one of the bright young scholars brought into the museum by Artamonov. During his student years, however, Tarassuk had put his knowledge of arms to a strange purpose. He had been tipped off, reputedly by his mother who worked in a government office, that a pogrom against the Jews was planned and decided that he would go down fighting. He had been born in Odessa on the Black Sea and it was there that he and a cousin stockpiled antique arms and hid them in the local catacombs.

Tarassuk went blithely back to Leningrad and forgot about the cache until he was rudely reminded of it by the KGB in 1959. They had found it by accident and laboriously traced responsibility back to him. They had also installed a microphone in his flat and caught him out regularly cracking jokes about the Party. He was arrested and could well have been shot for treason had not his colleagues at the Hermitage come to his aid. A secret collection was organised within the museum to pay for a top lawyer from Moscow to defend his case. The lawyer got Tarassuk off on two ingenious grounds. According to Russian law, you could say anything you liked to your family; uninhibited talk only became 'anti-Soviet propaganda' if those who were listening were not relatives. Secondly, the weapons he had collected were antique – of the nineteenth century or earlier – and could not possibly, the lawyer argued, be used for an armed insurrection (though that was what Tarassuk had intended). The disgruntled KGB sent him to prison for three years all the same.

On his release he was not immediately allowed back to Leningrad. He had been living with a prima ballerina at the time of his arrest and friends in the theatrical world engineered his return by making him a consultant on costumes and armour for Grigory Kozintsev's famous

1964 film of *Hamlet*. Meanwhile strings were being pulled at the Hermitage to get him back on staff, notably by Larissa Salmina, then academic secretary of the Western European Department. 'I suggested we rehire Tarassuk at a Party meeting,' she says. 'But, of course, it had already been decided higher up. Artamonov had fixed it.'

In 1972 Tarassuk launched himself into another political battle by applying for a visa to leave the Soviet Union for Israel. He wanted to take his ailing mother there for hospital treatment but, by this time, the political climate had changed, and the Hermitage could not help him. As was usual in such cases, he was sacked the day after he applied for a visa. It was left to the many Western friends he had made in the arms and armour field to battle for him. They issued a pamphlet explaining his plight. His 'abrupt dismissal', they pointed out, left him 'jobless, and undergoing an officially inaugurated crescendo of other punishments. His wife, a conservator of decorative arts, also employed by the Hermitage, was likewise dismissed. Dr Tarassuk's most recent book was removed from sale within twenty-four hours after his visa application was made.' A letter to the London *Times* signed by forty-two leading scholars and collectors from all over the world was the opening salvo of a major campaign. Hundreds of supporters wrote letters of protest to Soviet ambassadors in their own countries and the Minister of Culture in Moscow. Their strategy was to give the issue so high a profile that the Soviet government could not further punish Tarassuk without losing face. It worked.

Artamonov's reign at the Hermitage was not, however, exclusively devoted to political battles. The museum collection continued to expand, partly through the work of the many archaeological expeditions he encouraged and partly as a result of purchases from impoverished Soviet collectors. In the mid-1950s the Russian Department devised a form of 'expedition' whose rationale took its cue from the political environment. Experts began to spend their summers touring provincial towns and villages in search of Russian works of art. They would contact local teachers and librarians, give lectures, help with local museum collections, and in return they were introduced to local collectors who might sell works of art or just give them to the Hermitage as a means of saving their treasures for posterity. Art had little monetary value in Russia in Soviet times. Collecting was a dangerous business – you could easily be arrested for hoarding – so the Hermitage obtained a rich harvest at modest prices. The museum continued these summer expeditions right up to 1985–6.

The most exciting accretion of these years was the group of some 1,000 icons dating from between the thirteenth and the seventeenth centuries, for which a slightly different style of 'expedition' was mounted. Most of Russia's churches had been closed since 1929 and their best known treasures had already been annexed by the Tretyakov Gallery in Moscow, the Russian Museum in Leningrad, or the local museums of cities such as Novgorod. While some of the Hermitage icons came from private collections, a large proportion were literally rescued from abandoned churches. In 1954 the museum began to send summer expeditions to the remote villages of the Russian north to search out important works and either restore them on the spot or bring them back to the museum.

The present keeper of icons, Alexandra Kostsova, went on her first expedition in 1956 and ran most of the subsequent ones. Now well into her seventies, she recalls with passion the dangers and achievements of the early years. In 1958, for instance, they were following the River Onega which runs for 250 miles from Archangel and comes out in the White Sea. 'In 1958, it felt as if no human foot had trodden there. Just walking along the river, you felt out of time,' she says. 'As you walked along, trees had fallen across the path; you started to climb over and the tree collapsed under you. It had rotted where it fell, though it looked whole.'

They travelled along one section of the river by boat and noticed a little wooden church that wasn't on their map. The party jumped out into the water — including their eighty-year-old icon restorer — and waded across to it. 'The porch was collapsing under our feet as we went inside. It was full of sacks and there were some wooden planks lying on the floor — but they weren't planks. Four of them were completely black and two of them a little lighter — icons, all of which had been painted over in the twentieth century.' When the restorer, Fedor Kalikin, took one of the black icons in his hands 'he began to dance, an old man's dance. He said it was a very, very old icon, dating from the thirteenth century, and when he began to clean it, he proved to be right.' The four black 'planks' are now the oldest icons in the Hermitage, painted by an anonymous artist of the Northern School, working under the influence of Novgorod.

The restorer, Fedor Kalikin, continued to work at the Hermitage until his death at the age of ninety-five and, according to Kostsova, was the single most important reason why the Hermitage succeeded in identifying and saving so many important icons. He was an Old Believer and had worked as a painter and restorer of icons all his life. The Old Believers split off from the Orthodox Church in the seventeenth century, objecting to the modernisation of church practices, and Kalikin treated the early icons as objects of worship. He would pray to them before he restored them.

He knew where small groups of Old Believers had settled in the remotest areas and could have taken old icons with them. Moreover, he had acted as an adviser to several collectors before the Revolution which had given him a knowledge of how to search for icons. Finally, and most importantly, he knew how to tell the age of an icon from its feel – a knowledge he passed on to Kostsova.

I have often had to assess the date and value of an icon with my hands and not with my eyes. For example, when you were let into a church by a warehouseman and found it was used for storing sacks of flour – which was not unusual – you couldn't see the icons because sacks and sacks of flour were stacked against the iconostasis. So you climbed on the sacks and started to run your hands along the back and sides . . . The first thing you could tell by touch was what tools had been used, then from the knots what wood – pine, fir or lime. With later icons, the edge of the board has a groove to attach it to the iconostasis while the early ones had a runner attached by nails.

All these clues would add up to an identification of date and school. Icons were painted in egg tempera and when it darkened they would be painted over with oil to brighten the colours; then the oil itself would darken and, with the help of smoke from candles, the icons became almost black. From the earliest times, it was standard practice for the darkened surface to be repainted when it became too hard to see. Thus early icons have often been repainted eight or nine times. On getting an old board back to the Hermitage, a tiny area of the surface would be investigated, gently cleaning it off layer by layer to see what lay beneath – sometimes the original icon had been lost and sometimes merely painted over. In the latter case, it could be gradually revealed to view by an experienced restorer. By undertaking voyages through the most primitive regions of the Soviet Union – Kostsova tells the story of meeting two bears fighting each other outside one church filled with important icons – the Hermitage collection was painstakingly gathered.

The abandoned churches, used from the 1930s to the 1980s to house farm equipment and stores, were, of course, a political phenomenon and the museum collection of rescued icons reflects one of the many unlooked for opportunities thrown up by political upheaval. The negative impact of Russian politics on the Hermitage was, however, illustrated by Artamonov's battle to share the Shchukin and Morozov pictures with the public. Their exhibition, and his defence of the paintings against attack by the Moscow Academy of Art, are among the principal reasons why he lost his job – though officially his offence lay in condoning a 'subversive' exhibition of paintings by young Hermitage staff which was not even open to the public.

In art, as in other fields, Krushchev's 'secret speech' denouncing Stalin in 1956 had opened floodgates of freedom which, by the early 1960s, was beginning to frighten the party leadership. Krushchev was got rid of in 1964 and Brezhnev subsequently oversaw a return to coercive discipline without reinstating Stalin's terror tactics. The new artistic freedom of the late 1950s had made it possible to mount a show of the Shchukin and Morozov pictures, but in 1963 the whole Praesidium of the Moscow Academy of Art arrived at the Hermitage intent on closing it down. The Academy was fighting a rearguard action at the time against 'modernism' in contemporary painting.

At this time the older generation of Socialist Realist artists felt themselves under threat and the Academy had elected Vladimir Serov, a dyed in the wool conservative, as its president. Serov took Krushchev round the huge exhibition of avant-garde paintings that young artists mounted in the Moscow *Manège* in 1961, carefully adopting the route that would be most likely to shock him. Kruschchev was so horrified that he closed it down. After this initial victory, Serov turned his sights on the Hermitage and its exhibition of the art which had so dangerously influenced the younger artists.

The guide who had devised a lecture tour of the paintings, Nadezhda Petrusevich, was asked to take the visitors from Moscow round, giving them her standard explanation. She now works in the Hermitage Drawings Department and recalls the occasion poignantly; besides Serov, the Praesidium of the Academy included leading figures from the fields of sculpture, graphic arts, art theory and art criticism. They were accompanied by Artamonov, Levinson-Lessing, Izergina, and other senior Hermitage staff, including representatives of the Party Bureau. 'If I'd taken those colleagues round on any other occasion, I would have been tongue-tied,' she recalls. 'But in these circumstances their presence was comforting.'

After it was finished they all trooped down to the director's office.

The first speakers complained that too little had been said about Neoclassicism and the Barbizon school and too much about the later pictures. 'I wanted to explain that there was a natural crescendo to the tour,' says Petrusevich, 'but everyone kicked me under the table.' Each of the Praesidium, in turn, criticised the exhibition with varying degrees of passion and called for the removal of the innovative pictures that were so dangerously inspiring young artists.

Izergina then played her trump card. She quietly explained the history of the exhibition and, having asked the visitors' permission, read out the decree nationalising the Shchukin collection in 1917:

'Taking into account that Shchukin's art gallery is an outstanding collection of great European masters, above all French masters, of the late nineteenth and early twentieth century and through its high artistic value is of national significance in the matter of public education, the Council of People's Commissars have decreed that the art collection of Sergey Ivanovich Shchukin shall be declared the state property of the Russian Socialist Federated Soviet Republic and transferred to the control of the People's Commissariat for Education on the same basis as other State Museums.'

'Who wrote that nonsense?,' Serov exploded.

'It is signed Ulyanov Lenin,' Izergina sweetly replied.

'It's a provocation,' shouted Serov.

Pandemonium followed. 'Artamonov sat there calmly, with his arms folded,' says Petrusevich, 'a smile gently rising to his lips.'

The Muscovites retired but soon regrouped, issuing a decree on which paintings should be removed from exhibition. When Artamonov took no notice, he was summoned to the regional headquarters of the Party in the Smolny. Professor Abram Stolyar, Artamonov's pupil and faithful friend, heard what happened from Artamonov himself and gives this version of the story: 'the Party secretary pressed him to put the Moscow Academy's decree into effect, to which Artamonov replied: "As regards the decision of that company of drunken half-wits, the only place I could suitably find for their decree was the waste-paper basket." ' Stolyar says that the pressure was kept up for days and Artamonov was offered the highest honours – including full membership of the Academy of Science and the Academy of Art – if he would knuckle under and reorganise the exhibition.

The title of Academician was, and is to this day, most highly regarded in Russia but Artamonov remained unshakeable. Stolyar says that he told the Party secretary: 'The government appointed me director of the Hermitage and allocated me a pay cheque, and I will not disgrace it.' With hindsight, Stolyar may have exaggerated Artamonov's outspokenness. But his refusal to interfere with the Impressionist and modern paintings display is undisputed fact. And Stolyar is probably right in suggesting that this was the moment when the regional committee of the Party decided that Artamonov must be removed as director or they would never be able to deal with him in future.

It became a matter of finding a suitable pretext for Artamonov's removal. An exhibition of paintings by young artists, then working for the museum as labourers, mounted in a screened off section of the Rastrelli Gallery, which was not open to the general public, was chosen as a battleground. It has since achieved a legendary significance far in excess of its contemporary importance since one of the chief exhibitors and moving spirits was Mikhail Chemyakin, a dissident artist who left Russia in the 1970s and made a successful career in France and America. In the early days of perestroika the Russian authorities reclaimed him as a long-lost and beloved son and his sculptures have been placed in prominent positions all over St Petersburg – much to the annoyance of his many critics among the cognoscenti: a bronze statue of Peter the Great in the Peter and Paul Fortress, for instance, and two bronze sphinxes at the point on the Neva embankment where sewage from the KGB headquarters – 'and the blood of their victims', in Chemyakin's words – drained into the river.

The Hermitage 'labourers' are considered the lowest form of life in the museum – they carry heavy weights around, clear excess snow, and take on the dirty jobs no one else wants – but for more than forty years budding poets, artists and scholars have been included among their numbers. They represent a curious backwater of museum life. Pay levels have always been derisory but for the young intelligentsia of St Petersburg, association with the Hermitage and its treasures has always been a privilege. Two of the present deputy directors of the Hermitage began working in the museum as labourers. For Chemyakin and the other artists on the team, it also meant that they could copy paintings in the galleries after hours. To this day, Chemyakin's contorted, often nightmare images demonstrate a powerful debt to the Hermitage Old Masters.

In 1964 the main activity of the labourers was to carry water round the galleries and fill troughs under the radiators to maintain humidity levels, according to the poet Vladimir Ufliyand, who also took part in the famous 1964 exhibition. 'The paintings were fine when stoves were used for heating, but the radiators dried them out,' he explains. The labourers also had to clear the snow and ice from the pavement outside the Hermitage, carry marble statues round the building – 'many Roman emperors lost their noses because of us', says Chemyakin – burn old frames that had woodworm, clear stores in the basement that had been left untouched since the Revolution or World War II. Here, there were duplicate books and engravings suffering from the damp, according to Chemyakin, who admits to removing some of them for his own use.

Among the fifteen to twenty labourers who worked at the Hermitage in 1964, ten or so belonged to the intelligentsia and several have since become household names in Russia. Besides Chemyakin and Ufliyand, there was Konstantin Kuzminsky, a poet and literary critic who now lives in New York, the artists Vladimir Ovchinnikov and Oleg Ligachev, and the actor Valery Kravchenko. Five of these – all except Kuzminsky – took part in the exhibition. Kravchenko had been taught to make lino cuts by Chemyakin a matter of days before the exhibition and has never made art since, but Ufliyand was a good watercolourist as well as a poet. His drawings are particularly influenced by the work of Aubrey Beardsley.

The year 1964 also saw the Hermitage celebrate its 200th anniversary and there were many exhibitions and celebrations planned. A group of restorers had been allowed to hold an exhibition of their paintings in the Rastrelli Gallery and the labourers petitioned the directorate to be allowed to do the same. Artamonov himself was on holiday and his deputy, Vladimir Levinson-Lessing, gave permission for a three-day exhibition in the same venue. The old scholar was friendly with the young artists and wanted to encourage them. He checked the exhibits before the show opened and asked that two or three works, which he thought the authorities might consider provocative, be removed.

Although it was not supposed to be open to the public, the artists had printed their own invitations to the opening, a folding sheet with a linocut on the front, and many people came – an exhibition of unofficial art at the Hermitage was, at the time, a considerable event. All went well on the first day and the exhibition was undisturbed when the labourers came in to work next morning. But when they came back from their lunch break it had been closed. 'They just put a board up to close it off and put a printed notice on it,' says Ufliyand. 'I pushed aside the board and grabbed the drawings I had in the showcase next to it.

There was one of an idiot looking like Krushchev hanging up the Soviet flag to dry. They'd have got me for that.'

In fact, the principal charge against the exhibition was that it was 'abstractionist', a campaign against 'abstractionism' being in progress at the time. Chemyakin, according to Ufliyand, spent a lot of time trying to explain to the authorities that they were all figurative artists, and what the difference between figuration and abstraction was – to no avail. Later in the afternoon the KGB removed the exhibits and the visitors' book in which the guests at the opening had written words of appreciation. An office in the Hermitage was converted into an interrogation room where the exhibitors and their guests began to be grilled. The worst offenders were summoned to the Party headquarters in the Smolny. Ekaterina Furtseva, the Minister of Culture, is said to have asked for a film to be made of the exhibition, so that she could personally study it.

The interrogations were serious stuff and continued for several days but, in the end, none of the labourers was fired. That privilege was reserved for Artamonov. He returned to St Petersburg from holiday to learn about the exhibition, a project he had no knowledge of and had not sanctioned. Levinson-Lessing was being given a hard time by the KGB and the Party committee and Artamonov, a doughty fighter and man of honour, decided to take responsibility for the fracas himself, insisting that Levinson-Lessing should not be blamed.

There is little doubt that he understood that the KGB and the Party had ganged up on him, though they themselves seem to have got cold feet. Vasiliev, the Party secretary and KGB informer – whose power within the museum was second only to the director – is said to have pressed Artamonov to meet the high-ups and hammer out a compromise, but Artamonov refused. On a Monday, Artamonov's day off, the regional secretary arrived at the museum himself saying he wanted to clarify the situation with the director. They rang Artamonov at home three times, pressing him to come into the office but he refused. Artamonov's reaction, according to Stolyar, was 'they've got me in a corner and I can't back out.'

The announcement of Artamonov's removal as director was a further embarrassment to the authorities. On two occasions the staff were summoned to the Hermitage theatre to hear an announcement from the regional secretary, only to find the meeting had been cancelled. On the third occasion he still did not come but sent a letter.

The eighteenth-century theatre, with its pink marbled pillars and

Classical sculptures, was packed – even the attendants had forced their way in. The letter was read out from the stage. Then the staff began to make spontaneous speeches lauding Artamonov's outstanding contribution to the Hermitage. 'Anyone who hadn't known what was going on would have thought it was a meeting in honour of the director,' says Stolyar. The Party hierarchy was represented to make sure the meeting did not get out of hand but played little part in the proceedings. All the staff had brought flowers to present to Artamonov and he rose to speak amongst a sea of them. 'The years I have spent with you have been very dear to me,' Stolyar remembers him as saying. 'No decree can break the threads that bind us because they are too sincere and heartfelt.'

After this some 250 people poured out into the street to say goodbye to him. The emotional cavalcade set off down the Neva embankment towards Palace Bridge, stopping the traffic. Gradually the crowd thinned and by the time they reached the Café Sever on Nevsky Prospect there were some fifty or sixty people left. They turned into the café with Artamonov to drown their sorrows in vodka.

16

Piotrovsky and Son

*B*oris Piotrovsky initially refused to follow Artamonov as director of the Hermitage. In the highly charged atmosphere surrounding the sacking, no man of honour could happily have taken over Artamonov's chair. Piotrovsky refused repeatedly for over a month as more and more senior figures in the Communist Party pressed him to take it on. His son, Mikhail Borisovich, says it was a very hard decision – 'I was one of the people who told him he mustn't take it.' His misgivings and excuses finally drove the Minister of Culture, Ekaterina Furtseva, into a fury. 'What else have I got to do to make you take over?' she screamed at him.

Someone had to run the Hermitage and there was an ever present danger that a Party hack, rather than a scholar, would be appointed. Artamonov himself supported Piotrovsky's appointment and, despite his removal as director of the Hermitage, Artamonov was still a force to be reckoned with. He retained, until his death in 1972, the professorial chair of archaeology at Leningrad University where he was a much loved teacher.

Piotrovsky was the obvious choice. He had been Orbeli's deputy director and continued in the job for two years under Artamonov, only resigning in 1953 when, to his astonishment, he was appointed director of the Institute of the History of Material Culture. He had made a courageous speech praising Nikolay Marr's work as an archaeologist at the height of Stalin's anti-Marr campaign and, instead of being sacked, he found himself elevated to his first directorship. 'Someone in authority must have had a hidden agenda,' his son comments.

Piotrovsky loved the Hermitage. He had haunted it as a teenager, had helped the Egyptian specialists while a student, and worked there for over twenty years. He finally accepted the post which he had probably often dreamed of. The sacking of Artamonov thus ushered in the dynastic era of the Piotrovsky family. Boris Borisovich Piotrovsky was director of the Hermitage from 1964 to his death in 1990 and his son Mikhail Borisovich, the current director, appointed in 1992, looks set for another long run.

It is quite as unusual in Russia, as it is in the West, for a son to succeed his father as director of a great national institution. Moreover, the two Piotrovskys were appointed for diametrically opposite reasons. Boris Piotrovsky, who joined the Communist Party in 1945, was selected as a safe man for the job at the opening of the repressive Brezhnev era, while his son Mikhail was appointed by Egor Gaidar, Boris Yeltsin's short-lived reformist prime minister, because he was a dynamic, cosmopolitan scholar who looked capable of steering the museum through the rough water of perestroika.

Superficially, they could hardly be more different. Boris Borisovich was tall, patrician, full of friendly chat and an appeaser; Mikhail Borisovich is small, modest, with an irrepressible sense of humour and an iron will. But there is no question in the Piotrovsky family of a rebellious son in conflict with a harshly conservative father. The two of them were obviously devoted to each other, shared most of their attitudes to culture and politics and were always mutually supportive. Rather, they provide a fascinating example of a family traditionally devoted to the service of its country – irrespective of the regime in power.

The Piotrovsky family was of Polish origin but settled in Russia around the seventeenth or eighteenth century where it was numbered amongst the minor nobility. Both of Boris Piotrovsky's grandfathers were generals in the tsar's army; his father, a mathematician and soldier, ran a school for the orphans who roamed the streets of St Petersburg in the wake of the Revolution, before joining the staff of the Pedagogical Institute – thus earning Boris Borisovich a free university education. Following the family tradition of service to the State, Boris Borisovich became a symbol and propagandist of Soviet culture while Mikhail Borisovich, who speaks eleven languages, ensures international support for the Hermitage in an era when Russia, having abandoned Communism, is stumbling as it tries to find a new way forward.

The chameleon nature of the Piotrovsky clan is not without its critics. 'Boris Borisovich was an old fox who always knew which side his bread was buttered', or he 'was a good man who only did the evil that was necessary'; 'Mikhail Borisovich's internationalism is only skin deep – scratch him and you'll find a Soviet apparatchik', etc. No one who holds power over other people's lives can escape criticism. But the two Piotrovskys have clearly served the Hermitage with diligence, honesty and a fierce love. 'It may sound pretentious,' says Mikhail Borisovich, 'but I think we have always known that the Hermitage is bigger than those who work for it.' Most of the Hermitage staff feel the same way. They like to call themselves *ermitazhniki* ('Hermitageniks'), wryly implying that their devotion to the museum borders on lunacy.

The story of the Piotrovskys and the museum also upsets conventional Western attitudes to Russia – dissidents good, Communists bad; opening to the West good, residual Communism bad, etc. Both were active members of the Communist Party; Mikhail Borisovich ran the Party bureau at the Institute of Oriental Studies until the Party itself was scrapped in 1991. 'The Party went out of me, rather than me out of the Party,' he says. Boris Borisovich died of stroke brought on by the early struggles of perestroika – the museum staff formed themselves into a Workers' Collective which challenged the administration and demanded the right to rule. He was hurried to hospital after a stormy meeting of the Collective in the courtyard of the Winter Palace, arguing over the nomination of his successor. His son is the first to admit that it was easier to run the museum under Communism, as he battles to force the government to honour its budgetary undertakings – often without success. But he is a man who enjoys challenges and prefers the new era.

Boris Borisovich's widow, Ripsime Mikhailovna, recalls: 'Boris Borisovich and I joined the Party together in 1945. It was a matter of idealism.' The Soviet Union and its Communist Party had just won the Great Patriotic War and saved the world from Hitler's fanaticism, or so it would have seemed to the young couple. That the Soviet Union had received assistance from its allies would have looked unimportant when viewed from within the vast territories of the country itself; the sheer size of Russia is very important in imparting a sense of greatness to its patriots. Mikhail Borisovich echoes his parents' attitude: 'I joined the Party out of romantic patriotism: I was working in the Yemen just after their Revolution and felt I was experiencing the kind of idealistic, political ferment I had so often read about existing in Russia in 1917. It gave me a proud sense of how Russia had shown the way and could now help struggling countries like the Yemen – it was the romance of imperialism, if you like.'

He gives a deprecating smile and a little glint from behind his spectacles. 'It hasn't turned out how I dreamed as a young man. Now all my friends in the Yemen are trying to kill each other – and I can't turn on the heating in the museum because the Russian government won't pay the bill.' Which doesn't mean he has changed heart or lost faith. 'I still believe in socialist ideals,' he says, 'but we live with a new reality.' His widowed mother is even more emphatic. 'Of course I am still a Communist. What is happening is a tragedy. But I like to think that Russia, just like a building, is going through a period of restoration – that's why it's so uncomfortable to live in. It will be alright again once the work is completed.'

The Piotrovskys were not like the fanatical Communists portrayed in Western literature. Boris Borisovich made a personal contribution to the world of *samizdat* (illegal, unofficial publications) by teaching himself to visually memorise books which he could then repeat to his friends. He astounded Thomas Hoving, director of New York's Metropolitan Museum, in the 1970s by his ability to quote from Harrison Salisbury's *Siege of Leningrad* – the book was banned in Russia on account of its references to cannibalism.

Mikhail Borisovich explains that they had no anti-American feelings in the 1960s and 1970s, despite the barrage of propaganda. 'We always understood that Americans had liberty and the good life. Everyone knew that capitalism provided better material possibilities.' They knew it from books. His reading, he says, included Agatha Christie, Tennessee Williams, Micky Spillane, Henry Miller, Ian Fleming and Jack Kerouac, 'books that visitors had left behind in Russia which got passed from hand to hand or traded on the black market – most of them were banned.' The Piotrovsky family has dominated life at the Hermitage for so long that it is worth taking a closer look at them.

Boris Borisovich Piotrovsky was born in St Petersburg in 1908 but at the time of the Revolution his father was teaching in a military college in Orenburg in Kazakstan. In November 1917 the nine-year-old Boris celebrated the Revolution in the streets of Orenburg wearing red armbands; then the city was taken by the Whites, then by the Reds, then the Whites again. His schooling was interrupted, and took an original slant when the family returned to St Petersburg in 1921 to live in the Grand Hotel Europe. His father was running a school for orphans there which Boris duly attended.

At the time, many teachers spent the summer in Pavlovsk, the village associated with Paul I's great palace, where food was marginally more accessible than in the capital and it was there, over breakfast with one of his friends, that Boris Borisovich first met Nataliya Flittner, keeper of Egyptian art at the Hermitage. She would bring small figurines – *oushbati* – home to show the two boys and Boris Borisovich's imagination was fired. In the summer of 1922, at the age of fourteen, he bought his first book on Egypt. Flittner mounted a tour of the Hermitage collection for his class and he became a regular, unofficial helper in her department. The connection continued after he entered the university in 1925; while still a student he provided the illustrations for Flittner's 1929 guide to the Egyptian collection.

Having studied archaeology at Leningrad University, he entered Marr's Academy of the History of Material Culture as a graduate student in 1929 where he met the future director of the Hermitage, Iosif Orbeli. The patronage of two great cultural figures of the period, Marr and Orbeli, gave Boris Borisovich a flying start. He joined the Hermitage staff in 1931 without severing his links with the Academy and became the curator and researcher responsible for the art of the Transcaucasus, concentrating especially on Urartu. Having shared with Orbeli the sufferings of the siege of Leningrad and evacuation to Armenia, he became his deputy in the post-war years.

It was in Armenia that Boris Borisovich found his wife and the family's Armenian connection has become an important facet of its character – adding a dash of southern temperament, family ('clan') loyalty and independence. Ripsime Mikhailovna is also an archaeologist and was working in the History Museum of Yerevan when Orbeli found her and invited her to spend two months in the Hermitage to study the operation of the museum. She became friendly with Boris Borisovich and worked on his pre-war digs at Karmir-Blur from 1939 to 1941. He used to refer to her as 'the best artefact I found in my excavations'. Their friendship only ripened into romance, however, after Boris Borisovich was evacuated to Yerevan in 1942. Ripsime was small, pretty and full of temperament. Boris Borisovich, the tall, patrician northerner was the perfect foil. They were married in February 1944 and brought the present director of the Hermitage into the world in December.

Yerevan was to play a key role in the upbringing of Mikhail Borisovich. For two or three months in the summer his parents would decamp to the south to work on their – separate – digs. Ripsime was a medievalist and excavated at Dvin while Boris Borisovich continued to work at Karmir-Blur. Their two sons were parked with Ripsime's parents and ran wild around the back yards of Yerevan. The doting grandparents, however, provided them with as cultured a background as they had at home in St Petersburg. Like the Piotrovskys, Ripsime's family had belonged to the upper echelons of society before the Revolution. Though Armenian, the family lived in Nahichevan, now an autonomous region within Azerbaijan, where they had made a large fortune from running salt mines; Ripsime's parents escaped the 1918 Azeri massacre of Armenians by walking to Yerevan. They arrived with nothing, but struggled successfully with poverty and put all their four children through university.

Mikhail Borisovich and his brother Levon were encouraged by their parents to learn foreign languages – Armenian hardly counted, being as natural to them as Russian. Boris Borisovich considered languages as the key to an interesting life in the Soviet Union – they could open a window on a wider world. So Mikhail Borisovich and his brother – now a leading chemist – had German lessons at home before they went to school and, once they had mastered that language, moved on to English and French. Mikhail Borisovich is now also a fluent Arab speaker – he first travelled outside Russia as an interpreter. And his historical studies have required him to master several dead languages, from the ancient language of South Arabia, to Aramaic and Hebrew.

He explains his choice of specialisation with characteristic modesty. 'I had to find a subject my father didn't know, so I became an Arabist.' His father returned the compliment by taking obvious pleasure in his son's success: 'When they hear my surname in Arab countries they ask if I'm related to Mikhail Borisovich,' he would say with pride.

Mikhail Borisovich spent an undergraduate year at Cairo University – Colonel Nasser was friendly with the Soviet Union at the time – and it was while he was there that he came across the intellectual adventure that has shaped his scholarly life: the rediscovery of the forgotten history of Southern Arabia before the arrival of Islam in the sixth century AD. He began with the Yemen, a land of nomads, mountains and deserts which, in the 1960s, was still little changed from biblical times. In his own words, 'we Russian Orientalists gave them back their history'. The Yemenis had just thrown out the British imperialists and embarked on a Communist reconstruction, so the country was both accessible and politically exciting for a young Russian scholar. Mikhail Borisovich spent two years teaching ancient history at the Communist Party school the Russians had set up in the Yemen to help train a new ruling cadre.

Such an opportunity would not have been available to any young

Russian. It reflects the fact that the Party and the KGB smiled on the budding scholar and saw him as a 'good thing' for Russia. The fact that his father was an important cultural figure, well known to the Party bosses in the Kremlin, would have helped. He denies working for the KGB himself, adding with a disarming chuckle: 'If I had worked for them, do you really think I'd tell you?' A Russian who could speak the language and teach Yemeni history presented 'a good face for our country', he explains. He was one of two or three specialists who worked for the Party school but were not themselves members of the Party. 'It was the people without qualifications who were on the KGB payroll. Of course, if anyone asked me questions about life there, or the political situation, I would answer them, whether they were from the embassy or the KGB, no matter. And when I worked as an interpreter for Russian delegations, it was part of my job to write up their reports.'

It was not politics that took him to the Yemen but a group of seventh- and eighth-century manuscripts relating to its legendary past which are spread around the libraries of the world and were virtually unstudied before he began work on them. From the second millennium BC to the coming of Islam in the sixth century, there was a rich – but largely forgotten – civilisation in Southern Arabia, complete with kingdoms, monuments, and a written language. It had close links with the Babylonians and Assyrians and Mikhail Borisovich has written its history.

The manuscripts treated legend and folklore, combining elements of history with romantic imaginings. He set about the task of distinguishing fact from fiction by comparing the legends with other contemporary documents, including the Bible – a kind of historical detective work. The resulting book had a stormy reception. 'I was prepared for scholars to object to my finding any truth in the legends but not for the opposite objection from some literate Yemenis. They thought every word of the legends was true and banned the distribution of the book in their country.' He also explored the trade routes of the ancient Yemen, paying special attention to the inscriptions cut into the rocks by travellers – the equivalent of today's graffiti. Inscribed on the rocks in the ancient language used before the sixth century, they provide a living record of daily life. And he excavated at various ancient sites, collaborating with the Russian-Yemeni expedition from 1981 and 1990 and running it for the last two years.

After focusing on the Yemen, Mikhail Borisovich expanded his vision to take in the rest of Arabia. He wrote an analysis of the Koran, sorting fact from fiction in the light of the known facts of ancient history, using the same methods he had applied to the Yemeni manuscripts. Another major work, an anthology of studies of ancient Arabia by Russian scholars, which demonstrates (for the first time) that there was a great, unified civilisation in antiquity stretching from the Yemen to the Greek Islands, and importantly interacting with the rest of the world, remains on his former desk at the Institute of Oriental Studies – unpublished, since the Russian government has run out of paper, ink and finance for scholarly publications.

Mikhail Borisovich's need for paper and ink has now been sharply reduced. 'When I moved to the Hermitage,' he says, 'it was clear that I wouldn't have much time for scholarly work.' In abandoning the Institute for the museum he faced an easier decision than his father. Vitali Suslov, the new director, who had been his father's number two, invited him to join the museum staff as his deputy and designated successor. 'I thought about the offer for two or three days. But there are some things you can't refuse – and being director of the Hermitage is one of them,' says Mikhail Borisovich. In July 1992, after acting as deputy director for just over a year, he came into the office on a Monday morning to find a decree signed by the prime minister, Egor Gaidar, on his desk appointing him director in Suslov's place.

'I went and showed it to Suslov – it hadn't been sent to him – and the first thing he asked me was when it was supposed to go into effect. The document didn't say, so I rang the Ministry. "You're director now," they told me. "Sort it out for yourself." So Suslov and I sat down and discussed what to do.'

New statutes governing the national heritage, including how museum directors should be appointed, had just been introduced, following the closure of the Party. Gaidar used the opportunity they offered to remove Suslov who was considered to have blotted his copybook in a number of ways – notably over the Hermitage Joint Venture, of which more later. He became a consultant to the museum, the first director to relinquish his post but remain on the staff since Sergey Troinitsky.

When the Piotrovskys first took over the running of the Hermitage in 1964, it was a great, old fashioned museum organised on strict Communist principles for the enjoyment and educational improvement of the peoples of the Soviet Union. But the political 'thaw' with the West had begun and around 1970 the Kremlin realised that cultural exchanges could be used as a means of exploring new contacts abroad and establishing diplomatic links. Initially, Moscow would tell the

Hermitage in which country it was anxious to improve relations. 'We would get a telegram or telephone call,' Vitali Suslov remembers, 'saying it would be very good if you could arrange an exhibition in London, France or America . . . The next week it would be somewhere different.' Often the exhibition projects were linked to a state visit and many of the Hermitage exhibitions abroad were formally opened by presidents, prime ministers or other political figures.

The Hermitage would seek out a partner from among the national museums of the designated country and try to develop an idea for the exchange of art exhibitions. They always tried to get another exhibition back for each one they sent out. In almost every country an exhibition of the Shchukin and Morozov paintings was the first request. As a result, many of the exhibitions were organised jointly with the Pushkin Museum in Moscow, the owner of the other half of these great collections, and many of the foreign exhibitions that came to Russia would be shown in both cities. The development of the Hermitage's links with the rest of the world became the keynote of Boris Borisovich's period as director.

The first exchange exhibitions with foreign countries had begun under Artamonov – the exhibition of 'Painting in Great Britain, 1700–1960', sent to the Hermitage by the British Council in 1960, is still remembered as a visual eye opener – but the flowering of Russia's international exhibition policy was guided by Boris Borisovich and his opposite number at the Pushkin Museum in Moscow, Irina Antonova. 'Masterpieces of Modern Painting from the USSR' were shown in Japan in 1966–7. Matisse paintings from the Shchukin and Morozov collections were shown at the Grand Palais in Paris in 1970 – after exhibitions at the Hermitage and the Pushkin the year before.

At this time ordinary Russians had no opportunity to travel abroad. So Boris Borisovich set about bringing world culture to Russia. The exhibition of Tutankhamun's treasures from the Cairo Museum, already shown with sensational success in New York and London, arrived at the Hermitage in 1974. Boris Borisovich had negotiated that it should be paid for out of the Egyptian government's debts to Russia. In 1975 '100 Pictures from the Metropolitan' came to Leningrad and exhibitions from the Louvre and Prado followed. He also took the initiative in setting up special exhibitions for which he wrote the catalogues himself, including 'Colombian Gold' and 'Out of Nigeria', an exhibition of Benin bronzes and other sculptures.

Boris Borisovich in his role as cultural ambassador ended up visiting forty different countries. Having been denied the opportunity to travel in his youth – he was already fifty-six when he became director of the museum – these expeditions had a special significance for him. He kept diaries of all his foreign visits in which he meticulously recorded his impressions, day by day, illustrating them with spare line-drawings of the kind he used to illustrate archaeological reports – and letters to his children. The extent of his official travels is underlined by the fact that he left 133 of these diaries, ranging in date from 1964 to 1990.

Another major development of his period as director was the opening of a branch museum in the Menshikov Palace on Vasilevsky Island. Alexander Menshikov was Peter the Great's close friend and associate, the first governor of St Petersburg. Peter had intended that the centre of his city should be concentrated on Vasilevsky Island but his subjects' understandable preference for returning home without having to take a boat sabotaged this plan. Menshikov, however, built his own palace – the first palace that was built in the city – on the island. From the time of his disgrace, at the end of Peter's reign, until the Revolution the confiscated building was used as an extension of the nearby officer cadet school; the Bolsheviks gave it to the university for a while but then handed it back to the army.

By the 1960s its condition was very dilapidated but the city recognised that the building itself was a historical monument of the first importance. They began its restoration in 1966 and two years later brought in the Hermitage as consultants on the history of the building. The museum began archaeological-style research on it, finding many original features, such as doors, window frames, paintwork, even a whole painted ceiling in Menshikov's walnut-lined cabinet. As a result, the city decided to restore the building to its original eighteenth-century appearance. It was a mammoth restoration project, only completed in 1981, at which point the Hermitage was allowed to rent the building and install a display devoted to 'Russian Culture in the First Third of the Eighteenth Century' – Menshikov's time. The museum was finally given the building outright in 1994.

Menshikov, like Peter himself, was a great collector. His possessions, confiscated at the time of his disgrace, entered the imperial collections but were never identified in inventories as such. Many have probably survived in the Hermitage collections and the effort to identify them on the basis of contemporary documentation is a continuing challenge to its scholarly curators. The present display, however, is mainly drawn from Menshikov's period, rather than his own collection. Its 1981 opening came as a revelation to the citizens of St Petersburg. Peter's own Summer Palace had led them to believe that aristocratic taste was simple at this early period. The sumptuous decoration of the Menshikov Palace has dispelled this myth.

Ritzy taste has continued to be a feature of those who govern St Petersburg right up to the present day. Grigory Romanov, the Leningrad Party Secretary in the early 1980s and one of Gorbachev's rivals, was no exception to the rule. It was thus entirely in character when a rumour started to circulate that Romanov, in order to celebrate his daughter's wedding with suitable pomp, had borrowed one of Catherine the Great's dinner services from the Hermitage and broken several of the plates. Boris Borisovich denied the rumour but still it grew. And it has survived for over ten years, so thoroughly intact that it is now generally regarded as a 'fact'.

'There was never any truth in it,' says Mikhail Borisovich, 'but the rumour was very persistent and seems to have emanated from Moscow. My father denied it many times but very high-level journalists always came back with it. I think it was deliberately invented and distributed. Romanov was not loved either by the intelligentsia of St Petersburg or the Party leaders in Moscow. He was young and ambitious, and hoped to jump into Moscow politics on the basis of working-class support in St Petersburg. He was Gorbachev's chief rival and I think someone, maybe the KGB, must have fixed it.'

Romanov also resented Boris Borisovich's fame as one of the nation's leading cultural figures. There was not room in Romanov's Leningrad for a rival figure of such stature. He sabotaged Boris Borisovich's activities in every way he could manage and refused to speak to him about the Hermitage's problems. At one point the clash became so acute that Boris Borisovich sent a letter of resignation from the Hermitage. But a friend who outranked Romanov arrived from Moscow in the nick of time to rescue the situation. Romanov was forced to apologise. Boris Borisovich remained the director of the Hermitage and one of the nation's chief cultural ambassadors.

His freedom to travel was a reflection of the 'thaw' in Russia's foreign relations, but the apposite verb was definitely 'to thaw' rather than 'to melt'. The Hermitage library, for instance, had three grades of books: those openly available, those only accessible to museum staff, and those restricted to senior cadres with special permission. Virtually any book published in the West, the romantic biography of Catherine the Great by Henri Troyat, for instance, was only available to senior museum staff.

The offices habitually used by foreign visitors to the Hermitage were wired up by the KGB so that every conversation could be recorded. At one point, Boris Borisovich summoned his senior staff to ask them if they would kindly keep their conversations in those rooms to a minimum in order to reduce the work load of the KGB transcribers. For several days people tried anxiously to remember what they had recently said there. Among the designated rooms was, of course, the handsome director's office on the ground floor of the Old Hermitage, overlooking the river. The seventeenth-century Flemish tapestries on its walls provided ideal cover for listening devices.

The sound engineer of an American television crew recently told Mikhail Borisovich that he was picking up odd signals and asked if these devices were still active. 'I have no idea,' he told them. 'They are not my microphones.' Since then he has had his office checked and been told it's clean. 'But they also told me that microphones can't be detected unless they're switched on,' he adds, leaving other possibilities in the air.

Boris Borisovich's attitude to his staff's struggles with the system was sympathetic rather than combative. An older member of staff tells the story of a brush with the KGB. After refusing to become an informer, she was, in her turn, refused permission to travel by the KGB officer who had pressed her to help him – she had been invited to a foreign seminar. Erupting in a rage into the director's office – Boris Borisovich prided himself on keeping all three doors to his office open and being available to any member of his staff at any time – the curator demanded he help her. 'There are two things you could do,' he is said to have replied. 'Either you can write a letter of complaint to the Party Bureau, or you can wait until the KGB officer is promoted and then go abroad. I would advise the latter.'

Those who were allowed to travel were very strictly vetted. Anyone with family members who had been repressed, or who had spoken too freely on the telephone – most of the office phones were tapped, often so inefficiently that you could hear heavy breathing as the listeners clicked into place – was not allowed to travel. Many of the Hermitage curators did not get abroad until after perestroika. As recently as 1985, one young curator was reprimanded by his departmental chief for inviting an American graduate student working in the department out to coffee. She was pretty, of course. But no unofficial contact with foreigners was permitted.

On the other hand, well vetted Party members could drink as much vodka as they liked with well vetted foreign visitors. The official hospitality of the museum was not necessarily formal. And in the 1970s and early 1980s relations with the West had become sufficiently normal for tourists to start visiting St Petersburg in large numbers. It was regarded as an exotic venue and many cultured people were prepared to suffer package tours, then the simplest way of getting there, for the sake of visiting the Hermitage. Travel restrictions within the Soviet Union had also been lifted for Russians, while subsidies kept air and rail tickets at rock bottom prices. The result was a boom in internal tourism.

Under the combined impact of foreign and local visitors, the Hermitage began to come apart at the seams. At the high point, around 1981–2, the museum had some three and a half million visitors a year; the galleries were packed and queues were known to stretch round the building, across Palace Square and down as far as Nevsky Prospect. The imperial parquet floors, with their wonderful intricate patterns designed by eighteenth-century architects, began to be ground into dust. It became urgently apparent that something had to be done.

Whether Boris Borisovich or his deputy Vitali Suslov should be credited with responsibility for the grandiose development plan drawn up in the early 1980s to deal with the challenge of the tourist boom is a moot point. No doubt they both had a hand in it but the two men, by that time, were frequently at loggerheads. Boris Borisovich had handed some of the museum administration to Suslov when he first joined the staff and, over the years, Suslov had taken more and more into his hands – eventually, more than he had competence to handle. Boris Borisovich was already seventy-two in 1980 and eighty-two when he died in 1990. Over this final decade Suslov's role grew in importance.

Boris Borisovich had recruited Suslov as his deputy in 1967 to replace the ageing scholar Vladimir Levinson-Lessing who considered himself too old for the job – he died in 1972. Levinson-Lessing's erudition and charm are born witness to by all those who knew him, though his history of the Hermitage picture gallery, published posthumously, is his only major publication. His shortcomings as an administrator are also legendary. So it is understandable that Boris Borisovich should have looked especially for administrative qualities when seeking a new deputy.

Suslov was forty-three when he joined the Hermitage. The son of a coal mining engineer, he was born near Vladivostok, served in the navy during the war and only began to study at Leningrad University in 1946. He wrote a dissertation on the Russian avant-garde of the 1920s, then turned to Russian painting of the Soviet period, getting his first post-graduate degree (*kandidat*) in 1954 but never finishing his doctorate. Hermitage curators liked to point out that he was not a scholar. He now looks like a friendly, grey-haired bear and clearly sets great store by the reforms he attempted in the 1980s, seeing them as the introduction of 'modern Western' ideas into the museum.

When Boris Borisovich recruited him he had been deputy director of the Russian Museum for five years: 'I wanted to start a new life as an administrator. It was a whole new world,' he says. As a result, the two men worked together for twenty-three years. While superficially friends, relations between them became very strained. By the last five years or so, Suslov had managed to play his cards so well that he had effective control in many areas. The staff knew that if they got a 'yes' from Boris Borisovich and a 'no' from Suslov, or vice versa, Suslov's ruling would prevail. Meanwhile, Boris Borisovich struggled to keep the ship on course, though he was far beyond normal retirement age. According to his widow, 'he couldn't retire because there was no suitable successor'. A significant motivation for remaining in office was to keep Suslov out of the director's chair.

It seems curious that Boris Borisovich felt unable to dismiss a deputy who was usurping his power and making decisions with which he did not agree. The explanation probably lies with his innate dislike of confrontation, coupled with the absolute power of the Party. Suslov was a Party member and a member of the Party Bureau for his section of the city. He thus had powerful support both inside and outside the museum. Had Boris Borisovich tried to move him, it is anyone's guess who would have won the tussle for power; Suslov could have argued, with justification, that Boris Borisovich was too old for his job.

The grandiose development plan that the two of them dreamed up in the early 1980s has been the source of many problems, some of them still not resolved as I write. The prime motive for expansion lay in having galleries so packed with visitors that the visitors themselves could not see the displays or move about freely. Since potential gallery space was being used for storage, offices and restoration studios, it was natural to want to move these elsewhere and open up new exhibition areas. The potential for new displays was vast; only some five per cent of the museum's three million objects were on show. At the same time, contacts with Western institutions had revealed how technologically out of date the Hermitage had become – the need for temperature and humidity controls, new security systems, computerisation of inventory and so on.

The museum prepared several alternative plans for resolving their problems which they presented to the Ministry of Culture in 1980. Essentially, the decision lay between annexing adjoining properties to the museum or building new facilities on the outskirts of town. And after due assessment, discussion and many changes of mind, the national and city governments approved a development plan in 1985 which incorporated both.

It envisaged the building of a vast new complex to accommodate storage, restoration and education facilities at Novaya Derevnya, beside a big World War II cemetery on the edge of town. No one was thinking small. In addition to air-conditioned open storage, it was to contain a swimming pool, a cinema and a restaurant. Building began in 1989 and money ran out in 1991. The new administration has now altered the plans, trying to make them more responsive to current realities. But it still looks as if a white elephant is rising on the outskirts of the city, whose vast cost could be much better spent on reworking spaces in the centre – but whose facilities are so desperately needed that the construction must now be finished and the space brought into use. Naturally enough, staff who are used to working in a palace in the city centre are not keen to move to an ugly new building on the outskirts, inadequately served by public transport. Making the best of it, Mikhail Borisovich now speaks of establishing a cultural and exhibition centre that will serve the dormitory communities housed in multi-storey apartment blocks in this newly developed region.

The 1985 plan also envisaged the redevelopment of Quarenghi's theatre building to incorporate offices and restoration studios; the annexation of the apartment building next to the theatre, No. 30 Palace Embankment, and its redevelopment; and a vast new museum in the handsome buildings opposite the Winter Palace on Palace Square, built by Rossi in the 1830s to house the Ministries of Finance and Foreign Affairs. The government allocated the whole of this block for the Hermitage's use. The new museum that would be established there was to be devoted to the applied arts, thus freeing up the main halls of the Winter Palace and allowing them to be presented as 'palace interiors'.

As I write, only the theatre building has been completed. In addition to the elegant eighteenth-century theatre, sensitively spruced up, there is a new laboratory for restoring works on paper, modernised office space and a new display relating to the life of Peter the Great, on show in the remains of his original Winter Palace which were found and excavated in the basement during restoration. How far the more exciting opportunities for expanding into nearby buildings will be realised remains to be seen. One day, perhaps, the Hermitage will become the largest museum complex in the world, with specialised museums devoted to the applied arts, archaeology and Russian military history, its great library better housed and more accessible, its storage and restoration staff rescued from the outskirts and housed in buildings of outstanding architectural merit, comprising, in Suslov's words, 'an architectural museum in its own right'. This is the dream of the current director.

Mikhail Borisovich needs to dream as he is forced to watch the original development plan – which was expected to be completed in 1991 – limp forward, constantly sabotaged by lack of funds. All work on the new complex at Novaya Derevnya was suspended from 1992 to 1995. Then, after a short spate of renewed activity, building work slowed down again in late 1996, as promised government financing failed to materialise. As time passes, plans for its use are constantly revised. One of the new ideas is to create storage space with open access for the public – no museum has ever attempted to put its reserve collections on show on the scale that the Hermitage is projecting. There will be paintings hitherto considered too large to exhibit, imperial carriages, an embroidered travelling tent used by an eighteenth-century Persian shah, and quantities and quantities of furniture.

The attempts to restructure Russia's economic system which Gorbachev called perestroika had a noisy, painful but relatively superficial effect on the Hermitage. Since government financing for the much vaunted 'reconstruction' of the museum began to run out in 1991 – foreign currency allocations were cancelled before rouble funding – the museum and its staff were forced to continue in their old ways, working in cramped, old fashioned offices packed into corners of the palace buildings. They continue to busily prepare foreign exhibitions of Hermitage material and mount new displays in the museum itself.

However, two of Gorbachev's favourite schemes for revitalising the economy – joint ventures with foreign companies and workers' control of company management – caused turmoil in the museum between 1989 and 1992. The Hermitage Joint Venture, which was forced into receivership in America in 1995 and finally tipped into oblivion in Russia by Mikhail Borisovich in the course of 1996, was organised by Suslov with a buoyant desire to keep the museum in the forefront of the nation's economic change. 'My father knew something was wrong and didn't want to do it,' comments Mikhail Borisovich, 'but Suslov said it was a "modern" solution that would contribute a living dynamism to the Hermitage.' Government funding for the reconstruction of the Hermitage had run out and Suslov saw the Joint Venture as a potential source of huge earnings. Boris Borisovich signed its founding charter on 26 January 1989.

On paper, the aims of the Joint Venture between the Hermitage and the American company Transatlantic Agency were admirable. Its business was to include:

> the sale and distribution of products and services related to the State Hermitage Museum; buying and selling goods and services; operation of stores and businesses; registering, maintaining and defending copyrights, trademarks, tradenames and patents related to the State Hermitage Museum in the Soviet Union and throughout the world; defending licences in the Soviet Union and throughout the world; offering additional tourist services directly related to the activities of the Hermitage, including trips for the staff of the State Hermitage Museum abroad for educational exchanges; the organisation of exhibitions and doing other work; operating cafeterias, restaurants and hotels called 'The Hermitage' and other forms of services; various forms of education; organising and operating foundations funded by The Hermitage; and all other matters including acting as agents and consultants.

Unfortunately the Joint Venture turned out to be both too ambitious and too amateur. Rather than join forces with an established American company, Suslov linked the museum with the 'Transatlantic Agency', a company founded by a Russian émigré called George Garkusha and his American wife with the sole purpose of acting as a partner to the Hermitage. Garkusha had worked as a porter at the museum when he left school and was employed by the Soviet Trade Department in America after he moved there. In the various depositions he made in the course of legal disputes in America, he never revealed any other commercial experience.

What most impressed Suslov about Garkusha was that he produced a representative of the famous American magazine, *National Geographic*, as a third party to the deal. It was envisaged that *National Geographic* would publicise Hermitage exhibitions in America, help with catalogues and help fund some of the museum's archaeological digs. But *National Geographic* was never a direct party to the deal. The founding charter speaks of 'the Transatlantic Agency in association with the National Geographic Society' but makes no pretence that anyone other than the Transatlantic Agency was the American partner in the Joint Venture. *National Geographic* dropped out at a very early stage.

The museum's financial inexperience shows up in the split they agreed for the Joint Venture's profits. Transatlantic Agency – i.e. Mr and Mrs Garkusha – were to get 55 per cent and the Hermitage – a 200-year-old museum with 1,500 employees – 45 per cent. Garkusha was appointed managing director of the Joint Venture which took the dangerously confusing trade name of 'The Hermitage'. Suslov was appointed chairman of the board.

The commercial undertakings of the Joint Venture never prospered. It linked up with a Canadian firm to make high class photographic reproductions of pictures but the company closed down; it did a deal on reproducing furniture; imported antique furniture from Scandinavia to be restored at the Hermitage; took a *Catherine the Great* exhibition on a tour of America; and commissioned a paperback picture-book on the Hermitage from a British publisher. It was the latter deal that was the Joint Venture's final undoing, for it failed to pay for the 100,000 copies of this book that it ordered from the British publisher, Booth Clibborn. He took them to court in America and ended up the official receiver of the Hermitage Joint Venture and some one million dollars out of pocket. With its new publishing deals, the museum is now working with Booth Clibborn directly, avoiding the use of an intermediary.

The Joint Venture's commercial ventures in Russia included making pottery reproductions of Antique items in the Hermitage collection and running shops inside the museum, as well as a visitors' café, a staff canteen and hot-dog stands on Palace Square. None of these undertakings ended up yielding a profit to the museum.

In its progress from Great White Hope of Western-style financial salvation to Russian-style oblivion, the Joint Venture became one of the focal points of the battle between staff and management which erupted between 1989 and 1991. This again was a direct reflection of Gorbachev's economic reforms. His 'Law on State Enterprises' of 1 January 1988 encouraged the staff of state-owned enterprises to form democratically voted 'councils of the workers' collective' which would help direct the enterprise and have the right to hire and fire management. The Hermitage joined the fashion and started to organise such a collective council on the initiative of the Party Bureau in 1989.

Its progress was thoroughly documented by an in-house newspaper called *Panorama* which began publication in July 1989 and died in October 1991 – as a result of massive lethargy among the staff and the new political orientation of the country following the attempted coup of August 1991. The idea of democratic control and the opportunity to complain publicly about the bosses was an exciting novelty for Soviet citizens but it soon palled.

The head of the museum publications department, Sergey Avramenko, the son of a noted poet, had been very interested in wall newspapers in the 1960s and ran one at the Hermitage which included in-house news, poems and drawings. He lost interest in the Brezhnev years, when it was impossible to say what you thought, but he urged the Hermitage to reintroduce such a newspaper after Gorbachev proclaimed *glasnost* – freedom of expression. The Party bureau, however, preferred an ordinary newspaper and so *Panorama*, a single sheet folded in two, was born. It came out once a fortnight and had a circulation of 500.

The front page of the first issues announced that it was 'The paper of the Party Bureau, Trade Union, Komsomol Committee and Director's Office of the Hermitage Museum' but no one was happy with such a wealth of official backing and as soon as the Workers' Collective was up and running, in January 1990, the banner at the top of the front page was changed to read 'The Paper of the Workers' Collective'. The Party Bureau appointed an editorial committee of three people, Sergey Avramenko, who was not a Party member, his assistant Roald Rabinovich, and Evgeny Mavleev, the curator of Etruscan antiquities, who had recently joined the Party seeing, as he thought, an opportunity to contribute positively to change. He was to become the chairman of the Workers' Collective but retired sadly back to his antiquities when it came to nothing and died shortly afterwards.

It was Mavleev's idea, or ideal, that *Panorama* should represent all shades of opinion within the museum. But after so many decades of keeping quiet about what they thought, the staff of the Hermitage were understandably shy of putting their names to personal opinions in print. The most critical articles were generally written by Mavleev himself, while Rabinovich busied himself collecting the opinions that other people didn't dare express and Avramenko collected poems, obituaries, letters and memories.

It became a vivid hodgepodge. The fourth issue, dated 29 August 1989, for instance, carried Suslov's suggestions for how national laws should be changed to help museums raise funds privately, a message of special appreciation to the lady in charge of the toilets by the Jordan staircase who kept them squeaky clean and always supplied with toilet paper ('We thank her and wish her good health'), a list of the new books in the library, an obituary, a leading article on 'Problems about the reconstruction of the Hermitage', a veteran's memories of World War II and a complaint about the food in the staff canteen ('It would be terrible if they fed us well – we'd spend all the afternoon in there. It's so good of the Hermitage to arrange that the food is disgusting.') One of the Joint Venture's few positive achievements has been improving the food in the canteen.

The staff's concern about the Joint Venture and the reconstruction of the museum surfaced again and again. In November 1989 horror was expressed in *Panorama* at the Joint Venture's idea of leasing the extra building on Palace Embankment, which the city council had just given the museum, to a foreign company which would 'build a complex consisting of a first class hotel for foreign tourists (400 beds), a restaurant, a recreation zone and an administration block' – a scheme that never got off the ground. The article explained that the building was expected to return to the Hermitage after ten years, during which time it would have made an estimated profit of ten million dollars, half of which would go to the museum. The staff were capable of seeing that this moneymaking scheme was wildly unrealistic. They would, no doubt, have expressed even greater indignation had they known that the small print of the Joint Venture agreement gave the museum only 45 per cent of the proceeds, not even half.

In issue after issue *Panorama* complained that the staff had been given no information on the terms of the Joint Venture agreement – although they were being asked to prepare exhibitions, make catalogues, restore furniture, etc. in its name. Another *bête noire* was the new air conditioning equipment that had been ordered from a Finnish company called FLEKT. The equipment had been delivered before plans were completed on how to use it; the units were large and ugly and would destroy the harmony of the rooms, and – as the porters point out – had been piled up in the courtyard habitually used for playing volleyball, thus sabotaging the museum's sporting activities.

A whole issue was devoted to the open Party meeting held on 7 December 1989 at which Mavleev made a keynote speech vividly criticising the Joint Venture and the museum's reconstruction plans. In his report on the meeting, Evgeny Zeimal, the Oriental Department's expert on the ancient East, pointed out that the hotel scheme was only expected to bring in five million dollars when the overall cost of the

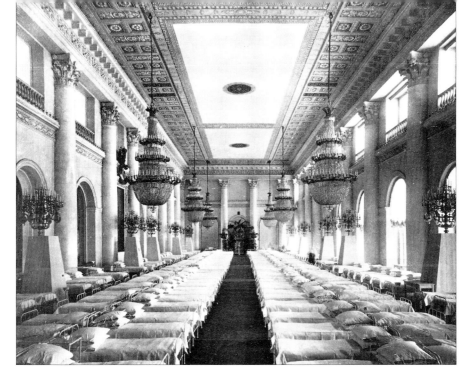

The Nicholas Hall prepared for use as a hospital ward during World War I.

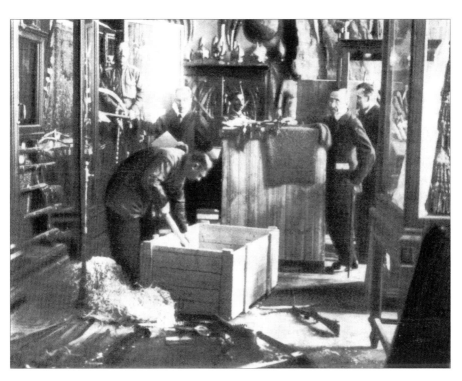

Packing arms and armour for evacuation during World War I,
left Eduard Lenz, curator of the Medieval Department, *right* Count Dmitry Tolstoy,
director of the museum.

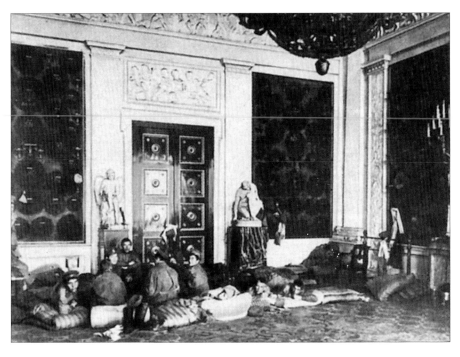

The *yunkers* camping in the Winter Palace in 1917 to defend Kerensky's Provisional Government.

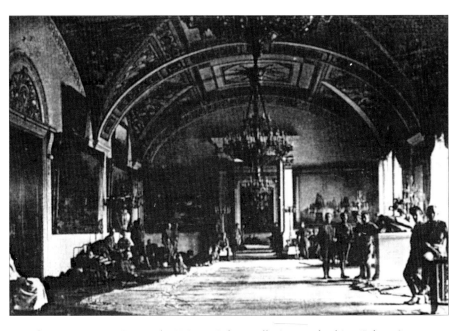

Above: Troops waiting in the Winter Palace galleries overlooking Palace Square to defend the Provisional Government from the Bolsheviks who stormed the Palace in November 1917.

Right: The office of Nicholas II after the storming of the palace.

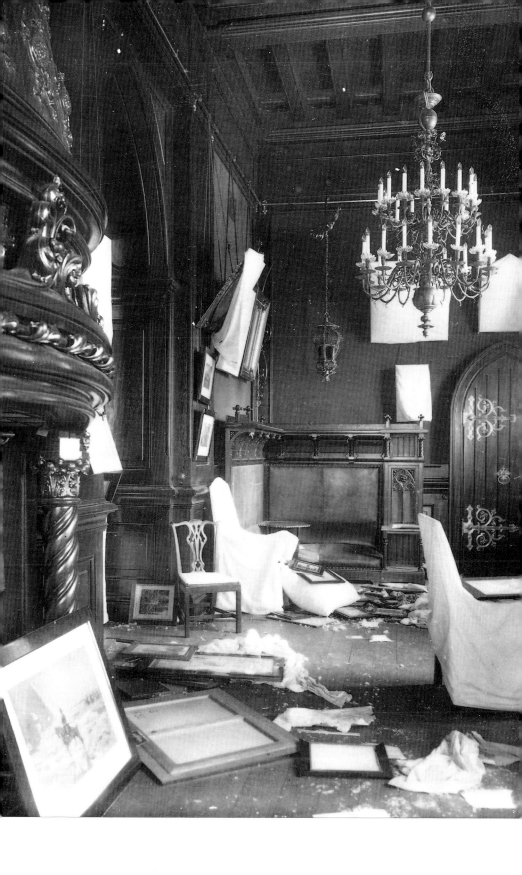

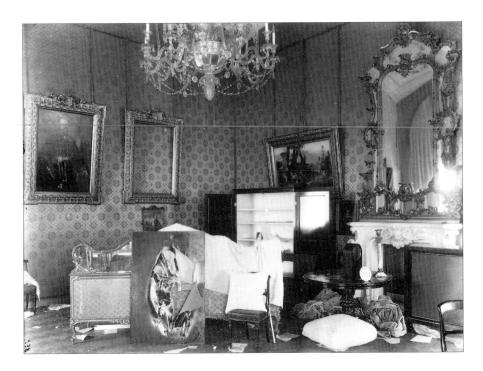

Empress Alexandra Fedorovna's sitting-room after the storming of the Winter Palace by the Bolsheviks in 1917.

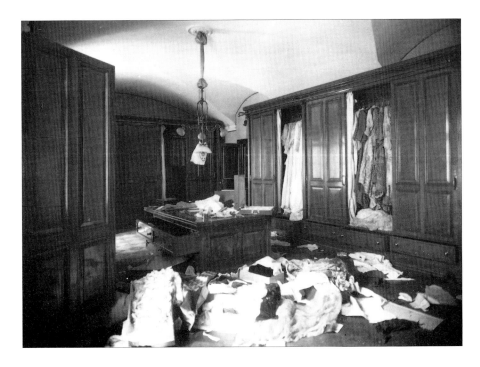

Empress Alexandra Fedorovna's *garderobe* after the storming of the Winter Palace.

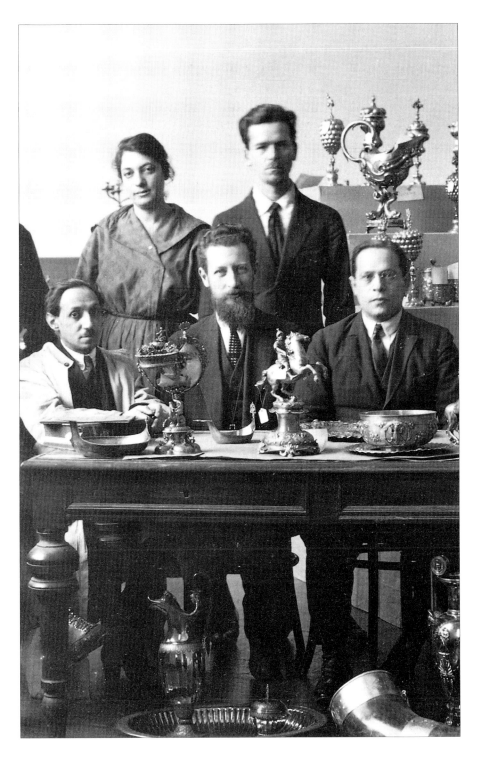

Sergey Troinitsky, director of the Hermitage, seated centre, with Moisey Lazerson, seated right, and other member of the Commission for the Classification of Antique Silver – mostly confiscated church silver – in the offices of Gokhran in 1923.

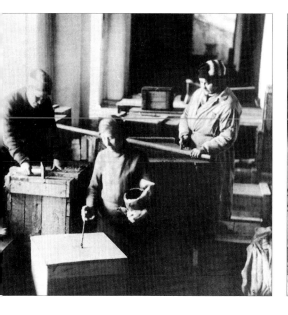

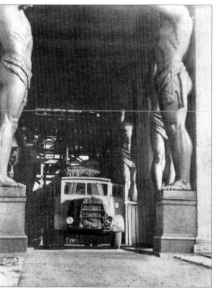

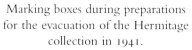

Marking boxes during preparations
for the evacuation of the Hermitage
collection in 1941.

A lorry of treasures, flanked by
Atlantes, as it left the Hermitage
entrance in 1941.

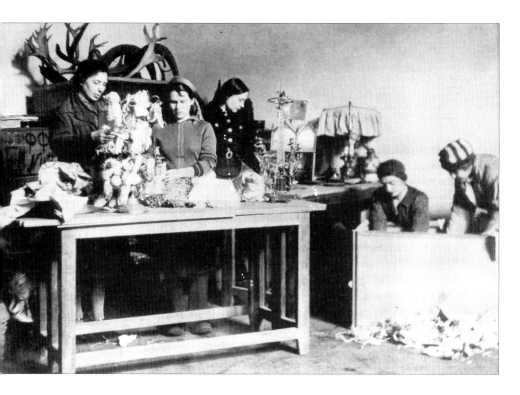

Hermitage staff packing the collection for evacuation to Sverdlovsk in 1941.

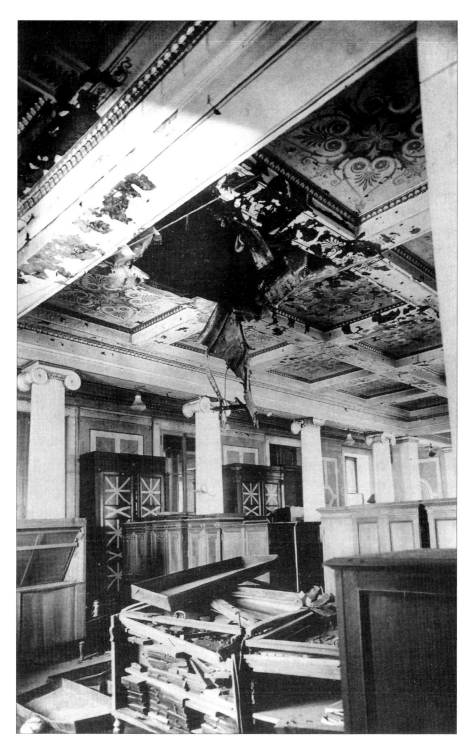

A hole in the ceiling of the Hall of Twelve Columns, caused by a direct hit from a shell in 1944.

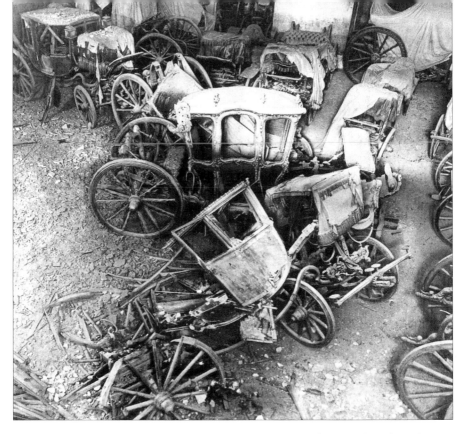

The effect of a 70-mm shell exploding among the coaches stored in the riding school on the ground floor of the Small Hermitage during World War II.

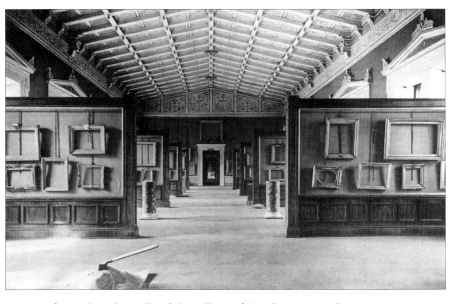

Empty frames line the walls of the gallery of Dutch seventeenth-century paintings during World War II. The paintings themselves had been evacuated to Sverdlovsk. In the foreground is a pile of sand and a spade in case of fire.

reconstruction plans was 150 million. 'It is clearly not enough, even if we can come to terms with this lump of pus, as the hotel was described at the meeting, attached to the Hermitage (or will the Hermitage be attached to it?). The conclusion is sad. Neither the Ministry of Culture of the USSR, nor the City Government, nor the museum administration know where to get the money from for the reconstruction of the Hermitage, the first during the years of Soviet power, a reconstruction already begun.'

Zeimal also drew attention to 'the clear lack of agreement between the activities of the director and his first deputy' – i.e. Boris Borisovich and Suslov – 'which has long been felt by all and which is affecting our work'. He thus flagged the battle for power which became one of the central issues with which the Council of the Workers' Collective concerned itself. A substantial group of staff wanted Suslov out, or at least out of the running for the directorship when Boris Borisovich should vacate his post – it was obvious to everyone that he was already too old for the job. There were a number of rival candidates for the succession. The jockeying finally became so aggressive that the Minister of Culture was invited to intervene.

A letter was sent to Nikolay Gubenko, Gorbachev's Minister of Culture, by the more conservative departmental heads and their deputies – Suslov's supporters – pleading for help. And when he arrived at the Hermitage to try to sort things out on 8 August 1990, the letter writers were invited to meet him, together with a token force from the Council of the Workers' Collective. Tempers were running so high that it was impossible to get all the participants to agree the minutes of the meeting and *Panorama* ended up publishing an unsigned report based on a tape recording. The keynote speech had been delivered by Natalya Gorbunova from the Department of Archaeology, and repeated 'what she had said in two previous articles in this paper, except that her criticism of the Council of the Workers' Collective was perhaps more sharp and her praise of the director's office, more fulsome . . . At the end of her speech Gorbunova said "one gets the impression that there is a battle for power" and those present shouted "Yes! Yes!" The people sitting round the long table joyfully accused the leaders of the Workers' Collective of trying to usurp power, without understanding that in expressing such a theory about a battle for power they were simply expressing their own interests and intentions.'

Gubenko came down on Suslov's side. 'The Gubenko meeting was a defeat,' Rabinovich says sadly. 'I was close to the heads of department and they had all been anti-Suslov. After the Gubenko meeting, they were all pro-Suslov. They were frightened that somebody new would introduce change. I was shocked by the reactions of my friends.' Boris Borisovich Piotrovsky died on 15 October 1990 and on 22 October Gubenko confirmed Suslov as the new director of the Hermitage. While the museum mourned, there was a pervading sense of guilt that the perestroika-style battles should have so distressed the old man that he suffered a mortal stroke. He had been mystified and horrified by what was going on. A faithful servant of the Soviet regime, he found the behaviour of the Hermitage staff outside the range of his experience.

Suslov had waited twenty-five years in the wings, a deputy looking forward to his turn in the director's chair. Under the Soviet nomenklatura system, the successor for every important post was nominated in advance and, until the final, noisy battle for power, Suslov would have known that the succession was his. As director, he now had the right to choose his own first deputy, subject to Ministry approval. And it is an extraordinary tribute to him that he let no petty resentment of Boris Borisovich's antagonism sway him against the best candidate. 'There were maybe four candidates inside the Hermitage. Delegations from each department visited me and pushed their man. I knew about the conflicts between the inside candidates. For me, it was better to have a good man from outside.' He chose Mikhail Piotrovsky.

Mikhail Borisovich's talents were obviously suited to the job. He had never worked at the Hermitage because of his father's position but knew it inside out. If asked when he first visited the Hermitage, his answer is 'when I learned to walk'. With his grasp of foreign languages, he had often helped his father entertain delegations and Suslov knew him well. 'I had often visited the family, dined there and drunk with Boris Borisovich and Misha. Maybe I had an intuition.' Maybe he also felt safer with a Piotrovsky as a running partner; he knew the family psychology so well. Both of them assumed when the appointment was made that Mikhail Borisovich would succeed him as director, but neither of them knew that it would be so soon.

The idea that Mikhail Borisovich would make a good director of the Hermitage was not Suslov's own. Its chief propagandist had been his father. When asked about a suitable successor, Boris Borisovich would laughingly suggest his son. He didn't push the idea. He aired it and it got around. The suggestion first came from Evgeny Primakov, now Russia's Foreign Minister, a former head of foreign intelligence, journalist, and director of the Soviet Academy of Science's Institute for Oriental

Studies. Primakov and Mikhail Borisovich had worked together on an Islamic dictionary – Russians became suddenly interested in Islam after the invasion of Afghanistan. In response to a plea from Boris Borisovich for advice on where to find a successor, Primakov is said to have responded: 'Try looking at home!'

It is, of course, too soon to pass judgement on his directorship. It can be said, however, that he works something like ten hours a day, seven days a week. Not only can he communicate with Westerners because of his remarkable grasp of languages, but he also charms them. No one comes out of his office without wanting to help. He is a scholar and cares about the scholarly standards of the museum's work, but is prepared to use up his own time on administration, propaganda and travelling the globe to make influential friends for the museum. He also works indefatigably with his contacts in Moscow to tease money out of the government. With the demise of the Party and the Council of the Workers' Collective, he wields almost autocratic power over the museum's destiny.

In his first three years Mikhail Borisovich managed to lift government funding for the museum from three to thirteen million dollars. He pioneered the publication of accounts – hitherto treated as secret – thus revealing that he had chosen to plough back almost all the museum's private sector earnings into salary and benefits for the staff. Government salaries are extremely low – an average of around £50 a month for Hermitage curators – but under Mikhail Borisovich the museum regularly pays out double, as well as providing assistance in kind, sometimes food, sometimes colour televisions and washing machines. His socialist principles are very clearly revealed. Although the museum is hugely overstaffed he does not regard slimming down as an option. 'I don't sack staff,' he says, 'though I may move them.'

The money the museum earns through operations abroad has increased sharply. At any one time, there are probably six or seven exhibitions round the world to which the Hermitage has contributed. Mikhail Borisovich takes a close interest in the scholarly quality of cataloguing for these exhibitions, as well as those mounted by the museum at home; he gets his friends abroad to help with translations for multi-language catalogues and chooses his publishers with care. He encourages scholarly seminars and conferences.

He has got the government to register the whole of the Hermitage as a 'national treasure'. 'Which means that if I'm asked to sell from the collection, I can say no,' he explains. Before the 1996 presidential election, he persuaded Yeltsin to sign a decree taking the Hermitage under the special protection of the Presidency – it is the only museum with such status. The decree also stated that the Hermitage should have a special line in the National Budget, rather than receiving money through the Ministry of Culture – the Ministry had, in the past, shown a tendency to spend money earmarked for the Hermitage on other causes.

The decree promised the Hermitage that the government would pay old debts and make good current funding commitments. Some of these undertakings were fulfilled while others weren't – like many election pledges. By the autumn of 1996, the battle for funding had become acute. The government announced it would only pay two-thirds of museum salaries; the museums, led by Mikhail Borisovich, threatened to close. When the Hermitage's heating bill wasn't paid, Mikhail Borisovich was seen walking round the museum in a natty, navy knit scarf – for the sake of television cameras and journalists. Under his unrelenting pressure, money continued to trickle into the Hermitage coffers and the museum stayed open. The bigger the problem, the brighter the light in his eyes. He is an indefatigable fighter.

Epilogue

*I*t's best to visit the Hermitage on a sunny day. Walking along the embankment to the entrance, the golden spire of the cathedral in the Peter and Paul Fortress holds your eye, glittering across the broad sweep of the river whose ripples are also sparkling. Or else the river is frozen and covered in snow with hooded Siberian crows stalking its surface. Again the golden rooves of the Fortress, the blanket of white snow and the blue sky lift the spirit.

Sometimes you approach the staff entrance along the Winter Canal. Then the view across the river is framed by the arch of the bridge that joins the Old Hermitage to Quarenghi's theatre. Reality and the vistas beloved of Canaletto and Bellotto, that hang inside the museum, merge.

In winter, when it's very cold, there is another delicious moment. In the four feet between the door from the street and the second set of swing doors, a barrier of especially hot air is maintained to avoid the draughts from the street interfering with the heating of the museum. Coming in from outside you are momentarily bathed in summer.

You clump the snow from your boots on a dirty mat and climb the stone steps towards a miscellany of younger personnel who are hanging round the ashtrays. Not so much ashtrays but ash tubs, placed symmetrically at either side, at the top of the steps. How long will smoking continue to be allowed in the museum? Not long, if American finance is allowed to rescue the Hermitage from the state of near bankruptcy it was experiencing as I wrote this book. I shall mourn for the place I loved if it gets cleaned up.

You can also smoke in the two lavatories, 'his' and 'hers', that flank the Council Staircase, a grand sweep of red carpeted steps leading up to the largest malachite vase in the world and the Rembrandt room. The doors, in addition to carrying the standard signs of an outline figure in a skirt or trousers, have a round disc with a cigarette in the middle which has not been crossed out. There is never any lavatory paper.

Going back to the staff entrance, you pass the smokers and push through another set of swing doors where you find a fashionably dressed girl at a desk and a uniformed policeman guarding the entrance to the directors' corridor. Security services have not yet been imported to Russia. A detachment of guards from the city police watches over the museum galleries.

Turning down the long vista of the corridor, likely as not, you'll see a cat licking its back in a shaft of sunlight. And if it's summer, the noise outside the windows will draw your attention to the courtyard where the porters and restorers are playing volleyball over a high net.

Mikhail Borisovich's office looks over the river. He has Alexander III's mahogany desk piled high with papers, telephones and computers. Below the huge seventeenth-century tapestries that line the walls – landscape vistas that notably retain their colour and, maybe, still conceal the KGB microphones – are imperial bookshelves piled with a miscellany of catalogues, papers and malachite vases. A long mahogany table, delivered to accommodate meetings of the tsar's ministers some time in the nineteenth century, and a matching suite of balloon-back chairs, now wait to welcome museum conferences.

If you climb the staff staircase, past the fashionable girl and the policemen on the ground floor, up the broad stone steps to the cloakroom, up another three sweeps to the level of the Raphael loggia and the theatre entrance, and up another three (passing a white marble nymph up to no good) you reach a large level space where fraying upholstered chairs made in the 1950s are gathered round another ashtray. This is where the Western European Department smokes.

A glass door leads into their corridor of offices. The first room with its samovar and outside telephone line is where they have tea, sitting round a marble table, with bread and cheese and biscuits. The offices mainly accommodate two experts each, except for that of Yuliya Kagan, keeper of Renaissance and later engraved gems, who shares her office space with Catherine the Great's gem cabinets. There are five made in London after designs by James Wyatt in satinwood, palm, ebony, stained maple and thuja wood – light Neoclassical confections with marquetry panels – and three majestic, show-off pieces by David Roentgen, cabinetmaker to all the crowned heads of Europe, in heavy mahogany, wreathed with ormolu flowers and foliage, brass stringing and railed galleries.

You enter the silver store, or any other store for that matter, by breaking the plasticine seal that holds two wires together. Each keeper has a stone or glass seal – in a ring or on a chain round the neck or in a pocket – which they press into the plasticine when their store is closed, to signify that it was locked up by its proper guardian. Marina Lopato's silver store is a narrow space with a high ceiling; imperial wardrobes, probably from the servants' quarters, line the walls densely packed with silver – including some Renaissance and Baroque pieces taken by the Russian army from Germany in 1945. The old-fashioned stepladders used to reach the higher shelves are branded with the imperial eagle.

One last visit. Boris Asvarishch, keeper of German nineteenth- and twentieth-century paintings and guardian of the 'Hidden Treasures' – the magnificent Impressionist paintings also taken by the Russians from Germany – has a modernised office in the theatre building. You can hear his two parrots chattering before you open the door. The imperial desk, settee, bookcase and chairs date from around 1900. Veneered in figured birch, they are richly mounted with floral plaques of gilt bronze. They were formerly used by the Party Bureau, he explains, but the bronze mounts snagged the ladies' nylons and he was kind enough to take them over. He has grown ivy up supporting wires and it hangs in festoons from the ceiling.

For anyone privileged to get an insider view of the Hermitage, there are two things that set it apart from the other great museums of the world: its echoes of imperial splendour and the dilapidated, makeshift, human dimension. In the public rooms you are everywhere reminded that this is a museum in a palace – by the glittering chandeliers, sparkling ormolu, malachite, coloured harstone, white marble figures contorted with mythical endeavour, paintings large and small – some so great that they open windows on the nature of life itself, some pleasantly second-rate. But when you pass into the staff quarters behind the galleries, you find that the palace, like an anthill, is alive with human activity. The curators are studying, arguing, making plates of bread and cheese, celebrating a birthday with a bottle of vodka, and starting romances which will breed another generation of Hermitage curators. This is the world of the *ermitazhniki*. May their shadows never grow less.

Appendix:
Hermitage Staff Prosecuted by the Soviet Security Services

*T*his material has been gathered from various sources, including Memorial, a Russian organisation set up to press for the release of information on political repressions and to rehabilitate the innocent, and from the archives of the former KGB, with the help of many members of the Hermitage staff, notably Vadim Zuev, and Yaroslav Vasilkov of the Institute of Oriental Studies.

In some instances very little information is available about the arrest of an individual, particularly if the arrest took place outside Leningrad or was dealt with in connection with cases in other cities. More information is coming to light about victims of political repression, and this appendix is subject to revision.

The most commonly used charges fell under Article 58 of the Criminal Code, which dealt with counter-revolution and treason. Although the earlier of the fourteen clauses are more or less in line with international standards, the later clauses are catch-all accusations, which could be widely interpreted by the police to give them the right to see counter-revolution in such simple acts as holding meetings and discussions, chance accidents at work (e.g. the loss of an unimportant file could be interpreted as carelessness with intent to weaken the Soviet State), or the possession of information even if it was necessary for work, and could be applied retrospectively. It is worth noting that Article 58 was only introduced in 1927, a full ten years after the Revolution, by which time Stalin had consolidated his power and the mass repressions were starting.

The fourteen clauses can be summarised as follows:

1 Actions intended to bring down or weaken official bodies, councils, or their elected representatives; any actions which damage Soviet military power or its independence as a state; spying, going over to the enemy, defecting from the country.

2 Armed uprising, or any action intended to bring about the seizure of any part of the Soviet Union.

3 Any connection with foreign states or their individual representatives with the aim of counter-revolution.

4 Any help whatever given to that part of the international bourgeoisie which does not recognise the Communist system and seeks to overthrow it; being under the influence of any group linked to the said international bourgeoisie.

5 Leading foreign powers, or any group within them, to declare war on the Soviet Union or take any other measures such as blockade, seizure of state property, the breaking off of diplomatic relations, etc.

6 Spying: passing on, or gathering for transference, state secrets, or economic information which is not a state secret, but which is not for publication by direct ban or order of state bodies.

7 Any action which interrupts industrial production, transport, trade etc., carried out with counter-revolutionary intent.

8 Terrorist acts against representatives of Soviet power, workers' leaders and peasant organisations.

9 Destruction or damage caused to railway and other transport, telecommunications, the water supply, warehouses, state or public property.

10 Propaganda or agitation which calls for the overthrow or weakening of Soviet power, also the distribution, production or storage of literature of such content.

11 Any organised activity intended to prepare for any of the above activities.

12 Not informing the relevant bodies of any counter-revolutionary act.

13 Activities against the working class and the revolutionary movement as an open or secret officer of the imperial system or other governments during the Civil War.

14 Sabotage, i.e. deliberately not carrying out one's duties, or being careless, with the aim of weakening the government.

The punishment for most of these crimes is described as 'The Highest Measure', i.e. execution, with confiscation of property, although in some cases the accused was simply imprisoned, again with confiscation of property, and even if released in due course, fell under the '101st kilometre ruling', which stated that they could not live in any of the major cities, being exiled literally to any place further than 100 kilometres from the city. Some articles also required that the accused be deprived of citizenship, and thus expelled, but this was rarely used in the 1930s.

Two Hermitage employees were arrested under Article 151, for homosexuality, but bearing in mind the period at which they were arrested and that others who were openly homosexual remained untouched, it is the opinion of their successors at the Hermitage that this was simply a pretext.

Other campaigns of persecution of particular importance and which affected Hermitage staff are:

1935: After the initial campaigns which followed the assassination of Leningrad Party leader Sergey Kirov – for instance the arrest of all those with the same surname as the assassin (see NIKOLAEVA) – came that against 'former people', i.e. those of noble origins, the 'exploiters of the people'. The victims were mainly exiled, amongst them Troinitsky, Kosinsky and Bykov, but some were rearrested at the height of the purges in 1937–8 and sentenced to death, e.g. Rostopchin.

The Slavists' Affair: One of the links in a campaign against the old Russian intelligentsia, the aim was not so much to annihilate as to frighten and humiliate those brought up with a different value system. Between September 1933 and February 1934 hundreds were arrested and accused of setting up a fascist Slav nationalist organisation which sought to overthrow Soviet power and establish a fascist dictatorship. The case expanded to cover the Soviet Union and in Leningrad thirty-seven leading scholars were arrested (more even than in Moscow), mainly from the Slav sections of the Russian Museum, but among them five employees of the Hermitage: Avtomonov, Lindros and Spassky, who were accused of supplying weapons for an armed uprising (see AVTOMO-NOV), the numismatist Fasmer and the archaeologist Gryaznov. All of those arrested in the case 'admitted' their guilt, with the exception of a very few, including Avtomonov, Spassky and Gryaznov. Those who had been let out by 1937 were lucky, but with the exception of Lindros, those still in prison were then shot.

After the death of Stalin in 1953, many former prisoners, both living and dead, were formally rehabilitated, and if still alive allowed to return from camp or exile. Those without relatives or friends to take their part had to wait until the mass rehabilitations which followed the first opening of KGB files in 1989, at the prompting of organisations such as Memorial.

ADJAN, Anton Arutyunovich 1904–8: Oriental Department. Specialist in the Near East and Turkish art. Head of Department 1937–8. Non-Party.* He studied at the Institute of the History of Material Culture under Iosif Orbeli, where Boris Piotrovsky and Gyuzalyan (see below) were friends and fellow students, all initially studying the culture of Urartu. He joined the Hermitage staff in 1929, becoming head of the Oriental Department in 1937. He was arrested on 5 February 1938, along with other Armenian intellectuals, and accused under Article 58–6/11. Sentenced to death on 11 October 1938, he was shot 17 October. According to fellow Orientalist Igor Diakonoff, Orbeli

---

*Whilst membership of the Communist Party did little to save anyone during the Purges, we have noted, where information is available, whether or not each individual was a member of the Party.

hurried to Moscow to protest at the arrest and waited in the office of Anastas Mikoyan, deputy chairman of the Council of People's Commissars, until 2 a.m. Mikoyan deceived him, telling him that Adjan had already been shot. Adjan's posthumous rehabilitation (18 June 1956) was fought for by Boris Piotrovsky.

ALABYSHEV, Nikolay Vasilievich 1898– after 1937: Numismatics Department. Specialist in Chinese numismatics. He studied Chinese at the Leningrad Institute of Oriental Languages, graduated in 1926 and went on to work at the Academy of Sciences. From 1932 to 1933 he was a post-graduate student in the Numismatics Department of the Hermitage. Alabyshev made an important discovery of Chinese silver ingots (used for payment). These were to be melted down at the mint to make Soviet coins, but the Hermitage was given the chance to select pieces for their collection first. Alabyshev picked out 515 pieces from the many hundreds of coins and managed to produce a card index for them before he was arrested on 8 September 1933 and charged with Article 151 (homosexuality). On 1 December he was sentenced to five years in a labour camp. The last that is known of him is that on 21 August 1937 he appeared in the Hermitage to remove his certificates of education from the Personnel Department. Nothing further is known about him. It is assumed that he was arrested again and died in prison.

ARIENT, Vsevolod Viktorovich, dates not known: Arsenal. Specialist in arms and armour. He took over the Hermitage Arsenal in 1933, after the arrest of Avtomonov (see below), but Orbeli disliked him and forced him to leave. He moved on to become scientific secretary of the Artillery Museum, attached to the Hermitage, but was himself arrested in 1937 and died in prison.

AVTOMONOV, Alexander Aleandrovich 1884–1938: Arsenal. Specialist in arms and armour. Professor of the Artillery Museum attached to the Hermitage. He was arrested 29 November 1933, in connection with the so-called 'Slavists' Affair'. A museum in Kharkov (Ukraine) had organised, in 1933, an exhibition of old weapons, borrowing some items from the Hermitage stores. Avtomonov and Lindros (see below) were then arrested and accused of supplying weapons to Ukrainian nationalists for an armed uprising, thus allowing the police to support the theory of a planned terrorist attack. They both also suffered because of their private (legal) collections of weapons. Avtonomov refused to admit his guilt (which was rare), despite being tortured, and was sentenced to ten years in Baikal-Amur Camps, but was later tried a second time and sentenced to death on 31 March 1938. No information is available regarding the date of execution. When the case was being reassessed in 1956, much attention was paid to the question of the supply of weapons, in the course of which all documents proving the legal despatch of museum objects for exhibition in Kharkov, and the legal right of both keepers to have decorative weapons at home, were found and presented. We know that

Hermitage director Mikhail Artamonov made the most positive recommendations to the rehabilitation tribunals of both Avtomonov and Lindros.

BAUER, Nikolay Pavlovich 1888–1942: Numismatics Department. Specialist in Western European and Byzantine coins. Head of Department 1931–5. Non-Party. Of German origin, he joined the Hermitage in 1912, becoming head of Numismatics in 1931, after Ilyin (see below) was temporarily removed by the Workers' and Peasants' Commission. In 1935 he was in his turn removed from the post, and was sacked on 22 August 1938, officially accused of hiding his membership of the 'bourgeois' Cadet Party in 1917. From 1939 to the day of his arrest he worked at the Institute of the History of Material Culture. In the lead up to World War II there was a mounting campaign against those of German origin, and Bauer was notable for having published nearly all his works in Germany, rather than in the Soviet Union. Arrested 8 July 1942, he was accused under articles 58–10/2 and 182–4, anti-Soviet agitation and the possession of a Finnish (flick) knife. On 8 September he was sentenced to death with confiscation of property, and was executed 18 September. His family believed until the 1980s that he had died of hunger during the Siege of Leningrad, but on her deathbed his widow told her son the truth. Bauer's grandson, Oleg Androsov (he was advised to take his mother's surname to avoid further complications with a German surname), is now head of modern painting and sculpture at the Hermitage. Bauer was rehabilitated in 1989.

BOROVKA, Grigory Iosifovich 1894–1941: Antiquities Department. Archaeologist, specialist in the Scythians and related cultures. His family was of German origin but had lived in Russia since the reign of Empress Elizabeth. The rest of his family emigrated to Germany after the Revolution. He studied archaeology and worked at the Hermitage as a student from 1912, helping Oskar Waldhauer with inventories of Antique vases and sculptures, and joined the staff in 1917. From 1921 he was keeper of Scythian art, conducting excavations in the Eurasian steppes and Mongolia. In 1927 he was elected a corresponding member of the German Archaeological Institute and the following year organised an exhibition in Berlin of artefacts from the Noin-Ula burial mounds. Always anxious to visit his family in Berlin, he worked on the Lepke sales of Hermitage antiquities in the late 1920s, and is said to have deliberately miscatalogued objects in the hope of discouraging purchasers. In early 1929 he was involved with plans for a joint Soviet–German expedition to study Goth culture in the Crimea. He was arrested 21 September 1930 as a German spy (in connection with the so-called 'Academicians' Affair'). On 17 October 1931, he was sentenced under article 58–6 to ten years in the camps. He studied palaeontology while in the camp at Ukhta (now Ust-Ukhta), and ran a geological museum. He gave lectures and put together a large archaeological collection (still in the local museum). On his release on 21 September 1940, he was restricted to living in the Komi Autonomous Republic, where he worked as a geologist and archaeologist. He was arrested again on 6 November 1940, as a socially dangerous element (because of his German origin) and shot at the end of the year, according to witnesses. His unpublished monograph on the Chertomlyk Barrow was seized by the OGPU and has disappeared without trace. He was rehabilitated in 1989.

BYKOV, Alexey Andreevich 1896–1977: Numismatics Department. Specialist in Oriental, mainly Arab, numismatics. Head of Department 1945–74. He was born in St Petersburg to a noble family, and studied at the élite Corps de Pages. He then went on to study in the ethno-linguistic faculty of the university. A student of Fasmer (see below), from 1923 Bykov worked in the numismatics sector of the Academy of the History of Material Culture, entering the Numismatics Department at the Hermitage the following year. He was arrested 16 March 1935, for his noble origins, and sentenced four days later to five years' exile in Samara as a 'socially harmful element'. He was lucky in exile, as he was able to work in the local museum, putting their collection in order and taking part in archaeological excavations. This exile was annulled 2 April 1936, and he returned to Leningrad. In 1941 he was in charge of the evacuation of coins to Sverdlovsk during the Siege of Leningrad, and on his return at the end of the war became head of department.

CHERNAVINA, Tatyana [Tatiana Tchernavin] 1883/4–?: Western European Applied Art Section. Specialist in French seventeenth- and eighteenth-century art. In 1918 the commercial school in which she was teaching was closed but the following year she was given charge of the archives at Pavlovsk Palace Museum, from where she moved to Peterhof Palace in 1920. In 1925 she became assistant keeper of the Applied Art Department at the Hermitage, but in October 1930 her husband, a marine zoologist, was arrested, and in March of the following year she too was charged with 'furthering economic counter-revolution'. By the time she was let out in August 1931, her job at the Hermitage had been filled, and in her memoirs she says that Boris Legran refused to take her back, and she was forced to take a job as a librarian elsewhere. In 1932 she and her son visited her husband in the camp at Kem, and that summer they walked over one hundred miles into Finnish territory and from there on to the West.

DERVIZ [Derwis], Pavel Pavlovich 1897–1942: Western European Applied Art Section. Specialist in silver. Head of *objets de vertu* from 1931. Non-Party. Born into the Baltic (German) nobility, related to a rich banker, himself a former baron and junior officer in the imperial army, he seems to have been arrested and/or suspended from work at the Hermitage sometime in early 1938. His surviving niece says that he was to be exiled but Orbeli had him pardoned and dragged him off the train. On 23 October, however, he was restored to his previous post as secretary of the Western European Department, only to be arrested again on 2 November 1938, accused under article 58–10/11 as a participant in counter-revolutionary groupings in the Hermitage. Whilst in the notorious Kresty Prison, he was beaten so severely that his lungs were permanently damaged. The case was dropped and he was released from prison on 11 April 1939, but the damage was done, and although he returned to the Hermitage once more a week later he was too ill to do much work. When the sarcophagus of Alexander Nevsky was due to be packed for evacuation, he begged to be taken to see it one last time, to say farewell. During the harsh conditions of the first winter of the Siege of Leningrad, his lungs soon gave out and he died in early 1942. His wife and small son managed to leave the city that spring, but his wife died on the journey. His orphaned son was later sought out and adopted by Marina Torneus, who succeeded Derviz as keeper of silver.

FASMER, Richard Richardovich [Roman Romanovich] 1888–1938: Numismatics Department. Arabist and numismatist. He graduated from St Petersburg University in 1910 and immediately entered the Hermitage. The country's leading specialist on Oriental coins, he created a new system for dating finds of such coins on Russian territory. Of German origin, he maintained a correspondence with his brother Max, an émigré who was a member of the National Socialist Party in Germany. He was arrested 10 January 1934 in connection with the so-called 'Slavists' Affair' and accused of articles 58–4/10/11; he was said to be part of a counter-revolutionary fascist organisation. Three points counted against him: the correspondence with his brother and other relatives living in Germany and the fact that in the summer of 1933 he had, at his brother's request, asked the pastor of a still functioning Lutheran church in Leningrad for confirmation of Max's Aryan origins and sent a document to this effect to his brother, inscribed 'Not for use in Soviet Russia'; a visit to his flat in 1932 by an employee of the German Embassy who had been attending Max Fasmer's lectures in Germany – interpreted by the NKVD as 'spying and transferring information'; receiving money from his brother through Academician Vernadsky, who travelled regularly to Germany and was also mentioned in the Slavists' Affair – interpreted as 'transferring money to finance the organisation of spying'. On 29 March 1934, he was sentenced to ten years' corrective labour in the Baikal-Amur Camps. He was soon moved to Tashkent, Uzbekistan, where he worked in the offices of the Central Asian Labour Camps. In 1935 his wife fought unsuccessfully for him to be permitted to work in the museums of Tashkent, which had many unsorted coins and medals collections, but he remained in camp and died of hunger 22 February 1938. Fasmer was rehabilitated in 1956.

Fasmer's sister-in-law, Mariya Nipp, who shared a flat with his family, was also arrested in connection with the case and was exiled to Bashkiria for three years.

FE, Olga Alexandrovna 1892–d. after 1967: Drawings Section. Art historian. Non-Party. Born into a noble family in St Petersburg, she completed higher education and worked in the libraries of the Stieglitz Museum and Academy of Arts. She entered the Hermitage in 1924, where she became assistant keeper in the Drawings Section. On 8 August 1930, she was arrested and accused under article 58–6/11. Her post at the Hermitage was liquidated 14 October 1930 'in view of her being held under arrest for over two months'. On 3 February 1931, she was sentenced to three years in camp, which was then commuted to three years' exile in Eastern Siberia. But the following year, on 26 May 1932, the sentence was changed again, this time to five years' exile in Ufa. From then on she remained in the Urals. Fe was rehabilitated in 1989.

GERTS, Vera Konstantinovna 1896–1975: Western European Painting Section. Specialist in Poussin and French seventeenth-century painting. From 1913 to 1916 she studied at drama school and until 1927 was an actress at the Intimate and Alexandriinsky theatres in St Petersburg. She retired from the stage due to ill health and then studied at the Zubov Institute of Art History and entered the Hermitage in 1929. On 4 March 1935, she was sentenced to five years as a socially dangerous element (the Alexandriinsky had been an Imperial Theatre, and her husband had already been arrested), but having spent a short period in exile in Astrakhan she was freed on 25 April 1936, on reconsideration of the case. Only in 1944, however, was she able to return to the Hermitage, where she worked until 1971.

GRYAZNOV, Mikhail Petrovich 1902–84: Prehistoric Department. Archaeologist, specialist in the Bronze Age. After initial studies at Tomsk University, in 1922 he moved to the Anthropology Section of Petrograd University, and also worked at the Academy of the History of Material Culture. In 1925 he joined the Ethnographic Department of the Russian Museum, taking part in excavations, and until 1933 he continued to work in both organisations, studying the Bronze Age cultures of Southern Siberia. Of particular importance was the excavation of Scythian barrows in the permafrost of the Altai region. Then came arrest on 29 November 1933, in connection with the so-called 'Slavists' Affair'. He was accused of being an Ukrainian nationalist, although he had never been to the Ukraine, and he was one of the few to refuse to admit his guilt. After three years in exile in Vyatka (Kirov), he continued his archaeological research for the local regional museum there, joining the staff in 1936. His release came on 25 December 1936, and he returned to Leningrad, joining the Hermitage as head of the Siberia and Kazakhstan Section of the Prehistoric Department; from 1937 to 1941 he was also at the Institute of the History of Material Culture. He was evacuated to Sverdlovsk with the Hermitage between 1941 and 1945, and on his return worked at the Hermitage and the Institute again, playing a leading role in the post-war excavations of the frozen barrows of Pazyryk and coming to occupy many high-ranking posts in the archaeological world. In 1948 he moved permanently to the Institute of the History of Material Culture, retaining a minor post at the Hermitage until 1960, after which he was a voluntary consultant. His most important discovery in this period was the excavation in 1971–4 of an old Scythian barrow at Arzhan in Northern Tuva.

GUKOVSKY, Matvey Alexandrovich 1898–1971: Western European Department; Library. Medievalist. He graduated from Petrograd University in 1923, and from 1922 to 1925 he worked on the scholarly staff of the Public Library. After a time in the Import Department of the North West Trading Organisation, from 1929 to 1933 he was Scientific Secretary of the Library of the Academy of Sciences. In 1934 he started teaching at the university, where from 1938 he was professor of the history faculty. In 1939 he became assistant rector, and during the war director of studies. Even before the war he was a consultant at the Hermitage, which he rejoined in 1945. From 1947 he was deputy director for research, until he was arrested by chance on 28 June 1949, during a holiday trip to the south, and was replaced by Boris Piotrovsky. The year 1949 saw the campaign against 'cosmopolitanism', which led to the arrest of hundreds of Jews like himself. Sentenced on 6 August 1950, to ten years in camp under article 58–10, Gukovsky actually spent five years in the camps, until the general amnesty after the death of Stalin, and was taken back on at the Hermitage in 1955, having fought for his own rehabilitation (1 December 1955). First he returned as deputy head of the Western European Department, and in 1959 became head of the Library until his retirement in 1969.

GUMILEV, Lev Nikolaevich 1912–92: Library. Historian, geographer, ethnographer and palaeographer. Although Gumilev joined the Hermitage after his arrest, he is a typical example of the talented scholars, victims of repression, who were given jobs at the Hermitage by Mikhail Artamonov in the 1950s. The son of two poets, Nikolay Gumilev (shot in 1921) and Anna Akhmatova, he could not enter university due to his social origin, so he worked as a junior assistant on expeditions. He finally got to university in 1934, but his first arrest followed in 1935. Although soon let out, he was not allowed back to the university and continued his studies into the history of the ancient Turks and Oriental languages independently. Restored to the university in 1937, he was arrested again in 1938 on invented charges, this time spending five years in prison in Norilsk. On his release he stayed on there to work on an expedition. In 1944 Gumilev finally received permission to volunteer and go to the front, and he entered Berlin with Soviet troops. He graduated after the war as an external student and started post-graduate studies, but problems once more arose, this time in connection with his mother, who was in 'disgrace' with the authorities. In early 1949 he joined the Museum of the Ethnography of Peoples of the USSR, but was arrested once more in November 1949, being sentenced to ten years in camps near Karaganda and then Omsk. After Stalin's death, in 1956 he returned to Leningrad, where he was taken on to the Library staff by Artamonov. From 1960 he taught at the university, and after defending his thesis in 1962 joined the permanent staff of the Institute of Geography and was able to publish his work. In the 1970s, during the Brezhnev era, he was once more unable to publish, but in the 1980s he became a popular figure with his books and vastly popular TV and radio programmes and interviews.

GYULAMIRYAN, Gaik Egyazarovich 1904–38: Oriental Department. Specialist in Armenia and Iran. He was born in Van Province, Turkey, from where the Armenians were expelled between 1914 and 1918. From 1926 to 1930 he studied at the State Institute of Armenia and then went on to post-graduate study in Leningrad at the Academy of the History of Material Culture. He entered the Hermitage in 1932 and on completing his studies in January 1934 joined the staff of the Academy. From February 1937 he devoted himself wholly to the Oriental Department of the Hermitage, but on 4 February 1938, he was arrested as a participant in a counter-revolutionary spy organisation, accused of articles 58–6/11, apparently as part of the same 'Armenian' case as Adjan, Gyuzalyan and others. He was sentenced 16 October 1938, and shot the following day. Gyulamiryan was rehabilitated in 1956.

GYUZALYAN, Leon Tigranovich 1900–94: Oriental Department. Specialist in medieval Iran, especially epigraphy. Born in Tiflis (now Tbilisi), Georgia, in 1929 he graduated from the Persian section of Leningrad's Institute of Oriental Languages, and joined Nikolay Marr's section at Leningrad University. From 1930 he worked at the Hermitage. He dealt with the culture of medieval Iran, particularly poetic inscriptions on tiles. For some time he studied Urartu rock inscriptions along with Piotrovsky and Adjan, even taking part in preliminary trips to the Transcaucasus, before finally settling on medieval Persian literature. He was arrested at the same time as Adjan, on 5 February 1938, and accused under articles 58–10/11 of participation in a counter-revolutionary terrorist organisation. On 2 September 1938, he was sentenced to five years in Usol Corrective Labour Camp, Perm Region. The war prevented his release in 1943, and he was let out only in 1945, returning to Leningrad in 1946. As he was banned under the '101st kilometre' ruling, he lived and worked in Luga, south of the city. Gyuzalyan was said to have been interrogated for days and pressured to denounce Orbeli but refused. Perhaps this was what led Orbeli to allow him to work at the Hermitage from 1947, despite the ban. He was officially rehabilitated on 16 December 1955, after the death of Stalin, and re-entered Leningrad University, where he worked until 1974, and after that the Oriental Department of the Hermitage, where he remained until his death. A brilliant and promising specialist, although his achievements were notable, all his work from before his arrest had been destroyed and he never fully recovered the ground he had lost.

ILYIN, Alexey Alexeevich, 1858–1942: Numismatics Department. Numismatist. Head of Department 1920–31. The major map publishing business which he inherited before the Revolution was nationalised in 1918 and he joined the Hermitage, putting to use his passion for coin collecting. He was arrested after the Workers' and Peasants' Commission reviewed staff in 1931, but protests by Orbeli led to his return to the Hermitage, although not as head of department. He donated his superb collection to the museum.

KAZAKEVICH, Vladimir Alexandrovich 1896–1937: Oriental Department. Specialist in Mongolian history. He studied at the Institute of Oriental

Languages and then the University, and himself taught Mongolian. He worked in Mongolia for the USSR Trading Representation from 1923 to 1925 and in 1927, and was part of the Mongolian Commission of the Soviet Academy of Sciences. In 1929 he joined the staff of the Oriental Institute and the Hermitage. From 1935 he worked full time in the Hermitage, whilst remaining secretary of the Association of Mongolian Studies at the Institute. Kazakevich was arrested 30 August 1937, accused under article 58–1a of association with Russian émigrés abroad during a study trip to Germany and France in early 1933 – in Paris he met with an old school fellow working as a doctor there – and for having assisted in 'bringing Hitler to power'. He was sentenced to death 16 December 1937, and executed 20 December.

KELLER, Alexey Pavlovich 1888–?: Historian of European and Far Eastern Applied Art. He graduated from the Academy of Arts in 1918 and went on to teach at the Zubov Institute of Art History. He worked as an expert for the Museums Fund and as keeper of applied art at the Hermitage. He was arrested 17 December 1933, accused under article 151.2 (homosexuality) and was sentenced to eight years' corrective labour. On 14 November 1937, he was sentenced to ten years in prison for some unknown reason, and released 13 October 1943 by decision of the Archangel Regional Court. He went to live in Georgia, firstly in Telavi, then Tbilisi, where he worked in a museum.

KOSINSKY Mikhail Fedorovich 1904–75: Arsenal. Specialist on arms and armour. Head of Arsenal 1936–8. His father was a baron and his nominal godparents were the Greek queen and a grand duke. From 1924 to 1928/9 he studied at the Zubov Institute of Art History, but also worked during the day, mostly in the port. In 1926/7 he started work at the Artillery Museum, then in 1934 at the Military History Museum of the Life of the Red Army, where he was in charge of banners. Arrested 13 March 1935, presumably for his noble origins, he was sentenced 23 March to five years' exile in Kazakhstan, but this was annulled 2 April 1936, allowing him to return to his job in the museum. In August 1936 he became head of the Arsenal at the Hermitage after the arrest of his predecessors (see Avtonomov, Lindros), and another Arsenal employee, Arient, was arrested the following year. Whilst Arient was in prison his nephew rang Kosinsky and asked if he would like to buy some of his books for the Hermitage, which he did, and was then accused of helping an enemy of the people by Zhanetta Matsulevich, head of sculpture and a fanatical Stalinist. On 10 July 1938, Kosinsky was arrested once more, and sentenced 10 November 1939, after torture which left him in hospital for a year, to five years in a camp. He was released early and was able to join the army in July 1943. When he returned after the war to the Hermitage, Matvey Gukovsky was in charge of the Medieval Section which included weapons. In 1949 Kosinsky was sacked, and in his memoirs he blames Gukovsky for his later arrest in January 1951, but Gukovsky was himself arrested in 1949 and this seems unlikely. Kosinsky was sentenced on 28 April 1951 to five years' exile in Kazakhstan. After Stalin's death, like Gukovsky, he was rehabilitated (1956), but again in his memoirs he blames Artamonov for not taking him back on at the Hermitage. From 1956 to 1966 he was chief keeper of the Museum of the Academy of Arts. Although Kosinsky's (often inaccurate) memoirs tend to blame others for his many undeserved misfortunes, the current head of the Arsenal rates highly the work he did both before and after the war to systematise and study its Western European material.

KRASNOVA, Nataliya 1889–1965: Western European Department. Specialist in Western European and Russian engraved gems, also Italian engravings. Krasnova started work in the library of the Medieval Section of the Hermitage in 1919 and later transferred to be keeper of glyptics. She was arrested in 1935, possibly because of her surname (General Krasnov, no relation, was a leading officer in the White Army), and was sent to camp for ten years, where she worked mainly as a nursing officer. This left the glyptics collection largely uncared for, and after it was re-evacuated after the war it remained in boxes. A post-graduate was taken on in the early 1950s and when Krasnova was allowed to return to Leningrad, and thus to the Hermitage, in 1956 she was immediately taken on as a consultant to train the new keeper (still in charge of the collection today), although she was by this time severely ill with tuberculosis. In 1961 she published a book on the Raphael School frescoes from the Palatine Palace.

KRUGER, Otto Oskarovich 1893–1967: Oriental Department. Egyptologist (specialist in papyruses). Candidate Party member. Of German origin, he graduated from Petrograd University and studied Armenian and Georgian under Marr, then entered the Hermitage, where he worked 1919–30 and 1933–48. From 1920 to 1938 he also worked at the Academy of the History of Material Culture. From 1932 Kruger was a candidate member of the Communist Party, but he was expelled in 1933 and then reinstated. In 1938 he received his doctorate, but on 6 November 1938, he was arrested and accused under articles 58–10 pt 1, 58–11; it was stated that he was a 'member of the German nationalist society "Verein", was in close contact with representatives of foreign diplomatic missions in Leningrad, and was a participant in a counter-revolutionary menshevik organisation'. On 10 November 1939, he was exiled to Kazakhstan for five years, but was only given his freedom in 1955, after Stalin's death, and rehabilitated in 1957. He returned to Leningrad, where he taught at the university and was in charge of post-graduates at the Academy of Sciences.

KRUGLOV, Andrey Pavlovich 1907 – d. after 1941: Prehistoric Department. Archaeologist, specialist in the Caucasus. From 1927 to 1930 he studied the history of material culture under Marr at Leningrad University and then entered the Academy of the History of Material Culture. From 1934 to 1935 he was head of the Academy expedition in the northern Caucasus, and it was at this time that he joined the Hermitage. On the night of 28 February 1935, he was arrested at a party in Peterhof, along with Boris Piotrovsky and Podgaetsky (see below). Only a week after his arrest he had been sacked from the Academy. He was accused of belonging to a terrorist organisation and remained in a special secret service prison until 10 April, when the case was dropped. That year a standard text was published under his name and that of Podgaetsky, which was well received both at home and abroad. L. S. Klein says that the book was in fact by Boris Latynin (see below), who was arrested on the eve of its publication, and thus the book appeared under the names of his very young assistants. Kruglov died at the front in the war.

LATYNIN, Boris Alexandrovich 1899–1967: Archaeologist and ethnographer, specialist in the Volga Region. Born into a noble family, he studied archaeology between 1920 and 1923. His first arrest came in April 1924, and after two months in prison he was sentenced to exile, which was then repealed. From 1926 to 1929 he was a post-graduate student at Leningrad University specialising in material culture and linguistics. He studied the peoples of the Caucasus and Central Asia, along the Volga. From 1929 he was at the Academy of the History of Material Culture, in 1932 becoming head of the Institute's committee on conducting excavations on the site of new construction. In 1934 Latynin was elected a full member of the Institute and head of field studies, and early the following year head of expedition research. But on 10 March 1935, he was arrested and on 15 March sacked from his job 'as an alien and antisocial element'. As a result, his new book was published under the name of his students, Kruglov (see above) and Podgaetsky (see below). Sentence came only on 21 September 1937: five years in camp for 'counter-revolutionary activity', extended to ten years on special directions, plus six years of exile. He spent some of this time in Kolyma and Nakhodka and returned an invalid, having lost a leg in the camps. He returned to the Hermitage in 1953 and revived his archaeological work in Central Asia. Abram Stolyar recalls that Mikhail Artamonov refused to allow anyone to offend Latynin because, he said, they had not suffered what he had.

LINDROS [Lindroz], Emil Ivanovich 1884–d. after 1956: Arsenal. Specialist on arms and armour. He was arrested 1 December 1933, in connection with supposed terrorist acts as part of the so-called 'Slavists' Affair' (see Avtomonov, above). His private collection was interpreted as 'the storing of weapons with the aim of using them in the organisation of an armed uprising'. Sacked from the Hermitage on 1 February 1934, because of his absence from work for over two months, he was sentenced to ten years in the camps, which he spent first in the Siberian Siblag, then at Ustizhma in the Komi Autonomous Republic. He was the only one still in prison in 1937 who was not retried and shot, but the war prevented his release until 1945, when he found work as a watchman in the forestry office of Pestov District, Novgorod Region. In 1949, the head of the local police recommended that due to his very poor health he should be allowed to return to the city, but this was turned down. He continued to work until his rehabilitation in 1956 – at the age of 72 – as he did not qualify for a pension.

MILLER, Valentin Friedrikhovich 1896–1938: Western European Department. Specialist in Poussin and nineteenth-century European art. Non-Party. Despite his noble origins and a period as an ensign in the imperial army (1916–17), from 1919 to 1921 he served in the Red Army as an aide to the Commanding Officer. He was connected with many literary figures, including those around the poet Nikolay Gumilev, father of Lev (see above). Miller worked part-time at the Hermitage until 1929, when he became a member of staff. He was arrested 26 October 1937 and held in a Leningrad prison, accused under article 58–6/10. Whilst he was there, on 27 December, he was sacked from the Hermitage, and then on 11 January 1938, he was sentenced to death, and executed 18 January. Albert Kostenevich, today's keeper of modern art, explains that Miller wrote a book on Courbet, a 'revolutionary' artist beloved in the Soviet Union, in which he said that, on the contrary, Courbet was a bourgeois with a passion for rich bourgeois women, thus contradicting official opinion. Kosinsky, however, albeit a less reliable witness, says that a Hermitage employee found a manuscript in Miller's office which mentioned the art of modern, i.e. Nazi, Germany, and denounced him. In any case, in July 1957 the case was finally closed 'for lack of evidence', and Miller was rehabilitated. Miller's wife worked in the picture gallery from 1929 to 1932, and from 1945 until her retirement in 1975 in the Education Department.

NEVSKY, Nikolay Alexandrovich 1892–1937: Oriental and Numismatics Departments. Specialist in Japan and on Tangut texts. He studied at St Petersburg University from 1910 to 1914 and then worked briefly in the Numismatics Department of the Hermitage before departing for Japan in 1915, initially for two years. As a result of the Revolution and Civil War he stayed until 1929. Thanks to his perfect knowledge of Japanese and his ethnographic studies, he is considered to be one of the founders of ethnography as a science in Japan. He studied old Shinto texts and sought to explain their origins and original meaning through comparison with ethnographic material. From 1925 he also worked on deciphering Tangut texts found in 1909 at Hara-Hoto by P. Kozlov. Nevsky came under increasing pressure from Soviet Orientalists and officials to return to the Soviet Union and he succumbed in 1929, leaving his Japanese wife and child to follow him (in 1933). In 1930 Oldenburg invited him to work in the Institute of Oriental Studies and from 1934 he was at the Hermitage once more, but he was unable to publish his discoveries on the Tangut texts. Arrest came on 3/4 October 1937, but he must have suspected what would happen because he had already agreed with N. Conrad, who was himself repressed at some point, that he, Conrad, would take on his small daughter, Elena. Despite heart trouble, Nevsky was kept standing for days until he signed a 'confession' that he had been lured into Japanese service and had set up a network of spies in Leningrad, gathering information on the sites and numbers of military zones, aerodromes, factories, and on staff and students of the Institute of Oriental Studies. During investigations in the 1950s, several participants in the case admitted there had never been any evidence of activity, simply admissions dragged from Nevsky through severe torture. In 1963 one V. M. Titiyanov, who had been in the same cell as Nevsky, recalled Nevsky's last days. Immediately after his arrest Nevsky entered into the 'cultural life' of the crowded cell, presenting lectures on the Hermitage collections, talking about the lost Tangut state and its culture; he returned very different from 'interrogation', his legs swollen, and said that he had a weak heart and he had signed some document they had given him. He was worried about his manuscripts, which had been disturbed during his arrest, about his wife who spoke no Russian, and his daughter, and expressed his regret that he had returned to Russia. On 19 November 1937, he was sentenced to death under article 58–1. Unaware that his wife had been arrested just four days after him, he was shot on 24 November, the same day as her and other Leningrad Orientalists such as Zhukov (see below). Nevsky was rehabilitated in 1957, opening the way in 1960 to the publication of his work on Tangut studies, which was hailed in the West as one of the most important philological discoveries of the twentieth century, and which forced the Soviet authorities to recognise his achievements. He was awarded the Lenin Prize posthumously in 1962. Of his manuscripts, some were seized by the NKVD, and a Japanese specialist sent in by them to sort out the rest is said to have handed them out to all and sundry. After Nevsky's rehabilitation, however, the Institute of Oriental Studies started gathering and publishing what survived. In October 1991, two of his manuscripts were transferred to the Institute in strange circumstances: there are two versions as to what happened. Either they had been found in the private library of the ageing Japanese specialist O. Petrova, or they had been returned via middlemen by the Administration of the Leningrad KGB. Several genuine Tangut inscriptions from Hara-Hoto which were at Nevsky's house for study purposes have disappeared without trace.

NIKOLAEVA, Vera Alexeevna 1899–1937: Antiquities Department. Egyptologist, art historian and historian. She worked at the Institute of Art History and in the Classical Orient Section of the Antiquities Department at the Hermitage. Arrested with her brother in December 1934, after the murder of Kirov, they were both victims of a mass round-up of those who shared a surname with L. V. Nikolaev, the assassin. The court case under a military tribunal ran from 31 May to 2 June 1935, and brother and sister were sentenced to ten years in prison under article 58–10, which was altered to the death sentence on 2 November 1937. They were executed 17 November 1937. Both were rehabilitated in 1960.

PIOTROVSKY, Boris Borisovich 1908–90: Oriental and Archaeology Departments. Archaeologist, specialist in the culture of Urartu, and Egyptologist.
Director of the Hermitage 1964–90. Party member from 1945. See chapter 16
for full biographical details. He was arrested on the night of 28 February 1935,
along with Kruglov and Podgaetsky, after a working evening-cum-Shrove-
tide party with fellow students in Peterhof, just outside Leningrad. Armed
soldiers and NKVD officers in civvies broke into the room and 'invited' all
those present to an interview, which resulted in the arrest of the hostess and her
friends, including the three archaeologists. The first interrogation that night
revealed that they were accused of participation in a terrorist organisation and
were expected to divulge their plans. This would seem to be part of the first
general surge in arrests after the assassination of Kirov in December 1934, and
Piotrovsky himself states in his memoirs that conditions were much better than
they were to be even a short time later when the purges gathered momentum.
All three were released 10 April 1935, for lack of evidence, but they had
meanwhile been expelled from the Academy of the History of Material
Culture. Piotrovsky and Podgaetsky fought this decision, even taking the case
to court, and were eventually reinstated at the end of September.

PODGAETSKY, Georgy (Yury) Vladimirovich 1908–41: Archaeologist, specialist in the Caucasus. Of noble birth, in 1926 he began studying the history of
material culture under Nikolay Marr at Leningrad University, graduating in
1930. He then started work at the Academy of the History of Material Culture
under Latynin, and from 1934 he was also employed at the Hermitage.
Arrested on the night of 28 February 1935, along with Kruglov and Piotrovsky
(see above) at a party in Peterhof, and accused of belonging to a terrorist
organisation, he was released with them on 10 April 1935, having by this time
been sacked from the Institute. Podgaetsky successfully sued to be reinstated.
Later that year Podgaetsky and Kruglov published Latynin's book under their
own name, as by now Latynin had himself been arrested (see above).
Podgaetsky died of dystrophy during the first winter of the Siege of Leningrad,
on 26 December 1941.

ROSTOPCHIN, Fedor Borisovich 1904–37: Oriental Department. Specialist in
Iran, the Kurds and Turks. At fourteen years old he volunteered for the Red
Army and took part in the Civil War (1918–21). From 1931 he worked as
secretary of the Persian Cabinet at the Institute of Oriental Studies in
Leningrad, compiling a Tadjik–Russian dictionary, and in the Oriental
Department of the Hermitage. Despite his revolutionary background (he was
also very involved in the study of the Central Asian area of the Soviet Union
and of 'the Revolutionary East'), he was arrested on 29 March 1935, and exiled
to Kazakhstan for five years for his noble origins (he was a count and his
relatives had occupied high posts in the imperial service). In January 1936 he
managed to be transferred to Bukhara, where he worked as a freelance at the
museum and continued his studies of Central Asia, but at the end of the year he

was deemed a 'socially dangerous element' and deprived of all rights. He seems to have protested this decision actively, thus bringing himself to the attention of the local security bodies, and on 11 February 1937, he was arrested and taken to Moscow, where he 'admitted' under torture that he was part of an 'anarchic-mystical terrorist organisation, the Order of Tampliers', and sentenced to death on 29 July 1937. He was shot the same day. Rostopchin was rehabilitated in 1991.

SHCHUTSKY, Yuliyan Konstantinovich 1897–1938: Oriental Department. Chinese linguist, historian of Chinese philosophy. Between 1915 and 1923 Shchutsky composed a number of musical works, in parallel studying at Petrograd University (1918–21) and working at the Institute of Oriental Studies (from 1920). With a knowledge of numerous Oriental languages, he translated and wrote many original works, but censorship after his arrest was to mean that they remained largely unpublished. Having started a new job at the Hermitage in 1936, he defended his doctoral thesis in 1937 and went off for a holiday at a dacha with his wife. It was there that he was arrested on 3 August 1937, accused under article 58–10/11. He was tied into the fabricated case of a supposed (but non-existent) anti-Soviet, anarcho-mystic and terrorist organisation known as the Order of Tampliers. He was sentenced to death 18 February 1938, and shot the same day. Shchutsky was rehabilitated in 1958.

SIVERS, Alexander Alexandrovich 1863–1952: Numismatics Department. Numismatist. It is known only that he was arrested in the 1930s as part of Orbeli's campaign against Zhebelev (see chapter 12) but was later freed, returning to the Hermitage where he worked until his retirement.

SPASSKY, Ivan Georgievich 1904–90: Numismatics Department. Numismatist, specialist in medals. Born in the provinces, he worked in local museums (Nezhin, Kharkov) until 1931, when he joined the Hermitage. He was arrested on 31 October 1933, in connection with the Slavists' Affair, and accused under article 58–10/11 as a participant in a counter-revolutionary organisation. He was arrested as part of a group within the Hermitage supplying weapons to terrorists (see Avtonomov above), although he had no involvement with the Arsenal, because he was an employee of the Kharkov Museum borrowing weapons from the Hermitage for an exhibition there and turned to his former colleague for help in acquiring packing materials. Spassky refused to admit his guilt (which was rare, due to the use of torture), and on 29 March 1934, he was sentenced to five years' corrective labour in the Baikal-Amur Camps, on completion of which he was exiled to Vologda, where he worked as a theatre designer, before going to fight in World War II as a military messenger/postman. He was taken back by the Hermitage in 1946, largely through Orbeli's efforts. At his rehabilitation by a military tribunal in 1956, Orbeli recalled the shouts of joyful greeting from Hermitage employees as Spassky entered his old workplace, still wearing his soldier's greatcoat. His second period in the Hermitage was longer than the first, and he was for many years chief curator and keeper of medals.

STRELKOV, Alexander Semenovich 1896–1938: Oriental Department. Specialist in the art of Pre-Islamic Central Asia, Iran and India. Strelkov was first arrested in Moscow on 24 May 1930, under article 58–10, but the case was dropped in November 1932. It was perhaps to avoid new arrest that he moved to Leningrad, where he worked at the Hermitage and the Academy of the History of Material Culture, mainly on Pre-Islamic art in Central Asia. The memoirs of Igor Diakonoff describe him as 'an elegant erudite Muscovite'. He took part in the 1935 Iranian Congress held partly at the Hermitage, in 1936 represented the museum on an expedition in Old Termez, but in 1937 was refused a permit to take part in excavations in the border region of Turkmenia, which was, as Boris Piotrovsky puts it in his memoirs, 'a usual signal' that something was up. On 17 February 1938, he was arrested under article 58–6, accused of 'spying activity for Germany on the territory of the USSR', and of 'links with I. A. Orbeli', 'who remained free'. It seems that the NKVD were pressuring him to denounce Orbeli, as they had pressured Gyuzalyan, but Orbeli was to remain apparently untouched. Strelkov was sentenced to death on 28 August 1938, and executed 6 September. He was rehabilitated in 1989.

SUKHOTINA, Vera Konstantinovna (née Grinberg), 1898–?: Oriental Department. Arabist. Party member from 1920. She worked at both the Hermitage and the Academy of the History of Material Culture, and was a member of the Administration of the Association of Arabists attached to the Institute of Oriental Studies. Her husband, S. Bykovsky, worked at the Academy and was also arrested. In the early 1930s Sukhotina was technical secretary of the Palestinian Society and in 1936 or 1937 took part in the Hermitage excavations of Old Termez, after which she seems to have been exiled to the north, where she lived in Salekhard. Then on 15 March 1938, she was sentenced to ten years in prison by the Omsk court, and returned to Leningrad in the mid-1950s.

TARTAKOVSKAYA, Elena Alexandrovna 1898–? 1938: Western European Department. Specialist on Rembrandt. She entered the Hermitage in 1929 and became keeper of Dutch painting in 1936. Arrested in 1938, her further fate is unknown.

TCHERNAVIN, Tatiana 1883/4 – ?: *See* CHERNAVINA.

TROINITSKY, Sergey Nikolaevich 1882–1948: Keeper of applied arts and *objets de vertu*. Director from 1918 to 1927. A leading specialist in the decorative arts, especially silver and porcelain, he became director of the Hermitage in 1918 when Tolstoy did not return from a 'family trip' to Kiev, but was removed in 1927, possibly after conflict with Orbeli. He stayed as head of the Applied Arts Department until 1931, fighting tooth and nail to protect objects from sale through the state antiques export organisation, Antiquariat, but was then sacked, probably in connection with the Workers' and Peasants' Commission, which was 'purging' the Hermitage staff. He then went to work as an expert for Antiquariat, but continued living in a Hermitage flat. He was arrested on 28 February 1935, as a socially dangerous element, for his noble origins, and on 4 March he was exiled to Ufa for three years. On his release on 8 December 1938, he went to Moscow, where from 1939 to 1941 he worked at Kuskovo Ceramics Museum, on the outskirts of the city (as an exile he was not allowed to live in the city itself), and from 1943 to 1945 as a consultant. He lived in terrible poverty, on the museum site itself. From 1941 to 1945 he was also a professor at the Theatrical Arts College. From 1944 to 1945, he taught at the Studio of the Moscow Arts Theatre through the efforts of the director, Vasily Grigorievich Sakhnovsky, with whom he had been in exile. At last, after the war, he was allowed back into the city proper, and from 1945 to his death in 1948 he worked first as chief curator, then as head of the Decorative Art Department (founded by him) at Moscow's Pushkin Museum of Fine Arts. Having had several wives (his second wife was formerly married to fellow *ermitazhnik* Sergey Yaremich, while his third was the daughter of the Russian Symbolist artist Viktor Borisov-Musatov), it was through the efforts of his mistress Alexandra Khokhlova, head of stage arts at the Moscow Arts Theatre, and mother of his son, that he was buried in the Khokhlova family vault at the prestigious Danilov Monastery. He was rehabilitated in 1989.

VEKSLER, Lyudmila Filippovna 1909–60s: Iranian specialist, philologist. She studied Persian in Kiev, then married an actor and moved to Leningrad in October 1933. In December she started work at the Institute of Oriental Studies and soon started work at the Hermitage (full-time from 1936). In 1935 she took part in the Iranian Congress. She was arrested in 1938 as part of a case against the Caucasian linguist A. Genko, but was released in January 1940 when the case was dropped (Beria, newly appointed chief of police, was getting rid of those loyal to his predecessor, Yezhov, which led to the release of many of those arrested by Yezhov's men at this time). Hers was a unique case in the history of the NKVD: she told friends that during questioning by two investigators a high-ranking officer entered the room and insulted her, to which she responded by 'slapping him round the face, so hard that he rushed into the corridor with a shout'. She was taken to a cell and when next called for questioning asked her investigators how their boss Yezhov was, and saw that they were unhappy with the question, the implication being that he had fallen foul of Beria's internal purge. Nobody believed her story for some years until a scholar looking into the arrest and execution of Genko found reference to the event in the relevant files. During the war she worked in Leningrad's Public Library.

ZHUKOV, Dmitry Petrovich 1904–37: Oriental Department. Specialist in Japanese History. Party member from 1929. A scholarship boy at the Tsarskoe Selo Commercial School, then at the School Commune, he was sent by the Bolshevik Party to Petrograd Communist University, from which he graduated in 1923. From there he was sent to Kingissepp in Estonia as an assistant in the political agitation department. In July 1925, Trotsky sent him to study in the Japanese Department of the Institute of Oriental Languages. From May 1927 to August 1928 he worked in the Soviet political mission in Japan. In December 1929 the Regional Party Committee sponsored his post-graduate studies at the Institute, where his supervisor was Nikolay Bukharin (expelled from the Party 1929, repressed 1939). He made a study trip to Japan in 1930, also sponsored by Bukharin. He completed his post-graduate studies in 1932 and was appointed scientific secretary of the Far Eastern Branch of the Soviet Academy of Sciences. From 1935 he was attached to the Oriental Institute, and became head of the Sector of the History of Oriental Culture and Arts at the Hermitage. He was set the special task of studying 'Japanese fascism', which was what he was doing until he was sacked from the Institute in October 1936, followed by his arrest on 29 May 1937. After torture, he admitted to being lured over to Tokyo's side and that he had brought the poets Nikolay Oleinikov and Wolf Ehrlich into his Trotskyite spy and terrorist group, along with the writer V. Matveev and many Orientalists. He was sentenced to death under articles 58–8/11 on 19 November 1937, and executed on 24 November along with Nikolay Nevsky. Zhukov was rehabilitated in 1956.

It was not only the scholars at the Hermitage who were arrested, but also many of the administrative and technical staff, of whom we include three examples:

DMITRIEV, Alexander Aleksandrovich 1880–1937: Assistant bookkeeper. He was arrested on 26 August 1937, sentenced 15 November, and shot 24 November.

OLEV, Filipp Dmitrievich 1892–1937: Master joiner. He was arrested on 11 August 1937, sentenced to death 26 August under article 58–10 and shot that day.

PRESNYAKOV, Vladimir Vladimirovich 1885–1937: Photographer. From 1926 he was the official photographer at the Hermitage, but in 1935 he was exiled to Orenburg for five years as a socially dangerous element. It was there, in 1937, that he and his wife were arrested and shot, leaving a small son. He was rehabilitated in 1957.

Select Bibliography

Russian-language sources are quoted (in transliterated form, with a translation in square brackets) only if the relevant information has not been published in a Western-European language.

General Background

Bown, Matthew Cullerne, *Art Under Stalin*, Oxford, 1991.

Chavchavadze, David, *The Grand Dukes*, New York, 1990.

Clark, Bruce, *An Empire's New Clothes*, London, 1995.

Deutscher, Isaac, *Stalin*, Harmondsworth, 1990.

Elliott, David and Valery Dudakov (eds), *100 Years of Russian Art*, exhib. cat., Barbican Art Gallery, London; Museum of Modern Art, Oxford, 1990.

Ellis, Jane, *The Russian Orthodox Church*, London, 1985.

Gerhardi, W. A., *The Romanovs*, London, 1940.

Gray, Camilla, *The Russian Experiment in Art 1863–1922*, rev. edn, London, 1986.

Hosking, Geoffrey, *A History of the Soviet Union*, 5th rev. edn, London, 1992.

Lawrence, John, *A History of Russia*, 7th edn, New York, 1993.

Lincoln, W. Bruce, *The Romanovs*, London, 1981.

Marshall, Richard, Jnr, *Aspects of Religion in the Soviet Union*, Chicago, 1970.

Remnick, David, *Lenin's Tomb. The Last Days of the Soviet Empire*, New York, 1994.

Russkii biograficheskii slovar' [Russian Biographical Dictionary], 25 vols, St Petersburg, 1896–1913.

Select Bibliography

Shapiro, Leonard, *The Communist Party of the Soviet Union*, London, 1970.

Tchernavin, Tatiana [Tatyana Chernavina], *Escape from the Soviets*, London, 1933.

Thompson, John M., *A Vision Unfulfilled. Russia and the Soviet Union in the Twentieth Century*, Lexington, Mass., and Toronto, 1996.

Books on St Petersburg

Custine, Marquis de, *La Russie en 1839*, Paris, 1843.

Georgi, J. G., *Versuch einer Beschreibung der Russisch Kayserlichen Residenzstadt St. Petersburg und der Merkwurdigkeiten der Gegend*, 2 vols, St Petersburg, 1790; trans. into French as *Description de la ville de St Pétersbourg et ses environs*, St Petersburg, 1793.

Kelly, Lawrence, *St Petersburg: A Traveller's Companion*, London, 1981.

Kennett, Victor and Audrey Kennett, *The Palaces of Leningrad*, London, 1973.

Ometev, Boris and John Stuart, *St Petersburg: Portrait of an Imperial City*, London, 1990.

Pylyaev, M. I., *Staryi Peterburg* [Old Petersburg], St Petersburg, 1889; repr. Moscow, 1990.

Pylyaev, M. I., *Zabytoe proshloe okrestnostei Peterburga* [The Forgotten Past of the Environs of St Petersburg], St Petersburg, 1889; repr. St Petersburg, 1996.

Reimers, H. von, *Petersburg am Ende seines ersten Jahrhunderts*, St Petersburg, 1805.

Ségur, Louis Philippe, *Mémoires, souvenirs et anecdotes par le Comte de Ségur*, Paris, 1824–6.

Volkov, Solomon, *St Petersburg: A Cultural History*, London, 1996.

General Books on the Hermitage

Arkhiv Gos. Ordena Lenina Ermitazha, Putevoditel' [The Archive of the State Order of Lenin Hermitage, A Guidebook], Leningrad, 1988.

Arzumanyan, A., *Brat'ya Orbeli* [The Orbeli Brothers], Yerevan, 1976.

Avramenko, S., *Vospominaniya ob Ermitazhnom teatre* [Reminiscences of the Hermitage Theatre], St Petersburg, 1992.

Belyakova, Alla, *Stories About the Hermitage*, Moscow, 1990.

Descargues, Pierre, *The Hermitage Museum*, Leningrad and New York, 1961.

Ducamp, Emmanuel (ed.), *The Winter Palace*, St Petersburg and Paris, 1995.

Ermitazh. Istoriya i sovremennost [The Hermitage. History and Modern Times], V. A. Suslov (ed.), Moscow, 1990.

Ermitazh. Istoriya stroitel'stva i arkhitektura zdanii [The Hermitage. The History of the Construction and the Architecture of the Buildings], B. B. Piotrovsky (ed.), Leningrad, 1991.

Fond Orbeli [The Orbeli Fund], St Petersburg Branch of the Archive of the Russian Academy of Sciences, Fond 909.

Fotoarkhiv Gos. Ermitazha [The Photo-archive of the State Hermitage], St Petersburg, 1992.

Gilles, F., *Musée de l'Hermitage impérial*, St Petersburg, 1860; rev. edn 1863.

Istoriya Ermitazha i ego kollektsii: sbornik nauchnykh trudov [The History of the Hermitage and its Collections: An Anthology of Papers], Leningrad, 1989.

Levinson-Lessing, V. F., *Istoriya kartinnoi galerei Ermitazha (1764–1917)* [The History of the Hermitage Picture Gallery (1764–1917)], Leningrad, 1985.

Lichnye arkhivnye fondy Gos. Ermitazha [Personal Archive Files in the State Hermitage], St Petersburg, 1992.

Piotrovsky, Boris, *The Hermitage: Its History and Collections*, London, 1982.

Piotrovsky, Boris, 'Moi predshestvenniki' [My Predecessors], *Iskusstvo Leningrada* [The Art of Leningrad], no. 4, 1989, pp. 5–26.

Piotrovsky, M. and O. Neverov, *The Hermitage: The History of the Collections*, St Petersburg, 1997.

Soobshcheniya Gosudarstvennogo Ermitazha [Bulletin of the State Hermitage since 1940].

Sorok let Sovetskogo Ermitazha [Forty Years of the Soviet Hermitage], Leningrad, 1957.

Trudy Gosudarstvennogo Ermitazha [Papers of the State Hermitage since 1956].

Varshavsky, S. and B. Rest, *Ryadom s zimnen* [By the Winter Palace], Leningrad, 1969.

Voltsenburg, O. E., *Biblioteka Ermitazha* [The Hermitage Library], Leningrad, 1957.

Voronikhina, A. N. and Lyulina, R. D., *Ermitazh v akvarelyakh, risunkakh, chertezhakh kontsa XVIII–serediny XIX veka* [The Hermitage in Watercolours, Drawings, Sketches beginning 18th–mid-19th century], Leningrad, 1964.

Voronikhina, L., *Art Treasures of the Hermitage*, Leningrad, 1961.

Voronikhina, L., *Gosudarstvennyi Ermitazh* [The State Hermitage], Leningrad, 1992.

The Collections of the Hermitage

There have been many publications covering the collections of the Hermitage, and the following is simply a very select list.

Select Bibliography

Benua, Aleksandr, [Benois Alexandre], *Galereya dragotsennostei imp. Ermitazha* [The Gallery of *Objets de vertu* of the Imperial Hermitage], St Petersburg, 1902.

Benua, Aleksandr, [Benois, Alexandre], *Putevoditel' po kartinnoi galeree imp. Ermitazha* [Guidebook to the Picture Gallery of the Imperial Hermitage], St Petersburg, [1913].

Derwis, Paul, 'Some English Plate at the Hermitage', *Burlington Magazine*, July, 1935, pp. 35–6.

Derwis, Paul, 'More English Plate at the Hermitage', *Burlington Magazine*, July, 1936, pp. 25–6.

Dukelskaya, L. A., *The Hermitage: English Art, Sixteenth to Nineteenth Century*, Leningrad, 1979.

Ivanov, A. A. et al., *Yuvelirnye izdeliya vostoka* [Oriental Jewellery], Leningrad, 1982.

Les émaux des Russes au 17e au debut du 20e siècle, exhib. cat., Limoges, 1988.

Penzer, N. M., 'The English Plate of the Hermitage', *Connoisseur*, December, 1958.

Peredol'skaya, A. A., *Krasnofigurnye atticheskie vazy v Ermitazhe* [Red-figure Attic Vases in the Hermitage], Leningrad, 1967.

Piotrovsky, Boris et al., *Egyptian Antiquities in the Hermitage*, Leningrad, 1974.

Potin, V. M., *Monety, klady, kollektsii* [Coins, Hoards, Collections], Moscow, 1993.

Russian Glass of the 17th–20th Centuries, exhib. cat., Corning Museum, 1990.

Slovar' numizmata [The Numismatist's Dictionary], Moscow, 1993.

Smirnov, Ya. I., *Vostochnoe serebro* [Oriental Silver], St Petersburg, 1903.

Sokolova, T. N. and K. R. Orlova, *Russkaya mebel' v Ermitazhe* [Russian Furniture in the Hermitage], Leningrad, 1973.

Suslov, V. (ed.), *The State Hermitage, Masterpieces from the Museum's Collections*, 2 vols, London, 1994.

Tarasyuk [Tarassuk], L. I., *Starinnoe ognestrel'noe oruzhie v sobranii Ermitazha. Evropa i Severnaya Amerika* [Old Firearms in the Collection of the Hermitage. Europe and North America], Leningrad, 1971.

Trever, K. and V. Lukonin, *Sasanidskoe serebro* [Sassanian Silver], Moscow, 1987.

Waldhauer, Oskar, *Die Antiken Skulpturen der Ermitage*, 3 vols, Berlin and Leipzig, 1936.

Two issues of the English art magazine *Apollo*, for December 1974 and June 1975, were devoted almost entirely to the Hermitage. Their contents were as follows:

Apollo, December 1974:
Editorial; 'Treasures of the North'
Tamara Sokolova: 'Interiors of the Winter Palace'
Yaroslav Domansky: 'The Scythian Theme in the Art of Ancient Northern Black Sea Cities'
Zhenya Gorbunova: 'Classical Sculpture from the Lyde Browne Collection'
Tamara Fomicheva: 'Venetian Painting of the Fifteenth to Eighteenth Centuries'
Nina Kosareva: 'A Terracotta Study of Gianlorenzo Bernini for the Statue of the Blessed Ludovica Albertoni'
Yury Kuznetsov: 'Rembrandt Discoveries at the Hermitage'
Zoya Bernyakovich: 'The Collection of Russian Silver'
Albert Kostenevich: '*La Danse* and *La Musique* by Henri Matisse. A New Interpretation'

Apollo, June 1975
Editorial: 'Russian Francophiles of the Dix-huitième'
Nina Nemilova: 'Contemporary French Art in Eighteenth-Century Russia'
Nina Kosareva: 'Masterpieces of Eighteenth-Century French Sculpture'
Kira Butler: 'Sèvres for the Imperial Court'
Nina Biryukova: 'Decoration and Diplomacy. Eighteenth-Century French Tapestries'
Marina Torneus: 'Elegance and Craftsmanship. The Eighteenth-Century French Snuff-box'
Irina Novoselskaya: 'French Drawings. From Watteau to Greuze'

The paintings of the Hermitage collection are being published in Moscow and Florence, in both English and Russian, in sixteen volumes, under the title *Catalogue of Western European Painting*. The following volumes have already appeared:
Vol. 1: Tatiana Kustodieva, *Italian Painting. Thirteenth to Sixteenth Centuries*, 1994.
Vol. 2: Tamara P. Fomicheva, *Venetian Painting. Fourteenth to Eighteenth Centuries*, 1992.
Vol. 5: Nikolai N. Nikulin, *Netherlandish Painting. Fifteenth to Sixteenth Centuries*, 1989.
Vol. 10: Inna S. Nemilova, *French Painting. Eighteenth Century*, 1986.
Vol. 11: Valentina N. Berezina, *French Painting. Early to Mid-Nineteenth Century*, 1983.
Vol. 12: Anna S. Barskaya and Albert G. Kostenevich, *French Painting. Mid-Nineteenth to Twentieth Century*, 1991.
Vol. 13: Larisa A. Dukelskaya and Elizaveta P. Renne, *British Painting. Sixteenth to Nineteenth Centuries*, 1990.

Vol. 14: Nikolai N. Nikulin, *German and Austrian Painting. Fifteenth to Eighteenth Centuries.* 1987.
Vol. 15: Boris I. Asvarisch, *German and Austrian Painting. Nineteenth and Twentieth Centuries,* 1988.

The following is a chapter-by-chapter list of the most useful bibliographical sources:

Chapter 1: *Catherine's Hermitage and Peter's City*

Androsov, O., 'Istoriya "Venery Tavricheskoi [The History of the Tauride Venus]" ', *Muzei* [Museum], VIII, 1987, pp. 122–33.
Gothein, Marie Louis, *A History of Garden Art,* London and Toronto, 1928.
Kaminskaya, K. G., 'Yu. I. Kologrivov i ego uchastie v sozdanii pervykh kollektsii skul'ptury v Peterburge [Yu. I. Kologrivov and his Participation in the Creation of the First Sculpture Collections in St Petersburg], *Muzei* [Museum], V, 1984, p. 136.
Massie, Robert K., *Peter the Great,* New York, 1980.
Maurice, Klaus, *Sovereigns as Turners,* Zurich, 1985.
Neverov, O. Ya., ' "His Majesty's Cabinet" and Peter I's Kunstkammer', in *The Origins of Museums. The Cabinet of Curiosities in 16th- and 17th-Century Europe,* Oxford, 1985.
Neverov, O. Ya., *Iz kollektsii petrovskoi Kunstkamery* [From the Collection of Peter's Kunstkammer], St Petersburg, 1992.
Peter de Grote en Holland., exhib. cat., Amsterdams Historisch Museum, 1996–7.
Rudenko, S. I., *Die Sibirische Sammlung Peter I,* Moscow and Leningrad, 1962.
Stanyukovich, T. V., *Kunstkamera Peterburgskoi Akademii Nauk* [The Kunstkammer of the St Petersburg Academy of Sciences], Moscow and Leningrad, 1953.

Chapter 2: *Catherine's Collections*

Alexander, John, *Catherine the Great, Life and Legend,* Oxford, 1989.
Castera, J. H., *Vie de Catherine II,* Paris, 1797.
Catherine the Great, *Memoirs,* edited by D. Maroger, New York, 1957.
Charles-Louis Clérisseau (1721–1820). Dessins du Musée de l'Ermitage, Saint

Pétersbourg, exhib. cat., Louvre Museum, Paris, 1995.

Cross, Anthony, 'The Duchess of Kingston in Russia', *History Today*, vol. 27, 1977, pp. 390–5.

Cross, Anthony, 'The Great Patroness of the North. Catherine the Great's Role in Fashioning Anglo-Russian Contacts', *Oxford Slavonic Papers*, vol. 18, 1985, pp. 67–82.

Falconet, Etienne-Maurice, *Correspondance de Falconet avec Catherine II*, Paris, 1921.

'Gertsoginya Kingston i eyo prebyvanie v Rossii' [La Duchesse de Kingston et ses séjours en Russie]', *Starye gody* [Days of Yore], June, 1913, pp. 3–35.

Grigorieva, Irina and Asja Kantor-Gukovskaja, *The Famous Italian Drawings in the Collection of the Hermitage in Leningrad*, Milan, 1983.

Makarov, V., *Chasy pavlin Ermitazha* [The Hermitage's Peacock Clock], Leningrad, 1960.

Maksimova, M. I., *Imp. Ekaterina II i sobranie reznykh kamnei* [Empress Catherine II and the Collection of Carved Gems], Petrograd, 1921.

Mayor, E., *The Virgin Mistress*, London, 1964.

Moore, Andrew (ed.), *Houghton Hall, The Prime Minister, The Empress and The Hermitage*, exhib. cat., Norwich Castle Museum, Kenwood House, London, 1996.

Neverov, O., 'The Lyde Browne Collection and the History of Ancient Sculpture in the Hermitage Museum', *American Journal of Archaeology*, vol. 88, 1984, pp. 33ff.

Penzer, N. H., 'The Great Wine Coolers', *Apollo*, vol. LXVI, nos 390–1, August–September 1957.

Rossiya-Frantsiya. Vek prosveshcheniya [Russia-France. The Century of Enlightenment], St Petersburg, 1992.

Scherer, Edmond, *Melchior Grimm*, Paris, 1887.

Stuffmann, M., 'Les tableaux de la collection de Pierre Crozat. Historique et destinée d'un ensemble célèbre, établis en partant d'un inventaire après décès inédits (1740)', *Gazette des Beaux-Arts*, vol. 72, no. 1194–6, 1968, pp. 11–55.

Tourneaux, Maurice, *Diderot et Catherine II*, Paris, 1899.

Treasures of Imperial Russia. Catherine the Great. From the State Hermitage Museum, Leningrad, exhib. cat., various venues, London, 1990.

Chapter 3: Paul and Alexander

Alle Origini di Canova, Ca d'Oro, 1991–2.

Androsov, O., 'O kollektsionirovanii ital'yanskoi skul'ptury v Rossii v XVIII veke' [On the Collecting of Italian Sculpture in Russia in the

18th Century], *Trudy Gos. Ermitazha* [Papers of the State Hermitage], vol. 25, 1985, p. 90.

Benua, Aleksandr [Benois, Alexandre], *Khudozhestvennaya zabava imp. Marii Fedorovny* [The Artistic Pastime of Empress Mariya Fedorovna], St Petersburg, 1913.

Canova all'ermitage, exhib. cat., Marsilio, Museo Correr (Venice) and Palazzo Ruspoli, Rome, 1991–2.

Coudray, A.-J. Chevalier du, dit 'le Chevalier', *Le Comte et la Comtesse du Nord, Anecdote Russe*, Paris, 1782.

Gielgud, Adam (ed.), *Memoirs of Prince Adam Czartoryski and his Correspondence with Alexander I*, 2 vols, London, 1888.

Grandjean, Serge, *Inventaires après décès de l'impératrice Josephine à Malmaison*, Paris, 1964.

Hartley, Janet M., *Alexander I*, London, 1994.

McGrew, Roderick, E., *Paul of Russia*, Oxford, 1992.

Oberkirch, Baroness, *Mémoires de la Baronne d'Oberkirch sur la cour de Louis XVI et la société française avant 1789*, new edn, Paris, 1982.

Palmer, Alan, *Alexander I. Tsar of War and Peace*, London, 1974.

Parkinson, John, *Tour of Russia, Siberia and the Crimea*, London, 1971.

Waliszewski, K., *Le fils de la Grande Catherine: Paul I, sa vie, son regne et sa mort*, Paris, 1912.

Chapter 4: Nicholas I and the New Hermitage

Antichnye Gosudarstva Severnogo Prichernomor'ya [The Antique States of the Northern Black Sea Area], G. A. Koshelenko (ed.), Moscow, 1984.

Asvarisch, Boris I., 'Friedrich's Russian Patrons', in *The Romantic Vision of Caspar David Friedrich. Paintings and Drawings from the U.S.S.R.*, exhib. cat., Metropolitan Museum of Art, New York; Art Institute of Chicago, 1991, pp. 19–40.

Aswarischtsch [Asvarisch], Boris, 'Franz Kruger in Russland', *Staatliche Museen zu Berlin. Forschungen und Berichte*, vol. 26, Berlin, 1987.

Borovka, G., *Scythian Art*, Leningrad, 1928.

Efimova, E. M., *Russkyi reznoi kamen' v Ermitazhe* [Russian Carved Stones in the Hermitage], with French résumé, Leningrad, 1961.

From the Lands of the Scythians, exhib. cat., Metropolitan Museum, New York; Los Angeles County Museum, 1975, (*Metropolitan Museum of Art Bulletin*, Special Issue).

Gilles, F., *Les Antiquités du Bosphore Cimmerien*, St Petersburg, 1854.

Godeonov, E., *Notice sur les objets d'art de la galerie Campagna . . . acquis pour le Musée Impérial de l'Ermitage*, St Petersburg, 1861.

Grigorovich, D. V., *Progulka po Ermitazhu* [A Walk Through the

Hermitage], St Petersburg, 1865.

Hederer, Oswald, *Leon von Klenze: Personlichkeit und Werk*, Munich, 1964.

Historicism in Russia. Style and Epoch in the Decorative Arts. 1820s–1890s, exhib. cat., The Hermitage, St Petersburg, 1996.

Karcheva, E. I., 'K istorii sozdaniya zala noveishei zapadnoevropeiskoi skul'ptury v Imperatorskom Ermitazhe' [On the History of the Creation of the Room of the Latest Western European Sculpture in the Imperial Hermitage], *Tezisy dokladov nauchnoi konferentsii aspirantov i soiskatelei* [Theses of Papers from a Conference of Post-Graduates and Doctoral Candidates], St Petersburg, 1994, pp. 26–8.

Kochelenko, Guennadij A., 'Entre Scythes et Grecs', *Les Dossiers d'archéologie*, no. 188, December, 1993.

Lincoln, William B., *Nicholas I*, London, 1978.

Makarov, V. K., *Tsvetnoi kamen' v sobranii Ermitazha* [Coloured Stones in the Hermitage Collection], Leningrad, 1938.

Mavrodina, N. M., *Kolyvanskaya vaza*, Leningrad, 1989.

Montpereux, Dubois de, *Voyage autour du Caucase*, 1843.

Piotrovsky, Boris, Lyudmila Galnina and Nonna Grach, *Scythian Art*, Oxford and Leningrad, 1987.

Rosowzew [Rostovtsev], M., *Skythien und der Bosporus*, Berlin, 1931.

Rostovtzeff [Rostovtsev], M., *Iranians and Greeks in South Russia*, Oxford, 1922.

Tarassuk [Tarasyuk], L., 'The Collection of Arms and Armour in the State Hermitage Museum, Leningrad', *Journal of the Arms and Armour Society*, London, vol. 1, no. 3, March 1959 and vol. 4–5, no. 5, March 1966.

Tiucheva, A. F., *At the Court of Two Emperors*, 1990.

Tsetskhladze, Gocha R., 'Greek Penetration of the Black Sea', in *The Archaeology of Greek Colonisation*, Oxford University Committee for Archaeology, Monograph 40, Oxford, 1994.

Vrangel', N. N., *Iskusstvo i gosudar' Nikolai Pavlovich* [Art and the Sovereign Nicholas Pavlovich], Petrograd, 1915.

Waagen, G. F., *Die Gemäldesammlung in der Kaiserlichen Eremitage zu Petersburg nebst Bemerkungen über andere dortige Kunstsammlungen*, Munich, [1864].

Wortman, Richard S., *Scenarios of Power*, Princeton, 1995.

Chapter 5: Twilight of the Romanovs

Bothmer, Dietrich von, 'Les Vases de la Collection Campana', *Revue du Louvre*, 1977, pp. 213–21.

Gaultier, Françoise, 'La collection Campana et la collection étrusque du Musée du Louvre', in *Les Etrusques et l'europe*, exhib. cat., Grand Palais,

Paris; Altes Museum, Berlin, 1992–3.

Hopkirk, Peter, *Foreign Devils on the Silk Road*, London, 1980.

Kryzhanovskaya, Marta, 'Alexander Petrovich Basilevsky', *Journal of the History of Collecting*, vol. 2, no. 2, 1990, pp. 143–55.

La Madonna Benois, exhib. cat., Florence, 1984.

Samosyuk, Kira Fyodorovna, 'The Discovery of Khara Khoto', in *Lost Empire of the Silk Road*, exhib. cat., Villa Favorita, Lugano, 1993, pp. 31–47.

Steinberg, Mark D. and Vladimir M. Krustalev, *The Fall of the Romanovs*, New Haven and London, 1995.

Stephani, Ludolf, *Die Vasen-Sammlung der Kaiserlichen Ermitage*, 2 vols, Berlin, 1869.

Vostochnyi khudozhestvennyi metal iz srednogo Priob'ya. Novye nakhodki [Oriental Metalwork from the Middle Reaches of the River Ob. New Finds], exhib. cat., The Hermitage, Leningrad, 1991.

Zapadnoevropeiskoe prikladnoe iskusstvo srednykh vekov i epokhi Vozrozhdeniya [Western-European Applied Art of the Medieval and Renaissance Periods], exhib. cat., The Hermitage, Leningrad, 1986.

Chapter 6: St Petersburg Collectors and Connoisseurs

Asvarishch, B. I., *Kushelevskaya galereya: Zapadnoevropeiskaya zhivopis' XIX veka* [The Kushelev Gallery: 19th-Century Western European Painting], exhib. cat., The Hermitage, St Petersburg, 1993.

Benois, Alexandre, *Memoirs*, London, 1960–4.

Brown, David Alan, *Madonna Litta*, 1992.

Dnevnik gos. sek. A. A. Polovtseva [The Diary of State Secretary A. A. Polovtsev], Moscow, 1966.

Etkind, Mark, *A. N. Benua i russkaya khudozhestvennaya kul'tura* [A. N. Benois and Russian Artistic Culture], Leningrad, 1989.

Furtwängler, A., *Sammlung Sabouroff*, Berlin, 1883–7.

Glinka, V. M., *Yusupovskaya galereya. Fr. shkola* [The Yusupov Gallery. French School], Leningrad, 1924.

Hamilton, George Heard, 'The Slavic Revival and Mir Iskusstva', in Hamilton, *The Art and Architecture of Russia*, Pelican History of Art, 3rd edn, Harmondsworth, 1983.

Iz kollekstii N. P. Likhacheva [From the Collection of N. P. Likhachev], exhib. cat., The Russian Museum, St Petersburg, 1993.

Karnovich, E. P., *Zamechatel'noe bogatstvo lyudei Rossii* [The Marvellous Wealth of People in Russia], St Petersburg, 1874; repr. Moscow, 1994.

Katalog vystavki serebra, fayansa, emalei iz sobranii grafini E. V. Shuvalovoi [Catalogue of an Exhibition of Silver, Faience and Enamels from the

Collection of Countess E. V. Shuvalova], exhib. cat., Stieglitz Museum, St Petersburg, n.d.

Kollektsionery i metsenaty v Sankt-Peterburge 1703–1917 [Collectors and Patrons in Saint Petersburg *1703–1917*], S. O. Androsov (ed.), St Petersburg, 1995.

Materialy nauchnoi konferentsii. Vipperovskie chteniya 1994, Vypusk XXVII: Chastnoe kollektsionirovanie v Rossii [Conference Material. Vipper Readings 1994, Issue XXVII: Private Collecting in Russia], The Pushkin Museum of Fine Arts, Moscow, 1995.

Muzei barona Shtiglitsa. Proshloe i nastoyashchee [Baron Stieglitz Museum. The Past and the Present], St Petersburg, 1994.

Noveishii putevoditel' po Stroganovskomy dvortsu [The Latest Guide to the Stroganov Palace], S. Kuznetsov (ed.), St Petersburg, 1995.

Petrova, M. V., 'Iz proshlogo grafov Bobrinskikh [From the Past of the Counts Bobrinsky], *Voprosy Istorii* [Questions of History], Moscow, 1993, no. 5, pp. 171–6.

Sternin, G. Yu., *Khudozhestvennaya zhizn' Rossii 1900–1910-kh godov* [Artistic Life in Russia 1900–1910s], Moscow, 1988.

Trever, K., *Stroganovskyi dvorets* [The Stroganov Palace], Petrograd, 1922.

Vizantinovedenie v Ermitazhe: K XVIII Mezhdunarodnomu kongressu vizantinistov, Moskva 8–15 avgusta 1991 goda [Byzantine Studies at the Hermitage: Towards the XVIIIth International Congress of Byzantinists, Moscow 8–15 August 1991], V. S. Shandrovskaya (ed.), Leningrad, 1991.

Weiner, P., E. Lipgart, J. Schmidt, et al., *Les anciennes écoles de peinture dans les palais et collections privés russes*, Brussels, 1910.

Western European Applied Art from the Hermitage Collection [Russian and English dual text], St Petersburg, 1996.

Yousupoff, F. F., *Lost Splendour*, 1953.

Chapter 7: The Shchukins and the Morozovs

Barskaya, Anna, *French Painting from the Hermitage Museum*, with an introduction by Antonina Izergina, New York, 1975.

Boguslavsky, M. M., 'Kommentarii. Isk Iriny Shchukinoi (o reshenii frantsuzskogo suda)' [The Suit of Irina Shchukina (on the Decision of the French Court)], *Moskovskii zhurnal mezhdunarodnogo prava* [The Moscow Journal of International Law].

Kean, Beverley Whitney, *All the Empty Palaces*, 1983; rev. edn. as *French Painters, Russian Collectors*, London, 1994.

Kostenevich, Albert, *Western European Painting in the Hermitage*,

Leningrad, 1987.

Kostenevich, Albert, *Monet to Picasso*, Folkwang Museum, Essen, 1993.

Kostenevich, Albert and Natalya Semyonova, *Collecting Matisse*, Paris, 1993.

Morosow und Schtschukin. Die russischen Sammler, exhib. cat., Folkwang Museum, Essen; Pushkin Museum, Moscow; The Hermitage, St Petersburg, 1993–4.

Ternovets, B. N., *Museum für Moderne Kunst des Westens*, Moscow, 1934.

Vollard, Ambroise, *Souvenirs d'un marchand de tableaux*, Paris, 1948, p. 158.

Chapter 8: The 1917 Revolution

Aleksandr Nikolaevich Benua i Ermitazh [Alexandre Nikolaevich Benois in the Hermitage], exhib. cat., The Hermitage, St Petersburg, 1994.

Benua, Aleksandr, [Benois, Alexandre], *Vybornye mesta iz dnevnikov 1916–1918 gg.* [Selected Moments from Diaries of 1916–1918], unpublished manuscript in the archive of the Benois Family Museum, a branch of Peterhof Palace Museum Reserve.

Gorky, Maxim, *V. I. Lenin*, Moscow, 1974.

Grabar', I., *Moya zhizn'* [My Life], Moscow, 1932.

Lapshin, V. P., *Khudozhestvennaya zhizn' Moskvy i Petrodgrada v 1917* [Artistic Life in Moscow and Petrograd in 1917], Moscow, 1983.

Moorehead, Alan, *The Russian Revolution*, London, 1958.

Pitcher, Harvey, *Witnesses of the Russian Revolution*, London, 1994.

Polovtsoff, Alexandre, *Les Trésors d'art en Russie sous le régime Bolchéviste*, Paris, 1919.

Reed, John, *Ten Days that Shook the World*, New York, 1919; Penguin repr., Harmondsworth, 1977.

Startsev, V. I., *Shturm Zimnego* [The Storming of the Winter Palace], Leningrad, 1987.

Tolstoy, D. I., 'Revolyutsionnoe vremya v Russkom Muzee i v Ermitazhe (Vospominaniya grafa D. I. Tolstogo)' [The Revolutionary Period in the Russian Museum and the Hermitage (Reminiscences of Count D. I. Tolstoy)], *Rossiiskyi Arkhiv* [Russian Archive], vols II–III, Moscow, 1992.

Troyat, Henri, *Gorky*, New York, 1989.

Varshavsky, S. and B. Rest, *Bilet na vsyu vechnost': povest' ob Ermitazhe* [Ticket to All Eternity: A Tale of the Hermitage], 3rd edn, Leningrad, 1986.

Zubov, Count V. P., *Stradnye gody Rossii. Vospominaniya o Revolyutsii (1917–1925)* [Russia's Years of Suffering. Reminiscences of the Revolution (1917–1925)], Munich, 1968.

Chapter 9: The New State Hermitage

Androsov, S. O. (ed.) *Skul'ptura v muzee* [Sculpture in Museums], Leningrad, 1984.

Conway, Sir Martin, *Art Treasures in Soviet Russia*, London, 1925.

Fitzpatrick, Sheila M., *The Commissariat of Enlightenment. Soviet Organization of Education and the Arts under Lunacharsky, October 1917–1921*, Cambridge, 1970.

Legran, B., *La Réconstruction Socialiste de l'Hermitage*, Leningrad, 1934.

Levinson-Lessing, V. F., 'S. P. Yaremich 1869–1935', *Soobshcheniya Gos. Ermitazha* [Bulletin of the State Hermitage], no. 2, 1940.

Muzei 1, 1923; *Muzei 2*, 1924 [Museum 1, Museum 2; short-lived annual with reports on the transformation of St Petersburg museums], Petrograd.

O'Connor, Timothy, *The Politics of Soviet Culture*, Alabama, 1983.

Philonenko, M., 'L'expropriation des biens des particuliers par les Soviets devant la justice allemande', *Journal du Droit International*, (Clunet), 1929.

Valdgauer [Waldhauer], O., *Etyudi po istorii antichnogo portreta* [Studies in the History of Antique Portraiture], Leningrad, 1938.

Zhukov, Yu. N., *Stanovlenie i deyatel'nost' sovetskikh organov okhrany pamyatnikov istorii i kul'tury 1917–1920* [The Establishment and Activities of Soviet Bodies for the Protection of Historical and Cultural Monuments 1917–1920], Moscow, 1989.

Chapter 10: Art Sales

Blumay, Karl, *The Dark Side of Power: The Real Armand Hammer*, New York and London, 1992.

Clarke, William, *The Lost Fortune of the Tsars*, London, 1994.

Foelkersam, Baron A. E., *Inventaire de l'argenterie conservée dans les gardes-meubles des Palais Impériaux*, St Petersburg, 1907.

Hammer, Armand, *The Quest of the Romanoff Treasure*, New York, 1936.

Larsons, M. J., [Lazerson, Moisey Yakovlevich] *An Expert in the Service of the Soviets*, London, 1929.

Mosyakin, Aleksandr, 'Antikvarnyi eksportnyi fond' [The Antique Export Fund], *Nashe Nasledie* [Our Heritage], 1991, nos II, pp. 29–42 and III, pp. 35–48.

'Mr Mellon Admits He Owns Ex-Hermitage Treasures', *Newsweek*, 2 March, 1935, p. 23.

Oldenburg, E. G., *Dnevniki* [Diaries], St Petersburg Branch of the Archive of the Russian Academy of Sciences, St Petersburg, Fond 208, Op. 2, delo 57.

Perdigao, José de Azeredo, *Calouste Gulbenkian, Collector*, Lisbon, 1969.

Runkevich, S. G., *Aleksandro-Nevskaya lavra 1733–1913* [The Alexander Nevsky Monastery 1733–1913], St Petersburg, 1913.

Twining, Lord [Edward Francis Twining], *A History of the Crown Jewels of Europe*, London, 1960.

Vasileva, O. Yu. and Pavel Knyshevskii, *Krasnye konkistadory* [Red Conquistadors], Moscow, 1994.

Walker, John, *Self-Portrait with Donors*, Boston, 1974.

Williams, Robert C., *Russian Art and American Money, 1900–1940*, London 1980.

Williams, Robert H. Davis, Jnr, and Edward Kasinec, 'Witness to the Crime: Two little known photographic sources relating to the sale and destruction of antiquities in Soviet Russia during the 1920s', *Journal of the History of Collections*, vol. 3, no. 1, 1991, pp. 53–9.

Zavadskaya, L., 'Raka Aleksandra Nevskogo v sobranii Ermitazha' [The Sarcophagus of Alexander Nevsky in the Hermitage Collection], in *Aleksandr Nevsky i istoriya Rossii. Materialy nauchnoi-prakticheskoi konferentsii* [Alexander Nevsky and the History of Russia. Material from a Scholarly-Practical Conference], Novgorod, 1996, pp. 84–92.

Zhukov, Yu. N., *Operatsiya Ermitazha* [Operation Hermitage], Moscow, 1995.

Chapter 11: Archaeology

Alpatov, V. M., *Istoriya odnogo mifa* [The History of a Myth], Moscow, 1991.

Artamonov, M. I., *Istoriya Khazar* [History of the Khazars], Leningrad, 1962.

Artamonov, M. I., *Treasures from Scythian Tombs*, London, 1969.

Artamonov, M. I., *The Dawn of Art*, Leningrad, 1974.

Dunlop, D. M., *The History of the Jewish Khazars*, Princeton, 1954.

Frozen Tombs. The Culture and Art of the Ancient Tribes of Siberia, exhib. cat., British Museum, London, 1978.

Gryaznov, M. P., 'The Pazirek Burial of Altai', *American Journal of Archaeology*, vol. 21, no. 1, 1931.

Gryaznov, Mikhail, *Sibérie du Sud*, Geneva, 1969.

Higgins, Reynold, *Tanagra and the Figurines*, London, 1987.

Koestler, Arthur, *The Thirteenth Tribe: The Khazar Empire and its Heritage*, London, 1976.

Miller, Mikhail, *Archaeology in the USSR*, London, 1956.

Mongait, Alexander, *Archaeology in the USSR*, Moscow, 1959.

N. Ya. Marr kak arkheolog [N. Ya. Marr as an Archaeologist], Leningrad, 1935.

Orbeli, J. (ed.), *IIIe Congrés International d'art et d'archéologie Iraniens*, Leningrad, 1939.

Piotrovsky, Boris, *Urartu*, London, 1969.

Rudenko, S. I., *Kul'tura naseleniya Gornogo Altaya v skifskoe vremya* [The Culture of the Inhabitants of the Mountainous Altai Region During the Scythian Period], Moscow and Leningrad, 1953.

Rudenko, S. I., *Kul'tura naseleniya Tsentral'nogo Altaya v skifskoe vremya* [The Culture of the Inhabitants of the Central Altai During the Scythian Period], Moscow and Leningrad, 1960.

Shnirelman, Victor A., 'From Internationalism to Nationalism: Forgotten Pages of Soviet Archaeology in the 1930s and 1940s', in Philip Kohl and Clare Fawcett (eds), *Nationalism, Politics and the Practice of Archaeology*, Cambridge, 1995.

Chapter 12: 'Enemies of the People'

This chapter has made use of the archives of the association for the rehabilitation of victims of political repression, Memorial, and through them limited access to KGB files, including the publication *Leningradsky martirolog: kniga pamyati zhertv politicheskikh repressii* [Leningrad Martyrology: Book in Memory of the Victims of Political Repressions], volumes 1–, 1995–.

Ashin, F. D. and V. M. Alpatov, *'Delo slavistov'. 30-e gody* ['The Slavists' Affair'.], Moscow, 1994.

Conquest, Robert, *The Great Terror*, London, 1973.

Dyakonov [Diakonoff], I. M., *Kniga vospominanii* [Book of Reminiscences], St Petersburg, 1995.

Formozov, A. A., *Russkie arkheologi do i posle revolyutsii* [Russian Archaeologists Before and After the Revolution], Moscow, 1995.

Getty, J. and R. Manning (eds), *The Stalinist Terror, a Reassessment*, Cambridge, 1993.

Guruleva, V. V., 'N. P. Bauer i ego vklad v vizantiiskuyu numizmatiky' [N. P. Bauer and his Contribution to Byzantine Numismatic Studies], *Vizantiya i Blizhnyi Vostok. Sbornik nauchnykh statei* [Byzantium and the Near East. Collection of Articles], St Petersburg, 1994, pp. 117–26.

Kosinsky, M. F., *Pervaya polovina veka. Vospominaniya* [The First Half of the Century. Reminiscences], Paris, 1995.

L'Hermitte, René, *Marr, Marrisme, Marristes, une page del'histoire de la linguistique soviétique*, Paris, 1987.

Neiman, M., 'Partiinaya zhizn', *Sovetskoe iskusstvo* [Soviet Art], 28 July 1938, p. 2.

Oldenburg, E. G., *Dnevniki* [Diaries], op. cit. (see chapter 10).

Serebryakov, I. D., 'Nepremennyi sekretar' AN Akademik Sergey Fedorovich Ol'denburg' [Permanent Secretary of the Academy of Sciences, Academician Sergey Fedorovich Ol'denburg], *Novaya i noveishaya istoriya* [New and Most Recent History], no. 1, 1994, pp. 217–38.

Tunkina, I. V., 'M. I. Rostovtsev i Rossiiskaya Akademiya nauk' [M. I. Rostovtsev and the Russian Academy of Sciences], *Skifskii Roman* [Scythian Romance], Moscow, 1997.

Vasilkov, Ya. V., F. F. Perchenok, G. A. Savina and M. Yu. Sorokina, *Vostokovedy v Gulage. Bio-bibliograficheskii slovar' vostokovedov-zhertv repressii v SSSR (1917–1991)* [Orientalists in the Gulag. A Bio-bibliographical Dictionary of Orientalists who were Victims of Repression in the USSR (1917–1991)], Moscow, 1997–8.

Zuev, V. Yu., 'Sud'ba ermitazhnika: Grigorii Iosifovich Borovka (1894–1941)' [The Fate of a Hermitage Employee, Grigory Iosifovich Borovka (1894–1941)] *Pamyat' B. B. Piotrovskogo* [Conference Papers in Memory of B. B. Piotrovsky], The Hermitage, St Petersburg, 1996.

Chapter 13: *The Siege of Leningrad*

Ermitazh spasennyi [The Hermitage Saved], exhib. cat., Sverdlovsk, St Petersburg, 1995.

Levinson-Lessing, V. F., *Nauchnaya i muzeinaya deyatel'nost' M. V. Dobroklonskogo* [The Scholarly and Museum Work of M. V. Dobroklonsky], Leningrad, 1959.

Orbeli, I., 'O chem dumalos' v dni i nochi blokady Leningrada' [What I Thought About During the Days and Nights of the Siege of Leningrad], *Druzhba* [Friendship], book II, Yerevan, 1960.

Salisbury, Harrison E., *The 900 Days. The Siege of Leningrad*, London, 1969.

Shlikevich, E. A., 'Odna neopublikovannaya rukopis' M. B. Dobroklonskogo: Gosudarstevnnyi Ermitazh za dva goda voiny' [An Unpublished Manuscript of M. B. Dobroklonsky: The State Hermitage During Two Years of the War], *Zarubezhnye khudozhniki v Rossii* [Foreign Artists in Russia], part 1, St Petersburg, 1991, pp. 3–8.

Sirkov, A. V., 'Zdaniya Ermitazha v gody Velikoi Otechestvennoi voiny i nachalo vosstanovitel'nykh rabot' [The Hermitage Buildings During the Great Patriotic War and the Beginning of Restoration Work], ed. V.I. Razdolskaya, *Soobshcheniya Gos. Ermitazha* [Bulletin of the State Hermitage], vol. V, Leningrad, 1948.

Varshavsky, Sergei and Boris Rest, *The Ordeal of the Hermitage*, Leningrad and New York, 1985.

The Hermitage

Varshavsky, Sergei and Boris Rest, *Podvig Ermitazha* [The Hermitage's Great Feat], 3rd edn, Leningrad, 1985.

Chapter 14: Trophy Art

Akinsha, Konstantin and Grigorii Kozlov, with Sylvia Hochfield, *Stolen Treasure: The Hunt for the World's Lost Masterpieces*, London, 1995.

Ilatovskaya, Tatiana, *Master Drawings Rediscovered. Treasures from Pre-war German Collections*, New York, 1996.

Knyshevsky, P., *Dobycha: Tainy germanskikh reparatsii* [Loot: The Secrets of German Reparations], Moscow, 1994.

Kostenevich, Albert, *Hidden Treasures Revealed. Impressionist Masterpieces and Important French Paintings Preserved in the State Hermitage Museum*, St Petersburg, New York and London, 1995.

Nicholas, Lynn H., *The Rape of Europa*, New York, 1994.

Volynsky, Leonid [pseud. of Leonid Rabinovich], *Sem' dnei* [Seven Days], Moscow, 1958.

Vystavka proizvedenii iskusstva iz muzeev Germanskoi Demokraticheskoi Respubliki [Exhibition of Works of Art from Museums in the German Democratic Republic], Leningrad, 1958.

West European Drawings of the XVI–XX Centuries. Kunsthalle Collection in Bremen, cat., tri-lingual edition (Russian, German, English), Moscow, 1992.

Chapter 15: The Post-War Years

'Artamonov, M. I.' [M. I. Artamonov], obituary in *Sovetskaya arkheologiya* [Soviet Archaeology], no. 2, 1973, pp. 322–3.

'Istoriko-bytovoi otdel' [The History and Everyday Life Department], *Trudy issledovatel'skogo instituta muzeevedeniya* [Papers of the Research Institute of Museum Studies], no. 7, 1962, pp. 240–84.

Kostsova, A. S., *Sto ikon iz fondov Ermitazha; Ikonopis' russkogo severa XIII–XVIII vv.* [One Hundred Icons from the Stores of the Hermitage; Icon Painting in the Russian North, 13th–18th Centuries], Leningrad, 1982.

Kostsova, A. S., *Drevnaya russkaya zhivopis' v sobranii Ermitazha* [Early Russian Painting in the Hermitage Collection], with English summary, Moscow, 1992.

Pamyatniki russkoi stariny: itogi raboty ekspeditsii po sboru proizvedenii drevnerusskogo i narodnogo iskusstva [Monuments of Russian Antiquity: The Results of Expeditions to Gather Old Russian Works and Folk

Art], exhib. cat., The Hermitage, St Petersburg, 1993.

Sivkov, A. V., 'Rekonstruktsiya Zimnego dvortsa' [The Reconstruction of the Winter Palace], *Soobshcheniya Gos. Ermitazha* [Bulletin of the State Hermitage], vol. IV, Leningrad, 1958.

Soloukhin, Vladimir, *Searching for Icons in Russia*, London, 1971.

Chapter 16: Piotrovsky and Son

Avramenko, S. I., 'Pyat' novell Ermitazhnogo teatra' [Five Novellas of the Hermitage Theatre], *Neva* [Neva], vol. 3, 1996, pp. 154–81.

Panorama Ermitazha [Hermitage Panorama], 48 issues, from 11 July 1989 to 8 October 1991.

Piotrovsky, Boris, *Stranitsy moei zhizn'* [Pages from my Life], St Petersburg, 1995.

Shkurovich-Khazin, Boris, 'Prosto Piotrovsky' [Simply Piotrovsky], *Dantist* [Dentist], vol. 25, no. 9, September, 1996.

Index

Index

Index

Index

Index